This Business of Music Marketing & Promotion

Revised & Updated Edition

TAD LATHROP

Contributions by Jim Pettigrew, Jr.

BILLBOARD BOOKS
An imprint of Watson-Guptill Publications/New York

Copyright © 2003 Grayson F. Lathrop

First published in 2003 by Billboard Books,
an imprint of Watson-Guptill Publications,
a division of Crown Publishing Group,
Random House, Inc., New York
www.crownpublishing.com
www.watsonguptill.com

Executive Editor: Bob Nirkind
Editor: Sarah Fass
Cover Design: Spencer Drate & Judith Salavetz
Design: Cheryl Viker
Line Art: Nancy Carroll
Production Manager: Ellen Greene

Excerpts from "Keeping the Dream Alive" by Bud Scoppa reprinted by permission of ASCAP
and *Next* magazine.

"Think Different" excerpt courtesy of Apple Computer, Inc. Used with permission.

Picture Credits:
Courtesy of Alligator Records: pp. 54 (Koko Taylor; designed by Matt Minde; photograph by
Chris Jacobs), pp. 56 (Shemekia Copeland). Courtesy of Astralwerks/Caroline Records: p. 56
(Fluke). Courtesy of Blind Pig Records: p. 145 (Norton Buffalo and Roy Rogers). Courtesy of
EvaLuTion Entertainment Marketing: p. 197. Courtesy of Imaginary Road Records: p. 56 (Will
Ackerman). Courtesy of Lance Cowan Media: pp. 95, 145 (Sam Bush). Courtesy of Mark Pucc
Media: pp. 146, 149. Courtesy of Morton Beebe & Associates: p. 113 (Windham Hill catalog
cover). Courtesy of Jacqui Naylor (photograph by John Lemon): p. 109. Courtesy of New West
Records: pp. 126, 156. Courtesy of Shanachie Entertainment Corp.: p. 56 (R. Crumb and His
Cheap Suit Serenaders). Courtesy of Smithsonian Masterworks Orchestra: p. 54. Courtesy of
Windham Hill/BMG Entertainment: pp. 56 (Will Ackerman), 113, 115.

Library of Congress Control Number: 2003106298
ISBN 0-8230-7729-2

Manufactured in the United States of America
6 7 8 9 / 11 10 09 08

For June Laura Howard Lathrop

Contents

Acknowledgments

This book benefited from the expertise and generous assistance of a number of talented music professionals. The following, in particular, deserve special thanks:

Bill Krasilovsky and the late Sid Shemel, whose book *This Business of Music* played a role in my career and remains, four decades after its first publication, a vital resource for all music-industry participants.

Jim Pettigrew, for his enthusiastic support and invaluable contributions to both editions of this book, especially in the narrative description of the marketing process provided in Chapter 2.

Bruce Iglauer, for his thoughtful review of the first edition and his continuing willingness to clarify some of the murkier aspects of the marketing process.

Roy Gattinella, for sharing knowledge accrued over many years in the front lines of music marketing.

Mark Pucci, for his expertise as an independent publicist.

Jacqui Naylor, for graciously providing clear and useful answers to key questions about self-marketing.

Tim Kolleth and Stephanie LeBeau, for insights into the radio promotion process.

Bob DePugh, for shedding light on the TV and film markets for music.

Marc Lipkin, for discussing his record label's publicity operation.

Thanks are also due to Carey Giudici, who edited and improved several key chapters of the revised edition; Nancy Carroll, for her graphics; Kerry Peace, for clarifying key points about distribution; Eva Dickenson-Post and Luann Sullivan Myers, for contributing materials and case studies; Lance Cowan, for supplying press kits and promotional items; Steve Savage, for updates on recording technology and practices; and Bob Nirkind, Ellen Greene, Sarah Fass, and Cheryl Viker at Billboard Books, for shepherding the manuscript through the publication process.

Finally, my love and gratitude to Jacqueline and Audrey Celenza, for making the space for completion of this work and providing warmth and support every step of the way.

TAD LATHROP
Oakland, California
February 2003

Notes on the New Edition

Transformation and volatility have been the operative forces in the music industry since the first publication of *This Business of Music Marketing & Promotion* four years ago. Online music has provided much of the impetus for change, with downloadable songs and popular file-sharing programs opening up new avenues of distribution and promotion to millions of consumers. The older, more established sector of the music business has been scrambling to brainstorm new marketing initiatives, including strategies for profiting from the Internet. In short, the music marketplace, always in flux, is now in a state of all-out self-reinvention to meet the challenges of increased competition and ever-evolving distribution methods.

The new, revised edition of *This Business of Music Marketing & Promotion* accounts for this transformation—and for the full integration of online sales and promotion into the standard music marketing mix. It also taps into a vast well of new marketing tactics, from innovative uses of e-mail to more intelligent approaches to generating sales on a Web site.

Do-it-yourself music makers have much to gain from smart marketing, and the revised edition of this book offers many ideas targeted specifically to those readers. Yet the basic principles laid out in the first edition haven't changed. Nor has the author's original objective: to present standard and nonstandard marketing strategies in the context of an overview of the music business, so that music makers can pursue their careers armed with the power of knowledge.

Preface

This Business of Music Marketing & Promotion, Revised & Updated Edition, is intended as a source of practical information for anyone currently involved in, or thinking about getting involved in, selling music to the listening public.

If you're a musician with some finished recordings, and you need guidance on how to get your music out to the world, you'll find it here.

If you're an entrepreneur aiming to launch your own music company, and you're looking for ways to set the business wheels in motion, you'll find ideas here.

If you're a manager wondering how to spin gold from the threads of a musical client's creativity, you'll find pertinent information in these pages.

If you're a record company marketer seeking ideas for expanding your marketing program, you'll find them here.

If you're a businessperson investigating what's involved in selling music on the Internet, you'll find sections here devoted to that subject.

If you're none of the above, but you're researching possible careers and want to know what goes on in the commercial end of the music field, you've come to the right place.

OVERVIEW OF THE CONTENTS

Chapter 1 provides an overview of the current music marketplace and the forces that are shaping it and providing new opportunities for resourceful entrepreneurs. Chapter 2 offers a behind-the-scenes look at a national marketing campaign as conducted by a midsize record company and a music publisher. This "big picture" summary lays the groundwork for the detailed guidelines to follow.

Chapters 3 through 19 deal with the specifics of music marketing and promotion. They present all the steps involved in planning and carrying out a complete marketing program, with separate chapters devoted to packaging, pricing, store-based and Internet distribution, direct marketing, promotion (including exposure in print media and the Internet and on radio and television), live performing, and managing the entire process.

Chapter 20 contains discussions with professionals active in the business of selling music. They offer a range of perspectives on marketing, from an independent artist's views to those of a veteran major-label executive, a midsize-label owner, a radio promotion specialist, a TV and film music licensing expert, and two publicity professionals.

The Appendix will guide you to other sources of information and professional assistance.

This Business of Music Marketing & Promotion is designed to be used however you prefer. It can be read from cover to cover for a complete "crash course." Or, it can be dipped into as needed and then kept on hand for future reference.

However you choose to use the book, I sincerely hope it proves helpful in your search for marketing ideas and guidance.

Note: This publication has been written with the aim of providing accurate and up-to-date information about the music industry. However, business customs, technology, and monetary values change over time. Furthermore, every business situation is unique; readers' circumstances will invariably differ from those I describe, even if the circumstances may appear similar. For those reasons, the author and the publisher bear no responsibility for actions taken by readers based on information provided in this book. Readers are urged to seek the current advice of appropriate professionals.

Chapter 1

Selling Music in the New Entertainment Marketplace

Most of us first get involved in music for emotional reasons. It's about joy, pure and simple, and for some of us, that pleasure becomes impossible to give up. Over time it tightens its hold and becomes, for many, an obsession.

A number of us decide to make music a livelihood. That's when we find ourselves facing the prospect of treating music not just as an emotional pursuit but as a business. We shift from making and appreciating music to trying to sell it.

You're making that shift, or getting ready to, right now, whether as a musician promoting your own songs or as a businessperson marketing a product line. And you'll find, if you don't already know, that it's a demanding, complex enterprise. It requires ingenuity, skilled decision making, expert use of all available information, and aggressive action.

Selling music may not be easy, but it can be done. It's being done all around us, worldwide, every day, to the tune of billions of dollars. People who sell music successfully have learned that there's a method to the process—a method that revolves around the twin activities of marketing and promotion.

They've learned something else, too: The business end of music, perhaps surprisingly, delivers its own emotional payoff. It comes in the form of an unmistakable surge of excitement when you see the positive results of your effort, measured in higher sales rankings on retail Web sites, larger audiences at shows, increased press coverage, and more.

MUSIC MARKETING AND PROMOTION DEFINED

Maximizing the sales and exposure of music is the bottom line of music marketing and promotion. Put differently, marketing and promotion are systematic approaches to following the money trail of commercial music—and doing it with as much precision and skill as a symphony conductor pulling musical riches from an orchestral score.

The marketing process involves shaping a "product" (as recorded work is termed in the music industry) and then getting it "rack space"—that is, making sure it's displayed and sold in record stores and other outlets, including many that weren't even dreamed of just a few years ago.

Music promotion is part of the marketing process. It involves increasing public awareness of and attraction to the product, with the goal of boosting sales. Each of the key media—print, radio, television, and the Internet—offers unique promotional opportunities and challenges.

The publicity side of the promotion field involves getting magazine and new media outlets to publish articles and stories about the artist and new releases, scheduling guest appearances on talk shows, and earning album reviews in the online as well as printed press.

Live performance is another kind of promotion. But it's also a kind of shelf space because the performer is also a product, offered to customers in this case via the concert stage.

That's the marketing and promotion arena in a nutshell. In upcoming chapter we'll explore its many sectors in detail.

THE CURRENT MARKETPLACE

"The only constant in the music business is that it's always changing. Always."

Record promoter

There's never been a better time to get into music marketing and promotion—or a more volatile one. The old music-industry structure is rattling under the forces of technological change, increased competition, rapidly shifting public tastes, and the globalization of music.

The rules of commerce—once dictated by a handful of corporations and the executives who ran them—have become infinitely more flexible. A new and increasingly creative generation of independent musicians, alternative record labels, maverick promoters, and Internet-based entrepreneurs are inventing entirely new distribution systems and ways of doing business. (It was a nineteen-year-old college student— Shawn Fanning—who created the software behind Napster, the online file-sharing service that shook the music industry in 2000.)

At one time, individual music makers had to rely on cadres of talent-hunting middlemen and music-business insiders to get their music to a broad audience. Now, of course, the Internet and other communication technologies provide almost unlimited direct links between music maker and music customer.

Independent record labels and entrepreneurs have long provided alternative marketing channels running parallel to the superhighways dominated by the major labels But these "indies" were the exception, not the rule.

Now, more than ever, individuals outside the mainstream music industry are gaining a real presence as leaders in marketing innovation. Sometimes even a non-music company can have an impact, as Apple Computer did in 2003 when it modeled a new Internet sales system with its iTunes Music Store.

How We Got Here

The music business has always been an industry of innovators—of individuals pushing their wares to the listening public using all existing methods and, when necessary, creating some new ones. This was true as far back as 1900, when the music business in the United States was a much simpler industry than it is today. It was a make-do environment back then, lacking the communication channels, institutions, systems, and regulations that structure today's commercial landscape. In many ways, it was a market free-for-all.

Sheet music was the key music product at the time, and music publishers marketed it largely through such retail outlets as the F.W. Woolworth chain. The publishers employed salesmen popularly known as song pluggers. Singers and performers themselves, the pluggers would belt out the songs right on the premises of the retailers, hoping to attract attention to the sheet music being sold. They energetically plugged the tunes in other settings as well, from music halls and bars to city streets—wherever they could hope to draw a crowd.

But over time, developing technologies opened the door to new and more sophisticated possibilities for music distribution and promotion. The phonograph record, pioneered in the early part of the 20th century by the Victor Talking Machine Company and Columbia, paved the way to mass distribution of music by allowing consumers to purchase recorded performances. Its invention was accompanied by Rudolph Wurlitzer's development of a coin-operated playback machine that could be used commercially in hotels, restaurants, and other public settings. It caught on, and by the early 1930s, so-called jukeboxes were being used across the United States.

Radio developed alongside the phonograph industry and proved to be a potent force. As with most new technologies, it initially posed a threat to established industries. At first, record-label brass feared that listeners would simply tune in their radios and stop buying records. But the opposite proved to be true: radio airplay greatly stimulated sales of the 78-rpm discs of the period.

With the growing number of ways consumers could purchase and listen to music came an increase in the number of ways creators could earn money. Tracking and collecting the income from those uses became a vital concern of artists. In 1914 a group of songwriters formed the American Society of Composers, Authors and Publishers (ASCAP) to ensure that music creators would be compensated for public performances of their work. Today, ASCAP and its chief competitor, Broadcast Music, Inc. (BMI), serve as central clearinghouses for the channeling of money from music users (such as radio and TV stations) to music creators. (See "ASCAP and BMI" on page 234.)

By 1950, the basic infrastructure of today's marketing and promotion system was in place: a set of formats for the commercial sale of music (at that time, phonograph records and sheet music) accompanied by communication methods (radio, movies, jukeboxes, and live performances) that exposed people to a range of performers and sounds and helped convince those people to purchase the records and sheet music.

The 1950s saw the beginnings of dramatic new ways that music was brought to—and could be enjoyed by—the public. Television, introduced in the late 1940s, revolutionized the entertainment field by bringing visual performances into the homes of mass audiences. Television had the side effect of boosting radio's use of recorded music. Prior to TV, radio concentrated largely on broadcasting live performances. As TV's early variety shows siphoned off radio's audience for live programming, radio had to focus more on playing records. Ultimately, stations began to specialize, "narrowcasting" their broadcasts to suit local listeners' tastes (such as for country music, rhythm and blues, show tunes, and, later, rock and roll). Radio programming became increasingly segmented, with different stations specializing in ever narrower music "formats."

The 1950s also brought the appearance of the 45-rpm "single" record and the 33 ⅓-rpm long-playing disc (LP)—the latter becoming popular in stereo by the early 1960s. By the mid-1960s, many radio stations were turning to stereo FM broadcasting for improved signal quality. Such innovations led to improvements in the music listening experience, to more choices for music consumers, and to the overall growth of the music industry.

In the early 1980s, Music Television (MTV) ushered in the era of the music video—yet another means of getting music to audiences. Digital recording technology began to eclipse traditional analog production methods, leading to the rapid and overwhelming acceptance of a new playback format, the compact disc (CD), which could store more music than an LP record and (arguably) offer higher-quality sound.

As the 21st century began to unfold, Internet music streaming and downloading captured the interest of consumers and sparked the creativity of musicians and music sellers. Like innovations of the past, the Internet promised reinvention of music production, packaging, and distribution to the public.

Challenges and Opportunities

Individuals and companies entering the music marketing arena today need to be aware of trends posing significant challenges and opportunities:

Development of New Forms of Entertainment. The music industry is increasingly challenged by new forms of entertainment competing for consumer dollars. Internet games, computer software, and almost-unlimited cable TV options are just a few of the current sources of competition for music sellers.

Consolidation of Supply-Chain Ownership. Increasingly, large media conglomerates are gaining ownership of the businesses that traditionally controlled the flow of products to consumers. Such domination of the marketplace by a few giant companies makes it more difficult for smaller companies to break into the business. (See "Vertical and Horizontal Integration" on page 84.)

Expansion of the Internet. The World Wide Web is providing a marketing solution for individuals and small businesses squeezed out by the conglomerates. Now any small business can bypass standard marketing channels and sell music directly to customers. But the market leaders aren't ceding this battlefield to the up-and-comers. Using all the legal and economic weaponry at their disposal, major record companies are fighting for control of cyberspace and setting up their own money-making sites.

Development of New Technologies. New technologies are continuing to change the face of music commerce. As just one example, listeners can choose music from the Internet's vast selection and copy it to personal hard drives or to portable players. This poses a direct challenge to brick-and-mortar retailers and CD manufacturers. (See "The Internet Music Shakeout" on page 125.)

Sources of Income

Today's marketplace—with its many product formats and music outlets—offers numerous possible sources of income for the music seller. Here are some of them:

- Retail sales of CDs, tapes, DVDs, and other formats
- Ticket sales for live performances
- Royalties and fees earned from performances of recordings on radio and television, on the Internet, in movies, and in commercial venues such as restaurants and nightclubs
- Royalties earned from cover versions (that is, other performers' versions) of music, created for use on records, in live performances, on television and radio, and in movies
- Fees for re-recording and play by Muzak and other background music companies, and for reproduction of music in music boxes and musical toys
- Retail sales income and royalties earned from sheet music
- Sales of T-shirts, jackets, tour books, and other promotional merchandise
- Subscription fees and other Internet-based income for artists and music sellers with their own Web sites, and licensing fees for use of music on others' sites

Approaches to Doing Business

How can a musician or businessperson use marketing to tap into these profit centers? As commercial channels have multiplied, several different approaches to doing business have become common.

The Traditional Approach. Until recently, artists and their representatives, with very few exceptions, have had only one viable option when it came to getting their music to the public. Here's what they've had to do:

- Sign a contract with a major record company, which handles the marketing and promotion process.
- Sign with a music publisher, which handles the administration and promotion of original music compositions.

- Affiliate with a performing rights organization (the largest are ASCAP and BMI), which tracks radio and TV airplay and handles the royalties for such use.
- Market through partnerships with an established management agency, which oversees all the career decisions of the performer-songwriter, and a large talent and booking agency, which handles the business of touring and live performance.
- Hire an independent publicity firm to support the record label's publicity efforts (mostly coverage in magazines and newspapers and on TV, radio, and the Internet).

The Alternative Route: Doing It Yourself. In recent years, the music business has seen more and more adventurous souls taking care of business themselves. An alternative or "guerrilla" strategy for getting music to an audience may include the following tactics:

- Recording music in a small studio using digital technology
- Burning CDs one by one, or ordering mass duplication and storage of CDs directly from a commercial outfit
- Using the Internet and local media to promote the music and the act
- Selling CDs via the Internet, direct mail, and/or phone orders
- Selling digital song files over the Internet through various kinds of Web sites
- Marketing the CD directly to smaller record stores and other retailers
- Personally booking live club dates
- Establishing a small publishing company to deal directly with a performing rights agency
- Devising brand-new music income sources

THE MARKET-AWARE MUSIC SELLER

So while some of the basics remain the same, many other aspects of the marketplace are changing at warp speed. The demands on the marketer have never been greater, requiring initial decisions about which route to follow and then many more tough decisions about how best to travel that route.

Regardless of the path you choose for your music, your success as a marketer will depend on your knowledge, skills, and attitude. Today, smart marketing requires

- knowledge of how to target and reach an audience
- awareness of all the current sources of music income
- knowledge of the established procedures of music commerce
- the ability to develop innovative new business procedures
- knowledge of how to take full advantage of technology
- willingness to take the initiative—to work proactively rather than passively wait to be "discovered"

In the current wide-open, rapidly changing business environment, you, the marketer, have to become a lifelong learner, market expert, media maven, pioneer, innovator, and—very importantly—self-starter. If you're a musician, no one is going to work as hard or apply as much dedication as you in getting your music across to an audience. You are always the best advocate for your creative work.

THE INDEPENDENT MUSICIAN'S CHALLENGE

If you're a musician planning to take your career into your own hands and use the tools of marketing to do it, keep in mind that you're vying with thousands of others for the attention of the listening public. This means you need to be realistic, smart, and persistent. A successful career requires the following:

- *Musical talent*—or at least an ability to connect with listeners, whether through personality, lyrics, or showmanship. Before doing any marketing, realistically assess yourself as a musician. As obvious as this seems, it's a step that many don't take before they expend resources on making and trying to sell CDs.
- *Desire to succeed,* which often means the willingness to make sacrifices in other aspects of life. At times, music-career demands may take a toll on your personal life, since working at night means frequently not being home. Make sure you can handle it.
- *Persistence,* and the ability to remain positive about your career even when the inevitable rejections come your way. Not everyone will like your music. But if *you* know it's good, and if enough others like it, forging ahead and staying in it for the long haul will almost certainly ensure eventual success.
- *Live performance.* Unless you plan to work behind the scenes—say, as a studio musician or a jingle composer—you'll need to work in front of audiences as regularly as you can. It both hones your musical skills and builds your fan base.
- *Recordings.* CDs and digital files are both key sources of income and tools for preserving your music in fixed and lasting form. Release new ones regularly.
- *Marketing.* With all the other elements in place, using the tools of marketing in a systematic, creative, and relentless way will ensure you emerge from the crowd as an attention-worthy musical professional.

The equation for success boils down to this:

$$\text{talent} + \text{desire} + \text{persistence} + \text{gigs}$$
$$+ \text{recordings} + \text{marketing}$$
$$= \text{likelihood of professional rewards}$$

As a musician, you may be inclined to pursue a record contract and leave the marketing to the label staff. You'd prefer to concentrate on your music and not have to concern yourself with the business side. But keep in mind that one way or another you'll have to deal with the business side, at least early in your career. Today, record companies are looking for artists who have already proven themselves in the marketplace, preferably with a CD that has sold respectably, and with a base of fans who attend performances.

On the plus side of handling your own business, you won't have to turn over most of your CD earnings to a record company, and you'll retain control over every facet of the enterprise, from creating the record to designing the album covers, press materials, and collateral. What's more, you'll learn much more about the business through personal experience than you would if you handed the reins over to someone else. If you do eventually sign with a record company, you'll have an insider's knowledge of how the business works.

THE MUSIC MARKETER'S ADVANTAGE

To recap, marketing music is a challenging process, but it's doable when handled systematically. In some ways, music is easier to market than other types of products. It has a powerful built-in appeal. Music has been used worldwide, through the ages, to heighten the experience of social occasions, religious ceremonies, and other events—and simply to provide entertainment. Whether the instrument is the human voice, an acoustic piano, or the latest electronic device, music reaches deep within human consciousness to arouse emotions, lift the spirit, and spark the imagination. That innate value is priceless—and a boon to anyone involved in music marketing.

Music can also reach across language and cultural barriers—more so today than ever, given current communication technology. American pop music, for example, is embraced all over the world, and music from any country can be found in the repertoires—and the markets—of any other country.

Armed with those unique selling points, with music you believe in, and with a commitment to succeed in the music industry, you're poised for action.

In the next chapter you'll get a behind-the-scenes look at the marketing campaign for a new recording. Then you'll explore what's involved in bringing your own product to market.

Chapter 2

Charting the Corporate Hitmaking Process

Not too long ago, the discovery of a record by a customer usually went something like this:

One night, while watching a news show on cable, a music fan catches a featurette on an interesting new band. He remembers that earlier in the day he read a rave review of the band's new CD in the local newspaper.

Then it's Friday—payday. After work, he stops by his favorite music store and stops to look at the new cardboard cutouts, mobiles, and posters just inside the doors near the front listening booths. He checks out a new CD the store is promoting—it's the one by the band he read about and saw on cable TV. He likes what he hears and decides it's going home with him. Waiting in the checkout line he reads the CD's jacket to get the story behind his new purchase.

Then on the way home, he turns on his favorite FM radio station and hears a song from the new release. He feels good about his purchase.

Today, the process may unfold in any number of ways. For example, a music fan may hear a track somewhere and download it as an Internet file without buying the CD.

But whatever form the purchase takes, it probably occurs in part thanks to a recent marketing and promotion campaign by a record label.

THE RECORD COMPANY MARKETING PROCESS

A record company relies on effective cooperation by several of its departments: marketing, advertising, sales, promotion, and publicity (as shown on page 10). Together, they strive to "sell through" or maximize sales of a given musical product.

Here's how the process works, in a fictional example.

On the Rise

For months now, the industry has been buzzing about a hot new blues-rock band called Four Gone Conclusions (4GC) that exploded out of the Tampa area.

At a music-business convention in New York, the band played live at a nightclub showcase and brought the house down. Before the night was over, negotiations had begun between the act's management and the vice president of A&R (artists and repertoire, or talent acquisition) of a national label, Rhythm Oil Records.

The completed contracts were signed at an exclusive party in Hollywood, with pop-music press and label brass and their friends enjoying Cuban food and local beer from Tampa while a sound system resonated with the group's first (self-produced) CD, which had sold several thousand copies.

Departments involved in marketing activities of a large record company. (Organization varies from company to company.)

Gearing Up

Now, with production of the first album for the label underway, the various gears of the label machinery start to move, and every one of the label's departments has plenty to do.

Corporate brass kicks off the marketing campaign by holding an interdepartmental meeting to plan activities in support of the album release. Following a general discussion of the act, participants present opinions, strategies, and ideas.

Then the marketing director shares some specifics of her marketing plan:

- The band's mix of sophisticated, bluesy originals and reworkings of classic blues tunes is expected to appeal to educated males and females, ages 18 to 50-plus.
- This demographic group should respond to the members' literacy, musicianship, and songwriting talent.
- The act's somewhat dark, mysterious image will be maintained, while its members will continue to do significant charity work. This has been

shown to appeal to fans in the targeted age and education bracket. It will also provide an "angle" for stories pitched to the press.

- The band, a mainstream electric blues act, will be cross-marketed to blues, jazz, and modern-rock fans.
- To build on the band's artistic depth and fan appeal, the label will mount a big-budget promotional campaign. The plan includes a contest on the Internet.

The label's decision makers listen to a couple of rough studio tracks from the band's new CD. They're encouraged by the announcement that famed producer John X. Smith will come out of retirement to finish 4GC's new CD. This will get plenty of media play.

Timing, communication, and teamwork by everyone at the label are vital now. The label might have a new marquee act here and the executives can almost taste it.

As the album nears completion, various departments begin to swing into action.

Marketing

Several key decisions have been made in the marketing department, with more looming in the near future.

CD Packaging. First and foremost are two critical decisions for any new act: the CD's title and jacket art.

The band's manager, although not part of the label, is pushing hard for the CD to be titled *Ybo Arising*. The track with this title is an eerie, haunting 12-bar ballad based on a true story in which members of the fiercely proud West African tribe the Ybo, having been brought to coastal Georgia on a slave ship in 1855, chose to commit suicide rather than face servitude. According to the legend, you can still hear the distant clanking of slaves' chains on moonless nights near Ybo Landing on St. Simons Island, on Georgia's marshy lowlands.

Everyone in marketing likes the song, and agrees that the story should appeal to their multiethnic target audience.

But band members and label brass aren't sure how to illustrate the CD jacket, until the lead guitarist mentions a painting he's seen that would be perfect: a depiction of the Ybo tragedy that contrasts images of the captives descending into water with a scene of the tribespeople back in West Africa, rising from the surf, joyous and free.

Right after the meeting, the marketing director locates and contacts the artist. At first, the artist refuses and tells the marketing director her painting is not for sale. But she eventually becomes intrigued with the band, especially its history of charity work. She agrees to release worldwide rights if the painting can be auctioned off with a $50,000 minimum. All proceeds will go to Lions Clubs International to support that service group's childrens' eye-care program.

The label brass agrees, and the painting is couriered from Jacksonville, Florida, to the label's Hollywood office.

An art director in the label's creative services department is assigned to design the CD cover, combining the painting with the band's name, its logo, and the album title.

Web Site Design. The marketing department works with the creative services department to create a Web site for the band—linked to the label's main site—with copy written by the label's publicity staff. Text, graphics, and sound are formatted to be installed and uploaded.

Every staff member helps to design an elaborate contest to debut on the Web site. The top prize: an all-expenses-paid weekend for two at the Chicago Hilton with a limousine tour of famed Chicago blues clubs.

Video Production. Working with creative services, an independent production company, and a well-known video director, the marketing VP plans the band's music video. Footage from Ybo Landing and computer-generated graphics will be featured.

With marketing in high gear, an all-department meeting is held to report on progress.

Sales

Down the hall in the label's sales office, another team of professionals is just as busy. The sales vice president makes a personal call to the VP of Warner-Elektra-Atlantic (one of North America's largest distributors) to alert him to the impending new release.

By now the sales team has checked the master calendar of retail stores around the country for rack space and extra (preferred) display areas, with their cost and availability noted.

The sales VP is astonished when his staff tells him that Crazy Joe's El Cheapo, a nationwide chain of music stores, has listening booth, front-of-store, and end-cap (prominent rack) space available for the period coinciding with 4GC's release. This chain's stores are frequented by members of the band's target audience, so he quickly reserves the chain's display areas nationwide for that period.

Meanwhile, sales personnel are diving into their contact databases and updating their copies of the master rack-space calendar, based on calls to key independent music stores around the country that operate in the band's core markets: Boston, Denver, Chicago, New York, Atlanta, and Tampa.

The sales department also asks marketing to create a set of attractive promotional materials such as cardboard cutouts, mobiles, and posters. The label president and the band's management agree to set the suggested retail price for the CD at the top new-release price of $18.98.

The sales vice president checks in with a mass-duplicating plant in Philadelphia to schedule an initial run of 20,000 CDs. Four thousand of those copies will be used for promotion to radio, the media, distributors, and key buyers.

In a meeting with the sales VP, the advertising department agrees to place a half-page ad in the trade weekly *Billboard* for three weeks to promote the CD's release at well as an "image" ad in *Rolling Stone*. Other ads will appear in *Spin, Down Beat,* and *Living Blues,* as well as in selected lifestyle and entertainment publications aimed at the target audience.

One advance copy of the semifinal mix is delivered from the recording studio and listened to by representatives of all departments.

Now key components of the release are coming together.

Promotion (Radio and Music Television)

All along, the promotion department has been hard at work on 4GC's radio and music-television campaign and the first single release of the CD's title track. Nationwide promotional efforts will focus on two key formats: AAA (Adult Album Alternative) and jazz/blues (including some programming produced for local stations).

The national promotion VP contacts the independent promotion company chosen to push the title song to key radio programmers around the country, including program directors for national radio networks. Personal calls also go out to the hosts of nationally syndicated music shows.

Coordination and timing are at the top of everybody's agenda as the VP contacts regional promotion personnel in urban markets from San Francisco to Miami. In daily conferences by phone and e-mail, the groundwork is laid for the CD's delivery to stations. To avoid leaving any key station or network feeling slighted, the deliveries will occur simultaneously.

The label's promotion staff is in constant contact with field reps to finalize details of special listening parties, tailored to the individual markets. These lavish events will woo local deejays, veejays, programmers, and press people.

Publicity

The publicity department has been hard at work on 4GC's media exposure campaign.

The vice president of national publicity spends hours each day glued to his phone and computer keyboard. Some two dozen priority media contacts around the country—influential music editors and album reviewers at key national magazines, news syndicates, major-market daily newspapers, and leading music Web sites—merit personal calls from the VP with advance information on the label's publicity campaign.

The scene is much the same inside the tour publicity office, where specialists from the label work closely with the group's independent talent agency to promote the live concert schedule. (Several weeks before a nightclub or large-hall date, local media in the surrounding area will receive colorful press materials and concert tickets.)

In addition, college-press publicity professionals work hundreds of college newspapers, large and small, all over the nation to get the word out.

With the important contacts in place and advance word traveling down the media grapevine, the national publicity VP sets into motion a carefully orchestrated publicity campaign supported by well-designed packets of PR materials, or "press kits." The process involves the following steps:

- A professional entertainment writer interviews the band and drafts the artist "bio." This includes the story of 4GC and its members: who they are, how they got together, and where they stand artistically.
- A noted music business photographer plans and shoots the group's publicity photos—three sets of studio portraits and live onstage shots, with some in black and white and some in color.
- A graphic designer creates a sleeved cardboard jacket featuring the logos of the label and the band. This colorful jacket keeps the other materials neatly organized (and noticeable on the most cluttered of desks).
- A marketing staffer prepares a one-page publicity fact sheet, which will be useful for TV appearances and interviews on live radio or in Internet chat rooms.
- The band's most favorable press clippings—mostly nightclub reviews—are laid out neatly on 8 ½-by-11-inch paper and photocopied onto high-quality paper.

While these materials are being mass-produced by a printer, the publicists get busy studying the computerized media list on a computer database to fashion a direct mailing list, tailored for the CD release. Names on the list will include national magazine music editors, daily-newspaper entertainment editors, college-newspaper music editors, lifestyle/entertainment weekly editors, and key freelance music writers in every major urban center.

International Markets

Four weeks before the CD's North American release, the label's VP of international affairs confers with overseas distribution partners in countries with good potential fan bases. These include Belgium, France, England, Brazil, Japan, and Malaysia. The VP promises to express-mail advance copies of the CD and press kits to each partner for preview.

Now all the components of the band's debut campaign are in place. Each department checks and double-checks its work, and regular briefings keep every employee up to speed.

Teamwork with Non-Label Partners

At the same time, the band's non-label representatives are busy with important preparations.

4GC's management firm has signed the band with SevenStars/Crown, a top talent agency specializing in modern blues and blues-rock that can book the act in key clubs across the country. The agency also gets the act on a prestigious twenty-two-city package tour of medium-size halls.

Management cuts a deal with Ol' Rattler, a popular Tampa local beer, to co-sponsor 4GC's part in the package tour. The beverage company will provide stage backdrops, posters, and tasting parties across the country as part of the brewer's own expansion program. The band will also be spokesmen for the beer company's new "drink responsibly" campaign.

Band management also completes an agreement with an established publishing house, Four Dogs Music of Austin, Texas. Four Dogs then arranges with ASCAP to handle the band's performing rights worldwide.

After weeks of teamwork, planning, and preparation, things are ready to happen. And the pace is about to get dizzying.

The Breakout: Release Day and After

The recording having been completed in the studio, the following events unfold:

- Master discs are couriered to the duplicator in Philadelphia for an initial run of 1,000 CDs. Advance copies of the final master are also rushed to the label president and the various department heads.
- The 1,000 CDs are boxed with jacket art and shipped to the distributor's warehouses around the country, along with promotional materials.
- The units are then delivered to stores or chain distribution centers so the displays and listening booths can be stocked.
- While staff members in key markets hand-deliver CDs and various promotional items to programmers, many more sets of materials go out to "reporting" radio stations by overnight courier. Then local promotional staff organize a flurry of sneak previews in markets across the country for reviewers and entertainment editors.
- The publicity people take delivery of their materials. Along with the CD copies and promotional items, the press kits are overnighted to key editors and reviewers. A nationwide mass mailing is completed.
- Review copies of the CD, press kits, and promotional items are delivered along with copies of the video to MTV, VH1, and other music television channels.
- Mentions of the new release begin to appear on national entertainment news programs, syndicated radio shows, and selected music Web sites.
- Publicity leverages the story of the title tune and the charitable destiny of the original jacket art to get maximum coverage. NPR's *All Things Considered* does a two-minute featurette on the new release and the band's upcoming charity auction.
- Publicity pulls out all the stops to get CD reviews and feature stories in national magazines, daily newspapers, and lifestyle weeklies. The label continues to show its commitment to the band, making numerous follow-up calls to programmers and editors.
- As the title song begins to appear in the various radio formats, band members are interviewed live on selected major-market radio stations to tell the background of the title track.

- The band's Web site, linked to the label's main site, receives a growing number of hits, many of which are click-throughs from Internet radio stations and other music Web sites. Growing numbers of visitors are downloading 30-second song excerpts.
- Increasingly, the band plays to sold-out clubs (with about 200 seats) and medium-size performance venues (about 500 seats).
- In one major-market promotional push by the tour sponsor, the Tampa beer company peppers the Tampa–St. Petersburg–Clearwater area with "co-op" TV, radio, and print ads that tag the band, the new CD, and the beer brand, and also include a message about responsible drinking that praises designated drivers.
- At colleges, listening parties organized for local media—also cosponsored by the beer company—generate a great deal of "street buzz" within the target audience.

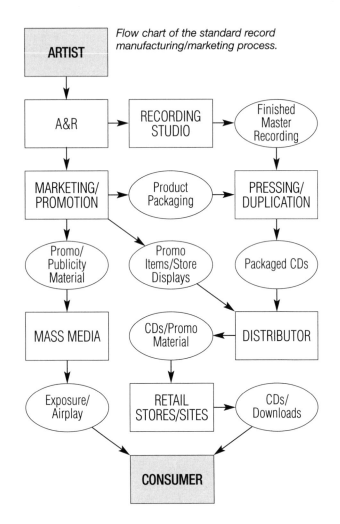

Flow chart of the standard record manufacturing/marketing process.

- "Feelers" come in from *The Tonight Show* and other national TV programs.
- The band receives an invitation to open for the Rolling Stones in Paris.
- The album's title song appears on *Billboard* magazine's Modern Rock Tracks chart.
- Back at the label, reports of brisk sales come in, along with reorders.
- In daily (and nightly) meetings, label executives and staff review promotional successes and strategies, then fine-tune their short- and medium-range plans. Everyone is invited to build on past decisions.

The End Result

Here's what has happened: A barrage of data about the band and the new CD has been hurled at the target audience. It's increasingly unlikely that anyone in the target market will be unaware of the band and their new CD.

Soon, the entire process will start all over again for this small army of marketing, promotion, and publicity professionals.

THE MUSIC PUBLISHER'S MARKETING PROCESS

With the record company's gears in motion, the band's management has attended to a different but equally important part of the band's career: their potential for earning money from an array of commercial uses of their music.

Management is well aware that every time a musical work is performed or broadcast on radio, TV, the stage, a jukebox, or any other medium, the songwriters earn royalties. That's why 4GC's general manager has signed each member (all are songwriters) with Four Dogs Music, the Austin-based music publisher. Working with 4GC on a 50-50 basis, the publisher will now represent the band's music in several important ways not handled by the record label.

Copyright

First, the publisher registers all the band's music with the U.S. Copyright Office. This provides legal protection from theft or plagiarism of both music and lyrics. It's a critically important step for any original music. (Although a composition is considered copyrighted at the time it is written, registering it with the Copyright Office adds legal weight to the claim of ownership.)

Performance Rights

Next, the publisher registers each band member and clears the members' respective songs with the American Society of Composers, Authors and Publishers (ASCAP), a performing rights organization based in New York. (The other large music rights house is Broadcast Music, Inc., also known as BMI.)

ASCAP will now oversee the calculation, collection, and payment of all performance monies due the band member–publisher team. For a popular song, money can come from a wide array of sources, including radio and TV airplay, Webcasting, cover versions by other performers, jukebox play, nightclubs, bars, restaurants, stores, and even parking lots that play recorded background music. (For more information on ASCAP and BMI, see page 234.)

Mechanical and Synchronization Rights

The publisher has also affiliated itself with the Harry Fox Agency in New York. This well-established company will now take care of all mechanical rights to 4GC music—which includes the collection and payment of licensing fees for new versions of the music used on other artists' CDs and tapes. (See "The Harry Fox Agency" on page 231.)

The publisher also promotes synchronization rights, which cover the use of the music in audiovisual media such as movies, television, and home video. This important side of music publishing can add a very lucrative dimension to a song's total earning picture. (See page 233 for more on synchronization rights.)

Tracing the Path of a Published Song

Let's go back to our original music fan who read a CD review in the newspaper, saw the band on cable that night, and then decided to buy the CD on payday.

While reading the CD jacket as he waits at the record store's checkout counter, he notices that the songs were written by members of the band—all except for one track, the title of which is followed by a name, Jakarta James, that the music fan doesn't recognize. For a split second he wonders how a song written by someone not in the band ended up on the CD.

He doesn't know it, but chances are a music publisher played a major role.

A Song Is Born. To trace the path of the song to the CD, let's return to the case of the Four Gone Conclusions.

Around the time 4GC is stirring up interest in Tampa, a year or so prior to their label deal, a local high-school student named Jakarta James is delighting her family, friends, and school music director with a song she has written. Titled "Cubano Skiffle," it's a lively dance tune about unwinding on a Saturday night. The excited music director is convinced the song has commercial possibilities, and he decides to help Jakarta get it to music publishers. Using a borrowed machine, he tape-records the girl singing and accompanying herself on acoustic guitar. He converts the recording to digital file and burns it onto a CD.

The music director composes a cover letter to an entertainment lawyer he knows, introducing the student and the song and suggesting a submission to Four Dogs Music, a company he found on the Internet. He sends a copy of the CD.

Two weeks later, to the astonishment of the school, the young lady receives a letter from the professional manager at Four Dogs Music. He's interested in the song. If she and a parent or guardian sign with Four Dogs, the tune will be cataloged, copyrighted, and registered with ASCAP. The letter includes the necessary forms to fill out.

The Right Song for the Job. Months pass, during which 4GC is signed to Rhythm Oil Records and Four Dogs Music. Soon, in a recording-studio planning meeting, it's discovered that the band is one song short for their new CD. Hastily, a search is launched for just the right number. Song after song is ruled out. This is a key decision because the cover song has to fit the image of the group and the context of the rest of the CD.

Back at the publisher, the professional manager hears about this and quickly begins searching the vaults. "It's a long shot," he decides, "but 'Cubano Skiffle' just might be the right song." A more professional demo is recorded locally and then overnighted to 4GC's producer and the label president.

A heated debate soon ensues. Is the tune too "pop" for the band's image? Would it have any single-release potential? Finally, a consensus emerges: everyone likes the lyrics; they're fun, upbeat. The problem is the arrangement.

Then, with Four Dogs' professional manager and arranger on a telephone conference call, the band and the producer iron out a suggestion: slow down the number slightly and turn it into a sexy, bump-and-grind shuffle (much like the Rolling Stones' version of the Buddy Holly classic "Not Fade Away").

Far into the night, the band experiments with tempos and such color-adding instruments as maracas, timpani, and steel triangle.

At the next day's listening session, everyone is enthusiastic about the latest "take," including the label president and the departments of promotion, sales, and publicity. "Cubano Skiffle" will round out the new CD. Quickly, the news travels to the publisher and then to Tampa, where Jakarta James and her music teacher are flabbergasted.

The Second Single Release. Flash forward to the present: Now that 4GC's first single release, "Ybo Arising," has peaked and is waning on the charts, it's time to discuss the all-important second release. From Austin, the publisher lobbies hard for it to be "Cubano Skiffle."

Both the publisher and the label brass begin the polling process, contacting key pop music programmers, club deejays, and reviewers across the country. The responses are positive.

As the responses come in, a couple of key pointers are discovered, sending the label into a tizzy: various major-market pop radio stations have started getting listener requests for the song; also, label reps in large cities have noticed the tune in dance clubs, both teen and adult. Phone calls and e-mail messages flash back and forth between the label and the publisher.

It's a Hit. The song is rushed into release, and soon it becomes obvious that the band has a major runaway hit on its hands. As one radio network after another adds the record to its playlist, the song spreads like wildfire in dance clubs across the country. It slips into *Billboard* magazine's top 10.

Building on Success. The publisher works swiftly to capitalize on the song's success and to generate revenues from additional sources, all of which will fatten the bank account of Jakarta James.

Arrangements are made to publish the lyrics in song-oriented magazines.

Notification comes in that pieces of the song will be heard in an upcoming episode of NBC's *Law and Order.*

ASCAP notifies the publisher that "Cubano Skiffle" has become extremely popular with cover bands across North America.

A feeler comes in from a Tokyo-based toy manufacturer. An agreement is then worked out allowing the company to produce a line of teddy bears with 4GC's logo; when squeezed, the toys will play the hit song's melody.

Finally, word comes in that Raven Della, an Argentine soap-opera star and pop singer with a huge pre-teen and teen audience all over South America, Central America and Mexico, will cover the song on her new CD.

But, like Rhythm Oil Records, Four Dogs Music won't rest on this success. On a daily basis the music publisher's staff will repeat this process with other songs from its catalog—songs both old and new, placed with a wide variety of musical artists.

Chapter 3

Previewing the Total Marketing Program

Before delving into the process of handling your own marketing and promotion, it's worth taking a look at what the competitive climate is like in the current marketplace.

Independent record sales account for a relatively small percentage of the entire music market. The lion's share has long been held by a handful of large music companies. In 2002, they were the Universal Music Group (UMG), the Bertelsmann Music Group (BMG), Sony Music Entertainment, the Warner Music Group, and the EMI Group.

Yet opportunities are multiplying for "indies"—sellers of music not affiliated with the above-listed "majors." The chief source of opportunity is the Internet. In the late 1990s, the Internet spawned a new kind of music distribution in which users could pull songs from vast collections stored online and play them on personal computers and portable storage devices. Because of its accessibility, the Internet has empowered music industry newcomers to set up online "presences" and sell directly to listeners.

But the Internet aside, there's always room in the marketplace for talented new entrepreneurs willing to take responsibility for their own success. Some examples:

- A small San Francisco–based label, Ubiquity Records, opened for business in the mid-1990s with only $1,000 in seed money. After several years the label achieved annual sales of over $1 million.
- Nashville-based Compass Records, run by a husband-and-wife team, succeeded by targeting a niche audience for eclectic roots music.
- New Albion Records, a company catering to aficionados of experimental music, got its products out by building one-on-one relationships with individual stores and later by using the Internet.

Thousands of other enterprising music makers and marketers have established firm footholds in the marketplace.

At the same time, there are plenty of roadblocks on the path to profitability in the music business. Not least among them is the trend toward consolidation—via mergers and buyouts—of players in the traditional music market, including distributors, retail chains, and radio networks. Fewer decision makers in the distribution pipeline means fewer marketing opportunities for small labels.

The greatest challenge of music as a profession may no longer be the creation of the record. Technology has advanced to the point where professional-quality sound can be achieved at low cost with relative ease. But with more people making records there's much more competition. Now the hardest part is getting the record into th hands of distributors, retail outlets, and customers who are already swamped with large quantities of new product.

Meanwhile, on the major-label side of the industry, business is no easier. Flattening CD sales and shrinking market share, combined with rising competition from Internet file-sharing sites, have lit fires under the people whose jobs depend on profits rising, not falling.

POPULAR PERCEPTION

The large, corporate record labels are almost impossible to compete against.
With the kinds of budgets and distribution systems commanded by the major labels, the small label has little chance of making an impact.

ALTERNATE REALITY

Small, independent labels, with their low overhead and ability to focus marketing efforts on fewer releases, can compete successfully. New outlets, including Internet distributors, are helping to level the playing field.

YOU, THE MARKETER

So where does this leave *you?* Presumably you've already come up with some high quality music. (This may not be your personal music; it could also be music that you'r representing as a manager, label owner, or employee of a large record company.) Now another big task looms before you. Your goal is to make the music earn some money

In your mind's eye is a transaction—an exchange in which someone happily pays money in return for the pleasure of listening to, and owning, your musical produc That money will, in turn, travel down a channel of people, offices, and banks unt it finally finds its way into your pocket. Sounds simple enough. But how do you make it happen?

The process of moving from the point of product creation to the other end of the commercial continuum—where you are on the receiving end of a sales transaction—is called marketing. And marketing is what you must do if you are to sell you musical product.

You will be most successful if your marketing program is clear and well thought out

THE NEED FOR A PLAN AND A PROGRAM

"Build it and they will come." This statement, paraphrased from the 1989 fantasy film *Field of Dreams,* pretty much sums up the way many music people imagine succe will come their way: "If I work hard enough on the music, eventually people will find out about it and start demanding copies of my CD."

But remember: the movie's title is *Field of Dreams*. If the movie were *Field of Reality*, the line would be: "Build something they want—then market and promote it—and there's a better chance they will come."

The point is, the musical product will just sit there unless you do the necessary marketing and promotion work.

With that fairly obvious point in mind, let's look at two contrasting ways of trying to sell a product: (1) using a "flying blind" approach and (2) using a more planned-out, systematic approach.

The "Flying Blind" Marketing Approach

One way to market a product is to release it into the marketplace blindly and hope it sells. In this scenario, the seller may have no hard information indicating that there is any demand for the product. There may be no specifically targeted audience—no identified segment of the populace that research or experience has proven is likely to purchase the seller's kind of product. The only basis for the sale is a gut feeling. The seller purports to have a finger on the pulse of current tastes and to know what kind of product will appeal. So the seller dives boldly into the marketplace, fueling the effort with self-confidence, faith, and raw nerve. Promotion is aimed at informing "the public" about the product in a general way.

Say, for example, you're planning to sell an album of music you'd categorize as electronica. You know from reading lifestyle magazines that electronica is currently popular. So you release the album with the sense that the album's quality will be self-evident and that people who purchase electronica records will find it appealing and will buy it. You place a few ads and hope that the project flies.

This "send it up and see if it flies" approach is risky. First, no matter how in tune with current popular tastes the seller may be, there is no way to predict with certainty how long those popular tastes will be in play. That disc you issued because it conformed to a current musical trend may wind up in a market that has already turned to a new and different trend.

Second, without relying on knowledge of a defined audience, your effort lacks focus. Your advertising and publicity may end up being too randomly dispersed to effectively reach specific groups that might find the record appealing. Your CD may get lost in the flood of equally attention-getting competitive products.

The Planned-Out Marketing Approach

In contrast, the second of the two basic sales approaches involves more fine-tuning of the effort. The seller has evidence that a specific group of people—people from a particular geographic region or age group, for example, or who have specific lifestyle preferences—are inclined to buy the kind of product being marketed. Before the release, the seller finds out as much as possible about the buying habits and tastes of that group, and packages the product to match those tastes. The seller then makes sure

that the product is distributed to outlets that cater directly to those people, and adver
tises and publicizes the product in media targeted to those buyers.

Say, for example, you're marketing a record by an artist with an established cul
following. By tracking sales of previous records, you've learned that the artist i
popular among college-age males located primarily in New England. It would be
reasonably safe bet to emphasize distribution in college towns in New England, t
set up tour dates in that region, and to advertise in publications that reach college
age males.

This approach to selling is far less chancy than the "flying blind" way. It involve
proceeding according to some established guidelines to ensure an informed and, t
the extent possible, *systematic* process of getting a desirable product to a receptiv
audience that has been made aware of the product and its benefits. This, more tha
the seat-of-the-pants approach, is what marketing is all about. When it comes t
staging a marketing campaign, avoid winging it, and you'll have a better chance c
winning it.

POPULAR PERCEPTION

The marketing of music is a loosely defined, make-it-up-as-you-go-along process.
Images abound of artists, managers, and record companies "winging it"—strategizing on a whim, exploiting momentary fads, and generating legions of one-hit (or
no-hit) wonders.

ALTERNATE REALITY

More and more, the marketing of music is a carefully planned process, with specialists
in the areas of artist development, sales, distribution, promotion, and publicity joining
forces in a single, methodical effort to break an artist and build a long-term following.

THE FOUR P's OF MARKETING

The music field has its own unique marketing requirements, as do other fields. Bu
there are some fundamental rules of marketing that apply to *all* fields, and it's helpfu
to be aware of them.

While the term *marketing* most simply translates as "selling," it has another, broade
meaning. It's a meaning that has developed over the course of time as the rationa
behind marketing has become less product centered and more customer focused–
based less on a "here's the product, now let's sell it" approach and more on the ide
"here's a customer need; let's create a product to satisfy that need and then make th
product readily available." Nowadays, marketing can really be said to encompass *c
activities having to do with transferring ownership of a product from the producer to the co
sumer in a way that meets consumer needs.*

Today, marketing refers to an entire *program* for selling—a program consisting of several key components. Those components have come to be known as the Four P's:

- Product
- Price
- Place
- Promotion

Product

All activities related to product development fall into this category. Product development involves ensuring that the product meets current standards of quality; that it has definable value to a definable group of people; that it offers something different from or better than competitive products; and that its packaging is appealing, economical, in conformance with legal and retail requirements, and relatively easy to produce.

Price

The price of the product must be set to achieve a balance of affordability to the audience, profitability for the seller, and competitiveness with similar products.

Place

Place really refers to *distribution*. The product has to be made available to, and easily obtainable by, the customers. Choosing sales outlets and setting up distribution systems to stock them are critical aspects of the marketing process.

Promotion

All the steps that must be taken to increase customer awareness of the product and to convince customers of the product's value come under the heading of promotion. This includes advertising and publicity, Internet exposure, and sales incentives.

The "Three W's and an H" Definition

As long as we're playing with letters of the alphabet, let's look at marketing in another way—in terms of Three W's and an H. The product can be considered the *What* of marketing. Distribution and placement can be thought of as the *Where*. Both promotion and distribution strategies can be boiled down to the *How*. That leaves one more W. Another crucial aspect of marketing is the timing—the *When*—of all the program elements, from production to distribution to promotion.

BEYOND THE FOUR P's:
THE FINER POINTS OF MARKETING MUSIC

Music, as stated previously, has its own special marketing and promotion requirements. Not surprisingly, the typical music marketing effort is more complicated than a simple set of Four P's would indicate.

Product development, for example, might involve coming up with several different product formats, permitting money to be earned from a number of different sources and in various ways. More and more, the marketing function views music a a raw unit of information—digital information, nowadays—that can be presented in multiple configurations, adapted to any media, sent through a variety of distribution channels, and used to establish multiple revenue streams.

A single album, for example, can be sold as a CD, a cassette, and a downloadable digital file. It can be combined with text and visual material in a multimedia format A song from that album can generate sales from the original disc, a separate single, a movie soundtrack, a television commercial, and many other uses.

Similarly, promotion in music represents a complex effort that includes publicity, advertising, sales promotion, live performance, radio play, Internet promotion, souvenir sales, television appearances, and more.

Music distribution involves not only retail store sales but just about any channel through which music is transferred to the consumer or reseller, including the Internet

And after the marketing program has been set into motion, it must be carefully monitored. Where ineffective, the program will need fine-tuning. The plan mus evolve according to market changes. Sales revenues must be managed. Expenditure may have to be reallocated.

Building the Perfect Marketing Machine

Whatever its final components, the marketing plan is created to achieve a goal. The goal, at its simplest, is to develop an audience base and to sell musical product. Along the way, a secondary aim is to build up the marketing program to the point where it momentum becomes almost self-perpetuating.

In music, as in many other fields, it is nearly impossible to completely separate th marketing categories of product, promotion, and distribution. As will be seen in late chapters, components of the marketing program tend to serve several purposes and to reinforce each other. Live performance, for example, is not only a direct source of revenue but also a promotion device, boosting retail sales of CDs. Television appearances generate both fees and publicity. Movie soundtracks do the same. When th components are working effectively, they function as a precisely calibrated system of interacting parts supporting a single money-generating engine, powered by audience demand. The engine's dynamics are summarized in the illustration on page 27.

Branding: Using the Machine to Build a Loyal Fan Base

As previously pointed out, the purpose of building this well-oiled machine is to generate sales. But is that all there is?

Marketing theory differentiates between the simple, one-time-only transaction—where all that matters is the immediate short-term sale (a kind of marketing hit-and run)—and a "transaction" that is more lasting: the establishment of ongoing relationship with customers, so that there will be repeat sales to those customers over the long term Ideally, customers will begin to view the artist (or occasionally the record company s a *brand* that they can trust to provide music that they like. This kind of long-term rust in a producer's products is often referred to as *brand loyalty.*

In music, building brand loyalty is an extremely important goal. In more familiar erms, it means building an audience. Establishing a base of loyal fans means having a ore group of customers who are nearly guaranteed to buy your new CD or show p for your live appearance.

For an example of brand loyalty in the music business, think of the Grateful Dead nd their fans. Deadheads, as the fans called themselves, consumed any product linked o the Dead, from concert tickets and records to trinkets, books, and neckties.

Fortunately, music is ideal for establishing deep emotional connections between rtist and audience. The connection is often felt on the most personal terms by the an. Think of your favorite musical artist and you'll know what this means. The music nd lyrics speak to you personally to the point where you feel a kinship with the rtist. One fan of the British singer Morrissey, for example, described him as "the only ne who understands."

In many cases, the connection is such that the musical artist becomes an absolute ecessity in the fan's life. In strictly commercial terms, this amounts to a one-to-one elationship between the seller and the buyer—the Holy Grail of marketing. It's the ind of brand loyalty that marketers of other types of products can only dream about.

Establishing that kind of audience loyalty and building on it is best done method-cally, by thinking through and then following a multitiered marketing program.

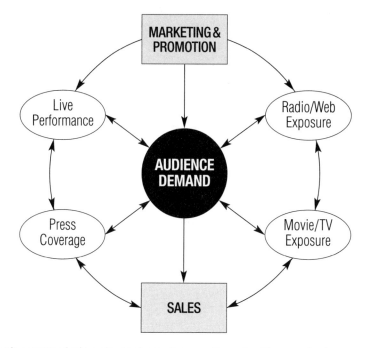

he marketing system fuels audience demand, generating sales. Success feeds energy back to the system, further boosting demand and sales.

COMPONENTS OF A MUSIC MARKETING PROGRAM

In music, the Four P's of marketing can be used as the basis for a more expanded set of building blocks for a marketing program. Again, the standard steps of traditional marketing may not always neatly match the requirements of the music business. But they can serve as a helpful point of reference. With that in mind, use the following as flexible guidelines that you can adapt to your particular marketing situation.

Product Development

The nucleus of any marketing effort is the product. In music, a key product is, obviously, a new recording. (As discussed in the next chapter, however, the core "product" also includes the performer.) As stated previously, product development involves all activities devoted to making sure the product is marketable. This process includes identifying the target audience, identifying and enhancing the product's selling points, differentiating the product from the competition, choosing appropriate delivery formats, packaging the product effectively, and setting the right price.

At What Stage of Product Development Does Marketing Begin? Consider the following two scenarios:

Scenario 1. An artist comes up with a completed master recording and sells it to a record company. The company then sets out to identify a market for the already recorded music and to develop a program for reaching the market.

Scenario 2. An enterprising label executive notices a lucrative new market—say, a market of adolescent female fans of the singer Pink. The executive then decides to develop another artist who will appeal to the same audience. The executive finds such an artist and oversees the recording process to make sure the CD matches the taste of those adolescent female fans of Pink.

In the first scenario, the core product—the music—is created before the marketing begins. In the second scenario, the *marketing guides the entire process,* including the creation of the product.

This begs the question: When should the marketing process begin? Should it start only after the product has been developed (as was once the norm)? Or should the marketing process begin at the same time as, or before, product development? In other words, should marketing be a consideration in the creation of the product itself? (I can already sense the artistic purists among you rising up in protest.)

Well, it all depends. In the case of art for art's sake—where the product embodies creative expression unencumbered by commercial considerations—the marketing would begin after. Captain Beefheart, for example, probably wasn't thinking much about marketability when he created his left-field masterwork *Trout Mask Replica.*

But in the commercial world, marketing is often an intrinsic part of the product development process. New artists get signed primarily because of their sales potential. A set of tracks may be chosen for a CD because they're radio-friendly. In a classical concert series, "Mostly Mozart" is likely to sell more tickets than an Elliott Carter tring quartet and for that reason is chosen for the programming. A jazz musician decides to create a rock band because she can earn more money that way. Marketing decisions occur at any and every stage of product creation and dissemination.

Where *you* begin the marketing process depends on your approach to your music. Are you interested mostly in pursuing your artistic vision, and secondarily in selling o whomever may be interested? Or are you interested in sales from the start, in which case you would think hard about the appeal of the music before you recorded or performed it?

POPULAR PERCEPTION

Marketing comes only after the music is already created.
The Beatles, for example, had songs written and a repertoire established before catching the ears of George Martin and issuing their first records.

ALTERNATE REALITY

The Beatles assembled their repertoire and wrote their first songs while they were playing in clubs—testing what worked and what didn't. To the extent that they chose material that they thought would be appealing, they were involved in self-marketing.

Whether you do it before or after creating the product, it's vital to ascertain the workability of the commercial idea before committing money, time, and effort to a marketing project. You have to know that the product has a chance in the marketplace—even if only a small chance.

With those considerations in mind, it's time for an overview of what happens in product development.

Defining the Target Audience. The workability of a given commercial venture depends on customers: Is there a group of people who will buy the product? If so, who are they? And how large is the group?

The group of people identified as the probable customers for the record is the *target audience.* You may wish to target broadly, aiming for a mass audience. (The textbook terms for dealing with a mass audience are *market aggregation* and *undifferentiated marketing.*) Or you may wish to narrow your focus, precisely targeting only a portion of the mass audience. (The terms for this focus are *market segmentation* and *target marketing.*) Such a portion of the larger market may consist of people in a particular age bracket, people who live in a particular region, people of specific nationalities, people who fall into specific income brackets, people who subscribe to particular lifestyles, and so on.

For marketing purposes, it is essential that there be some sense of the audience for a given musical product. Ideally, the marketer should be able to define the audience precisely, in words, on paper. That makes it possible to create sales messages and pro motions tailored to the audience's interests and characteristics.

Determining the Product's Selling Points. Music speaks for itself, right? Of course—that is, until you have to sell it. Then you need to take stock of the specific reasons why someone in the target audience would want to spend their hard-earned money on it. Having a clear idea of the product's selling points—the matrix of qualities that the audience will find valuable and appealing—is vital for effective marketing. The selling points can be emphasized in the packaging and serve as the basis for headlines and messages used in publicity and advertising.

When you begin to determine selling points, it's important to look beyond just the music. Audiences are attracted to more than melodies: they may fall for the performer's personality and look. They may feel a kinship with the lifestyle and philosophy expressed by the performer's songs and stance. Music as a product can be powerful symbol for the tastes and beliefs of a defined group of people.

Punk rock, for example, symbolized rebellion against the establishment, and against corporate rock in particular. Everything about punk rock's presentation, from ragged guitars to ripped T-shirts, underscored the symbolism. Those elements appealed primarily to listeners who imagined themselves as outside mainstream culture.

Successfully selling a product means having a handle on *all* its sales points, both overt (the music and performer[s]) and hidden (the underlying messages conveyed). The more you can define and communicate these aspects, the more accurately you'll be able to market the product to the correct audience.

In the case of a classical string quartet, for example, the *overt* selling points might be these: the group has won several prestigious awards; it performs adventurous new music; the members dress in outlandish style. The *hidden* selling point might be this: buying the group's recording will reinforce the customer's perception of himself as being culturally sophisticated and in tune with the avant-garde.

Differentiating the Product from Its Competition. Part of establishing a product's value involves setting it apart from the competition. Why would someone buy this jazz CD instead of another? What makes the product unique? Again, these are points that can be emphasized in both product packaging and promotion.

Packaging the Product. Having identified the product's audience and selling points to whatever extent possible, the marketer needs to answer the following question: Given the finished recording, what can be done to package it so that it appeals to the audience most likely to buy it?

The product packaging—the CD cover art, for example—can be designed to emphasize the qualities that target customers will find attractive. It can also be used to explicitly draw attention to the key selling points. The main design and selling points can be reused on ancillary material such as posters, retail display items, Web sites, and souvenir merchandise. They can also be reinforced in advertising.

Visual appeal isn't the only factor in packaging, however. Other considerations are cost of production, speed of production, size and shape requirements for retail display, and legal requirements.

Pricing the Product. The price of a product obviously has an important bearing on its sales success. A product may be priced so high that it is beyond the reach of the targeted customer. On the other hand, if it is priced too low, the seller may not earn a profit. And if its prices are different from those of similar competitive products, the sales effect could be very significant: increased sales with a lower-than-the-competition price; fewer sales with a higher-than-the-competition price. To cover all these bases, the seller has to balance three factors when setting a price: the cost of production, the value of the product set by the customer, and the price of competitive products.

In music, this is made easier by the fact that pricing is relatively standardized: the top price for a new CD as of this writing is $18.98. The industry, collectively, has found this to be a desirable price for covering costs and earning a profit; at the same time, it is a price that customers have been willing to pay (although options available on the Internet have made standard CD pricing seem less attractive). So that for the music marketer, the focuses in pricing will often be on (1) keeping costs down to ensure maximum profit on the generally accepted price, and (2) offering discounts on that price as sales incentives.

Distribution

Between the product and the customer lies the question of how to connect the two. The answer to that question is distribution.

It wouldn't do much good to know the audience if the marketer didn't then place the product in retail outlets—stores—that catered to that audience. It's an obvious point, but worth stating nonetheless: Sell the product in places people go to buy such products.

In the music field, identifying those places isn't difficult. Most people buy records at large record stores, whether on the street or on the Internet. The process of getting records into those stores, however, is not quite as straightforward. Normally, the seller of a record must first secure the services of a distributor—a "middleman" or third party whose job is to serve as a one-stop for distribution to numerous retail outlets. For a price, the distributor takes your CDs and sells them to its retail accounts.

The chain of entities involved in moving the product from the seller to the customer is called the *distribution channel*. Each part of the chain—the seller, the distributor, and the retailer—functions as a member of a team, and all stand to win when the team works well. There are a number of approaches to setting up distribution channels, and choosing the right ones—and the right channel members—is a crucial part of marketing. (See Chapter 7, "Distributing Through Stores and Their Suppliers.")

If you are a one-person operation, or close to it, your approach to distribution may be to bypass the usual multi-member channels. You'll be setting up an order system through the Internet using e-mail, a phone number, and/or an online order form.

You'll be visiting smaller music stores—possibly in person—to place CDs in their racks on consignment. You may be creating a brochure with an ordering coupon, which you will mail to names on a targeted mailing list.

Music Promotion

An essential part of any marketing plan is a promotional strategy. Promotion boils down to informing the world about the product, persuading potential buyers of its value, and continually reinforcing public awareness of the artist and product. Without promotion, you could have all other components—product, distribution, and audience—in place or identified, and the enterprise would still go unnoticed by the public. In the world of music, promotion takes many forms, including live performance, radio play, television, Internet activity, free media coverage (publicity), and paid advertising.

Management of the Marketing Program

As pointed out previously, once the marketing program is in play, it can function as a well-oiled machine, with promotion and concerts fueling new record sales, and increased demand leading to more radio and television play, wider distribution, ever-expanding press coverage, and even more sales.

But the machine requires constant attention and fine-tuning. Changes in the market require changes in the marketing program. For example, if an artist's style of music goes out of fashion, there may be a need to adjust musical direction and to recast the tone and focus of promotion. Similarly, once a product is no longer "new," it will require a new set of tactics to ensure that it continues to generate sales. And finally, it may be that a product or artist is simply not catching on. The marketer has to have a sensitive hand on the pulse of the market to know when this is the case, and to accurately assess when to curtail active promotion and begin winding down the enterprise.

Management of the marketing program might also mean monitoring the incoming flow of money from the various revenue streams—that is, from retail sales, television use, movie use, and any other sources that have been tapped—and executing accounts payable to any subcontractors, vendors, and royalty participants. While in a large company it is the financial division that administers accounts receivable and accounts payable, the marketing people also monitor and scrutinize the sales figures. The numbers are the bottom line, the final indication of the success or failure of the product launch and marketing plan.

For a small company, this process may be hands-on and entirely do-it-yourself. As such, it can be an accounting nightmare, but think of it this way: if you're in the enviable position of administering accounts receivable for your up-and-coming music business, it's the best nightmare you may ever have.

With all these bases to cover, it's helpful to begin the process with a rough blueprint of elements that will shape the marketing plan and guide the overall program. It can serve as an ongoing point of reference—and can be revised at any time as needed. The following example outlines several of the items that can be included in such a blueprint.

PRODUCT MARKETING INFORMATION SHEET

Title of Product:

Name of Artist:

Format(s) of Product:

Price(s) of Product (itemize all formats):

Brief Description of Product:

Targeted Audience:

Estimated Quantities of Product (itemize all formats):

Release Date:

List the main selling points of the product:

Describe what makes the product unique or different:

Where will the product primarily be sold?

List secondary market outlets (specialty stores and catalogs, direct mail, music clubs, special sales, and so on):

Describe the promotion, publicity, and/or advertising strategy:

Upcoming chapters provide more detail on how this chapter's marketing-program model can be used to make your music start bringing in money. The first order of business is to look at a basic music product—a piece of recorded music—and examine its role in the overall marketing scheme.

Chapter 4

Defining the Basic Product and Its Audience

Before starting a marketing and promotion campaign, you have to know what you're selling and who you're selling it to. This is more involved than simply deciding you're "selling CDs to people who buy CDs." It means understanding and being able to describe all the appealing qualities of the music you're selling, so that you can vividly communicate and promote those qualities. And it means identifying and understanding the kinds of people most likely to appreciate those qualities. Only then can you target people with effective messages, reach them where they reside and shop, and provide them with your music in the form they want.

So before going any further, start thinking objectively about your music as a product to sell. You'll need to choose the form in which to sell it—the product *format* or *configuration*. And you'll have to identify the selling points to emphasize in promotion.

You'll also need to focus on your target audience. This means identifying the kinds of people who would like your music, building a list of specific names of people to whom you will market directly, and taking steps to create bonds with your core audience.

Let's look at these processes in detail.

THE CORE PRODUCT

Understanding the difference between a product format and the core product is crucial. A compact disc is a case in point. On one level, it's a product. On another level it's simply a format for delivering a core product: music.

Music is raw information that can be configured in different ways and marketed in different ways. And music, as a product, has several different aspects that have a bearing on marketing. The core product has three components: (1) the performer, (2) the performance, and (3) the music composition.

The Performer

Performers appeal to audiences with their personalities, looks, and other characteristics. In a sense, the performer is the long-term product to be sold and promoted, with records serving as vehicles for generating income and building the career. Direct sale of the "performer" part of the product occurs through concert engagements, television and movie appearances, books, and any other context in which the performer as a personality is exposed to audiences.

Elvis Presley, for example, was sold to the public through records, radio, television, and movies. In a sense, Elvis was a product, and his records were by-products.

The Performance

The performance is the audio, and sometimes visual, expression of the performer's personality. People pay to hear a particular performer play music in a particular way. They like the sound of the voice, the style, the instrumentation, and other distinctive qualities. Thus the performance is a distinct product that can generate income by being used on a CD, broadcast on the radio, presented in a movie or video, showcased in a commercial—the list goes on.

The Composition

The performer and performance are nothing, however, without the musical composition, a product all on its own. It's *intellectual property*—a mental creation that earns money primarily when offered to the public in a performance, on a recording, or on paper. A song can be licensed to any number of different performers, licensed to producers of TV shows and movies, and sold as sheet music. There are myriad other uses that can generate song income.

The Total Marketable Package

These core product components are the primary focus of most music marketing programs, whether the format being sold is a CD, tape, or digital file. A complete marketing program taps into the revenue-generating potential of the total core product.

Think about all the components of your musical endeavor. Is your focus on original songs? Is the onstage performance a key aspect? What about the singer's physical appearance? Knowing what you'll be selling will help you to determine any marketing campaign's direction.

CHOOSING PRODUCT FORMATS

You'll probably end up selling a mix of formats to meet the varied preferences of a wide range of customers. When choosing formats for your music, emphasize the hottest formats—including visual formats if visual style is an important part of the product.

Primary Formats

The most common format for selling music—apart from live presentations in concerts or clubs—is a recording in physical form or in a digital file.

New product formats are always emerging, but the most widely accepted hard-copy format is the compact disc (CD). Its older sibling, the audiocassette, is fading into entertainment history. And the once-primary format, the vinyl record, has become a little-used specialty item.

Music in digital form is increasingly popular. Buyers can stream it from an Internet site, download it to a personal computer, burn it onto a CD, or copy it to a portable playback device.

Most customers purchase music in one of these formats. (Of total non-downloadable music sales in 2001, according to the Recording Industry Association of America [RIAA], 91 percent were compact discs, 4.6 percent were cassettes, and 4.4 percent were other formats, including vinyl and DVD.)

Additional Delivery Formats

You can increase a product's sales-generating capacity by selling it in more than one format. Each unique format meets a different customer need—say, for one or two songs rather than an entire album.

Additional formats also increase the product's visibility in the marketplace by requiring more retail shelf space and by getting the product into stores that specialize in each particular format.

Audiocassettes. Cassettes were once a primary format but now account for less than 5 percent of music sales. Some artists still issue them to meet the needs of people who listen on their old cassette players—in cars, for example.

Vinyl Records. Some artists and specialty record labels continue to issue limited quantities of product on vinyl. The market, though tiny, consists mostly of audiophiles who believe that the analog sound embodied in vinyl records is warmer and more expressive than the digital audio of compact discs.

Singles. Instead of, or in addition to, releasing an entire album, you can release a disc with fewer songs, targeting customers who may resist buying a complete album but are willing to purchase a song they heard somewhere and liked.

Other than Internet downloads, the format for issuing only a few songs is the *single*. During their heyday in the 1950s and '60s, singles were issued in 7-inch vinyl with two songs—an A side (the intended hit) and a B side. Today's CD "singles" may contain from two to five tracks, making them today's equivalent of the EP (extended play), a multi-song format favored especially by alternative bands in the 1990s. As of this writing, CD singles range in price from $3.99 (for two tracks) to $10.99 (for four or five tracks).

Internet downloads have largely replaced singles. (In 2001, CD singles represented less than 2 percent of all music units sold, about half the share they held in the previous year, according to the RIAA.)

Multiple-Album Sets. A multiple-album set may be a two-disc release of new music. It might also be a five-disc compilation of previously released recordings. Whatever the musical content, multiple albums sell in significantly fewer numbers than single discs, simply because their prices have to be set much higher.

A rule of thumb when thinking about using a multiple-album format is that they generally only work if the artist is already extremely popular, with a core audience of customers ready to snap up a new release regardless of the cost. (Bruce Springsteen's 1986 five-disc live set sold well due to pent-up demand for records of his legendary concerts.)

Audiovisual Formats. Most people who enjoy an artist's recordings also enjoy seeing the artist in action. An opportunity to do this—other than at a live appearance—is offered by audiovisual product formats. The most popular of these are videocassettes and DVDs (digital video discs). Generally, music artists don't sell videos and DVDs until after they've built an audience for their music.

IDENTIFYING THE PRODUCT'S APPEAL

Marketing begins at the product development stage with an effort to pinpoint the performer's unique strengths and identify the music's marketable qualities—the selling points you will promote in e-mails, press releases, and other marketing mechanisms.

In some cases, as discussed in Chapter 3, this happens *before* the record is created, affecting the approach to creating the album or single.

Before singer Amanda Latona completed her first album for Clive Davis's J Records, her handlers were "still trying to decide what kind of platinum-selling pop sensation she should be," according to *New York Times* writer Lynn Hirschberg. Artists-and-repertoire director James Diener found himself trying to find "the right spot" for Latona, whose voice could accommodate a wide range of styles. "I'm thinking there might be room [in the marketplace] for a cool, young beautiful girl in the spirit of Shania Twain," Diener told Hirschberg.

You may have a good handle on your own assets. During the pre-recording stage of marketing, try to pinpoint the aspects of your style that people find most appealing. What you learn may have an impact on your recording decisions.

Whether you already have a recording or are still at the pre-recording stage, make sure your product meets the following criteria:

- The music can be categorized for sales purposes.
- It has selling points that can be described.
- It can easily be differentiated from competing products.

Defining the Musical Category

It's important, for marketing purposes, to ascertain the musical category of your product. Is it country? Jazz? Classical? A mixture of several styles?

Some acts object to being identified with one category. But marketing is largely driven by such categories, beginning with product placement in stores. How else will retailers know which rack to put your music in?

Having a clear notion of the musical category and style also helps you communicate it to sellers through promotional material and product packaging. By labeling
your music, even in the most general way, you're simply helping retailers sell your
product. And that's one goal of marketing.

If in doubt about where your music might fit in, go to the nearest entertainment
superstore and look at how the music is shelved. One outlet used the following basic
categories in 2002:

Pop, Rock, and Soul	Oldies	Folk	Latin
Hip-Hop	Easy Listening	Bluegrass	Tex Mex
Electronica	Jazz	Gospel	World Music
Indie Rock	Blues	Reggae	Classical
Vocals (Pop)	Country	New Age	

Determining the Music's Selling Points

What about your music will attract potential buyers? You should be prepared to
answer the following question: Why will people buy this product?

Begin with some obvious selling points. If the artist is a high-energy live performer known for drawing wild crowds, a selling point of the CD might be that it
"captures all the energy of the live performances." For an artist known for writing
sophisticated songs that appeal to older, college-educated crowds, emphasize that the
CD offers "more of the insightful, perceptive lyrics and heartfelt music for which [the
artist] has been embraced by discerning listeners everywhere."

Here are some selling points for real-world artists: To sell Iggy Pop to a new generation of punk-rock fans, the sales point might be: "He's the Godfather of Punk, the
original pioneer of extremism on stage, on disc, and in life." The band Asleep at the
Wheel could be sold with the statement that "they're the leading contemporary pur-
veyors of western swing." The appeal of singer Shawn Colvin could be traced to her
"expressive folk-pop vocals in the Joni Mitchell tradition." A selling point for Pat
Metheny is that he's "a poll-winning guitarist whose compositions blend jazz
improvisation, Brazilian rhythm, and rock textures."

After extracting the obvious selling points, look beneath the surface for the not-
so-obvious ways the product might attract the targeted audience. Remember, the
musical product is only partly about music. It's also about lifestyle (as in the Beach
Boys' '60s paeans to sun, surfing, and cars); social identification (Bruce Springsteen's
evocations of working-class America); and various cultural factors (James Brown's
"Say It Loud—I'm Black and I'm Proud"). The hidden selling point might be the
product's appeal to the customer's self-image as a member of a particular culture or
social group.

Think back to the selling point cited above for the writer of "insightful, perceptive lyrics and heartfelt music embraced by *discerning listeners* everywhere." The hidden
selling point here is that by purchasing the record, the buyer can feel like a member
of the club of sophisticated "discerning listeners."

Consider also the following example, from the world of high technology. In a 1997 newspaper ad, Apple Computer directly addressed its message "to the crazy ones":

"Here's to the crazy ones. The misfits. The rebels. The troublemakers.
The ones who see things differently. They're not fond of rules. Because
they change things. We make tools for these kinds of people. Because
while some see them as the crazy ones, we see genius."

In this case, Apple apparently targeted its core market of creative professionals, appealing to their self-perception as unconventional and inventive. (The ad included photos of Albert Einstein and Mahatma Gandhi, implying that Apple users are members of an elite group that includes these two.)

A rock group's "unseen" selling point might be its raggedness and loudness, which appeals to teenagers rebelling against their parents' old-fashioned tastes. A heavy-metal band's unseen selling point might be that its screaming guitars appeal to aggression-spewing teen males. A singer-songwriter can be given an extra selling point by labeling him "indie," thus making him attractive to the masses of people who like to think of themselves as nonconformists. (One great marketing success of the 1990s was the use of the word "alternative" to describe essentially conventional products so they would appeal to groups noted for rejecting so-called mainstream values.)

Always bear in mind the different ways you can leverage obvious, overt selling points and hidden selling points. The overt kind ("award-winning concert pianist") is often explicitly used in promotional materials. Hidden selling points are mostly used "behind the scenes" as guidelines for linking the product—via visual and other means—with ideas, fashions, social groups, and activities embraced by targeted customers.

The following chart links selling points to particular target groups.

Musical Product	Target Audience*	Audience Characteristics*	Product Selling Points
New-age piano music	Mature; progressive	Domestic interest; health and spirituality focus	Unobtrusive; ambient; soothing
Young male pop group	Females aged 13–15	Concern with independence, appearance; onset of puberty	Musicians are attractive; songs are romantic
Punk rock with antisocial themes	Underemployed singles aged 19–24	Informal socializing; channeling anger at economic status	Angry, loud; provides role models
Electronic dance tracks	Young adults aged 19–s24	Dance and club hopping; dating	Long, uptempo songs; good for dancing

* Audiences and characteristics are hypothetical examples.

After you've identified your key selling points, keep a record of them for future product packaging, image building, advertising, and anything else used to communicate with a target audience.

Differentiating the Product from Its Competition

In a print advertisement for the Brodsky Quartet, the classical string quartet that collaborated with Elvis Costello on the 1993 album *The Juliet Letters,* the headline labeled the group "The Garage Band of Classical Music." This catchy wording accomplished three things at once: (1) it identified the Brodsky Quartet as classical musicians; (2) it positioned them as hipper than other classical music groups; and (3) it cued rock fans that this is one classical music group they'll like. In essence, it set the Brodsky apart from the usual, stereotypically buttoned-down classical string quartet, while positioning them to appeal to an audience—in this case rock fans—outside the core classical market.

Figuring out how to do this—how to set your product apart from similar products—is another key task in the early phase of marketing. "My job," said J Records marketing director Tom Corson to *New York Times* writer Lynn Hirschberg, "is to differentiate our artists. Many acts have a close demographic: what makes one boy band different from another? Why is Busta Rhymes different from Jay-Z? My job is to clarify those subtle distinctions for the consumer."

Just as you peeled back the layers of the product to extract potent selling points, so should you examine your music for characteristics that make it unique.

The most obvious way to differentiate your product from the competition is to present some *evidence* that this music is the best—or near the best—of its kind. Without plausible evidence, any extravagant claims about the music may cost you credibility and sales. Evidence of superior quality may include a list of awards, quotes from positive reviews, and endorsements by other musicians.

Another way to set the product apart is to focus on its unique qualities: A punk rock band may incorporate surf music in its tunes. A jazz big-band leader might claim he was born on the planet Saturn (as did Sun Ra). A classical pianist may have a special way of interpreting Beethoven sonatas. Your music and performer also have unique qualities. Look for them.

Again, keep a list of key differences between your product and the competition. These points can be used with other selling points in product packaging and throughout the promotional campaign.

Test Marketing and Using Focus Groups

Before committing money and time to marketing, try to get constructive feedback from others on how your music is perceived. Find people whose opinions you trust along with as many people as you can find who would simply be willing to respond to a somewhat time-consuming request. Then mail your informal focus group a few works in progress—an unfinished CD, a few MP3 files—and ask for their opinions. Weigh their responses and take them into consideration as you proceed to the next phase of your project.

In such a marketing test, a pattern of comments may emerge, as one music producer discovered after sending MP3s to members of an Internet newsgroup to get their opinions. A number of listeners complimented the singer and vocal harmonies with adjectives such as "earthy," "friendly," and "warm." Several described the songs as "thoughtful" and "wistful," and the style as "intelligent pop rock." The producer was then in a position to focus his selling points and key characteristics on the recurring themes from the respondents.

IDENTIFYING THE AUDIENCE

Identifying your audience as precisely as possible is key to marketing success.

Professional music marketers learn a lot about music audiences. Marketers of new rock music, for example, know that their audience is mostly young, style-conscious, and perhaps youthfully rebellious. Marketers of classical music also make it their business to know their core listeners' distinct characteristics.

Your music, too, has qualities that will appeal to certain people. Its very category—whether jazz, pop-rock, or something else—may have a built-in constituency. Within that group, at least one segment may be especially drawn to your unique approach.

Discovering who these people are gives you a powerful marketing tool. The more specific the audience information, the better you'll be able to tailor promotional messages, direct-mail pieces, packaging, and product placement to audience preferences. Then you can avoid expending time, energy, and money on unknown consumers who may not even like music, let alone your music.

How do you identify a target audience? Start with the most obvious group: your family, your friends, and others who share a personal connection or an interest in your music.

The informal test-market group used by the producer mentioned in the preceding section shared more than just general observations. Members of the group also shared demographic characteristics. By noting the kinds of people who responded most positively to the music—mostly middle-aged, college-educated women, as it turned out—the producer could begin to identify a target audience. Further research would help him more precisely define that group, for more productive target marketing.

Researching Audiences of Music Similar to Yours

Of course, you need to sell music beyond the core group of friends and immediate contacts. To effectively position your product for a wider audience, you must expand your research.

First, study the magazines, Web sites, Internet newsgroups, radio stations, and organizations devoted to or linked with your musical style, or with a specific performer who shares your style. Their audiences are probably the ones you should focus on at the beginning of your marketing campaign. Later, with more feedback and research results, you can more precisely pinpoint a fruitful customer base.

Estimating the Size of Your Audience (and Ballpark Sales Figures)

In addition to researching your target audience, you'll also want to estimate the size of the audience for projections of how many CDs to press, for example. There are several ways to "ballpark" this figure.

Get the circulation figures of magazines that specialize in your kind of music. Media kits from well-established organizations—often on their Web sites, or available by ordering over the phone—contain this information. There are also directories such as the *SRDS Consumer Magazine Advertising Source* (online at www.srds.com), the *National Directory of Magazines,* and the *Standard Periodical Directory.* Links to specific magazines can take you to their circulation data. (Make sure the directory is recent or you may be looking at outdated material.)

Contact associations related to your kinds of music, including fan clubs of similar musicians, and get counts of their membership. A good source for such organizations is the *Encyclopedia of Associations.* Look in the index under "Music" to find everything from the Country Music Association to the Jerry Jeff Walker Fan Club.

Get the sizes of audiences for radio stations that play your kind of music from the stations' Web sites. Or request the information from Arbitron, a company specializing in radio and television market research (its phone number is 212-887-1300, and it's on the Web at www.arbitron.com).

Past sales of CDs similar in style to yours are also good indicators. Record companies don't ordinarily give out sales information to the public, but the local outlet of a nationwide record retail chain might.

The numbers you gather tell you something about the size of your target audience. (But don't add together the numbers from different sources: two different groups you've checked out—magazine readers and record buyers, for example—probably overlap.) The largest numbers you find—audiences for free media such as radio and the Web—can be considered your universe of potential listeners. The smaller numbers, representing paying fans of music similar in style to yours, are closer to your immediate target.

If you can only afford to promote within a limited geographic region (a typical problem for new bands), reduce the estimated size of your audience accordingly. If possible, gather regional numbers for your kind of music based on regional media audiences and retail sales.

You won't sell to each and every individual in your targeted group. A general guideline for direct-mail sales to a list of targeted customers (see Chapter 8) is that between .1 and 10 percent of these people will buy. Thus, if you can reach 75,000 potential customers, you may sell them between 75 and 7,500 units.

BUILDING A MAILING LIST

One powerful marketing tool is a mailing list of customers, existing and prospective. Names on the list make up a database of "likely prospects" to whom you can send product information, newsletters, questionnaires, coupons, and other marketing pieces. Over time, you'll build your own proprietary "house list," which you may augment with a targeted list rented from a magazine, music organization, or commercial list broker for mass mailings.

In music, your house mailing list represents your core—make that *hard-core*—audience. And remember, the core people within this core audience are those with a personal connection.

Did you perform in college? An alumni directory of people in your age group, who might have heard you way back when, would be a good free source of names for a start-up mailing list.

As you collect names, organize them in a computer database program such as Microsoft Access or FileMaker Pro. Your easily updatable customer list will lend itself to storing such information as past purchases and comments about individual customers' preferences in music and media. And the information can be sorted in a number of ways to support your marketing—say, by region if you're planning a mailing to a specific geographic area.

You can expand the list by bringing a notebook or large address book to your live performances and asking interested audience members to sign it, or by leaving blank name-and-address cards on the club's tables for customers to fill out. (As a motivator, offer a free CD to one lucky respondent.) Collect the cards at the end of the night and add the names to your mailing list. Other techniques for getting more names on your list are packaging business reply cards (BRCs) with your CDs and putting a sign-in form on a Web site.

BRCs, Web forms, table cards, and other data-gathering tools should include questions about the customer's tastes and preferences, age, sex, number of records purchased

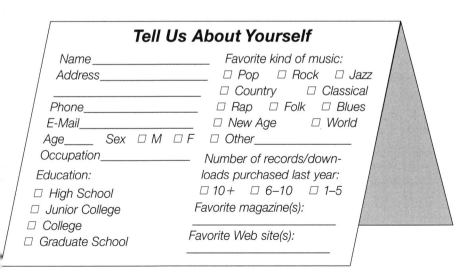

Name-and-address table (tent) card to be filled out by club-goers at a live performance.

in the past six months, and other useful data. Such information will help you assemble profiles of the people who like your music. Developing customer profiles—identifying commonalities in groups of people attracted to your music—will enable you to focus on those commonalities in your advertising and promotion.

These kinds of brief questionnaires are really informal methods of conducting market research. Sources of information about more formal market research methods are provided in the Appendix.

Remember: There may be times when you need to enlarge your list by renting targeted lists of customers from commercial list brokers or from the same magazines, Web sites, radio stations, and other organizations you used to research your target audience. (For information about renting mailing lists, see page 107.)

BUILDING BONDS WITH YOUR AUDIENCE

Gathering a mailing list of audience members is only one part of the audience-building process. You must also connect with the audience, bond with it, and understand it.

The most successful marketers of products for targeted audiences know their audience so well that they feel they can almost reach out and touch them. Editors of music magazine, for example, may know exactly who their readers are, because they share many of the same interests. Knowing precisely the kinds of information their readers seek, they shape the magazine to suit the readers' preferences (which, in turn, generates greater sales).

A band with a local following should have a clear sense of its audience, based on direct feedback and having literally touched their customers. Knowing who likes them and who doesn't, the band can create the kind of product that fans will expect from them.

The band Phish, for example, maintained close ties with its audience through newsletter, an official Web site, and a telephone hotline. This enabled the Phish organization to make artistic and business decisions carefully tailored to meet—or expand on—the fans' expectations.

So the more extensive the marketer's knowledge of target consumers' tastes and buying habits, the greater the marketer's ability to make the product appealing to them.

Getting to know your audience begins with looking at some broad parameters that start with the general characteristics of that audience, including age range, economic status, education level, geographical location, lifestyles, and cultural preferences. (Lifestyle factors are sometimes broken down into activities, interests, and opinions, or AIO.) To find out about characteristics of your potential audience, go to sources of information linked with your musical style: periodicals, record companies, and radio stations.

As mentioned earlier, magazines and Web sites that deal with your type of music are a great resource. Become familiar with them. Try to envision details about the readership by analyzing the tone and sophistication level of the articles; study the ads and imagine the people they target, such as young professionals with disposable income or teenage girls. And the magazines' media kits describe typical readers in terms of age, gender, annual income, Internet access, and other criteria.

Radio stations also have media kits with valuable information about their audiences. Choose stations with formats that are appropriate for your music by checking directories like the *Broadcasting and Cable Yearbook* and the *Gale Directory of Publications and Broadcast Media.* Many stations' Web sites also feature information about their listeners' demographics.

One useful source of information on U.S. radio stations and the music they play is the radio Web page of the *All-in-One Media Directory,* located at www.gebbieinc.com/adintro.htm. (Gebbie also publishes the hard-copy *All-in-One Directory,* a comprehensive listing of radio and TV stations, newspapers, magazines, and other media.)

As mentioned earlier, Arbitron, the radio-market-research company, has a Web site (www.arbitron.com) that provides basic demographic information on leading radio stations across the United States.

Two market information sources that deserve special note are MediaFinder (www.mediafinder.com), a Web-based library of media information that has listings of magazines, directories, mailing lists, and more; and the Ultimate Band List (ubl.artistdirect.com), a more music-specific Web site with information on radio stations, record labels, magazines and e-zines, as well as record stores.

One-to-One Marketing

Marketing increasingly emphasizes the value of market segmentation (target marketing, or niche marketing) over undifferentiated marketing (mass marketing). The ultimate form of market segmentation is one-to-one marketing, which strives for a direct one-to-one relationship between seller and customer. Using this approach, the seller can learn precisely what the customer wants, then customize the product to match the customer's needs. Increasing customer satisfaction leads to a long-term customer-seller bond, brand loyalty, and repeat sales.

The costs of this approach for a large producer have long been prohibitive. (It's cheaper and easier to develop one product with one marketing program for a large number of customers than to spend extra money and effort creating multiple products targeted at individuals.) But it's a valuable concept to bear in mind.

Today the World Wide Web is a hub of one-to-one marketing, because its interactivity permits individual customers to submit detailed preferences to the manufacturer. In some cases they can even customize a product before buying. (An example of a customized music product is a CD made up of tracks individually chosen by the customer, as offered by many music sites.)

Such personalized marketing can be as simple as some sort of direct communication or contact with customers comparable to politicians "pressing the flesh" during campaigns. A hand shaken is considered a vote taken. It establishes a personal bond.

How can one-to-one marketing apply to you? You can establish personal contact when you perform live, going out of your way to meet people in the audience between sets. Shake hands and ask audience members how they liked the music, then ask them to add their names and addresses to the mailing list you set up near the main entrance to the venue. Such steps help you build and solidify your audience base.

Chapter 5

Packaging the Product

"The most important marketing element is the packaging. It's the number one reason consumers make a purchase."

That's the majority opinion of a group of retailers surveyed by New Line Home Video, according to a marketing executive interviewed in *Billboard* magazine. Retailers ought to know, since they're right on the front lines of music commerce.

When we talk about "product package," we're obviously referring to a protective container in which a product is shipped and displayed—a CD jewel box, for example. But packaging involves more than that. From a marketing perspective, it can serve several purposes: to attract customer attention, tout the value of the product, position it amid the competition, and more. That's why packaging is a key part of the product development and marketing equation.

For illustration, look outside the music field for a moment. Take a batch of corn flakes. There are few things in life as vulnerable to crumbling, as indistinguishable from other similar products, and as plain boring to look at. Before cornflakes can be sold in a store carrying other brands, something has to be done to help them survive and succeed.

Here's some of what it takes:

- The flakes have to be packaged in a wax paper bag so they won't spoil, and then placed in a box so they won't be crushed during transport.
- The box has to be an appropriate size and shape to fit on the supermarket's cereal shelves.
- The label on the box has to be large and readable, so that people know what they're buying and who the manufacturer is.
- To meet legal requirements, information about nutrition and ingredients has to be printed somewhere on the package.
- A bar code has to be printed, so that the cereal box can be electronically scanned at the checkout counter.

And that's not all. Why would a customer choose this box of cornflakes over Brand X in the adjacent stack? Customers have to be given a reason. This can be done with the design (the "look") of the box. First, it's got to be visually attractive. Second, it has to be attractive to the right people. If the flakes are supposed to appeal to kids, the box should depict kid-friendly things like cartoon characters or their favorite heroes. If the flakes are aimed at adults, other images would be more appropriate. Finally, the esign should in some way suggest the aspects of the flakes that make them special, ifferent, and perhaps better than that sugary cereal down the aisle.

It's easy to see that packaging involves more than just providing a container. Getting all the elements of packaging exactly right is a complex process that requires erious attention.

Just as with flake-makers and their cornflakes, music manufacturers do not send heir CDs naked into the world to fend for themselves. They give them protective lothing, identification, and attractive decoration.

Music downloaded over the Internet amounts to a separate product category— ne that doesn't involve packaging in the traditional sense. But as of this writing, CDs re still the dominant format, so you'll need to plan for sleeves, boxes, folders, and ther packaging elements.

THE PACKAGE AS MARKETING TOOL

rom a marketing standpoint, the package is the image that the product presents to he outside world. It is the main means for communicating information about the roduct to potential buyers, and for emphasizing the aspects of the product that will ppeal to the targeted audience. All of the marketing factors you have previously iken into account—from the product's selling points to the tastes of potential buyers— vill inform your decisions about how best to package your music.

In many ways the jacket of a music recording is a summation and a highly focused xpression of the seller's (that is, your) beliefs about the nature of the music and how : should be presented in the marketplace. That's why in the corporate world the ackage design process gets the concentrated attention of nearly all parties involved 1 the product launch, from the art director, the product manager, and the marketing 1anager to the recording artist (depending on the artist's clout). Each party makes a onstructive contribution of his or her expertise toward a common goal: to create a uccessful package that informs and attracts.

You, on the other hand, may not be in the position of working with a marketing taff, a staff art director, a product manager, or even a separate artist (after all, *you* may e the artist). What this means is that you'll have to oversee the creation of the design. s the head honcho in charge of product development, it's your responsibility to stay n top of everything that goes into designing an effective package.

KEY FACTORS IN PACKAGING DESIGN

s previously indicated, the aspects of the design that are meant to inform and attract re only part of the picture. The process of designing a package takes into account an ntire range of criteria:

- physical requirements
- information requirements

- attractive, high-quality design
- adaptable design
- stylistically appropriate design
- persuasive design
- cost

Keeping in mind that for now you are working with the basic product configurations of CDs and, to a lesser degree, cassettes, let's go through the key packaging factors one by one.

Physical Requirements

There are three main physical requirements for packaging: (1) the package must protect the product from damage during shipping and display and after purchase, (2) the shape and size of the package must be such that the product can be effectively displayed in the store, and (3) the packaging must permit clear identification of all components of the product.

Protection from Damage. Obviously, with all the handling of a typical CD prior to purchase, the packaging has to protect against smudging, scratching, and other kinds of damage. Compact discs are packaged in a plastic container commonly known as a *jewel box*. The jewel box is still the industry standard, but you can opt for more eco-friendly alternatives like cardboard packaging in a wide range of configurations, or Digipak®—a cardboard package with a glued-in plastic tray to hold the CD. The standard cassette package is a plastic container called a *Norelco box*. The vinyl record uses a paper or plastic dust sleeve and a cardboard or heavy-paper-stock jacket. All formats are covered with shrink-wrap.

Appropriate Shape and Size for Effective Display. The package has to fit easily in the standard racks and shelving units used by retailers. For this reason, packaging formats are standardized in the industry, and if you match your packaging to these standards you will have no problems. Manufacturers and package producers provide this information on their Web sites and/or in their printed brochures.

Surfaces for Identification of All Product Components. The packaging must provide areas for printing identification of all parts of the product.

In the case of jewel-box CD packaging, this means including a *tray card*—a paper insert that fits under the plastic tray section of the jewel box and folds onto the spine (the thin edge of the box that is visible when CDs are stacked sideways). The tray card is meant to stay in position in the jewel box, and carries printed information about the CD. The package also includes a paper insert or booklet that slides into the front section of the jewel box and provides detailed information about the music. Some of the information on the package may also be printed directly on the CD. (Think of any blank area as potential "real estate" for posting valuable information.)

Other CD packaging formats—including cardboard packages with sleeves or ockets for the CD—offer many options for the number of printed panels and nsert pages.

In the case of cassettes, packaging includes a printed insert called a *J-card,* which olds to fit inside the plastic container. Additional information is printed directly on ne cassette shell (the plastic unit that houses the tape reels) or on a self-adhesive label pplied to the shell.

For vinyl records, the album jacket is used for primary information about the ecording. Additional information, such as song lyrics, may be printed on the dust .eeve or on a separate paper insert that slides into the jacket. The record should have paper label with identifying information.

nformation Requirements

'here's certain information that you need to include on the package, and other info nat is optional, as follows:

lame of Artist and Title of Album. This information should ideally be printed on the ont of the CD (near the top), on the spine, and, at least with standard jewel boxes, n a label stuck to the top spine, so that it will be readily visible to a customer flipping through a rack of products. This positioning is especially important for a new rtist. For well-established or world-famous acts, there is quite a bit more leeway in ne kinds of information to include and how visible you need to make it; sometimes photograph is sufficient identification information.

ompany Information. Display the name and address of the record company. (This is a egal requirement in most states.) And include the company logo, if you have one.

rademark. Company names that are considered trademarked should include the ymbol ™ after the name. If the trademark is registered with the U.S. Patent and rademark Office (USPTO), use ® instead.

For information about registering a trademark, contact the USPTO at (703) 308-IELP or on the World Wide Web at www.uspto.gov.

rogram Information. Provide a numbered list of tracks arranged in playing order. (For assettes and records, supply separate lists for the different sides.) For each track, indiate the song title, writer(s), publisher(s), ASCAP or BMI affiliation (more about this n page 234), and playing time.

opyright Information. Separate copyright notices must be provided for the composiions and for the recorded performance of the compositions. These indicate owner-nip. Copyright of a composition is indicated with the symbol © followed by the year f publication and the name of the owner (that is, the publisher); for example, ©2003 y John Doe Music, Inc. The performance copyright is the same idea, except that

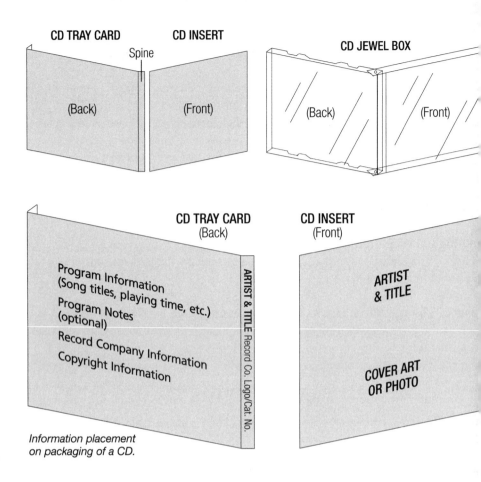

CD TRAY CARD   **CD INSERT**

Spine

(Back)   (Front)

CD JEWEL BOX

(Back)   (Front)

CD TRAY CARD
(Back)

CD INSERT
(Front)

Program Information
(Song titles, playing time, etc.)
Program Notes
(optional)
Record Company Information
Copyright Information

ARTIST & TITLE   Record Co. Logo/Cat. No.

ARTIST
& TITLE

COVER ART
OR PHOTO

*Information placement
on packaging of a CD.*

instead of a © you would use a ℗ symbol. The owner of the recorded performanc
is generally the record company.

Copyright of the cover design should be provided when the artist requires it. (
design created by a record company's in-house designer is generally owned by th
record company.)

Catalog Number. Assign your album a unique number, to facilitate tracking through
out the ordering, distribution, and billing process.

Universal Product Code (UPC) and Bar Code. Most packaging includes a *bar code*: verti
cal bars of different widths representing a 12-digit number. The bar code is a mean
of standardizing computerized tracking of sales and inventory. At a store checkou
counter, the bar code is scanned (via SoundScan technology, detailed on page 102
and a computer database is updated to reflect the sale. The information is usable b
you, the retailer, and the distributor to accurately record sales, and by the SoundSca
company to compile industrywide sales statistics.

A bar code is not absolutely required, but it is highly recommended, since so many retailers use the bar code scanning system.

The 12-digit number on which the bar code is based is called the UPC, or Universal Product Code. To get a UPC number, you'll need to order it from the Uniform Code Council (UCC), which requires that you first pay to become a member. Many commercial CD manufacturers provide a bar code for less money than the UCC, but it will only apply to the single product. If you're starting a small label with multiple releases planned, join the UCC, which will get you a permanent company code and the ability to generate many bar codes.

The 12 digits of the UPC number represent the following information: The first six digits are your permanent and unique UCC Company Prefix, which you will use on all products. The next four digits are an Item Reference Number you choose for your specific product (for example, the Four Gone Conclusions' album *Ybo Arising*). The next digit (the 11th) is a standard configuration code that identifies the medium of the product (CD, audiocassette, videocassette, and so on). The UCC will send you a list of configuration codes when it sends you your company code. The last digit is a "check character" that verifies the accuracy of the entire 12-digit code. It is supplied by the firm from whom you order the bar code.

Let's clarify that last point. When you schedule a product for manufacture, you have to order the bar code "art" for that product from a bar code supplier, not from the UCC. (The UCC can recommend companies in your geographic area.) You provide that company with the UPC number containing your chosen four-digit product code and the configuration code. The bar code company then provides you with film of the bar code for incorporation into your package design.

Alternatively, the bar code company can provide you with a digital file so you can print bar code labels yourself.

In addition to including the bar code art on your product, you should print the UPC number on all sales materials, including price lists, invoices, and shipping labels. To avoid confusion with your separate catalog number, you might want to use the same digits for both the catalog number and the product portion of the UPC number.

Got all this? If not, the UCC will spell it out. You can contact the Uniform Code Council at (937) 435-3870 or on the World Wide Web at www.uc-council.org. Their address is 7887 Washington Village Drive, Suite 300, Dayton, Ohio 45459.

Manufacturing Information. Indicate where the disc was manufactured, by country. For example: Manufactured in the U.S.A. (That's refreshingly straightforward, isn't it?)

Ordering Information. You wouldn't want to pass up an opportunity to promote additional sales, would you? Be sure to provide the address, phone number, fax number, e-mail address, and/or Web address where a company catalog and other company products can be ordered. (And it wouldn't hurt to include an insert showing some of the additional products.)

The Spine. Since the spine (the thin side surface of the CD package) is often the part of the package that is visible in a store's display, make sure it clearly shows the following information: artist name, title of album, company name, and catalog number. In addition, provide a top-spine stick-on label that names the artist and album and includes the catalog number and bar code. (The top spine is the topmost edge of the CD package.) Your CD manufacturer will prepare the top-spine sticker at your request, usually for a few additional pennies per CD.

The Disc or Cassette. The minimal information to print on the CD, cassette shell, or record label is the artist name and the title of the album. Beyond that basic information, you may include the following: the titles of songs, record company name, catalog number, side number or letter (not applicable to CDs), and copyright notices (both the © and the ℗). Additionally, you can include the writer's and publisher's name, the producer's name, the playing time, technical recording information (digital/analog information and the kind of noise reduction used), and just about any other information you'd like to include—as long as it will fit.

For CDs, you may opt to include the "compact disc" logo, which may also be printed on the CD tray. One thing to bear in mind when considering any design to be printed directly on the CD: *keep it simple.* Silkscreening (the printing method used in this case) cannot adequately capture fine detail or subtle color treatments.

ARTIST/ TITLE
CD Song Titles

Information placement on a CD.

Record Co. Logo/Compact Disc Logo
Copyright & Manufacturing Info
Catalog Number

Program Notes. Provide additional commentary or facts about the music as you see fit. Biographical information about a new artist is always worthwhile. In the case of a well-established performer, such facts wouldn't be needed since they're already common knowledge. Alternatively, or in addition, you could include complete lists of the contributing musicians and instruments played, lyrics of all the songs, and names of the producer(s) and other supporting personnel.

And you don't have to stop there. This is your record, isn't it? Budget allowing (words take up space, after all), you could declare your undying gratitude to everyone from your Aunt Mildred to the cooks at the all-night greasy spoon near the recording studio. Or you might include extra art. It's up to you. Just use good judgment.

1. **Iggy Pop "The Passenger"** (4:42)
   Courtesy of Virgin Creative Projects
   Published by Bug Music (BMI)
   Written by James Newell Jun Osterberg
   and Denis Roderick Gardiner
2. **Lou Reed "Dirty Boulevard"** (3:32)
   Courtesy of Warner Special Products
   Published by WB Music Group (BMI)
   Written by Lou Reed
3. **The Replacements "Alex Chilton"** (3:15)
   Courtesy of Warner Special Products
   Published by WB Music Corporation (ASCAP)
   Written by P. Westerberg, T. Stinson, and C. Mars
4. **American Music Club "Johnny Mathis' Feet"** (3:42)
   Courtesy of Warner Special Products
   Published by I Failed In Life Music (BMI)
   and Songs of Polygram International (BMI)
   Written by Mark Eitzel

Program information provided on a CD package.

Attractive, High-Quality Design

A '60s rock star who shall remain nameless, and who had been out of the public eye for quite some time, staged a modest reappearance in the mid-1990s. He went on the road with a small band and performed a set of new songs interspersed with a handful of his classic hits. The music sounded terrific. He had also recorded a new CD, which you'd guess had the same high quality of his live sound. But there was a problem. The packaging of the CD was extremely sloppy. The photo used on the front insert was out of focus. The design looked as though it had been slapped together on a computer by an amateur after a few too many sleepless nights. It made a good recording artist look bad.

The point is, whatever design approach you take, the packaging—illustration, photo, layout, typography, printing, and everything else—should be of the highest quality possible. It's the first impression you present to the public, and it should be a good one.

The way to ensure high quality is simple: hire a professional designer to create your graphics. (See "Choosing a Designer" on page 62.)

Adaptable Design

In addition to the album package, you may plan to create promotional material, either at the same time or at a later date. When creating a range of visual material, it's usually a good idea to use one design theme in all the elements. This helps to fortify the concept and image you want to present to the public. (Creating a single reusable design

Two examples of consistently designed CD packages and promotional items. The Smithsonian material (above) employs a retro design with Art Deco–style lettering. Koko Taylor's package (below) plays up her "blues royalty" quality with clean, elegant design and typography.

concept is especially important when you're trying to establish a strong brand identity, a concept that is discussed in detail later in this chapter.)

So for your CD and/or cassette release, make sure that the design used in the main product packaging is adaptable to other formats. Such formats might include

- posters
- flyers
- postcards
- bumper stickers
- Web pages

To make a design adaptable, make sure it looks good at various sizes. (Keep in mind that if an image is very intricate at a large size, chances are the detail will get lost at a reduced size.) The main portion of the image should be usable in both horizontal and vertical formats. It also wouldn't hurt if the original color image also looked good in black and white, for those occasions when it is printed in a newspaper as part of an ad or review.

Adaptability is especially important when you're creating a logo, since you'll be using it on a wide range of materials. A logo is a symbol or image used to identify a commercial entity. When you meet with a designer to discuss the creation of a logo, have a list of every conceivable way it might be used, so that the designer doesn't go ahead and create something that looks good only on, say, a large, vertical, four-color poster.

Getting back, for a moment, to the issue of when to create additional material like posters, stickers, and promo matter, keep this point in mind: it's more cost-effective to produce and print all items at the same time.

Stylistically Appropriate Design

It wouldn't make much sense to create a high-tech, space-age cover design for a CD of Appalachian folk songs. Nor would it be wise to use an infantile depiction of cavorting cartoon animals for an album of Bartók string quartets.

Make sure that the design of your package is appropriate for the music on the CD, as well as for your target audience. If the music is rustic, use a design that suggests rusticity. If the music is gritty urban rock, go for an image that conveys urban grit. For humorous music, go with a visual idea that matches the concept of the humor.

When you're operating on a tight budget, you may not be able to afford original artwork, custom photography, or lavish, full-color printing. Even so, you can convey a lot about style and mood using just typography and limited color. And stock photography—preexisting images that you can choose from the catalogs of stock-photo companies, for less money than you'd spend for a new photo—can go a long way toward enlivening a design if original photos aren't an option.

When relying primarily on typography to get your message across, it is especially important to make sure the designer is absolutely clear about the idea and tone you wish to convey.

◄ A CD cover using a sleek mechanical image is appropriate for the electronic sound of the band Fluke.

Power

Cartoonist R. Crumb's ► design matches the old-time Americana repertoire of his band.

◄ Will Ackerman's soothing new-age guitar music is evoked by a spare design and abstract image.

Original artwork © Michaela Harlow

A no-frills head shot captures ► the raw energy of blues artist Shemekia Copeland.

Persuasive Design

One step beyond appropriate design is *persuasive* design. Any package design that increases the customer's desire to buy the CD is effectively persuasive.

In the extreme, a persuasive design may be a design that panders. An album cover with a sexy girl in a bikini is meant to be persuasive. (The marketer knows that sex sells—even though it may have nothing to do with the music.) A series of albums by the Ohio Players released in the 1970s all featured seductive photos of female models. The point was to get people to buy those records.

But there are plenty of other, perhaps less blatant, ways to attract consumers through package design. The idea is to use the design to emphasize the attractiveness and uniqueness of your music.

Here's an example of an album design that really worked, and helped sell the artist. The pop singer Cyndi Lauper first emerged in 1983. Her image was that of a wildly garbed free spirit. The cover of her first solo album, *She's So Unusual,* helped to build this image by depicting her in a multicolored dress dancing against a background of vivid primary colors. The back cover had a close-up shot of the soles of her shoes, which displayed sections of the Van Gogh painting *The Starry Night.* All of these images supported the idea of Lauper as effervescent and slightly daffy—a persona that also came through in her music.

To use design in a persuasive way, start by recalling the music's selling points and unique qualities that you identified earlier in the marketing process. Then work with a designer to come up with visual ways to express those qualities. (Remember that you're not limited to pictures. You can always come right out and say it. Look at the title *She's So Unusual.*)

Here are some examples to get you thinking:

Artist/Album	Selling Point/Quality	Image
Bruce Springsteen, *Born in the U.S.A.*	Springsteen as American working-class hero	Springsteen in jeans and T-shirt in front of an American flag
Cocteau Twins, *Echoes in a Shallow Bay*	Atmospheric, mesmerizing music	Colorful, swirling abstract imagery
The The, *Infected*	Lyrics about urban decay, human suffering, and other dark topics	Abstract art of person screaming amid urban chaos
George Winston, *Forest*	"Rural folk piano" style	Simple photo of sunlit forest

A more subtle approach to persuasive design is to present images that are linked with the preferences of the targeted audience. For example, if the targeted audience is young professionals with disposable income, the artist might be depicted on the cover surrounded by the luxurious material rewards of financial success. This connects

A cover design that uses only type.

with the consumer's economic aspirations, and establishes a bond between artist and customer. It can help to sell the record.

In the 1970s, singer Boz Scaggs departed from his blues roots and went for a sleeker, more polished, "uptown" sound. This was during the disco period, when urban glamour and glitzy nightlife were the rage. The cover of one of Scaggs' albums, 1980 *Middle Man,* seemed directly targeted at seekers of the upscale "good life": an urbane looking, well-tanned Scaggs is shown in jacket and tie, lounging luxuriously with his head resting on a woman's elegantly stockinged leg.

The technique of appealing in a somewhat subliminal way to a target market's preferences and self-images is used mostly in advertising, and actually not too often on album covers. Here's why: record makers know that this approach can easily backfire. Audiences are often able to recognize a heavy-handed attempt at manipulation. As a result they may reject the artist permanently, even if they sense that the record marketers were the ones who were actually responsible. For example, portraying an established multimillionaire performer as a dressed-down "kid from the 'hood" in order to attract a lower-income audience might generate derision rather than sales.

On the other hand, there's nothing wrong with emphasizing values and lifestyles that are genuinely represented by the artist. If the artist subscribes to a school of thought or identifies with a particular social group, and expresses those affiliations on stage and disc, it may be well worth communicating the fact to potential buyers who have similar preferences.

Cost

Another factor to take into account when creating packaging is cost. No surprise there! Generally, the more lavish and complicated the packaging, the more you'll have to spend.

The number of colors used in the design affects the cost: the more colors you use, the more expensive the printing. Also, special design elements like holograms and tin foil reflectors add significantly to the cost.

The more inserts you use, the more you'll spend. And an insert with lots of folds r many pages will cost you more than a simple one-page insert.

Any package formatting that departs from the standard formats will also add to our cost. This would include odd-shaped record jackets, elaborately printed slipcases or CDs, and custom boxes for sets of CDs or LPs.

You'll probably have a wish list of packaging and design preferences when you meet with the designer to plan. Talk it over with the designer to get an estimate of the cost, and be prepared to let go of your idea for a television-shaped album jacket camped with a hologram of your smiling face.

AMPLE COSTS OF PRODUCT PACKAGING*

OVER DESIGN AND PRODUCTION (For CD, cassette, and/or LP)

esign (CD, cassette, LP cover):	$300 to $9,000
ustration or photography:	$500 to $7,000
ause[†] fee:	25%–75% of standard initial fee for anticipated use

Secondary use, as in advertising collateral.

D INSERT PRINTING

ull-color outside panels, black and white on inside; includes separate tray card)

Quantity	2-Panel	4-Panel	8-Page	16-Page
500	$175	$275	$525	$625
1,000	250	350	600	750
3,000	525	650	825	1,250
5,000	675	800	1,250	1,525
0,000	1,100	1,350	2,050	2,475

D MANUFACTURING (Includes jewel box, shrink wrap, and printing on disc)

Quantity	Initial Order	Reorder
500	$900	$550
1,000	1,200	1,000
3,000	2,650	2,375
5,000	3,950	3,500
0,000	7,500	7,300

All fees are averages as of 2002. Preparation of film for printing is a separate cost, and is handled either by a special service bureau or the printer. Contact vendors for current prices and fees.

VISUAL BRANDING

A *brand* is a recognizable name. *Branding*—or building a brand—is important if you product isn't just a one-shot deal and you're planning to release a string of record over time. Using appropriate imagery in packaging and repeating it in promotion, materials can help to build your brand. Over time, branding can boost custome loyalty and help to ensure repeat sales over the long term.

Let's define a brand more specifically. A brand is a collection of goods—such as line of records—identifiable through a unique name, logo, and/or other symboli element. When that name and logo are printed on a product, the customer know that the product is of a certain type or has a level of quality associated with previ ously purchased products of that brand. For example, buyers of Alligator Recor products know they're buying the blues. Rounder Records customers know th company specializes in American roots music. Rhino Records listeners expect com pilations of vintage tracks.

Branding can apply to an artist as much as to a company—more so, in fact, sinc audiences are more likely to build an attachment to an artist than to a label. (Hov many people do you know, for example, who will buy a CD simply because it is pt out by Columbia Records?)

The hope in creating a brand is to build *brand loyalty.* It works like this: The fir several products issued under the brand name establish an identity (musical style c styles) and a level of quality. Succeeding products reinforce the identity and maintai the quality. Eventually, the customer begins to automatically link the brand with th style and the quality, and will respond positively to new products that carry the bran name and logo. The customer has developed brand loyalty.

A distinctive brand logo or design makes it easy for customers to identify, at glance, any products marketed by the brand. (Think of the Rolling Stones' lips logo And, if the brand is well regarded, the logo gives the products a sales boost.

In cases where you are trying out spin-off projects or new products that depa from your established identity, stamping them with the brand name and logo ma help to get them accepted in a market where they would otherwise be viewed unproven products of unknown origin. (The term for a new product category give the brand name of an existing category is *brand extension.*)

Establishing a visual brand identity doesn't necessarily mean all products have t look exactly the same. You can also use different designs that conform to an overa style. For instance, Windham Hill Records, in its early new-age incarnation, ofte used photographs of landscapes or other natural subjects on its album jackets. Simil layouts and photographic subjects gave all the albums an identifiably "Windhar Hill" look.

Sometimes a logo alone, or another type of visual image, is sufficient to establis brand identity. The band Kiss used its distinctive typographic logo on its variou products. A rendering of a dancing, fiddling, or otherwise active skeleton graced man Grateful Dead album covers.

Establishing a visual brand identity is not a strict marketing requirement. In fact, if you're releasing a variety of very different products, it may not even be desirable. But just keep it in mind as another potentially useful ingredient in your marketing mix.

STEPS IN PACKAGE CREATION

Whether you're a marketer in a large company or doing everything yourself in a small firm or as an independent musician, you'll be involved in some aspect of package development—even if just to put in your two cents about the design concept. Here's an outline of the creation process, from conception to physical production.

Deciding What Elements You Need (or Would Like)

At the outset, you need to envision your ideal set of package elements. Will you be producing only CDs (the most widely used of the available formats)? Do you want to produce cassettes as well, even though they are becoming less popular? And what about vinyl records, which some audiophiles still prefer?

You then need to plan the package inserts. For CDs, you can choose to go with a cheap single-sheet insert and a tray card, or you might want to splurge and prepare a multi-page booklet. (Alternatively, you could go with a cardboard slipcase instead of a plastic jewel box with an insert.) For cassettes, you might opt for a simple single-panel J-card, or you may lean more toward something with multiple panels so you can print all the song lyrics or other information.

(At this time it would be wise to think about any other promotional items you might want to produce, from posters and postcards to bumper stickers. Batching them with the CD package production process may save you money on design and printing.)

Then you'll think about color versus black-and-white art for the cover image—or perhaps a duotone photo, where the black-and-white photo is reproduced using black and some other color, often to eye-catching effect.

At the same time, you need to envision the style of design. For ideas, you can go to a number of art and photo sourcebooks. *American Showcase Illustration* is a good source of illustration styles, while *Klik Showcase Photography* serves the same purpose for photo images. An excellent book that showcases a wide range of album design approaches is *The Ultimate Album Cover Album,* by Roger Dean and David Howells (Prentice Hall Press). It contains hundreds of album covers created over a 45-year period. Any of these books, and numerous others available in libraries and bookstores, can help to get your creative wheels turning. Simply browsing in record stores can also be helpful.

While thinking about the design style, make a decision about the kinds of information to include on the packaging. Simplicity could be the way to go. Or you might want to cram the package with text about the artist, the songs, the musicians, or other products available.

Choosing a Designer

You can save money by hiring your art-student friend to design the album cover. C
you can make sure you end up with a professional product by hiring an experience
pro. For reasons stated previously, going with a pro is the preferred route.

How do you find one? Start by checking the design credits on printed pieces yo
like and then calling the company that issued the printed piece and ask how t
contact the artist. You might also check local chapters of the American Institute c
Graphic Arts (AIGA) for information about its members. (It's a plus if the artist
affiliated with a professional organization such as AIGA, since it indicates a high leve
of professionalism.) Additionally, you can get artist contact information—and vie\
samples of their work—in such directories as *Black Book Photography, Black Boo
Illustration,* AIGA's online designer directory (www.aiga.org), and *Art Directors Annu*
(though people listed in them may be beyond your budget). Lastly, you can chec
your local Yellow Pages or the Web and look under Promotional Design.

Once you have found a few names, contact them and make arrangements t
review their portfolios or view their work online. Choose someone whose portfoli
includes samples similar to what you're looking for in an album design. You shoul
also consider the designer's depth of experience in promotional design—especiall
music promotional design.

Before making a final decision, check some of the designer's references. Verify tha
the work he or she supplied was satisfactory, on time, and met the agreed-upon budge

Initial Meeting with the Designer

Once you have hired a designer, set up an initial meeting to discuss your design idea

In this meeting you'll lay out the types of elements you need designed, from CI
folders to J-cards to LP covers. If a logo is to be created, now is the time to bring
up. The same is true of any collateral material—such as stickers, postcards, T-shirts, an
posters—that you may wish to have designed at this time. Cover all the bases. Hav
all your information available at the beginning of the design process.

Provide the designer with precise size specifications for all the elements include
in the packaging. CD and cassette manufacturers will have information about all the prope
dimensions along with specs for the positioning of type. They will mail them to you o
request, or you can sometimes download design templates from a manufacturer's Web sit

Clarify the form in which you would like to receive the finished design: electroni
files on a removable storage medium such as a Zip® or Jaz® disk (along with the plat
form used, whether Mac or PC), camera-ready mechanicals, or final film. The forr
you choose will depend on the method of reproduction you will be using. Th
designer should consult with the vendor (the printer, T-shirt silk-screener, or othe
manufacturer) to determine the required medium or format.

In the initial meeting with the designer, you'll also discuss the budget. The designe
knowledgeable about the costs and technical aspects of graphic production, will b
able to tell you what is and isn't possible to achieve on your budget. He or she wi
also be able to suggest alternative approaches that would be affordable for you.

If possible, supply the designer with visual reference material. If you have a strong notion of the kind of design you'd like, provide examples of similar designs. Also, give the designer a sample of the music.

If you wish to include a specific photograph, provide it at this meeting. Also give the designer a copy of the text that you wish to have included. Provide it electronically—on disk or via e-mail.

Don't forget to discuss the schedule. Set up deadlines for sketches, rough layouts, and delivery of final art.

Be sure to write down all terms of the agreement—including the schedule, form of delivery, fees, and rights granted (whether all rights to the art or only the rights for limited use)—in an official letter of agreement, a purchase order, or an "estimate and confirmation" form. An excellent source of standard contracts for graphic design work is the *Graphic Artists Guild Handbook: Pricing and Ethical Guidelines* (available from the Graphic Artists Guild at www.gag.org or [212] 791-3400).

Reviewing Rough Layouts and Sketches

At the next meeting, the designer will return with several options for the cover design for your review and, hopefully, approval. The ideas will often be presented in the form of sketches. The presentation of the concept may include recommendations for illustration or photography (which might involve hiring a separate illustrator or photographer, whose work will be overseen by the designer) or possibly a simple type-only approach.

Important: if you approve a sketch or idea, make sure you really mean it and won't change your mind later. Designers will charge you for partially completed work that you decide, after the fact, is "in the wrong direction." Therefore, think long and hard about that initial sketch. If you don't like it, it's expected at this stage that you ask for another. If you do like it, great. Let the designer know he or she has your full okay to go ahead and develop the idea.

Reviewing Photos and/or Illustrations

If you've agreed to use illustration or photography, review the recommended artist's portfolio before work begins, to make sure you like the general style and approach. After you've given the go-ahead, approvals of the art proceed as follows: In the case of photography, the designer will provide it to you for approval when it's done. For illustration, you'll approve roughs before giving the green light to rendering final art. The same caveat about sketches applies to this stage, only more so. Don't approve a finished piece of art and later decide it's "not quite right." If necessary, refine your vision further before moving forward and incurring more unnecessary costs.

Reviewing Layouts

Here's where the designer shows you the near-final layout, with all the items in place, from titles and text to images. You will either approve it or suggest changes, requiring a revised layout for your review.

If text changes are needed (for example, a song has been dropped from or added to the program), now is the time to provide the revised copy to the designer. (Do this as soon as possible, since any change in text has the potential to affect the layout, and thus your costs.)

Completing the Production Phase

Following approval of the final layout the designer will prepare the final version. This will most likely be in the form of an electronic file in a page-layout program such as QuarkXPress or a physical board called a mechanical, which shows all the elements in their exact "camera ready" positions, ready to be converted to film.

Preparation of Film

Your agreement with the designer may have encompassed creating film of the final art (from which the printing plate will be "burned" or etched). If so, all you have to do is get the film from the designer and ship it to the printer.

If the contract with the designer is only for final mechanicals or electronic files on a removable storage medium, you'll have to arrange for film output yourself. Getting from the mechanical stage (the traditional method) to final film involves processes called stripping and color separation. Getting from electronic files to final film involves the following operations: image reproduction and manipulation (scanning, color correction, special effects, and proofs); digital prepress (trapping, registration, and film imposition); and output (final proofs and film).

Many printers (or even CD manufacturers) will provide these services as part of their package deal. If not, you'll need to find a separate "service bureau" to output the film. Find a vendor that handles commercial art and performs digital prepress services professionally.

Checking Proofs

Whoever prepares the film—designer, service bureau, printer, or CD manufacturer— will provide you with a color proof of the art for your approval. This is your last chance to note mistakes. At this point, there should be no errors in the type, the position of the art, or the color fidelity.

Do pay special attention to the colors and "registration" of the images. (Images should be sharp and clean; there should be no double images. Blurring can result if the color separations that make up the final film are not precisely aligned in relation to each other.) If color fidelity is essential for your project, be sure to request a *color accurate* proof.

Printing

Printing will be handled by either a printing company or the CD manufacturer— usually your choice. If it is handled separately from the CD manufacturing, you will instruct the printer to ship the finished CD inserts and J-cards (and whatever else) to the manufacturer at the time they do the CD pressing and/or cassette duplication.

The manufacturer will then assemble the finished packages and ship them to the location you designate.

Your designer may oversee the printing process, either by reviewing proofs or (if it's geographically feasible) via an on-site press check.

The Easy (and Cheapest) Way

Instead of having the separate parts of the packaging process handled by separate vendors, there is an easier and cheaper way. That is to hire a full-service CD manufacturer. Full-service companies specialize in producing the entire CD-and-cassette package. You supply them with your finished master recording and your ideas for packaging, including all the text and any photos or art you wish to have included. The company will take care of package design, printing, CD burning, cassette duplication, package assembly, collateral design and printing, and shipping to your warehouse (or garage, as the case may be).

All the production steps outlined in the previous paragraphs will still occur, but the fact that they are being handled by a single supplier may make your life a whole lot easier.

Here's a cost comparison: If you were doing the CD design separately from the manufacturing, for a quantity of 5,000 you might pay over $6,500. Alternatively, if you went with a full-service manufacturer, for a quantity of 5,000 you might pay $6,000.

Full-service manufacturing is cheaper, but you'll probably get a better design and more control over the process if you hire a reputable independent designer.

If you do decide to use a full-service supplier, research it very carefully, check their references, and review samples of their work.

Chapter 6

Pricing, Payouts, and Profits

At some point before setting a commercial recording project into motion, you should determine whether the enterprise has a chance of being profitable. This requires a few vital calculations using information you've already collected. You start with your estimated audience size and translate it into a specific quantity of recordings that you hope to sell. Once you have this number, you factor it in with a product price and your total costs. At this end of the process you have your likely answer.

There's no way around it: At some point you have to translate your marketing plan into hard numbers.

PRICE

In music, it's easy to overlook the importance of the price factor in the profitability equation. After all, the music industry's standard top retail price for a new compact disc is $18.98. Seems straightforward enough. You could just set that as the price of your CD.

If your thinking stopped there you'd be ignoring an important marketing tool. Plenty of companies are out in the marketplace adjusting price points to make sure their products sell. To compete for consumer dollars, you'll need to fine-tune your marketing program. Pricing is an important way to do it.

In the planning stage, the price of your product is a "control" number you can use to calculate your profit after subtracting your costs. This calculation forces you to cast a cold eye on the grand marketing plans you've envisioned and view them strictly in terms of dollars and cents. Those numbers, you'll find, either work or don't. And if they don't, you'll have to begin rethinking your plan (or be willing to invest in your project with no expectation of financial return).

Later, when the marketing plan is under way, the price becomes an ongoing mechanism that can be adjusted upward or downward to increase short-term profits, to affect market penetration, or to influence market behavior in any number of other ways.

The Balancing Act of Pricing

In standard marketing theory, there are several factors that may be taken into account when you're trying to establish a product price as part of a profit calculation. The factors are sometimes referred to as the "Three C's" of product pricing: Cost, Competition, and Consumer.

Cost-Based Pricing. Calculating a price on the basis of cost means starting with what you've paid to produce the product and then establishing a price high enough to ensure a profit over and above your cost.

Competition-Based Pricing. Arriving at a price based on competition means looking at what competitors charge for your type of product and then setting your price to match or compete with it—to undercut it, for example. Your costs would be a secondary concern; if they were too high to permit your desired price, you would have to find a way to cut them.

Consumer- or Value-Based Pricing. Computing price on the basis of the consumer essentially means setting your price based on what the market will bear. If the consumer perceives a product as having a given dollar value, that's what you can charge for your product.

CONVENTIONAL WISDOM

Set your price as high as the market will bear.
If people will pay it, why not charge it? Ticket prices for concerts by world-famous performers are often set as high as possible, and people still buy them.

BREAKING THE RULE

To make themselves available to all of their fans, the band Fugazi refused to play in clubs that charged more then five dollars a ticket. What the band lost in short-term sales they gained in fan loyalty, which translated into a solid core customer base.

For a CD you'll set a *suggested* retail list price (SRLP), but the retail store will determine the actual price that best meets its needs to win customers while earning a profit.

In the real world, working the price factor into your marketing equation means attempting to balance all of the above elements—cost, competition, and consumer. You have to base price on cost because what you earn has to be greater than your expenses in order for you to make a profit. Both you and the retailers who sell your CDs have to be aware of the competition, because if your price is much higher than the competitors', their products may be chosen over yours. And finally, if your price is higher than consumers are willing to pay, then your product won't sell.

In the music business, suggested retail list prices (again, SRLPs) are standardized to some extent. So your balancing act will focus mainly on controlling costs and, as will be discussed, balancing cost with estimated sales quantities and desired profit margins.

But the place to begin "running the numbers" is most often in the area of your costs. Let's go there now.

COST

To figure out if you're going to make any money on a recording project, you have to look at what it will cost. Once you know costs, you can determine how many copies of your record you'll have to sell at a given price in order to break even (earn back the money you've spent).

If the needed number of copies is greater than the estimated size of your audience, then you'll have to figure out how to reduce your costs, so that you can break even with fewer sales—either that, or keep the costs the same and raise your price. (But raising the price may deter some people from buying the record. Welcome to the real world of trying to make the numbers work!)

Providing specific dollar figures for the cost of certain items is beyond the scope of this book (and would probably be out of date by the time you read this). Yet it's worthwhile to look at a general breakdown of what you'll be spending on a project. Costs fall into six main categories: (1) recording costs, (2) packaging costs, (3) manufacturing costs, (4) promotion costs, (5) royalties, and (6) distribution costs.

These cost breakdowns are primarily for people involved or interested in the total manufacturing process. The rest of you can skip the next discussion and go right to the section on "Competition" (found on page 75).

Recording Costs

Recording costs aren't limited to the hourly costs of booking a studio. They include a range of items, which vary considerably depending on how you approach the recording process.

Studio Time. The cost of using a professional recording studio can range from $35 an hour to $300 an hour. So, if you're recording a full album of, say, 10 songs and it takes you 15 hours per song (150 hours for all 10 songs), you're looking at a bill of anywhere from $5,250 on the low end to $45,000 at the upper level.

Now, you may be the kind of hands-on pro who owns a project studio, capable of outputting broadcast-quality master recordings. If so, you've eliminated the need to pay for studio time for the individual recording project. (The cost of equipment is an expenditure, of course. But that cost can be amortized—spread out—over a number of projects for a period of years.)

Musicians. The cost of musicians depends on a number of factors. Your musicians may be band members or close friends who are willing to donate their time as an investment in the ultimate success of the record. In that case, there might be zero payment for the recording time. Instead, they might be given a percentage of the artist royalty, to be paid when albums sell. (Similarly, you may be the *only* musician, if you're one of those do-it-all types who can arrange, sing, play several instruments, and work out additional instrumental parts on a sampling synthesizer. In this case, obviously, no musician fee is paid.)

An alternative is to pay musicians an hourly rate. The fee would depend on your budget, and on whether or not the musicians were members of the musicians' union (American Federation of Musicians, or AFM). If not working with union players, you could pay a low-ball hourly wage of, say, $25 an hour. If working with union musicians, you would have to pay union scale, which is around $100 per hour. ("Name" musicians can command up to triple scale, or around $300 an hour.)

If you estimate five hours of recording basic tracks for each of the 10 songs, you'd have a total of 50 hours for basic-track recording of, say, four musicians (drums, bass, keyboard, guitar). That would add up to 200 payable hours. Then figure five additional hours per song for overdubs, probably recorded by one musician at a time. Total overdub hours payable would be 50. Your total musician payable hours would be 250. At $25 an hour, your bill would be $6,250. At union scale, it might be around $25,000.

An alternative to paying by the hour would be to set a fee for the entire job for each musician, depending on the extent of the person's contribution.

Producer. The producer is the person who oversees and directs the recording and makes sure the final product is not only professional sounding but the best possible performance that can be eked out of the music, the players, and the studio. If this person is you, your cost will be zero. If you choose to work with an outside producer, your cost could be anywhere from $200 per song (a total of $2,000 for 10 songs) or a low-end hourly rate of $30 ($4,500 for 150 hours) to a higher $1,000-per-song rate ($10,000 for the entire 10-song project). As we'll see later, some producers are paid via royalty. And at the very high end, they can earn upwards of $50,000 per album plus a percentage, usually 3 percent, of sales earnings.

Engineer. For the person who operates the recording console and takes care of all the technical aspects of getting the music on tape, expect to pay a low-end figure of $25 per hour ($3,750 for the 150-hour project). More experienced engineers command $75 an hour and up. Another approach is to pay a flat fee for the entire project. Once again, if you do the work yourself, you will eliminate this cost.

Mixer. The person who shapes the raw recorded tracks into a well-balanced, sonically pleasing whole—adjusting the volume levels of the voices and instruments, positioning them in the stereo mix, adding sound effects, and optimizing equalization—is called the *mixer*. In the one-person studio, this person may be you. Cost: zero. If you hire a professional mixer, expect to pay $50 to $75 an hour. A well-known mixer might charge $2,000 to $4,000 per song, and even command a small percentage of sales earnings.

Storage Media. The standard used to be 24-track tape, which was very expensive. Today, works in progress are stored and transported on portable hard drives. These cost around $300 as of this writing. A typical album project also requires plenty of recordable CDs for reference throughout the project. You may need to spend $10 on these.

Mastering. The final polishing and tweaking of the finished tape to prepare it fo replication is called *mastering*. It includes evening out the audio levels and tone an sonically "sweetening" the tracks. A ballpark fee for mastering an entire album woul be $500 to $5,000. For purposes of our present calculations, we'll assume masterin costs are included in recording studio costs (although mastering is often done by separate specialist).

TOTAL RECORDING COSTS

Item	Low End	Midrange	High End
Studio Time	0	$7,500 ($50/hr.)	$37,500 ($250/h
Musicians	0	6,250	25,000
Producer	0	4,500	20,000
Engineer	0	3,750	11,500
Mixer	0	3,750	15,000
Storage Media	400	400	600
TOTALS	**$400**	**$26,150**	**$109,600**

Packaging Costs

As discussed in Chapter 5, packaging costs vary depending on the designer fee, typ of design used, lavishness of the production, and quantity of packages produced.

A low fee for a design would be $300. What you'd get would be a very basic, type only treatment—no photos or illustrations. On the higher end, you might pay $2,00 for the services of a graphic designer plus $4,000 for an original photograph or piec of art.

Printing cost will depend on the quantity of units to be printed, the number o colors (black and white, two colors, or four colors), and the complexity of th element (single-page CD insert versus six-page booklet, for example).

Let's say you're planning to press 20,000 CDs, based on your estimate of the siz of your market. Several years ago you might have manufactured cassettes, too, bu today the demand for cassettes is too insignificant to justify including them as part o a midsize pressing. (For a large pressing of music by an established artist, it still make sense to manufacture a limited number of cassettes to meet the needs of fans who stil use cassette players.)

On a bare-bones budget, you would opt for a two-panel insert and a tray card. You cost could be around $2,000. If you were willing to spend more, you might opt for four-panel insert and a tray card. In this case, your cost could be around $2,350. On the high end, you might go for an eight-page brochure. Here, your cost might run $3,500

TOTAL PACKAGING COSTS

Item	Low End	Midrange	High End
Design	$300	$2,000	$6,000
Printing of CD Insert and Tray Card	2,000 (2-panel)	2,350 (4-panel)	3,500 (8-page)
TOTALS	$2,300	$4,350	$9,500

Manufacturing Costs

The cost of manufacturing compact discs is relatively standard throughout the industry. For 20,000, you can expect to pay around $15,000.

Promotion Costs

The topic of promotion is discussed in detail in Chapters 10 through 13. But for purposes of analyzing overall costs in the context of profit calculations, promotion expenses need to be summarized here. (Bear in mind that, as always, all dollar figures are rough estimates, and that actual figures will depend upon the suppliers that you choose.)

Press Kits. The press kit will be your primary promotional device. It ordinarily contains a minimum of the following: a fact sheet about the album release; a biography of the artist; a clipping of a newspaper or magazine article about the artist (if available); a photo; and, in most cases, a copy of the CD. (For details about press kits, see page 143.)

A low-budget presentation might include 100 sets, each with a cover letter; a black-and-white photograph ($250 for the shoot, $125 for duplicates); a bio ($300 for writing); clippings; and a fact sheet. Add about $30 for 100 photocopies of the cover letter, bio, clipping, and fact sheet.

With a middling budget, you might go for 500 press kits, each with a pocket folder ($375); a more expensive photo ($500 for the shoot, $450 for dupes); a bio by a more established writer ($500); clippings; and a fact sheet. Photocopying would add about $150.

A higher budget for your press kit mailing might yield 1,000 (or more) copies of the following: a folder imprinted with a logo ($850, plus $500 for the logo design); a yet-more-expensive photograph ($1,000 for the shoot, $850 for duplicates); a biography by a well-known writer ($750); clippings; and a fact sheet. Photocopies would cost approximately $300.

Collateral. Collateral material might include posters, flyers, promotional postcards, and bumper stickers.

A low-budget approach might involve printing 500 black-and-white flyers ($50) and 500 postcards ($100).

On the more expensive side, you might opt for 1,000 units of each of the following full-color 11-by-17-inch poster ($800), full-color flyer ($600), full-color postca ($300), and one-color sticker ($100).

On a high budget, you could choose to print 5,000 units of a full-color 18-b 24-inch poster ($2,200), full-color flyer ($1,000), postcard ($1,500), and bump sticker ($825).

Other promotional items include logo-bearing T-shirts, coffee mugs, and a rang of other products (see page 224). For simplicity's sake, we'll limit the current discu sion to print material.

Stationery. Whatever the budget, professional-looking stationery will be a necessit The stationery set will include a main sheet with your letterhead, a blank secon sheet, an envelope, and a business card. The whole package should cost around $55 for 1,000.

Newsletter. A newsletter sent periodically to people on your mailing list is a good wa to keep in touch with your core audience. A simple two-sided sheet is all you real need. The cost of design might run about $150 per issue. On a tight budget you coul either not do a newsletter at all, send one via e-mail, or manually print out 500 copi on a laser printer for the cost of a ream of heavy-stock paper (about $18). For mo money you could have 1,000 copies professionally printed ($350). On a higher budg you might opt for 5,000 copies, professionally printed ($950). When you calculate th cost, make sure to factor in that you'll be spending this money periodically—that i each time you publish an issue of the newsletter. For the purposes of our current ca culations, let's assume there will be one newsletter connected with the album releas

Mailing Lists. As previously discussed, mailing lists are vital components of your mar keting plan. Lists of media and music industry contacts can be assembled by you fc a minimal cost—your time and energy. Customer mailing lists, on the other hanc can be rented for between $75 and $300 per 1,000 names. If you're really pushing direct-mail campaign, you might opt for 10,000 names, at a fee of roughly $75 (assuming $75 per thousand).

Mailing Costs. Press kit mailing costs will run roughly as follows: $200 for 100 envelope (at 50¢ each) plus postage (around $1.50 per package); $950 for 500 envelopes plu postage; $1,800 for 1,000 envelopes plus postage. These postage costs assume you' be including a CD in each press kit.

Postage will be an ongoing cost for mailing newsletters, flyers, and other materia For now, we'll assume $200 for a medium-budget promotion campaign, and $1,00 for a big budget.

Record Promotion. Initially, the cost of record promotion will be included in the pres kit budget. When your marketing plan begins to pick up steam and the record appear o be attracting attention, you may want to hire an independent promotion firm. A fee of $5,000 is not unusual for this service. (Really high-end independent record promoters can charge as much as $50,000 per single that they promote.)

Publicity Campaign. As your marketing campaign takes hold, you also may want to hire an independent publicist. Fees can range from $2,000 to $8,000 per month and more. On a limited budget, you might utilize the services of a publicist for a month. For a more concerted PR effort, a three-month commitment would be an option.

Advertising. Advertising is expensive. On a bare-bones budget, you may be doing none at all. For purposes of this cost calculation, we will set aside advertising and assume that it will be an option if there proves to be leeway in the overall budget.

Tour Support. To ensure that the recording artist builds an audience and thus helps to increase sales of a record, the record label will often provide dollars for tour support. Amounts vary widely. Let's assume that for a medium-budget project the amount will be $20,000, and for a higher budget, $40,000. (Bear in mind that costs will include hotels, travel, food, equipment, support staff, and other items depending upon the level of the act and the size of the tour.)

TOTAL PROMOTION COSTS

Item	Low End	Midrange	High End
Press Kit	$700 (100)	$1,975 (500)	$4,250 (1,000)
Collateral	150	1,800	5,525
Stationery	550	550	550
Newsletter	——	500	1,100
Mailing Lists	——	75	750
Mail/Postage	200	1,150	2,800
Record Promotion*	——	5,000	20,000
Professional PR*	——	3,000	15,000
Tour Support*	——	20,000	40,000
TOTALS	**$1,600**	**$34,050**	**$89,975**

* Excluding long-distance telephone charges.

Royalty Costs

Royalties are percentages of sales dollars, or fixed fees, payable to certain participants in the project. They are monies that are earned at the point of either sales or distribution, depending upon the recipient. You'll need to account for royalty payments as a deduction from estimated sales income.

For retail sales of recordings, two main categories of royalties come into play: (1) royalties paid to the recording artist, and (2) royalties paid to songwriters and publishers (mechanical royalties).

In some cases producers get royalties, and these days even some superstar mixers command royalties. But payment of these royalties usually comes out of the artist royalty. (See "The Way the Industry Does It," page 80.) So for now, focus on the two detailed below.

Artist Royalties. If you, the music marketer, are also the recording artist, outgoing payments of artist royalties will be zero. All profits go directly into your pocket. If, on the other hand, you're marketing an album recorded by an artist other than yourself, you'll pay the artist a royalty on each copy of the record sold.

A portion of the expected royalty is generally paid up-front to the artist in the form of an *advance*. Once the record begins to sell, the artist is paid no further royalties until the advance is *recouped*—that is, paid back to the record company (you) out of royalties earned on actual sales. After the advance is fully recouped, the artist is sent royalty checks for any additional sales.

For simplicity's sake, let's assume that for your recording project the artist's royalty rate is an even 10 percent of the SRLP. (In the more complex real world, percentages vary depending on the type of sale, as we'll see later.)

Mechanical Royalties. If you're recording songs written by people other than yourself, you'll need to obtain what is called a *mechanical license* to use each song. This license, obtainable through the Harry Fox Agency (see page 231) or from the music publisher, calls for payment of royalties by you for each copyrighted song you use on the album. You send payment to the Harry Fox Agency, which distributes the payment to the publishers. (If the publisher is not a Harry Fox affiliate, you pay the publisher directly.)

The amount of the standard mechanical royalty changes periodically. The royalty rate for 2004–2005 is 8.5¢ per song or 1.65¢ per minute of playing time, whichever is greater, per CD, tape, or record made and distributed.

Note the word *distributed* rather than *sold*. While recording artist royalties are paid for records sold, mechanical royalties are paid for records distributed, *whether or not they sell through*. (This means that you could distribute 10,000 copies, sell none of them, and still technically owe mechanical royalties on all of them.) According to the Harry Fox Agency's Web site, such royalties are also payable "on units that are given away").

For purposes of our upcoming calculations, we're going to assume that half the songs on your proposed recording project are original (written by you), while five others are owned by other writers and publishers and require that you pay mechanical royalties. The royalty you'll have to pay for each record distributed will be 42.5¢ (five songs multiplied by 8.5¢). Got that? I'll provide further explanation on page 77.

Distribution Costs

The costs tallied so far can serve as the partial basis for deciding on a retail price. If, for example, your cost works out to $5 per CD (including royalties), you'd want to set a price high enough so that you'd earn a profit over and above that $5.

But whatever your price, the money you'll actually *receive* for the sale will be what's left after allowances for the distributor and retailer—generally about 35 to 50 percent of your SRLP. Before you finalize any price you need to know the pricing structure of your distribution channel and what per-unit dollar amounts you'll actually receive. (More about this in Chapter 7.)

COMPETITION

The retail price has to be within the ballpark of standard pricing within the industry. Currently (as of 2003), the standard top retail list price for a new CD is $18.98. But a visit to your local record store will reveal that price points cover a range. There are "mid-priced" CDs set at around $12.98 and "budget" CDs selling for $10.98 and lower.

Retailers adjust prices of front-line and other albums to meet their own competitive needs. Different stores may sell the same CD for different prices. Setting a price in relation to the industry standard sometimes means underselling—setting the price lower than the standard to make the product more attractive to consumers.

CONSUMER

Whatever the final price, it will also have to be within the range of what consumers are willing to pay. If a record has been on the market for some time and sales have begun to dip, it may be that customers will now only buy the record at a lower price. On the other hand, a recording artist with a fiercely loyal cult following may be able to command a relatively high price for a new album release. Gauging customer reaction to product pricing means having an intimate knowledge of the target audience and its relationship to the artist. (For example, an artist known for keeping prices low may lose core customers if he or she shifts policy and begins to charge top dollar for new products.)

CALCULATING PROFITABILITY

It's time to take a close look at the kind of juggling that goes on when you try to balance the cost, quantity, and price of a record release (while keeping in mind the competition and the consumer) to make sure that you'll be able to achieve marketing and sales objectives.

Let's assume for the moment that the objective is simply to sell as many copies of the record as possible, as soon as possible, and at the highest possible price. (There are other types of marketing objectives, but we'll save discussion of those for later in the chapter.)

Remember that in the world of big-time record companies, the marketing perso would not ordinarily be the one performing these calculations. However, at a sma record label, where the owner may also be the marketing person (and the A&R direc tor, product manager, CFO, receptionist, and coffee runner), this kind of numbe crunching would be part of the job. Either way—whether large operation or sma mom-and-pop—it's helpful to be aware of this process. (But if you'd rather not clutte your mind with such details, feel free to skip ahead to "Additional Factors Affectin Price," on page 82.)

The essential purpose of the calculation is to make sure that expenditures and pro jected income balance out in such a way that there is a reasonable chance for th enterprise to achieve profitability, or at least stay within the realm of fiscal sanity.

Bear in mind that the components of any one project will be unique. The real-worl calculations you'll apply to an actual project will undoubtedly differ in their specific (recording costs, for example) from the ones presented here. Use the following exampl only as a general model of the kind of thinking that goes into "running the numbers.

Running the Basic Numbers

Let's begin. We're assuming that you've found a promising musical act with whor you'll record five songs that you've written and five songs written by others. On th basis of research, you've estimated you'll need to manufacture 20,000 copies of th record. (Don't forget it's only an estimate. See "Reality Check" on page 78.) You'v decided to sell only CDs, given today's dwindling demand for cassettes.

You'll start with the idea of using an SRLP of $18.98. For simplicity, we'll roun off the price to $19.

You'll probably be giving away about 4,000 copies. They'll be sent to the distrib utor, key radio stations, reviewers, and what-have-you. So you need to subtract thes from the number you'll actually be selling. You're left with 16,000 units.

To calculate total receipts generated by sales of the 16,000, you'll multiply tha number by your $19 price. Your total would be $304,000.

But wait! You won't be receiving the full SRLP. Your actual receipts may be 50 t 65 percent less, depending on your distributor's wholesale price. (We'll use the roun figure of 50 percent in this example, even though in the real world the amount yo receive will be smaller unless you're in a strong negotiating position. More on this i Chapter 7.)

Let's try the calculation again, using the dollar amount you'll actually receive. A $19 minus 50 percent, you'll get $9.50 per CD. Selling 16,000 will earn you $152,000

Right about now you're thinking that $152,000 is not too shabby a return. True but it's still not your final income. In fact, you won't know what you'll really ear until you subtract all your other costs.

Start by subtracting royalties. You've already figured on an artist royalty of 1(percent of the SRLP. For a CD, that will be $1.90 per unit ($18.98 × 10%, rounde off). The total artist royalties due, if you sell out all 16,000 copies (artist royalties ar not payable on those 4,000 free copies), will be $30,400.

Do the math: Sales receipts of $152,000 minus artist royalties of $30,400 equals 121,600.

Now you have to subtract mechanical royalties—the money you have to pay the Harry Fox Agency for the use of those five non-original songs. Remember that the calculation was 42.5¢ for each unit that you distribute (8.5¢ per song × 5 songs). On 20,000 units (4,000 freebies are considered "distributed" by Harry Fox, although many labels reportedly disagree), the full amount is $8,500. Subtract that from your ever-dwindling sales dollars and you're now down to $113,100 ($121,600 - $8,500).

What about all the other costs—recording, packaging, and promotion? You need to subtract them, too. Let's assume you've planned on moderate expenditures for production and promo. Using dollar figures from the charts shown earlier in the chapter, you come up with these figures:

Recording Cost	$ 26,150
Packaging Cost	4,350
Manufacturing Cost	15,000
Promotion Cost	34,050
TOTAL	$ 79,550

Subtract $79,550 from your remaining receipts of $113,100 and you get a grand total of $33,550. This amount is called the *gross margin*.

What percentage of $113,100 is $33,550? Just under 30 percent ($33,550 ÷ $113,100). This is your *gross profit,* expressed as a percentage.

Here's a summary of the calculations:

Receipts from distributor for 16,000 units	$ 152,000
Less artist royalty	– 30,400
Subtotal	$ 121,600
Less mechanical royalty	– 8,500
Subtotal	$ 113,100
Less costs of recording, packaging, manufacturing, and promotion	– 79,550
GROSS MARGIN	$ 33,550

Well, now what? That depends on how you feel about your profit. You may want it to be higher. (Remember: you haven't yet accounted for your *overhead*—namely, ongoing costs like rent, utilities, and other expenses that would exist with or without the album project.)

To increase your profit, you have a choice of raising your price, manufacturing and selling more units, or cutting costs.

If you raised your price, you'd be going too high. (Remember that you started ou with the top going price for new CDs.)

If you manufactured and sold more copies, your cost per unit would be less, an your profit per unit would be greater. (Cost per unit would be less because you'd b spreading your fixed recording costs over more units—recording costs stay the same no matter how many copies you have pressed—and manufacturing cost per unit goe down as quantities increase.)

That sounds wonderful until you remember your original estimate of th number of copies you expected to sell. If you pressed more than. 20,000 copie you'd be exceeding that number. There's a chance you could sell the extras, but you' be taking a risk.

The third option, trying to cut your costs, would seem to be the appropriat action in this particular case.

What if you felt that the profit of $33,550 was *more* than you really needed at th outset? Here you'd have some interesting options. You could set your retail pric lower, thereby making the product more attractive to buyers and potentially sellin more copies. You could spend more on promotion, and even buy a few print ad You could opt for a more lavish recording. Or you could manufacture fewer copie thus reducing your risk of excess inventory.

Reality Check: Putting Estimates in Perspective

Bear in mind this very important point: Calculations of quantities sold and profit expected are, at this stage, only *estimates,* the purpose of which is to give you a genera sense of the feasibility of your planned enterprise. What happens in the real world thanks to the unpredictability of the music market, may bear little resemblance to th numbers you've put down on paper.

It would be a mistake to assume that you're really going to sell the total number c CDs in your estimate. One industry safety measure is to try to delay placing an orde to manufacture copies until actual distributor orders come in, then manufacture 10 t 20 percent more than the distributor orders, and reorder as inventory goes down (Promo copies, of course, are manufactured ahead of time to use in creating deman for the hoped-for big orders.) As one industry veteran put it, "Hold on to your mone until the last possible minute. Don't press on a guess of what you'll get orders for."

Return on Investment (ROI)

In the preceding calculation, you started with fixed costs, a fixed price, and an esti mated sales quantity to calculate your profit. Another way to analyze the finances o your project is to start with the profit. You focus first on a fixed *return on investmen* (ROI)—that is, you establish a fixed profit percentage that is the minimum accept able for the viability of your project. Then you calculate your price and costs to mak sure that the ROI is reachable.

One way to do this is to use what is called a *target-return* approach. You estimat the number of records you expect to sell and determine the desired profit. Then you djust price and cost to guarantee the profit. In our number-crunch example, you stimated 16,000 sales units. If you established 50 percent as your desired profit, here's vhat you'd come up with: Based on a suggested retail list price of $19 and net receipts f $113,100, a 50 percent gross profit would be $56,550. But, as you already discovered, your current production/promotion costs of $79,550 would allow a profit of nly 30 percent. What to do? Either cut your costs by $23,000 or raise your prices.

Another approach is called *cost-plus pricing*. In this case you start with your fixed ost, establish a desired markup above the cost—say, 100 percent—and then set the rice according to that markup. If, for example, you had a fixed cost per unit of $5.50 nd you wanted to earn back a 100 percent markup on that cost ($5.50 × 100% = 5.50), you would need to receive $11 per unit. That, in turn, might require a retail rice of around $22 to allow for the amount deducted for distribution. (As you can ee, in this case the ultimate price to consumer would be higher than the norm. You vould have to do one of the following: cut costs, reduce your markup percentage, nd a cheaper distributor, live with the higher price, or cancel the project.)

The problem with these approaches is that in the music industry it is exceedingly ifficult to ensure a fixed return on investment. Trends come and go too quickly and udience tastes are constantly changing. To counter the unpredictability of sales, the est strategy is to keep costs down, find the best distribution deals, delay manufacturing until the last possible minute, try to sell the maximum number of records, and romote like crazy.

Break-Even Analysis

'ou can shed more light on the financial viability of your project by performing a *reak-even analysis*—that is, determining how many CDs you will need to sell in order o earn back your expenditures. This number of units is called the *break-even point*.

In your calculations, your estimated production and promo costs were $79,550 and our mechanical royalties were $8,500. One item that wasn't factored in was the artist *dvance against royalty*—the amount the artist will be paid up front, to be recouped from oyalties on sales. Since the general rule is that advances are nonrepayable (the artist ets to keep the advance even if it isn't fully recouped from royalties), you have to conider it an expenditure until it's recouped. Let's establish a $21,300 advance (roughly 0 percent of the hoped-for $30,400 in artist royalty earnings).

Adding all these figures together, you come up with total expenditures of 109,350 ($79,550 + $8,500 + $21,300). To break even, you would have to sell 109,350 worth of units. That would require selling approximately 11,510 CDs at a etail price of $19 (assuming you'll receive about $9.50 per copy).

Bear in mind that when you lower the price, the break-even point increases (you'll eed to sell more units to earn back your investment). When you raise the price, the reak-even point decreases (it takes fewer sales to earn back the investment).

Given this information, you can decide whether it is better to try to sell more CDs t a lower price or fewer units at a higher price. Your decision will depend largely on ow you think price will affect the customer's decision to buy.

The Way the Industry Does It

If you were serving strictly as the record label—not the recording artist—there would be another way of calculating costs to compensate for the risk associated with large up-front expenditures. Surprising as it may seem, you'd be conforming with standard music industry practice if you were to charge packaging costs, recording costs, and even some of the promotion costs back to the artist.

Here's how it often works: the record company advances money to the artist, who uses it to pay the studio, musicians, and other participants. An alternative scenario has the record label exerting more direct control over recording expenditures. Either way, *these costs are then recouped from artist royalties.* In other words, the recording cost ultimately comes out of the artist's pocket, not the record company's.

(Keep in mind, though, that companies get the money back only if the record is successful enough to generate artist royalties from which to recoup. If the record doesn't sell sufficiently, the record company loses the amount it invested.)

Also deductible from artist royalties is payment for a producer. In the record-biz big time, producers are often paid via royalty—usually around 3 percent of the SRLP. This amount may also be shifted to the artist side of the ledger. The artist might be guaranteed a 15 percent royalty, but he or she would be responsible for paying the producer's royalty (and advance) out of that money.

The charge-backs to the artist don't stop there. A portion of third-party promotion costs—ranging from 50 to 100 percent—may be recouped from artist royalties. The same is true for 100 percent of money provided for tour support.

It's also standard for a record company to deduct an amount of money from royalty-bearing sales receipts to cover the cost of packaging. This amount is usually 25 percent for CDs. So, if the retail price of a CD is $19, the "packaging deduction" would be 25 percent of that, or $4.75. The artist royalty would be calculated on $14.25 ($19 - $4.75) rather than the full $19. In other words, the artist is helping to pay for the packaging.

In addition, record companies do not pay the artist royalties on "free goods" shipped to retailers or wholesalers. This refers to the practice of offering 15-percent discounts or thereabouts to retailers or wholesalers as a kind of sales incentive, but treating it as 15 percent of an order given away as free or bonus records. Categorizing 15 percent of shipped records as "free" means the record company only pays artist royalties on the 85 percent "sold." (If it was treated as a 15-percent discount on the full order, they'd have to pay royalties on 100 percent of the units.)

None of this is particularly good from the artist's perspective. But record companies justify such deductions and charge-backs by pointing to the high-risk nature of the record business: Labels take the initial financial risk on an album, but most records fail to recoup their costs. So to stay in business, labels compensate for their flops by ensuring maximum profit on those products that do end up selling.*

Now let's see how the numbers play out using this approach.

---

* The record-label accounting practices described in this section have long been a point of confusion (to put it diplomatically) between labels and artists. In 2002 several companies, including BMG and Universal, responded to continuing pressure from high-profile artists by indicating they would begin simplifying and clarifying their accounting procedures.

tail price of CD	$	19.00
% packaging deduction	–	4.75
mount subject to royalty payment	$	14.25
tist 10% royalty per unit		1.43
16,000 units		22,880.00
ss 15% "free goods"		– 3,432.00
TAL ARTIST ROYALTY	$	19,448.00

In this case, the artist royalty is $19,448. That's $10,952 less than the royalty calcu-
ted in your original number crunch.

Of your original costs, $54,150 will, in this new computation, be recouped from
tist royalties. (That's $26,150 in recording costs, $20,000 in tour support money,
,000 in independent PR, and $5,000 in record promotion.)

Again, let's do the math to see what you'll earn:

ceipts for 16,000 units less 15% "free goods"	$	129,200
ss mechanical royalty	–	8,500
btotal	$	120,700
ss costs of production and promotion*	–	79,550
OSS MARGIN	$	41,150

*ncludes a $26,150 advance to the artist to cover recording costs.

But what about the artist royalty of $19,448? We've previously determined that
cording costs, tour support, and some promo money—totaling $54,150—are
coupable from artist royalties. Since $19,448 is less than that, the record company
eps it. (In fact, the artist still owes the company $34,702 out of that $54,150, which
e record company will recoup out of future royalties.)

For the record businessperson, how you calculate artist royalties, and whether you
hoose to charge recording, packaging, and promotion back to the artist, depends on
our sense of fairness and how you define your role as a record company. If you view
e record company's role as simply providing administrative services, manufacturing
xpertise, and distribution clout, then you might justifiably charge back items that
on't fall into these categories. Further, you may feel that maximum profit should be
our compensation for taking the financial risk.

For the recording artist there are two ways of looking at the above approach to
oing business:

1. It bears similarity to joint ventures in which all costs are recouped before
   either party receives profits, except that joint ventures are often 50-50

deals, whereas this deal ranges from 90-10 to 75-25. The only way to compensate for the above-listed royalty deductions is to obtain the highest base royalty rate you can negotiate.

2. It makes releasing and marketing your own records, rather than signing with a label, look a lot more attractive.

ADDITIONAL FACTORS AFFECTING PRICE

Earlier, we assumed your objective was to sell as many copies of the record as poss ble, as soon as possible, and at the highest price possible. But there are other types marketing objectives, and they have an effect on the price point you choose.

Your objective may be *early cash recovery*. In this case, you would set a low initi price to maximize sales and cash early in the marketing program.

You might opt for a *market skimming* approach. Here, you would secure maximu early profit by setting a high price, based on the knowledge that core customers w want to be among the first to own the product, regardless of the cost. (Of course, yc have to be certain these customers exist.)

Another possible objective is *market penetration,* where you set a low price ensure purchase by a large segment of the potential market.

Mid-Priced and Budget Albums

You may encounter a situation where you want to boost sales of *back-catalog produ* meaning CDs that have been on the market for a while, are no longer being active promoted, but are still for sale. You can use a price adjustment to achieve such objective. Generally, you'll sell these products as either mid-priced or budget items

Mid-Priced Albums. A mid-price is one adjustment down from the standard price (th is, the SRLP) of a top-line new release. A mid-price is used to encourage custome to buy older product that the company believes still has sales potential. An examp is an early album by a still-popular veteran performer.

A mid-price is generally 20 to 40 percent below the standard price of a ne release. Thus, a CD priced at $18.98 when new would be mid-priced somewhe between $10.98 and around $14.98.

Artist royalties are usually 75 percent of the rate for a new album.

Budget Albums. It may be that an old album won't sell unless the price is reduced eve further. In that case, you'd set the price at the budget level, which is generally und 65 percent of the new-release price. For a CD priced new at $18.98, the budget pri would be any price lower than around $12.50.

Artist royalties for budget records are typically one-half to two-thirds of the ra for a new album.

If a budget record fails to sell, you have the option of slashing prices even furth to encourage retailers to take your "excess inventory" off your hands.

Chapter 7

Distributing Through Stores and Their Suppliers

You may have a CD full of brilliant music. And you may have packaged it with eye-popping artwork. But the audio brilliance and visual dazzle will be lost on all but immediate friends and colleagues unless you take the next important step. The music has to be delivered to the public at large. And the term for getting it to the public *distribution*.

Distribution is the "place" part of the Four P's of marketing: Product, Price, Place, and Promotion. (And, as long as we're dealing with letters of the alphabet, is also the "where" of marketing's Three W's and an H: the What, Where, How, and When.)

Distribution is the part of the marketing program devoted to getting rack space. It's where you make sure the musical product is displayed in sites visible and accessible to your target customers, so that they can purchase it—and so that you can make money. That's why your distribution scheme will be a cornerstone of your marketing effort.

It is also the first step in the marketing program where you'll confront a significant obstacle. So far, in the product development stage, nothing (other than budget) has stood in the way of your creating the ideal musical product you have envisioned. Now you'll face distributors and retail personnel who need to be convinced your product has commercial potential before they'll agree to work with you.

There are many effective approaches to distribution, including direct-mail sales to customers (discussed in Chapter 8) and distribution on the Internet (Chapter 9). This chapter focuses on conventional retail and wholesale distribution (translation: getting CDs and other product formats into stores).

The notion of distribution sounds simple enough. But of course, nothing is particularly simple—in life or in the music business. In keeping with that axiom, the store distribution part of marketing involves several stages, and several different types of participants. In fact, store-based distribution involves a *chain* of participants, each of which moves the product one step forward on its way to the final customer. This chain of distribution entities is often called the *distribution channel*. For now, let's go right to the last and best-known segment of that channel: the retail outlet.

TYPES OF RETAIL OUTLETS

The *retailer* is the segment of the distribution channel that deals directly with the fin
customer. An example is the store on the street—the place where individual cu
tomers go to buy records. (Retailers are differentiated from *wholesalers,* which we
get to in a minute.) As you probably know, there are many different types of outle
that carry recorded music.

Where do *you* want to sell your music? Let's go out on a limb and guess that you'
more than willing to sell records wherever people will go to buy them. Fine. B
before jumping headlong into the retail maelstrom, let's first identify some of the di
ferent store options, bearing in mind that there are probably a few types you haven
previously considered, including non-music stores that might be ideal for reachir
your target audience.

At the top of the food chain in the retail sector is the large chain record store. /
of this writing, Tower Records, Wherehouse Records, Virgin Megastores, Borders, ar
Musicland are the principal players in this category. They're the department stores •
the record world, handling large amounts of stock covering a wide range of music
styles, and dealing also in audiovisual products like DVDs, videocassettes, and con
puter games.

The chain stores have outlets across the United States and in other countries, ar
they service the largest number of music customers. Tower Records, for example, h
about 180 stores in seven countries. Musicland, which also owns Sam Goody ar
other sub-chains, has about 1,300 stores in the U.S., Puerto Rico, and the Virg

VERTICAL AND HORIZONTAL INTEGRATION

One of the giant entertainment chains, Virgin, is a case study in the organizational
system known as *vertical integration,* where a single company controls all links in the
commercial supply chain—creative, production, and distribution. Virgin, for example,
not only runs a record label, through which it creates new product, but also owns
more than 80 Virgin Megastores in the United States, Europe, Japan, and Australia.
This enables Virgin to distribute its own product and thereby maximize its profits at
each stage of the enterprise.

Sony is an even more striking example. It creates the *content*—the entertainment
property—through its Sony Music record labels (including Columbia) and Sony
Pictures film studio. It also manufactures the *hardware,* from CD and DVD players to
televisions, with which buyers listen to and/or view the content at home.

A related system is *horizontal integration,* involving the merger of similar—perhaps
formerly competing—businesses under a single corporate owner.

Both vertical and horizontal integration characterize the structure of the media conglomerates—from Viacom and Disney to AOL Time Warner—that dominate the new-
millennium entertainment industry.

lands. Wherehouse Records runs more than 400 stores in the U.S. Barnes & Noble, the bookseller, also sells music in many of its more than 500 superstores. The HMV Group, which is based in the United Kingdom, operates more than 300 stores in the U.S., Europe, and the Far East. All of these chains maintain sites on the Internet, as discussed in Chapter 9.

It's important to note that chain stores—because of the quantities of product they purchase and the resulting lower prices they can offer customers—control most of the retail market.

It's truly a quantum leap from these entertainment megacompanies to the next type of retailer on our list. Struggling alongside the retail giants are smaller, independent record stores, sometimes called mom-and-pops. The typical mom-and-pop has a much smaller stock than a chain store, a more limited musical selection, and a smaller customer base that is drawn from the immediately surrounding neighborhood. It typically offers more personal service and, often, expertise in a particular musical area or genre.

That pretty much sums up the most obvious places to sell records. How about some less obvious ones? You've probably noticed that chain stores of other types, like Target, Wal-Mart, and Kmart, sell limited selections of records—mostly chosen from current top sellers and mainstream music releases. These general-goods stores can serve as a way to reach customers who don't ordinarily visit record stores. (Consumer electronics chain stores may also sell music. BestBuy is one that does, both in its retail outlets and online).

And you've probably come across the occasional specialty music store, the small retailer that supplies specific types of music—say, reggae, jazz, hip hop, or electronica—to aficionados of those styles. For many small record labels, these are excellent places to make product available to targeted customers.

Further off the beaten path are non-record stores that cater to specialty customers. These stores occasionally carry music product that fits the theme of their primary products. For example, a retro clothing boutique might set the mood with vintage swing sounds. A store that specializes in new-age products—gifts, crystals, and books of "fantastic" art—might also carry recordings of new-age music. Craft and health-food stores might also sell albums of acoustic music. Stereo equipment stores might feature a selection of audiophile recordings. The resourceful marketer will seek out these nontraditional outlets as a way of broadening distribution and reaching customers who might not otherwise become aware of the product.

GETTING PRODUCT TO THE RETAIL OUTLETS

Question: How do you get your product into the racks and shelves of these retailers?
Answer: With a lot of effort. So much effort, in fact, that an entire segment of the music business is dedicated to relieving creative and other non-sales personnel of this immense responsibility. Businesses that cover this sector of the commercial music industry are called, not too surprisingly, *distributors*. They are the middlemen

(and -women) who specialize in taking shipment of product from record labels and making sure it gets into the proper retail outlets. The chain of distribution, in its simplest form, is shown below.

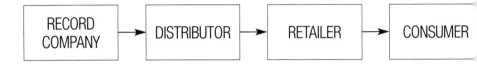

The Do-It-Yourself Method

Since lining up distributors takes a certain amount of salesmanship (and is helped by having a track record of previous sales), small, fledgling labels often start out by trying to handle local distribution on their own.

The key word here is *local*. As the Coalition of Independent Music Stores (CIMS) puts it: "We always recommend building a local story before going nationwide....As an independent artist, it is *always* best to focus your energies on a handful of areas in which you can build your audiences and develop relationships with night club bookers, store owners, and radio staff."

Tales of people who have done it abound. Norma Gatton, the mother of guitarist Danny Gatton, ran her own label that consisted entirely of her son's music. Mrs. Gatton started NRG Records in 1977 by pressing a thousand 45s, taking them around to local record stores, and asking the owners if they'd be willing to sell some. She kept at it over the years, working out of her garage, taking orders for CDs and tapes from individuals over the telephone, shipping to specialty record stores, and finally hooking up with a couple of large distributors. Twenty years after she began, Gatton's one-year sales exceeded 25,000 units.

Another example: The Boulder, Colorado, band Big Head Todd and the Monsters pressed 2,000 copies of their initial album—all they could afford. They personally delivered them to record stores, and checked back weekly to see what sold. The band eventually achieved enough success with two independent releases to attract the attention of a major label. They went on to platinum sales.

If you're a beginning music marketer handling a small quantity of CDs for an equally small label, the do-it-yourself route may be where you launch the distribution process. Look at the Internet option, of course. But human interaction in the brick-and-mortar marketplace should be a key factor in your overall distribution effort.

Hands-On Techniques

Here's one way to approach your hands-on retail distribution: Start by making a list of all the small record stores that operate in the vicinity of your home base. These are your prospective retail "accounts." (The small stores will be more open to stocking independently distributed CDs than large chain outlets would be.) Then use the following steps to get your product through their doors.

Prepare an Information Sheet. Before contacting the stores, prepare an 8 ½-by-11-inch information sheet. It can be as simple as text-only on your company letterhead or elaborately designed, with eye-catching imagery and typography. (This item is roughly equivalent to the "distributor one-sheet," described later in the chapter.)

The sheet should list such vital data as

- name of album (or single)
- name of artist
- available product formats with suggested retail list prices (SRLPs)
- product catalog numbers and UPC codes
- name, address, and phone number of record label
- some biographical facts about the artist
- listings of past and upcoming concerts in the area
- summary of radio activity (if any)

In addition, if the artist has been reviewed or featured in the print media, photo-copy one or two of the articles (positioned neatly on another sheet or two of 8 ½-by-11-inch paper) and staple them to the main information sheet.

The purpose of all this is to show that you're a professional and you mean business. And, as much as possible, you want to demonstrate to prospective buyers that the music you're peddling is saleable.

Visit Stores in Person. Just as professional sales reps do, you'll need to visit these prospective accounts in person.

In each case, ask to speak to the manager or the product buyer. Explain who you are, and that you'd like to know if the buyer would be interested in stocking some of your CDs to sell on a *consignment* basis. This means that the store pays you nothing for the records unless they sell. If they do sell, the store keeps a percentage of the sales receipts (50 percent is not unusual). (Consignment is far from an ideal arrangement for you the seller—retailers tend not to put much effort into selling products in which they haven't invested cash—but it's a way for start-ups to begin building a distribution track record. And it's best to get used to the arrangement, because, as you'll soon learn, even the mainstream industry's payment system is a kind of consignment.)

Assuming that the store's buyer hasn't abruptly cut you off in mid-sentence, describe the recording artist and his or her activities in as succinct and convincing a way as possible. For example: "This is [the artist's] first full-length CD. [The artist] has been playing in the area for several years, most recently at [name the venue], and has a lot of fans. Bookings are solid over the next few months, at [name some more venues]. We're plugging the CD at all the gigs. Also, [local radio station] is currently playing one of the tracks. On top of that, we're planning some advertising in the local press, and we'd be happy to list your store in the ads."

The point is to communicate the key selling points without monopolizing the manager's time. Offer a copy of your information sheet as a source of more detailed product information.

If the store is interested in stocking your product, ask if they'd be willing to display any of your promotional material. Also offer to create a rack divider with the artist's name on it, so the discs don't get stashed with many others in a general alph[a] letter section.

Make this entire process as easy as possible for the store manager. Whatever aspect you can handle yourself—such as tacking up a flyer—you should offer to do. And b[e] professional and self-confident in your interaction. Remember: you're not there to be[g] for help; you're offering a reasonable opportunity for both of you to make some money.

Put It in Writing. Be sure to put your agreement in writing. Specify the time perio[d] after which unsold goods are to be returned to you. Specify the condition th[e] merchandise must be in if the retailer returns it. Specify the retailer's promotiona[l] activities, if any. (Usually there are none, but if you can convince the retailer to pu[t] down a deposit on the merchandise, recoupable from sales, you will have created a[n] incentive for them to put some effort into promotion.) And, obviously, specify th[e] percentage of sales income each party is to receive.

Expand Beyond Music Stores. In addition to targeting record stores in your area, mak[e] a separate list of non-record stores that you feel cater to a clientele that would be inter[-]ested in your music. Then pay each a sales visit, following essentailly the same approac[h] that you would with a record store.

Keep in mind that CD sales in these types of stores will be significantly booste[d] if the store actually plays the CDs as background music. That's worth a suggestio[n] to the product buyer—as is the fact that customers often don't realize that CDs ar[e] for sale in such non-music stores, making some sort of promotional display a near[-] requirement.

Build Business Relationships. Once you've placed CDs in a store, think of it as th[e] beginning of a business relationship that requires ongoing attention.

Make sure you keep in frequent touch with each of your new accounts. Stop b[y] the stores weekly, or at least monthly, to check on sales. If discs have sold, you ca[n] request payment at the same time as you offer to replenish their stock. You can als[o] offer stores the option of displaying new flyers or posters.

Be aware of some of the obstacles you'll encounter. A big one: With large recor[d] chains taking over the retail market, it's become more difficult to get ahead b[y] working the small-store, one-to-one sales approach.

"For the first ten years I was in this business, all you had to do was find someon[e] in a record store who cared about music," Foster Reed, founder of the small classica[l] label New Albion Records, told *San Francisco Chronicle* writer Joshua Kosman. "If the[y] could see that a record was good, then automatically you had sales," Reed said. "Bu[t] with the independents gone...instead of dealing with a great store in Portland, Maine[,] you're dealing with a corporate buyer in Michigan who's selling to a chain. So yo[u] can't get that kind of one-on-one relationship."

All the more reason to approach local retailers with professionalism and a willingness to work hard to drive their sales.

The door-to-door, person-to-person sales approach may not be for you. You may prefer to focus entirely on the Internet. Or you may already be at a stage where professional distribution is an option. But if you're starting out and taking the do-it-yourself-on-the-street route, think of it this way: You're laying the groundwork for a future sales pitch to a distributor. Being able to say "We sold X amount of records in X local retail outlets over several months" can be an important buying incentive to someone who has the capability of lifting you to the next stage in the retail hierarchy.

That next stage is having a distributor pushing your product.

TYPES OF DISTRIBUTORS

As mentioned previously, distributors are the go-between entities that transfer product from the record label to retail outlets. They are *wholesalers* insofar as they distribute the product to entities other than the final consumer—in other words, to other businesses in the distribution channel.

There are a number of different types of distributors, some of which are wholly owned divisions of established record companies, and some of which are independent operations. There are also sub-distributors—companies that buy from distributors and then service off-the-main-path retailers.

Major-Label Distributors

Just as sales in the music industry are dominated by major record labels, so is the record distribution system dominated by a handful of distribution networks directly affiliated with those major labels. As of this writing, there are five of these major-label distributors: Bertelsmann Music Group (BMG), Universal Music Group, Sony Music Entertainment, EMI Music Distribution, and Warner-Elektra-Atlantic (WEA). They store product from record manufacturing plants and distribute it to large chain record stores, one-stops (defined on page 90), and rack jobbers (also defined shortly).

The major-label distributors handle the product of each label's subsidiary companies and partners. Universal, for example, handles Geffen, A&M, Island Def Jam, MCA, Motown, Philips, Polydor, and Verve. BMG distributes Arista, J Records, RCA, Windham Hill, and the Zomba Label Group. Sony distributes Columbia and Epic. WEA handles Warner Bros., Elektra, Atlantic, and Rhino. EMI distributes Capitol, EMI, and Virgin.

Independent Distributors

Independent distributors are just that: businesses that are not necessarily affiliated with the major labels. (I use the phrase *not necessarily* because there are many different types of business links between the independents and the majors, including ownership of an indie by a major.)

Independent distributors vary in size. All of them specialize in smaller, independent record labels, taking delivery from the labels' manufacturers and then distributing product to many of the same entities reached by the major labels: one-stops, chain stores, and smaller mom-and-pops.

Some independent distributors offer specialization in particular musical genres or in specific types of products. There could be a "boutique" distributor handling alternative rock, hardcore, ska, and roots music. Another might focus on oldies, classical music, or ethnic music. There are indie distributors that specialize in imported product, and indies that claim expertise in children's and educational music. The point is that, in aggregate, they offer retailers a more diverse selection than can be ordered from the five major-label distributors. Most important, the indies provide distribution services for the smaller specialty labels that don't have access to the major-label network.

Because indie distributors have close ties to small, specialty retailers, major labels have been known to buy or partner with these distribution firms. This provides the majors with access to "fringe" audiences they wouldn't otherwise have the expertise to reach.

For an informative introduction to the workings and procedures of an independent distributor, visit the Web site of Redeye Distribution at www.redeyeusa.com. The company's "Label Handbook" provides details about preparing for and following up on distribution.

See "Music Distribution" in the Appendix (page 290) for a list of companies that distribute independent labels.

One-Stop Distributors

One-stops are essentially *sub-distributors*—they buy in bulk from the majors and large indies and then sell in small numbers to mom-and-pops and specialty stores. One-stops provide "one-stop shopping" for retailers looking for a range of products that they can buy in small quantities—quantities too small for the larger distributors to be concerned with. They may also fill back-catalog orders for major record chains, and may service the record departments of large book chains like Barnes & Noble. One-stops also provide musical product to jukebox operators.

Rack Jobbers

As already mentioned, some chain general-goods stores like Kmart and Wal-Mart sell musical product. Rather than maintain their own staff to stock and manage a music section, these retailers may obtain such service from independent entities called rack jobbers.

Rack jobbers purchase records from large music distributors. They sell them by leasing sales space in department stores, discount stores, and other outlets, essentially setting up and managing a record department in a store that wouldn't otherwise have one. They pay the store rent and/or a percentage of sales income and then keep the profit.

The records chosen by rack jobbers are the most mainstream, broadly popular titles available—the ones currently situated high in the airplay and sales charts (for more about charts—especially the ones published in *Billboard* magazine—see page 260).

Rack jobbers play an important role in the distribution system: they specialize in retailing beyond the sphere of music specialty stores, and thus help to get records to a wider audience.

Chain Stores

The large chain stores discussed previously—Tower, Virgin, and others—can also be considered sub-distributors. They run central offices through which they buy product from the major labels and distributors. These central offices then ensure that the product is distributed to all the individual retail outlets in the company chain.

Naturally there are going to be differences in the inventory requirements of different local stores due to varying regional tastes. The companies deal with this by using centralized, computerized inventory systems that track individual store sales and automatically order new stock in product categories that are selling well in those stores.

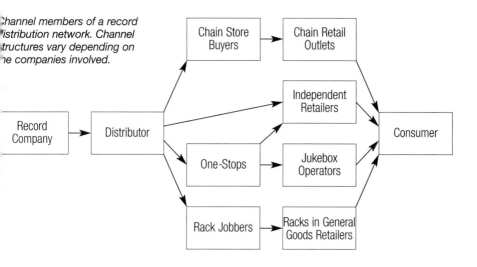

Channel members of a record distribution network. Channel structures vary depending on the companies involved.

SERVICES PROVIDED BY DISTRIBUTORS

You may be wondering why you need the services of distributors. What do they do that justifies their share of sales dollars? The answer can be summarized in two words: convenience and clout.

Rather than dealing with hundreds of retailers one by one, you can work with a distributor, and let it handle the details of mass dissemination. That's the convenience part.

The clout part is this: Chances are you're an individual or a small label with a limited track record of sales. With all the other record labels vying for store rack space, why should retailers choose your product? Just because you say it's good? They'll need more convincing than that. And that's where distributors come in. For the most part, they have longstanding business relationships with the stores. They're familia with what sells and what doesn't. Their acceptance of and confidence in your musi will go a long way toward convincing retailers that your product is worth a shot.

Record chains, in particular, tend to deal only with approved suppliers, and wit as few of them as possible. A one- or two-record label is unlikely to be approved as vendor. Thus chains may be off-limits to small labels that wish to sell to them directly— an excellent reason to seek representation by an established distributor.

So the main service that distributors provide is to stock your product, get it int retail or other outlets, and pay you when the product sells.

A key part of this job is convincing the retailers to accept your product. The dis tributor's sales representatives contact individual accounts (which might include one stops and rack jobbers in addition to retail stores) in person, by e-mail, or vi telephone. They provide buyers with their catalog of products (including your CD along with other product and promotional information culled from materials tha you have provided them (including one-sheets, which are described a bit later). The provide information about prices, different types of discounts, and in-store promo tion preferences. They then take orders. Later, they keep in touch to make sure th order was received, to monitor the progress of sales, and to check inventories.

In addition, distributors can provide you, the record label, with information abou sales promotion packages—such as prime display space—offered by retailers. (Se page 101 for more information about prime retail display space.)

For some distributors, the basic service stops there ("basic service" includin accounting and payment to you, of course). Other distributors provide more.

Some, although very few, offer promotional services beyond simply promoting t the retailer. They supplement the efforts of the record label (you) by helping wit radio promotion and publicity. Most distributors help set up what is called co-o advertising, where store and record label are promoted together in print ads (mor about which on page 188). In general, however, the responsibility for promotion fal on the shoulders of the record label, not the distributor.

A small number of distributors offer quite extensive services. Some, targetin indie music makers, claim to provide guidance through all stages of developmen and sales, from record mastering through CD artwork, bar-coding and labeling manufacturing, printing, radio promotion, retail promotion, publicity, and ultimatel distribution. (Prospective customers would be remiss in not checking the legitimac of such claims.)

If you're working with a major-label distributor, it will have the capability of pro viding both pressing and distribution services, as well as marketing. More about th a little later in this chapter.

WHAT KIND OF DISTRIBUTOR IS RIGHT FOR YOU?

The kind of distributor you choose will depend upon the size and extent of you enterprise. A well-established label may be best served by partnering with one of th major-label distributors. (See "Other Distribution Arrangements" on page 103.) A small specialty label, on the other hand, will seek the services of one of the independent distributors, with expertise in the label's style of music.

Let's backtrack, for a moment, to the process of hand-distributing to local stores described earlier. If you've done this for a while and have achieved some success—selling a respectable number of discs both in-store and on gigs, for example—you may be ready to work with a distributor. (You may also be ready *without* going through the hand-distribution process—you've created some buzz about your music in other ways. The point, though, is that being ready for a distributor means being able to present convincing indicators of potential for success.)

A distributor or one-stop *that handles product such as yours* would be the most appropriate type of entity to contact first. Later, you might add distributors to cover a greater range of accounts, thus creating your own international distribution network.

If you're just starting out, consider working with an Internet-based distributor such as The Orchard (www.theorchard.com), an indie-accessible organization that supplies product to brick-and-mortar retailers as well as online megastores.

HOW TO FIND A DISTRIBUTOR

The process of researching distributors can be relatively straightforward. If you're starting out locally and have been dealing directly with record stores, ask them the names of distributors they work with. Call the major record chains and ask them who they buy from. If you have friends or acquaintances who are involved in the record business, ask them for recommendations. Look at the list provided in this book's Appendix (page 290). If you have access to the Internet, type in the keywords *record distribution,* and scrutinize the sites you find.

Billboard, the weekly home-entertainment trade magazine, publishes a yearly directory called *Billboard's International Buyer's Guide.* It contains a state-by-state listing of a large number of distributors.

Visit the Web site of the National Association of Recording Merchandisers (NARM) at www.narm.com, view its list of distributors, and request access to information about them.

The Association for Independent Music (AFIM) puts out an annual directory that lists independent distributors. It also holds an annual convention in partnership with NARM. If you attend, you'll be able to meet directly with a number of distributors who handle indie labels. Bring along your promotion material and sample recordings, and you may be able to get some distribution interest right at the convention. If not, you'll at least come away with expanded knowledge of the distribution system and its participants. For information, visit the AFIM Web site at www.afim.org.

The important thing in finding a distributor is making sure that they handle the kind of music you are trying to sell. Specialists in your genre will have an inside track to the customers most likely to be interested—that is, your target audience.

HOW TO APPROACH A DISTRIBUTOR

After you find a distributor, the next step is to approach them to see if they'd be inter ested in working with you. Approaching a distributor is essentially a process of sellin them on the value and commercial potential of the product you're offering. They' be investing time and energy in the distribution process, so they'll want to be sur that the effort has a reasonable chance of paying off in the form of sales—both t retailers and to the end customers. (A product isn't really considered sold until it sel to the final customer.)

POPULAR PERCEPTION

If a CD "ships platinum," it's a huge success.
It's not unusual for retailers to order large shipments of new releases by well-known artists.

ALTERNATE REALITY

The release may ship from the distributor to retailers in large quantities, but it may not sell to the final customer in large quantities. When this happens, unsold copies are sent back to the distributor and the record company, with no money earned for those copies. A record isn't a success until it sells through to the public.

Many established distributors don't deal with untested newcomers. As the distrib utor Baker and Taylor says on its Web site, "BTD does not provide distribution serv ices for artists not established in the industry." This means that if you're a start-up you'll have to begin with a small distribution outfit.

Preparing a Sales Presentation

Because finding a distributor involves selling, you'll need to carefully prepare you presentation to any prospective distributor. Just as you'd do in selling directly to record store—or even in trying to get a recording deal with a major record label— you have to take stock of all your promotional assets and assemble them into both concise piece of printed communication and a brief list of talking points.

The promotional information that's most impressive to a distributor is a trac record of successful sales. If you've sold a few hundred or, better yet, a few thousan discs on your own (on store consignment, by direct mail, and at concerts, for example) emphasize that fact. This will support your claim of future saleability.

If you have no track record of sales, your job will be more difficult. To convinc a distributor to work with you, you'll just have to assemble whatever other sellin points you can think of. Current radio play, current touring, and media coverage i the form of newspaper and magazine articles—all of these are valuable.

Bear in mind, too, that most distributors want to know not only that you're serious about promotion and that your record will sell but also that you plan to have a continuing series of releases. They want to be sure you'll be a reliable customer and won't suddenly pull out of the business, leaving them holding stacks of unsellable records. For this reason you should probably refrain from trying to launch your own label if you're intending to sell only one record.

Distributor One-Sheets

The form in which to present your product information and sales points to the distributor is called a *one-sheet*. The one-sheet is an 8 ½-by-11-inch sheet of paper containing two kinds of information: (1) basic facts about the product (such as the title and UPC number), which the distributor will enter into its computerized accounting records, and (2) important sales points that will convince the distributor to buy the product. The distributor, in turn, will use the one-sheet to convince retailers to buy the product. Or, in some cases, *you* may supply the one-sheet to retailers. In any event, the following information should be included:

- Artist name (and logo, if any) and album title
- Picture of the CD cover
- Name of musical category or style
- Brief description of the artist and the album (including all noteworthy information, such as the names of any well-known participants, whether producer, songwriters, or musicians)
- Release date
- Bulleted list of the following selling points and marketing information:
    - Publicity plans and schedule
    - Radio airplay plans (including independent promotion) and schedule
    - Touring or live-performance plans to support the release (including schedule)
    - Advertising plans and schedule
    - Additional marketing and promotion plans and ideas
    - Artist's track record of previous sales
    - Record company's track record of previous sales
    - Description of the artist's audience, major markets, and size of following
    - Merchandise availability
- Record company logo and contact information, including Web address
- Product catalog number and UPC number
- Bar code
- Suggested retail list price (SRLP)

Most one-sheets are attractively designed. For a sample, visit Redeye Distribution at www.redeyeusa.com.

After you've prepared your one-sheet, you're ready to begin contacting prospective distributors. Make contact by phone or by mail, and try to set up an appointment to discuss the product.

Some distributors ask for press kits, have you fill out forms that detail the information provided in the one-sheet, and make you jump through a few other hoops.

Remember that you're competing with a glut of other independent labels trying to get distribution. You've got to do everything you can to "sell your product to the seller"—that is, the distributor.

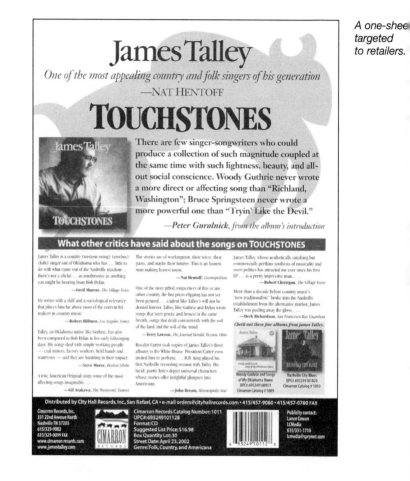

FINANCIAL ARRANGEMENTS WITH DISTRIBUTORS

What kind of financial arrangements will you need to make once you have received a positive response from a distributor?

Deals come in an assortment of configurations. Here's a common arrangement: The distributor agrees to take your product on consignment and try to sell it to retailers at a wholesale price based on your suggested retail list price (SRLP)—the wholesale price generally being greater than half the amount of the SRLP. (How much greater varies from company to company.) After the distributor makes sales, it pays you the wholesale amount minus a percentage and expenses. This agreed-upon distributor percentage—essentially a sales commission—might typically be between 18 and 35 percent. So depending on the overall distribution price structure, what you end up getting is typically somewhere between 35 and 50 percent of the SRLP.

One distributor sells to its retail contacts for about $10 per CD and pays the label $7. (If the label's unit cost is $4, it makes $3 profit. The distributor also makes $3. If the retailer sells for $13, it too earns $3.)

Other less common arrangements have you selling to the distributor at a discount off the SRLP. The discount is negotiable depending on your clout, but it generally runs from 55 to 65 percent.

Whatever the financial deal, you may need to supply the distributor with a number of free goods as an incentive they can use to secure a sale to retail. The number of free goods is often 15 percent of the total order. (For more information on free goods, see page 80.) The distributor will undoubtedly want some additional free copies for promotional use.

Promotional copies of recordings are given by the distributor's field reps to retailers, who generally use them for in-store play. (You should mark the packaging of promotional product to ensure that it doesn't get returned by the record store for credit.)

Now here's the catch: the distributor doesn't necessarily pay for all the records it orders from you. It only pays for the records shipped out of its warehouse to retailers—minus records that end up not selling through to consumers.

A FEW BUSINESS ESSENTIALS

If you're launching your own label, you'll need to take care of a few business essentials before focusing on selling your product.

The first is to obtain a *Fictitious Name Certificate* for the name of your venture. You can obtain one by filling out a simple form at your local county clerk's office. This establishes your exclusive right to use your chosen name in your geographic area. (At some point, you may want to register your business name as a trademark. To find out information about this process, contact the United States Patent and Trademark Office at (800) 786-9199 or (703) 308-HELP or on the World Wide Web at www.uspto.gov. To verify that your name is available for trademark registration—that is, it hasn't already been registered by someone else in your trade category—you can conduct a trademark search online through the USPTO's Trademark Electronic Search System (TESS), through an attorney, or by checking patent and trademark databases at public libraries.

The second task is to obtain a *seller's permit,* if you work in a state that assesses sales tax. This allows you to buy materials from suppliers without paying sales tax. (Tax is reported and collected at the retail level.) You can obtain a seller's permit through your state board of equalization.

The third is to set up a unique *catalog number* for your release. Additionally, you should obtain a *Universal Product Code (UPC)* from the Uniform Code Council at (937) 435-3870 and bar code film from your local bar code supplier. (See page 51 for details about UPCs and bar codes.)

Furthermore, it doesn't pay for these shipped records immediately. There's usually a negotiable billing schedule of 30, 60, 90, or 120 days. The length of time you can negotiate depends on your clout, and chances are (if you're a small start-up label) you won't have much bargaining power at the beginning. (Be aware that some distributors may count the days until their payment date not from the actual order date but from the last day of the month in which the order was placed.)

When payment comes due, there is a further deduction. The distributor will hold back a *reserve fund* as a hedge against records that are returned unsold. More about this shortly, but first let's take a look at the arrangements between the distributor and the retail outlet, and how they affect you.

Impact of Arrangements Between Distributors and Retailers

The retailer buys from the distributor at the wholesale price and sells to the public at the SRLP or at a discount off the SRLP. The retailer also agrees to pay the distributor within a negotiated time period (often 60 days) for the quantity of product shipped. (Discount incentives to pay earlier may be offered.) Like the distributor, the retailer will withhold a percentage of the payment (a reserve fund) to cover unsold goods.

The lag time between shipment and payment at the retail level is the reason the distributor doesn't pay you immediately. Essentially, the distributor wants to get paid by the record store before it pays you.

Assuming an established relationship with a distributor, and generally healthy sales at the retail level, it's not uncommon for the distributor to submit statements and checks to the record company on a monthly basis.

Returns Policies

It's entirely possible that some of the records stocked in retail will not *sell through*—that is, customers won't buy them. Here's what happens if records don't sell through: Retail stores are allowed to return 100 percent of unsold or defective product to the distributor for full refund or credit. (The retailer's reserve fund set aside to cover unsold goods, usually capped at 20 percent of the original shipment, will be applied to the refund or credit.) When the distributor receives the returns, and is unable to sell them elsewhere, it can then send them back to you without owing you any money. This arrangement is in fact spelled out in your distribution agreement: *100 percent of unsold goods are returnable to you.* And the distributor withholds up to 20 percent of its accounts payable to you as a hedge against any returns.

Here are two scenarios—good case and bad case—that might unfold from this arrangement.

Good case: You sell 5,000 CDs to a distributor on a 60-day payment schedule. The distributor sells them to retailers on a 45-day payment schedule. The CDs all sell through quickly. The retailers do their part and pay the distributor in full within 45 days. The distributor then pays you in full within 60 days and places an order for more CDs. Because you have been paid, you can afford to pay your manufacturer and have more copies pressed for the distributor. Everyone is happy.

Bad case: You hire a manufacturer to press 5,000 CDs on a delayed-payment schedule of 120 days. You sell these CDs to a distributor on a 90-day payment schedule. (You figure that when the distributor pays you, you'll have enough time to pay your manufacturer.) The distributor sells only 3,000 of the CDs to retailers, on a 60-day payment schedule. Sixty days pass, and the CDs have sold to customers only in dribs and drabs. The retail stores get cold feet, and ship everything back to the distributor as unsold goods (paying, of course, only for the units that did sell through). The distributor receives the returned shipments to its warehouse. It tries to sell them to other retailers but fails. Having paid you nothing so far, it decides the product is a loser. Per its agreement with you that allows it to return 100 percent of unsold goods, it ships back to you all the returns received from the retailers, along with the 2,000 that it wasn't able to move in the first place. Your warehouse (or garage, as the case may be) is now inundated with boxes of returned CDs that couldn't be sold. You receive a paltry sum from the distributor for the several hundred that did manage to sell through. Suddenly the bill comes from the manufacturer for the cost of pressing the full 5,000 copies. Because of the poor sell-through and the 100 percent return policy, you don't have enough money to pay the total amount. You pay what you can and then—in a spasm of fiscal panic—you shut down your business.

What can you do to prevent such a disaster? For one thing, don't manufacture a greater number of CDs than you're reasonably sure can be sold. (If possible, wait until you get an actual order from the distributor before pressing.) Be conservative—at least initially. If your first order does sell well, you can always go back and order more. This assumes, of course, that you have the money to do so. To make sure you do, focus like a laser on the distributor's payment to you, first negotiating a payment schedule that allows you enough time to pay for repressings, and second, staying on the distributor's back to pay you within the established time frame (not always easy).

Techniques for Ensuring Payment

This brings us to a common pitfall for independent labels: the problem of distributors not paying on time—or simply not paying at all. When that happens it puts the label in a financial squeeze when its own bills come due.

For example, one San Francisco-based independent label secured a pressing and distribution deal (a concept explained later in this chapter) with an independent distributor. When it came time for payment, the distributor went out of business, leaving the label with empty pockets. Small labels with no clout are the most vulnerable to this problem.

The way to handle this is to use any leverage that is available. The most effective, of course, is having a product that is selling well, so that the distributor wants to order more copies from you. In this case, you'd make a reorder contingent upon the distributor paying you in full for copies already shipped.

To increase the likelihood of this happening, limit the quantity you initially provide to the distributor. That way, sell-through occurs more quickly, prompting the distributor to request a reorder sooner than it otherwise would.

Before making a deal with a distributor, be sure to check references and get opinions of the distributor's business practices from other clients.

WHAT YOU NEED TO PROVIDE TO THE DISTRIBUTOR

When the distribution process gets under way, you'll be doing your part if you provide the following elements:

Invoice. Mail the distributor a notice of payment due, and send it separately from the shipment. It should contain the following information: invoice date, invoice number, distributor's purchase order number, product number (UPC or catalog number is standard), brief product description, ship date, unit price, quantity ordered, total amount due, and due date (terms of payment). The purpose of this is to enable the distributor to correctly cross-reference the bill to the order on their accounting system.

<table>
<tr><td colspan="2">YOUR COMPANY NAME
Street Address
City, State 00000
Country
TEL. NUMBER E-MAIL ADDRESS
FAX NUMBER WEB SITE URL</td><td colspan="4">INVOICE

Invoice Date:
Invoice No:
Purchase Order No:</td></tr>
</table>

SOLD TO:	SHIP TO:
COMPANY NAME/ACCOUNT NO. Street Address City, State 00000 Country Contact Person/Contact Phone	COMPANY NAME/ACCOUNT NO. Street Address City, State 00000 Country Shipped via:

PRODUCT NO.	DESCRIPTION	DATE SHIPPED	UNIT PRICE	QUANTITY	PRICE
0000000	Description	00/00/00	00.00	00,000	$ 000,000.00
0000000	Description	00/00/00	00.00	00,000	$ 000,000.00
0000000	Description	00/00/00	00.00	00,000	$ 000,000.00
0000000	Description	00/00/00	00.00	00,000	$ 000,000.00
0000000	Description	00/00/00	00.00	00,000	$ 000,000.00
0000000	Description	00/00/00	00.00	00,000	$ 000,000.00
0000000	Description	00/00/00	00.00	00,000	$ 000,000.00
0000000	Description	00/00/00	00.00	00,000	$ 000,000.00

TERMS Net 30 days			
	Subtotal	$	000,000.00
	Shipping	$	000.00
	Federal Tax	$	000.00
	State Sales Tax	$	000.00
	TOTAL	**$**	**000,000.00**

Packing Slip. Each shipment that you send to the distributor (or order a manufacturer to send) must be accompanied with a packing slip. It contains all the vital information about the shipment, including a description of what was ordered, the distributor's purchase order number, and a list of the shipment's contents.

Some distributors offer the option of manufacturing your CD, in which case invoices and packing slips aren't needed, since you're not shipping.

Other Items. As mentioned previously, provide an informational one-sheet. If you plan to have the distributor assist with in-store promotion you should also provide it with display items like posters, banners, and anything else that might be used by the retailer to attract attention to your product.

Any distributor that offers in-house marketing and promotion assistance will instruct you on exactly what you need to provide them, and they'll give you a timeline for providing it, too—to allow for thorough planning in advance of the release date.

SECURING PRIME RETAIL DISPLAY SPACE

Naturally, you'll want your product displayed in the most visible sections of stores, rather than just in the racks. Promotional space in stores includes table space near the front of the store, end caps (prominently featured display stands), wall displays, window displays, and listening posts.

There's huge demand among record labels for the limited amount of promotional space in stores. And what happens when demand increases? You guessed it: people pay large amounts of money. Today, record labels must pay for the privilege of having their products featured in store displays and at listening posts. How much? For a single store they might pay several hundred dollars per CD release. For a national campaign, the cost may run into many thousands of dollars. ("Payment," by the way, is usually in the form of a credit to the retailer's account with the distributor, who then subtracts the amount from its account with the record company.)

Bruce Iglauer, the president and founder of the blues label Alligator Records, describes his approach to securing display space:

> *"There are a number of things we do. First of all we do play this game.*
> *We spend anywhere from ten to twenty thousand dollars on a new release*
> *for price positioning, listening posts, end caps, and anything else related to*
> *retail placement.*
>
> *"With Borders, they have a thing they call a gondola, which is a free-*
> *standing display rack that costs a thousand dollars a month to be in.*
> *Sometimes it's a sale table; sometimes it's a front rack when people walk*
> *into the stores; sometimes it's a listening post. So we spend money there."*

It's possible for labels to arrange deals in which substantial discounts are offered on shipments in return for promotional space in the store combined with co-op advertising in local media. (For more about co-op ads, see page 188.)

Small labels have limited access to in-store promotion. Fortunately, some independent retailers have banded together to address this problem. The Coalition of Independent Music Stores (CIMS) has instituted a policy of employing custom marketing initiatives to promote developing artists. Their programs include "adopting several artists each month and promoting their releases with in-store play, display and advertising.

SUPPORTING THE DISTRIBUTOR'S EFFORTS

Once you've established a relationship with a distributor, treat it as an ongoing one. Support the distributor's efforts by keeping your part of the bargain. Follow through on the marketing and promotional plans you described in your one-sheet.

Also, keep in touch. Keep the distributor informed about your unfolding plans. Supply it with press clips when they become available. Let it know about local radio coverage, including interviews. Keep it abreast of your act's performance schedule. Knowing when and where a performance is to occur will allow the distributor to provide retailers in the area with extra stock of the product and promotional items so they can meet any increased customer demand.

Be liberal in supplying promotional items to the distributor—especially copies of your recording. Having an ample quantity will help the distributor sell your product.

When possible, establish personal contact with the sales representative who handles your material. Provide that person with detailed information about the product. Make the salesperson feel involved in your success effort. This will be appreciated, and will make the product stand out in the salesperson's mind rather than get lost in the vast quantity of product he or she handles.

NIELSEN SOUNDSCAN

Nielsen SoundScan, launched in 1991 as SoundScan, is a system of electronically tracking and counting retail record sales. Each sale is counted when a product bar code is "read" at a store cash register. The aggregate information—which is used by record companies and by *Billboard* magazine in its music popularity charts—provides a highly accurate picture of what's selling at any given time. The statistics can be sorted in numerous ways to indicate sales trends, such as regional sales performance, and to measure the sales performance of individual artists.

Nielsen SoundScan's impact on the music industry has been enormous. Before SoundScan's arrival, information was tallied using methods that left lots of room for inaccuracy. The actual sales figure reported by SoundScan revealed the market potency of such previously lower-charting genres as hip-hop and country.

With Nielsen SoundScan, record companies have a reliable means of determining their success at the retail level. This in turn helps companies to make more effective business decisions.

To ensure tracking of your sales, add your music titles to the Nielsen SoundScan database by filling out its Title Addition Sheet, available online at www.soundscan.com.

It can also be a good idea to go straight to the stores. Staff at Alligator Records, says Bruce Iglauer, regularly call retailers just to check in:

> "For example, I have two people who do nothing all day but call
> retail stores. And the irony of that is that we don't sell to retail stores.
> We sell through distributors. We're a real independent company.
> We don't sell around our distributors at all. But we call up stores
> and just talk to them about our new releases, about artists coming
> into town, about numbers on SoundScan reports. We talk about radio
> play in their market or other media in their market. We invite them
> to gigs, basically greasing them. Shmoozing them. Getting them
> to remember our product, talking to them about bringing titles in.
> I don't think that there's anybody else at our level of the independent
> industry who works so closely with retail."

Some distributors actively encourage you to promote at the retail level to pave the way for the distributor to sell to that retailer. One distributor, Redeye, sees it as the label's job to create retail awareness and demand, and the distributor's job to make sure the product is available to fill that demand. Redeye provides labels with its "Powerhouse List" of key retail accounts and instructs the label to send promo kits to each of those accounts (some 250) five weeks before the release date. A week later the distributor starts soliciting those accounts for orders. After orders have been shipped, Redeye has its labels make *tracking calls* (follow-up calls) to the retail accounts to find out if the product is selling and to provide any new promotion information.

Each distributor has its own way of working. But in all cases it'll be based on a working partnership with you, the label.

Another list for you to set up—in addition to a customer mailing list—is a list of retail accounts to stay in touch with on a regular basis, with fields for date of contact and purpose/result of contact.

OTHER DISTRIBUTION ARRANGEMENTS

It's possible for independent record labels or production outfits—the music makers—to enter into business relationships that go well beyond standard distribution agreements as described above. They include licensing, label deals, pressing and distribution deals, and joint ventures, as well as many permutations of these. All involve an indie music maker harnessing the distribution clout of an established record label.

All these deals are as challenging to set up as getting an artist deal with a record label. Mostly, they fall under the category of "what you can do once you have a track record." And they generally apply not to the independent musician with one CD to sell but rather to a person or group acting like a label, planning and putting out multiple products.

Distributing Through Another Label

A good way for a start-up or one-record operation to get distribution when it othe wise can't is to enter into an arrangement with another label, small or large, that alreac has distribution. For a percentage of sales income, the distributing label includes yo CD (or CDs) among the products it sells to its distributor or through its own di tribution arm. The percentage of sales income you give up to the host label depen on your clout.

Many of these types of arrangements are *licensing agreements,* specifying limite time frames, a defined number of products, and/or a specific market segment. An ir demand self-producing artist may decide a licensing agreement for his CD is preferab to entering into a recording contract.

Singer-songwriter John Hiatt, for example, licensed his album *Crossing Mud Waters* to Vanguard Records for distribution to record stores. Another compar handled Internet distribution.

Label Deals or Production Deals

Instead of licensing CDs for a limited time period, the independent record label c production company can have an ongoing arrangement with an established (c "major") label. In one such deal, the indie label or production company is under cor tract to provide products—in the form of master recordings—to the larger labe which provides recording funds and handles packaging, distribution, marketing, an promotion. The distributing label's name may appear on the products in addition t or instead of, the production company's or producing label's name. Payment occu in the form of a royalty to the producing company—a royalty large enough to allo some profit to the producing company after its subpayment to the recording artist.

When envisioning a production company with this kind of deal, think of a Quinc Jones, or some other well-known producer a major label would entrust with the tas of independently "packaging" a commercial record—that is, finding talented artis and recording them to best advantage.

Pressing and Distribution Deals

A less cozy variation of the label deal involves you—the indie label or productio company—providing the distributing label with the master recordings and finishe artwork, having paid for these to be produced. The distributing label manufactur the products, sees that they are distributed, and pays you the sales money minus a dis tribution fee of 17 to 30 percent and minus manufacturing and printing costs.

With the right deal, you can make more money per unit this way than if you man ufactured the record yourself and went straight through a distributor. And it's tw tasks—manufacturing and distribution—handled by one company.

This can also be a distribution-only arrangement, where you manufacture the CD and the major label distributes them to whatever sub-distributors, one-stops, an retailers it normally services.

Joint Ventures

In a joint venture, you partner with a distributing label to make and sell records and split profits after all costs have been deducted. The division of responsibility—who fronts recording costs, who carries out marketing—varies depending on what capabilities you and the partner label bring to the table. The responsibilities are spelled out in the contract.

After monies are received from retail, expenses are deducted and reimbursed to whoever paid them. The pressing and distributing label, for example, gets paid back for its costs related to distribution, manufacturing, and operation. Whatever remains after expense reimbursement is the profit, which the two parties split on a 50-50 basis or in another agreed proportion.

Choosing the Right Deal

If you're in a position to take advantage of any of the above-listed alternative distribution deals, you've already made some marketing headway. It may be worth your while to continue along the same path you've been taking.

But if you want to work with a more powerful label, choose the deal carefully. Run the numbers for each type of deal and see which one works best for you. One might work better for modest sales while another might deliver the biggest bang for the buck when sales rocket to the stratosphere.

And think about the profile, identity, and business practices of the label you're evaluating as a business partner. It should match the profile, identity, and business needs of your own outfit. In other words, make sure the partnership is a good fit.

Finally, be careful of contracts that limit your ability to maneuver through the marketplace. Leave yourself room to grow, to avoid getting into debt to the partner, and to retain maximum flexibility to make other advantageous deals when the deal on the table doesn't fulfill all your requirements.

Chapter 8

Direct Marketing and Non-Store Sales Methods

Successful marketers rack their brains to find and exploit every possible means of reaching customers. Part of this task is seeking methods that will supplement (or in some cases replace) standard retail store distribution.

There are at least three reasons for supplementing store distribution: (1) other distribution methods may reach customers who don't regularly shop at record stores; (2) other distribution methods may permit more precise targeting of prospective customers; and (3) the marketer might not have access to retail store accounts, due to lack of distributor interest in the product.

An example of a pioneering "alternative" marketer is Windham Hill, the record company originally known for new-age music. In its early years, the label had difficulty cracking the standard channels of record store distribution. It turned to off-the-beaten-path approaches, which included sending catalogs of its products directly to names on the label's mailing list. The silver lining was that exploring these alternative channels—the label also placed their CDs in bookstores, health-food stores, and other specialty outlets—helped Windham Hill to define its market niche and eventually develop an unusually loyal base of customers. Along the way, the label marketer gained a clear understanding of the "customer profile" of the typical Windham Hill buyer, enabling the company to market more effectively by distributing through outlets connected to customers' special interests. Success in its niche market eventually gained Windham Hill access to mainstream record stores and the mass market.

As Windham Hill discovered, and as many other small labels have found out, a number of effective sales channels exist outside the realm of retail store distribution.

Direct marketing, for example, accomplishes just what its name suggests: it employs techniques for bypassing the traditional wholesale-retail distribution chain and offering purchasing opportunities to core and prospective customers directly. For some small companies that specialize in niche markets (specific segments of the population, rather than the mass populace), direct marketing is the primary marketing method.

The Internet offers a popular tool for direct marketing. Its uses are discussed in detail in Chapter 9. The non-Internet sector of the marketplace still offers widely used tools for direct marketing, as any recipient of a postcard announcing a local singer's next gig will tell you. This chapter focuses on the non-Internet tools. For

xample, record clubs offer one means of marketing music outside the retail distri-
ution system. Another way of reaching potential buyers directly is to sell CDs and
ther product formats at live performances.

These are just a few of the common additions to the music marketer's distribu-
ion repertoire. You're encouraged to uncover more, but first, let's get the creative
uices flowing by looking at these main methods in detail.

DIRECT MARKETING

Direct marketing is any method of creating buying opportunities by providing information about the product directly to the customer (other than in person) and including
n that information a way for customers to place an order.

The most common types of direct marketing are direct mail and direct-response
dvertising. The advertising may be in print or via broadcasting.

Direct marketing is really a combination of distribution and promotion. The promotion part is providing information about the product along with persuasion and
ncentives to buy. The distribution aspect is the customer request to purchase and the
ulfillment of the order.

Direct Mail

For the small label, an accessible method of distribution is through the mail, which
eliminates the need for an outside distributor. It involves creating a postcard, informational brochure, promotion piece, or catalog and sending it to names on a targeted
mailing list.

The mailer should include instructions for ordering the product via mail, telephone, fax, e-mail, or the Internet.

Use of Mailing Lists and a Customer Database. The key to successful selling by mail is
having a carefully targeted list of customers. Use your house list—your collected
names of people who have indicated strong interest in your music by signing your
mailing list at performances, filling out tent cards, returning business reply cards that
you've included in CDs, replying to previous mailings, and subscribing to your
newsletter (if you have one). (For more about mailing lists, see page 42.)

The database program you've used for your house mailing list undoubtedly has a
"mail merge" function, which allows you to print out mailing labels automatically. It
should also allow you to sort the list by region—helpful if you're sending a region-
centric message such as a plug for an upcoming tour stop.

For some mailings, you may want to augment your house list so you can reach a
broader base of potential customers. Additional names may consist of likely prospects—
people who fit the profile of your typical customer as closely as you can determine.
You can obtain these names for a fee from music magazines, radio stations, and other
sources specializing in your style, or from commercial mailing-list brokers. This list
can be invaluable for large-scale mailings. It consists of people who have demonstrated

a strong interest in your kind of music, have spent money on it in the past, and are likely to spend money on it again in the future.

Magazines and other media outlets gather information on their audiences and sell that information in the form of mailing lists. These companies provide *list cards* that describe their mailing lists, segment them into categories, and provide prices. What you'll pay will depend on the category of recipient, since some categories are deemed of higher quality than others. Categories within lists may focus on business customers, residential customers, paid U.S. subscribers (*paid* being the crucial word here, telling you that the customer is reliable), and international subscribers.

You can order a company's list card by e-mail from the company's Web site or by calling the advertising department. (MediaFinder, on the Web at www.mediafinder.com, is a good source of information on music-related magazines that rent mailing lists.)

Commercial list brokers are companies that focus entirely on mailing lists. They provide catalogs with subject indexes from which you choose your category of customer. Hugo Dunhill Mailing Lists, for example, offers lists of individuals categorized by music preference. (MediaFinder, cited above, also lists commercial mailing list catalogs and directories.)

Usually, you can rent mailing lists for between $75 and $300 per thousand names, generally for one-time use, such as for a single direct-mail or e-mail campaign.

Lists rented for a fee are provided to you in the format you choose. You can get them in the form of printed labels or on CDs, diskettes, or e-mailed files from which you can print labels.

Bear in mind that response to targeted mailings follows relatively predictable patterns, running between .1 and 10 percent. If you have a very good core-customer list—a list of hard-core fans—a 10 percent response would be a smashing success. For the "likely prospect" portion of your list—the names purchased from a commercial mailing-list broker, for example—a successful response would be in the range of 1 or 2 percent. If you had a mailing list of 80,000 names (a not-unusual number for an enterprising niche marketer), 800 to 8,000 responses would indicate an effective effort.

Keep those percentages in mind when you contemplate renting a mailing list. Your returns may not justify the investment.

Postcards. To inform customers about a new CD or upcoming show, the simplest tool is a postcard, as shown on page 109. It's cheap to produce and mail, and recipients are more likely to read it than they are to open an envelope that looks promotional.

On the front of a 4-by-6-inch card (or larger), you can provide attractive artwork— a photo of the artist, for example, or a reproduction of the new CD cover—with or without a short message or headline.

The flip side includes, of course, the mailing surface on the right half of the card. On the left side, include the following information:

- *For a show:* the artist's name and the performance location, date, time, ticket price, and ticket-ordering information

- *For a new CD:* the artist, CD title, record label and catalog number, release date, and how to order
- *For all postcards:* contact information, including artist Web site; record company logo, address, phone number, e-mail address, and Web site; and additional promotional material, such as descriptions of the music, quotes from reviews, and any discount offers or special deals

Flyers and Brochures. If your direct mail program is aimed at selling a single product, such as a new CD release, or even a limited list of products, the most effective mailing tool would be a simple flyer or brochure.

In designing the flyer or brochure, you have two goals: (1) to convince the customer to buy the product, and (2) to make it as easy as possible to place an order. If you provide a postage-paid return envelope, for example, the recipient will be more likely to purchase than if he has to find an envelope, address it, and buy a stamp.

A simple solution is to create a one-page flyer with a tear-off order form. (For details about what kind of information to include on an order form, see page 114.) The bulk of the flyer promotes the product, as in the example on page 110. Include the following basic elements:

- Artist's name (and logo, if available)
- Product photo or graphic element pulled from the CD cover design (if affordable)
- Album title
- Item or catalog number
- Announcement of availability
- Descriptive copy

Postcard (front and back) *used by jazz singer Jacqui Naylor to advertise a nightclub engagement.*

Additional elements might include an eye-grabbing headline, an endorsemen quote from a magazine or individual, and a quote from the artist, commenting o some aspect of the album.

However you choose to promote the musical product, be aware of the followin time-tested formula—often called the AIDA formula—for successful direct mail:

- Grab **a**ttention (the "Look at this!" part of the promo)
- Spark **i**nterest ("Imagine this...")
- Create **d**esire ("Here's what it can do for *you*!")
- Call to **a**ction ("Order now!")

Whatever approach you take (and tone, wording, and style will vary tremendousl depending on the music and the targeted audience), the attention–interest–desire action elements are at the heart of every direct-mail piece. (For more about copy an headlines, see the section on "Direct-Response Advertising" on page 117.)

Since the flyer in this example is meant to be simple, you'd just fold it and seal with a sticker, stamp and address the reverse side, and mail it as is, without an enve lope. (Any mailing piece that can be mailed without an envelope is called a *self-mailer*

If you mail the flyer in an envelope, you then have the option of inserting a sel addressed, postage-paid (or postage-needed) return envelope.

A one-page flyer with an order form.

A convenient but more expensive mailer is a one-page flyer with a detachable return envelope built in. You address the *back* of the return envelope to your customer and add your postage. The *front* of the return envelope (which is not visible when you send the mailer out) is printed with your business address and a box for a stamp, a "No Postage Necessary If Mailed in the United States" message, or a bulk rate indicia. (See "U.S. Postal Regulations and Rates," above.)

The non-envelope portion of the flyer may be both a promo piece containing additional product information and an order form that the customer can fill out and return to you in the envelope provided. (For an example of an order form with return envelope included see the photo on page 115.) It's worth noting that this type of mailer requires more complex manufacturing, and should be handled only by a printer who specializes in it. Local printers or print brokers can refer you to qualified printers, or you may consult the Printers section of the Yellow Pages. Be sure to compare estimates from several printers and get samples of similar jobs they've handled in the past before making a final decision.

There are a number of variations on the single-product mailing piece. Here are just a few:

- A postcard that provides information and also serves as an order form to be placed in an envelope and mailed back to you
- A letter plus an order form
- A glossy, heavy sheet of 8 ½-by-11-inch stock that folds once into an 8 ½-by-5 ½-inch mailer. The customer address goes on the outside back. The outside front delivers the main message. The inside contains more promo and an order form that can be removed.
- An 11-by-17-inch sheet that folds into an 8 ½-by-11-inch "brochure." Attached to the center is a business-reply-mail envelope. One panel of the brochure serves as an order form, which the customer can cut out and

insert into the return envelope. Two panels are devoted to the product announcement and promo. Finally, the piece folds again into an 8 ½-by-5 ½-inch mailer that can be taped closed. The customer address prints on one of the exposed panels.

- A more elaborate piece that could include a glossy, full-color information sheet, a personalized cover letter laser-printed on company letterhead, a separate order form, and a postage-paid reply envelope.

The envelope in which you send the mailing can also be an important promotional tool. It might include an attention-grabbing headline to make the recipient want to open it. It might be in a special shape or size to make it stand out from other mail (although this can be expensive).

Also keep in mind that you want the customer to pay *before* you send them the product. What does this mean for the design of the brochure or flyer? It means that if you expect a buyer to send a check, make sure you provide the means to send it—either a return envelope or instructions to use their own envelope.

There are many other possible mailer sizes and folding styles, but it's beyond the scope of this book to list them all. For more information, refer to one of the many available guidebooks that focus on direct marketing. A good online source of information is Inside Direct Mail (www.insidedirectmail.com).

The only limitations to mailer design are your imagination and your budget. Remember: the simpler the mailer, the cheaper to produce.

Newsletters. Another effective approach to direct mail sales is to use a newsletter. The beauty of it is that the recipient will be less likely to toss it out as junk mail. The fan receives it as a valuable source of information about the artist, or label, or whatever the subject may be. Contained somewhere in the newsletter is product information and an order form.

The people managing the rock band Phish sent out a newsletter, *Doniac Schvice*, several times a year, reaching many thousands of fans. Most of the publication dealt with Phish news, like upcoming tour dates and recording schedules. It also contained a letters section, for that "interactive" touch. In addition, it included a tear-out order form, letting fans purchase T-shirts, stickers, posters, and hats.

E-mail newsletters have largely replaced the hard-copy mailing. But value still exists in tangible booklets of band information that sit on someone's coffee table for weeks and get read by others who happen to notice them.

Catalogs. When you have a full line of CDs to sell, you can promote and sell directly by creating a catalog. At its best, a catalog presents the CDs attractively, provides easy options for ordering, and gives persuasive reasons for ordering now.

Today, most record companies display products on the Internet rather than in paper catalogs, since the Web is a favored information source for the teens and young adults who make up the target audience of many record labels. With Internet catalogs

u can also provide audio excerpts of tracks, news about artists, chat rooms for fans, d other interactive promotional material not available in the world of paper. (See hapter 11 for more on Internet promotion.)

Still, hard-copy catalogs can be an effective direct-mail tool when you're aiming r older customers—or others—who prefer to peruse your wares by flipping pages. nd it's not uncommon for customers to "window shop" in a paper catalog and then ace orders on the Web. "We have found that the catalog and the Internet have a nergistic effect," said one e-commerce executive in 2002. Record clubs (such as olumbia House and BMG Music Service)—which rank high among successful line retailers—routinely sell via hard-copy catalogs.

If you do publish a printed catalog, send updated copies to customers on your ailing list, and supply copies to retailers and your distributor. Before it shifted to the ternet, Windham Hill sent its catalogs to mailing-list customers several times a year.

Another benefit of print, according to a successful e-commerce executive: It] can make something look so gorgeous you want to cry. We can't do that on a mputer screen."

In catalog design, use artwork or photography that reinforces the label's image. 'indham Hill, for example, goes for a cool, atmospheric quality reflecting both the nbient aspect of much of the label's music and the graphic approach used on many

of their album covers. They did this on their printed catalogs (see page 113), and th
do it on their Web site.

Use clear, straightforward profiles of each release, with a capsule descriptio
format(s) and price(s), the catalog number, and a reproduction of the album cover.

Provide the URL for ordering your product on the Web, and do it on every pa
spread. Do the same for ordering by phone. If you have a large enterprise, you m
want to consider setting up a toll-free number. (A detailed discussion of toll-free pho
numbers can be found on page 115.)

The order form can be formatted in any number of ways. In its catalog, Windha
Hill designed the order form as a separate insert with a tear-off return envelope. T
insert was stapled to the center of the catalog. (See page 115.)

Order Forms. The essential tool of the direct-mail piece is the order form. It can l
simple or complex, but it must contain at least the following elements:

- Space for the customer's name and address (pre-printed, if possible).
- Space for the customer to write the "Ship To" name and address (usually the same as above).
- Your mailing address, fax number (if available), e-mail address, Web site URL, and phone number—toll-free, if you have it.
- Space for the customer to list the item(s) ordered. This should include separate spaces for the item number, item title, price per item, quantity ordered, subtotal price (unit price multiplied by quantity ordered), state sales tax (if applicable), shipping and handling fee, rush charge (if applicable), and total amount due (subtotal + shipping/handling + tax).
- For the customer's reference, a list of shipping and handling fees for differe amounts ordered; for example, $4.50 for orders up to $19.99, $6 for order between $20 and $49.99, $7.50 for orders from $50 to $79.99, and so on. You determine the shipping and handling charges by combining the posta fee with reasonable labor costs for packing. *Note:* Some order forms on th Web provide choices of mailing options (standard, overnight, express mail, priority) with precise fees for each.
- Information about discounts (if any).
- Expected delivery date (for example, "Allow 4 to 6 weeks for delivery"). (See "The FTC Mail-Order Merchandise Rule," below.)

THE FTC MAIL-ORDER MERCHANDISE RULE

The Federal Trade Commission (FTC) has specific regulations governing stated delivery dates of mail-order merchandise. If you fail to ship within your stated time period, you must seek the customer's consent for a delayed shipment. If you can't get consent, you have to refund the money paid for the unshipped merchandise.

For more information, consult the FTC's Web site at www.ftc.gov.

- Space for the customer to indicate payment method. Typical options are check or money order. (Indicate that it should be made payable to your company.) If you are set up to take credit cards (see page 116 for more information), provide space for the type of card, the card number, its expiration date, and the customer's authorizing signature.
- A code (in numbers and/or letters of your choice) that tells you where the customer got the order form. Each type of mailing piece and each separate print ad should be assigned its own code (printed on the piece). This will enable you to determine how many orders each type of mailer or ad generated and therefore how successful each was.

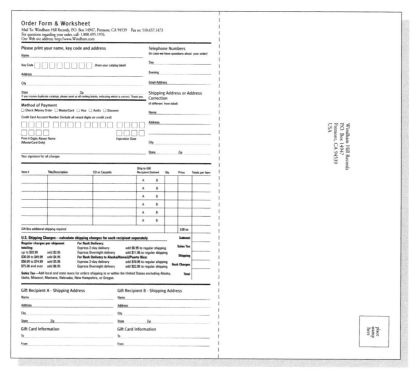

Tear-out order form used in the catalog of an established record company. Note the built-in return envelope.

etup and Use of Toll-Free Phone Numbers. If you wish to provide customers with the ossibility of ordering by telephone toll-free, you'll need to set up a phone line for is purpose (known as an 800 number, although 888 and other area codes are used). Vhen you do, you'll pay a monthly service charge plus a per-minute usage charge henever a customer calls you. That is, you, not the customer, will pay for the call. or this reason, many small labels don't use toll-free numbers.

Toll-free numbers can be made memorable by having them spell out words, such 1-800-RECORDS. Toll-free service providers call these "vanity numbers." Options

depend on availability, and, as you might imagine, not many memorable words a
still available.

If you want to, you can set up toll-free service by calling the business service offic
of your local telephone company. Typical rates are around $10 for a monthly servic
charge and an 8¢-per-minute usage charge, with a monthly minimum.

There are companies that specialize in these services and that offer competitiv
rates for toll-free lines. Before choosing a service provider, do some comparison shop
ping via the Yellow Pages and the Internet.

Credit Card Payment. Phone orders and Internet orders require payment by cred
card. In mail orders, credit cards provide an alternative option to payment by chec
Whatever the ordering mechanism, people are more likely to make spur-of-the
moment purchases if they can pay by credit card. If you want to provide this cap.
bility, you should set up a credit card processing system.

To do so, have your bank set you up with a business account for merchant cred
card processing via phone order, mail order, or Internet. There are also commerci
services, called credit card processing agencies, that can help you set up and use
system for accepting cards from all the major companies. Whether you go through
bank or a dedicated service, they will provide you with computer software or Intern
tools for registering each transaction.

Credit card transactions work as follows: When a customer orders by credit car
the funds are transferred to your account, usually within 30 to 60 days (althoug
some banks offer next-day availability of funds). The bank or processing service ma
charge you a setup fee, a transaction fee, a percentage (the "discount rate") of the gro
dollar amount of each transaction, a service fee, a fee for a monthly statement, and
fee for purchasing or leasing software. Setup and software alone can cost sever
hundred dollars, and with monthly fees and extra charges if your transactions don
meet a defined minimum, the credit card option is worthwhile only if you'll be har
dling a significant volume of those transactions on an ongoing basis.

Discounts and Other Purchasing Incentives. Sometimes it's not enough just to infor
the customer about the product. In order to nudge the customer over the final hurd
to decide to buy, you often have to give them something extra, a special break
some kind, a bit of added value.

Here are some examples:

- Discounts on quantity purchased, such as 10 percent off if the customer
  purchases X number of CDs, or a free CD when the customer purchases
  more than X CDs
- Discounts linked to time periods, such as 10 percent off if the customer
  places an order by a certain date
- Awarding points to customers for each product purchased, and providing a
  discount or free CD to customers who accrue a defined number of points

- Providing a T-shirt, a poster, a subscription to your newsletter, or some other piece of merchandise for free if a customer buys a given quantity or makes a purchase within a given time period

Direct-Response Advertising (Print)

Placing ads in magazines and newspapers can be very expensive—and even distasteful to some people. "I don't like advertising," Windham Hill's Anne Robinson once admitted, "because I don't think it's inherently honest. Second, we didn't have the money. Third, it's hard to sell music in a print medium."

Actually, though, when you compare the cost of an ad in a magazine that reaches 40,000 people with the cost of mailing a brochure to 40,000 people, the ad may be the more cost-effective, and easier, choice. This is especially true if you're promoting a single CD release. (For a full line of products, you'll need a brochure or catalog.)

In direct-response advertising, the goal is to ignite a purchasing decision and provide a response mechanism—an easy way for the customer to place an order. Usually the response mechanism is a phone number, an e-mail address, or a tear-out order form.

Note: If you're selling through stores, placing an ad that brings you direct sales and bypasses the store may create a conflict. Keep business-partner relations in mind whenever making a marketing move. For now, let's assume you're not going to rile any salespeople by running a direct-response ad.

Choosing the Right Publication. The most important choice you have to make is whether to advertise in a publication with a small but very targeted readership or a mass-market publication with a larger but less definable group of readers.

For example, if your music has a Brazilian jazz flavor, putting an ad in *Brazilian Jazz Now!* magazine might not get you to a lot of customers, but you'll know for certain that they're inclined toward your type of sound. Advertising in *Women's Wear Daily,* on the other hand, will get you a huge audience, but you won't know what percentage of that group listens to jazz of any kind, let alone yours.

These are extreme examples, and most often the decision will be less cut and dried. But it's one you'll have to make. For a tiny company, the decision will be easy: the targeted publication will be all that you can afford.

Whatever you choose, make certain the publication reaches your kind of audience. Here's a good fit: advertising a guitar virtuoso's album in *Guitar Player* magazine. And here's a bad one: advertising the Flower-Power Peace and Love Ensemble in *Soldier of Fortune.* You get the idea.

One way to save money is to set up a cooperative deal with the magazine. You pay them only for actual inquiries or sales leads received from the ad. This is called *per-inquiry (PI)* advertising. The publication keeps a tally of inquiries that come via the Web or a toll-free phone number and provide you with a report. Per-inquiry is not the standard print-advertising approach; usually you pay on the basis of ad size. So you'll have to check for availability of PI at your targeted publication.

If you're running ads in several publications, assign each a separate code and print it on the order form. That way you'll know which magazine generated the sale, enabling you to make better-informed advertising decisions in the future.

Headline and Copy Guidelines. As pointed out previously, the heart of any direct response piece (and this includes print ads) is the AIDA formula: grab attention, spark interest, create desire, and call to action. When writing headlines and copy, there are numerous other rules to consider (and to break, if it serves the purpose of your sales approach). Here are some of them:

- A headline should hook the reader. As much as possible, it should be about something that matters personally to the reader—something that relates to an emotional need (being popular with friends, for example) or appeals to self-interest. (It's been said that there is one headline *guaranteed* to interest John Doe the reader. That headline is: "This Ad Is All About John Doe.")
- A headline should also be easy to understand, and it should be written for the right audience.
- The body copy (that is, the main copy that follows the headline) should speak directly to the customer, as if you were talking one-on-one. Try to keep an image of the ideal customer in mind as you write. Read aloud whatever you write to make sure it flows conversationally.
- The body copy should relate logically to the headline (that is, explain the headline or answer the question the headline poses).
- Copy should be short and simple—unless the product demands more-detailed information.
- Avoid using long words, and try to use words that create mental pictures and sensations—so that readers *experience* what you're talking about.
- Avoid exaggerated claims, overblown adjectives, and hype.
- When possible, provide proof of quality by using endorsements.

Direct-Response Advertising (Broadcast)

You've seen the ads on television late at night as you're starting to doze off in your easy chair. A familiar hit from the 1990s jars you back to consciousness in time to see a lengthy list of song titles crawling up your TV screen. The announcer is peddling the complete three-CD set *The Nebulous Nineties* for "only $29.99!" Your finger twitches on the remote but the announcer's voice stops you: "And if you order now, you'll get a special bonus CD, *Millennial Memories,* for $5 off the regular price! That's right! An $11.99 value for only $6.99! Call toll-free, 1-800-765-4321—now, while supplies last!" You're sold. You make a dive for the telephone.

Well, maybe not. But ads such as these do tend to generate healthy sales.

The ad described above would have been placed by a company that obtained licenses to the original songs for the purpose of compiling them into a "nineties" package. Most TV ads for music are those that are selling such packages.

Financially, TV and radio ads tend to be way out of reach for the small marketer. Although I recall once seeing a local TV spot for a guitar teacher. It ran at about :30 a.m.)

If you're able to afford broadcast ads and they're appropriate for your product, the guidelines for providing information, incentives, and response mechanisms are essentially the same as for direct mail and print ads (minus the tear-off coupon, of course).

Direct-Response Advertising (Internet)

Internet advertising options have included banner ads, pop-up ads, and simple hyperlinked blocks of text on high-traffic Web sites to advertise phone-order numbers and to direct surfers to the advertisers' sites, where orders can be placed.

But pop-up ads have been condemned as the most disruptive feature of the Web, causing annoyance, outright anger, and a resistance to their messages. Using them can generate negative impressions among audiences.

The better approach is to use a display ad embedded into a popular Web page. In terms of copy, treat it as you would a print ad. But include a hyperlink to a site where your CD can be ordered on the spot. (See page 193 for details about Internet advertising options.)

CATALOG MARKETING THROUGH OTHER COMPANIES

Another approach to distribution (and promotion) is to have your musical product advertised in the catalogs of other companies. These may be music catalogs, such as Collector's Choice Music, or general-goods or gift catalogs that also include music recordings.

The concept of the latter is similar to selling your music in general-goods retail outlets or specialty retail stores that reach your targeted audience—except in this case the channel is mail order. Catalogs that fall into this category include *Signals* (the gift catalog affiliated with Public Television).

Generally, the catalog company buys product from you at your wholesale price and sells at the retail price. To get your CD listed in one of these catalogs you'll have to contact the catalog's product buyers and send them promotional information so that they can evaluate whether they want to include it. The key, of course, is choosing a catalog that reaches the appropriate audience.

LICENSING TO RECORD CLUBS

Record clubs are mail-order and Internet-order organizations that offer members regular opportunities to purchase, directly from the club, the products of a variety of different record labels. A club typically offers prospective customers first-time membership deals of several initial recordings for free or at a low price contingent upon agreement to buy a specified number of additional recordings over a given time period.

A typical arrangement is this: After the customer becomes a member, he or she periodically receives a mailing (either paper or electronic) describing a "feature selection" or a "selection of the month." If the customer does nothing, he or she is automatically sent the recording and charged for it. A customer who doesn't want to buy the recording has to take action by mailing a cancellation card back (or responding online) to the record club by a specified date.

Record clubs generate a very large percentage of total mail-order music sales and a significant percentage of total industry CD sales—10 percent, according to a 2000 article in *Business Week Online*.

The leading clubs are BMG Music Service and Columbia House. It's worth noting that in December 2002, Columbia House was the fourth-highest-ranked retailer on the Internet, bested only by eBay, Amazon.com, and Wal-Mart, according to a Nielsen/NetRatings report cited in the *New York Times*. BMG Music Service was number 15. And that's among *all* e-tailers, not just music-dedicated ones.

For record companies, the deal works as follows: A record company licenses its recording to the club. The club pays the record company a royalty on each copy sold (a typical arrangement is 9 ½ percent of receipts on 85 percent of the total number sold through to the customer, less a packaging charge).

A substantial number of copies distributed by the club are free goods. That's because many are sent out free as part of the initial membership deal, and other monthly mailings are simply never paid for by customers. This matters to record companies because they receive no royalties for free copies. For this reason, labels sometimes include in their contract a stipulation that free copies cannot exceed a certain number. (That number, by the way, is typically high: 100 percent of the number of records sold.)

The benefit of clubs to record labels is that clubs help labels reach otherwise inaccessible or hard-to-reach segments of the marketplace.

To place a record with one of the clubs, contact the club directly. You'll need to send promotional material as evidence of your product's commercial viability.

SELLING RECORDINGS AT LIVE SHOWS

Perhaps the most immediate form of distribution outside the retail realm is selling your recorded product at live performances. You're pitching the product (the music) as you perform it, and if the audience likes the sound they can buy copies of the CD on the spot.

A key benefit is that the profit for the seller is higher than in retail—even if discs are sold at a discount to customers. One owner of a small label pointed out that "if you're a band selling [CDs] at gigs for $12, it's cheaper for buyers, but you're still making about $10 profit on each. You can pay for the pressing in about 200 CDs— that's pretty easy to do if you're a gigging band."

Bear in mind that once an artist has achieved substantial commercial success and is performing to large audiences, the record company may prohibit sales of CDs at

oncerts because of the potential for cutting into retail sales. But given no such con-
ict, selling CDs at shows is a great way to capitalize on the performance.

One successful singer had a routine of setting up a table in the nightclub lobby
fter her show and autographing CDs (issued on her own record label) for anyone
who wanted to buy one. She usually had quite a long line of customers—and raked
n a nice monetary supplement to her performance pay. Those customers, by the way,
were likely to remain or become core fans—champions, if you will—as a result of the
irect contact with the singer.

Chapter 9

Distributing over the Internet

The Internet is an integral part of today's music distribution system. Moreover, it
the primary marketing alternative for unsigned musicians who want to distribut
original music.

Jeff Patterson, co-founder of the Internet Underground Music Archive (IUMA), pre
dicted in 1998 that the Internet is "going to change the music industry as we know it

And so it has. Much for the better, too—at least if you're an independent musi
cian or a startup label.

The Internet makes it possible to get your music to millions of potential onlin
customers directly, without the say-so, the approval, the backing, and the direction o
the corporate network of music industry conglomerates. All you have to do is get th
music you create (whether in your home studio or at a professional facility) onto th
Internet and then draw attention to it through a variety of means. The rest is up t
the people who hear your work. They either like it or they don't—a refreshingl
simple equation compared to the complex series of approval procedures you had t
go through in the past.

POPULAR PERCEPTION

Marketing and distribution cost a lot of money, even on the Internet.

ALTERNATE REALITY

On the Internet, you can do it on the cheap, using your own Web site, linking to distribution sites, and using e-mail to inform people. The effort takes time, and time is
money, but any cash-strapped outfit should be happy to make the investment.

Now, the Internet is even helping newer artists challenge the market dominanc
of established superstars, according to a 2002 article in the *Washington Post*. Researche
who tracked Internet use and college students' buying habits found that down
loading songs from the Internet boosted sales of CDs by new artists and cut int
sales of music by established stars. "Up-and-coming artists and groups now have
better chance at chart success because of (new) technologies," a research analyst sai
in the article.

With major labels and retailers staking out their own cyber-terrain, the Web is set to benefit all music participants. But its ease of entry and its global reach have proven especially useful to independent record labels.

"When the Web site [of classical-music label New Albion Records] launched in 1995, we immediately got three orders—from Australia, Uruguay, and Kansas, the three hardest places on earth to find our records," Albion's Tom Welsh told *San Francisco Chronicle* writer Joshua Kosman in 2001. "It showed me that there is interest in non-mainstream music. We have this tiny little beacon out there now, and anyone can find it."

The power of Internet distribution is that it can be done cheaply, and it can reach pockets of listeners that would otherwise be overlooked. But most importantly, the Internet has generated a range of new options for selling customers the music they want in the way they want it.

GETTING MUSIC TO FANS THE WAY THEY WANT IT

The Internet has helped make it possible to customize music delivery to meet every kind of music preference—that is, to achieve the ultimate marketing goal of satisfying customer needs. What the Internet has promised music fans—and is well along the way to providing—is maximum choice in the way music can be purchased and enjoyed.

Now it's about more than just listening. Now part of the fun for online users is manipulating and programming the music. Now people don't have to limit themselves to the narrow playlists of radio. Instead, they can choose the music they want online and have it streamed to them. Now people don't have to go to a store to pick out music during business hours. Instead, they can draw from a store's worth of music right on their computers twenty-four hours a day, and then burn it onto a CD or a portable listening device. And now sharing music with friends is more than lending them a CD. It's sending them links to music files over the Internet.

In short, the Internet meets the customer need for maximum flexibility.

The Internet's newness and technical innovation have also whetted imaginations and appetites for "playing with new toys," adding a whole new dimension to the music experience. Now, for many, enjoying music is as much about obtaining and using the downloading, file-sharing, and playback tools as it is about hearing the music itself. And it's also about being part of a community of users who share knowledge and kinship with others on the cutting edge of new technology use. (As of this writing, music downloading and file-sharing is essentially a lifestyle for many people.)

OVERVIEW OF INTERNET DISTRIBUTION

With all that as background, what are the options for Internet distribution? The idea is to give the customer maximum choice by doing any or all of the following:

- Sell a CD by letting users select and order it online, then mailing them the CD.
- Sell a single digital song file—say, for a dollar—and allow the user to download it, burn it onto a CD, or do whatever else the user wants to do with it. The file becomes their property.
- Sell a subscription to your music, for a monthly fee paid by credit card, that allows the user to stream either a fixed maximum number or an unlimited number of songs per month.
- Sell a subscription that also permits downloading songs to a computer hard drive—either an unlimited number or up to a fixed maximum.
- Sell a subscription that also permits burning songs onto a CD or transferring to a portable listening device—either an unlimited number of songs or up to a fixed maximum.

What most of these options do is allow users to create their own playlists. I essence, users customize albums—rather than having to take what's fed them on fixed CD that may have two songs they like and fourteen others they hate.

In addition to the various types of sales, the Internet offers different kinds of site where such sales can be made. As a seller of music, you might aim for any or all of the following options, starting with the most accessible to independent musician and ending with options controlled by major labels, requiring affiliation with on of them:

- Create your own Web site, and use it to sell your music.
- Distribute through an established music site that sells music by independen artists (and may also do peer-to-peer file-sharing).
- Become affiliated with a mainstream music-industry subscription site.
- Sell via mass-market online retailers.
- Sell via niche-market online retailers.

A complete Internet marketing strategy uses all or a combination of these option detailed in the following discussion.

OPTIONS FOR ONLINE TRANSACTIONS AND PURCHASES

The overriding music innovation of the Internet has been electronic transmission of music in the form of digital files, providing an alternative or supplement to hard-cop CDs and brick-and-mortar record stores.

Initially embraced as free-file-sharing, Internet transmission of music has sinc been regulated and brought under market control—at least to an extent—via record industry lawsuits and corporate economic muscle so that money can be made i various ways.

Some online sales methods still involve hard-copy CDs, while others are full electronic, from ordering method to product format.

Fuel for the rise of music on the Web came primarily from peer-to-peer file-sharing, an activity spearheaded in the late 1990s by a company called Napster. File-sharing sites allow users to search for and download music from the computers of other users in the same network, and do it for free.

Napster revealed the Internet as an outlet for getting music to a vast audience. It also prompted an attack on free file-sharing by corporations and artists, who viewed it as piracy and copyright infringement—essentially as stealing commercial product and intellectual property. (Some artists, however, supported free file-sharing as a way to spread their music to a large audience.)

But there were differences of opinion on whether online file-sharing would ultimately help or hurt sales of music in CD form.

One on hand, some researchers concluded that sampling music by downloading it from a file-sharing site encouraged the customer to go out and buy a CD by that artist.

On the other hand, a survey by the Recording Industry Association of America (RIAA) found a link between an increase in file-sharing and a *decrease* in CD sales. In an Associated Press article, the RIAA reported a 7 percent decrease in CD sales in the first half of 2002. (Ironically, some vertically integrated companies who lost revenues from CD sales gained them in sales of hardware used in file-sharing.)

The decline of CD sales suggested that the future of music marketing would not be store based but, rather, Internet based. Bolstering that idea was a 2002 report by research firm Ipsos-Reid that some 40 million U.S. individuals over age 12 had used a file-sharing program.

To ensure a stake in that future, and to control sales of their own music, the major record labels battled free file-sharing and scrambled to participate in new kinds of sites—subscription sites—where their songs would be transmitted for a fee.

According to a 2002 *New York Times* article, analysts from Jupiter Research predicted that over the next several years, digital subscription sites would be the places fans most often go for music.

But the researchers made that prediction before the arrival, in 2003, of Apple Computer's music service, the iTunes Music Store. Compared to the byzantine deals offered by many subscription services—with different price points for different levels of service, from listening to Internet radio to copying songs onto a CD—the Apple system boasted elegant simplicity: choose from a huge library of music, buy a song for a dollar or an album for $10, and use the music with few restrictions. In its first few months of operation the site proved successful, bringing to the music market yet another model for Internet sales.

CDs by Mail, Selected Online

If you have hard-copy CDs to sell, the Internet is one of the outlets for selling them. Whatever Web site you use (options discussed later) serves as a combination virtual storefront and catalog. You display your selection of products, provide sound clips to sample, and offer a range of ordering and payment options, whether using a phone number, a printable order form, or an onsite electronic transaction. When you receive payment, you ship the CD to the customer.

Phone Order. The simplest ordering system involves posting your phone number on the Web site and instructing customers to call it to order. When a customer calls, take the customer's credit card number and mailing information over the phone (see page 116 for details on credit card payment), or have them mail you a check. When the payment is credited to your bank account, ship the CD.

Printable Order Form. Post a form similar to the one illustrated on page 115, and instruct the customer to print it out, fill it out, and mail it in with payment. Provide space for the customer to write a name and address; CD title(s), item number(s), and price(s); and the total of all prices, plus sales tax (if any) and shipping fee—extra for shipping internationally. Provide checkboxes for choice of payment (personal check,

New West Records' online order form.

or credit card) and, if applicable, type of credit card along with spaces for credit card number, expiration date, and authorization signature. *Note:* Keep abreast of current rules about Internet sales tax, which always have the potential to change.

Online Order Form. Avoid paper altogether—and make ordering easier for customers—by providing an online method of CD selection and payment. (Some Web-hosting companies provide e-commerce services that include secure order forms.) In this method, the customer clicks on a CD title to select it, verifies the order before continuing the transaction (some sites gussy up this process by naming the list of selections the "shopping cart"), then clicks an Order button. The Order window provides fields for the same kinds of information requested on the printable form. Finally the customer clicks a Send Order button (or whatever the particular site calls it).

Subscription to Music Site

Rather than charging a single fee for the one-time purchase of a song or a CD, some sellers offer subscriptions to their music sites. The subscription covers a set time period—say, a month, three months, or a year. During that time the customer may be entitled to use music in different ways for different fees: streaming, downloading to a hard drive, or burning a download onto a CD.

The artist and producer Todd Rundgren proposed a similar idea in a 1997 issue of *Music and Computers* magazine: He talked about using the subscription technique to connect the artist with the customer directly (with the then-revolutionary side effect of bypassing middlemen like record companies). An artist would have a dedicated Web site, through which customers could subscribe to the artist for a specified period—say, a year. During that time, the artist would upload music to the site as it was created, and the subscriber could download it. At the end of the period, the artist would send the customer a collection of all that music, like an album.

Now subscription sites are the norm—even if they're mostly multi-artist sites.

Streaming. One option you can offer for a fee ($10 a month was about the average in 2003), is unlimited streaming of music. Streaming is essentially playback over the Internet without the option of downloading or making a copy: the listener has to remain connected to your site. Clean playback requires high Internet bandwidth, such as that provided by DSL or cable modem. (Web radio is an example of streaming audio; see "Internet Radio Licensing" on page 134.)

Setting up a music streaming option isn't difficult. It takes three basic steps:

1. Load (record) your music into computer-based music software.
2. Upload the finished file to a host server.
3. Set up a system for making the file available to online listeners using a playback system such as RealPlayer or Windows Media Player.

Downloading. As a no–extra-cost option or for a slightly higher fee, the seller might permit downloading—the U.S. Copyright Office calls it "digital phonorecord delivery"—of a finite number of songs per month or another set period of time.

Unlike streaming, in which the song is stored on a computer other than the user's, downloading allows the user to copy the file from your site onto his own hard drive.

This has a couple of benefits: The user doesn't have to be connected to the Internet to listen to the music. The sound quality is generally better than that of a streamed playback (the larger the file, the better the audio quality; hard drives can store larger files than low-bandwidth Internet connections can stream quickly enough to avoid audio "choppiness"). Also, with downloading the user gets to keep the file (except when companies offer limited-time, expirable downloads), allowing more control than streaming does, such as setting up custom playlists and listening to them when desired.

Making a downloadable music file involves the following steps:

1. Start with a finished CD, or record and master your music on computer-based music production software.
2. Open MP3 conversion software such as RealJukebox. Use it to automatically create an MP3 from the file on the CD you've inserted into your computer's CD bay or the digital file you've got on your hard drive. Apple's iTunes also allows you to convert files to MP3s.
3. Name the MP3 file, upload it to your host server, and set up a link to it on whatever Web site you're using.

An excellent source of information on streaming and downloading music files is available online at www.techtv.com/audiofile/musictech and at www.CNET.com.

Portable Downloads. The seller may choose to allow the user, over the period of subscription, to burn a limited number of downloads to a CD or copy them to a portable listening device. The user then has the right to "keep" the music and listen to it on a machine away from the computer. This option may be presented as a fee-per-song or a "platinum subscription" option, or offered as part of the standard subscription package.

Single Song or CD Download, One-Time Payment

In the simplest start-to-finish electronic transaction, you post a digital file of a single song on a Web site. You may also choose to provide a "free taste" in the form of a brief streamed excerpt (usually 30 seconds to one minute). The customer purchases the song with a single payment (doing it online makes sense since the product itself is electronic). The customer is essentially obtaining the right to download the music file onto a computer's hard drive for playback and burn the file onto a CD or copy it onto a portable playback device. This system served as the model for Apple Computer's innovative iTunes Music Store, and it has proved attractive to consumers.

TYPES OF INTERNET SALES OUTLETS

In the years of the Internet's evolution, it has evolved from a network for free exchange of ideas and files to an increasingly market-controlled commercial zone. The process yielded today's vast variety of sites—some approved by the music industry, others considered "outlaw"—devoted to finding and sharing music, streaming music, downloading music, and coming up with ever more ingenious ways to make the music experience convenient and fun. Now the Internet offers distribution options for music sellers at every level, from start-ups to commercial veterans.

As a marketer-distributor, you've got several options:

- Set up your own "storefront"—that is, build your own Web site and take care of business yourself.
- Place your product with an established multi-artist distribution and promotion site—a Web site that is a collection or archive of different types of music by a variety of artists.
- License your music to a site that offers subscriptions to stream or download music. (This includes collecting statutory licensing fees from Internet radio sites through the RIAA's fee collection-distribution entity SoundExchange.)
- Go through a standard distributor to get your CDs onto some of the mass-market and niche-market retail stores that maintain sites on the Web, or get on them directly where permitted.

Your Own Web Site

For many musicians and music sellers, a proprietary Web site—an Internet "home" for the seller's own music—is a good starting point for online distribution. It's practically free to create a Web site, assuming you have access to a computer and simple Web development software. You'll pay a monthly fee to an Internet service provider (ISP) and may choose to pay a professional Web designer to craft and build your site. Beyond that, the cost comes in time spent to maintain the site and keep it fresh and up to date.

CONVENTIONAL WISDOM

Giving away music, as in free file-sharing, is a mistake that will deny you profits.

BREAKING THE RULE

For new artists and startups, free distribution, at least at the beginning, may be a good way to build an audience whom you can sell to later.

To sell the music, you can use any of the options outlined in the preceding section—charge for a mailed CD, charge for a file transfer, charge for a monthly subscription, or put together a package that combines elements of all. The key is to present your products clearly and attractively, with cover artwork if possible, and to offer easy-to-execute instructions for ordering.

The value of selling through your own Web site rather than the online distributors and retailers discussed next is that you keep all the sales revenues—there is no need to pay a cut to a middleman.

As with all Internet distribution, you'll need to publicize and promote the site to the maximum to make sure it doesn't get ignored. (See Chapter 11 for details about Internet-based promotion.)

Established Sites for Independent Artists

Other outlets for independent artists and small labels include already established, professionally run multi-artist sites that offer distribution services—and in some cases file configuration, promotion, royalty accounting, and other services.

If you choose, you can have one of the multi-artist sites take care of the entire e-commerce process for you. This includes warehousing your CDs, order taking, accounting, and shipping—along with electronic distribution.

Many of these sites also offer peer-to-peer file-sharing—basically an interface for accessing the music collections of other users logged onto the site. It was this function, pioneered by the company Napster, that brought the vast potential of Internet distribution to the attention of the major labels.

Because peer-to-peer file-sharing is free, it won't bring royalties to artist or record label. (That's why the commercial side of the industry did battle with it, leading to a shift toward fee-based sites.) File-sharing may be good for promotion, but it's the other services of indie-artist sites that have potential for bringing in some revenues.

How Indie Artist Sites Work. One of the pioneering Web sites for independent musicians, IUMA (Internet Underground Music Archive) (www.iuma.co) offers a deal in which it enables you to set up a Web page at the IUMA site, from which you can promote yourself and offer music for downloading and streaming. You can view how you're doing online by going to a Site Stats section that tracks your page views and downloads. The basic idea is that by affiliating with IUMA, you have a better chance of being noticed than if you "fly solo."

Through IUMA's parent, Vitaminic (www.vitaminic.com), you can go beyond promotion to sales. Vitaminic enables you to push your music through a variety of channels including free streaming and a subscription service. After registering with Vitaminic, you post your music on a home page. Visitors have a choice of streaming it for free or paying for it at a price you set. Vitaminic also bundles your music in a catalog sold via subscription to third parties. In both types of sales, Vitaminic splits the proceeds with you.

Internet sites come and go with blinding frequency. Here's a snapshot of sites active as of this writing—with procedures subject to change at any time:

- The Orchard (www.theorchard.com) distributes CDs, tapes, vinyl, videos, and DVDs by independent artists and record labels. It sells these products to online stores as well as to brick-and-mortar retail accounts and one-stop distributors. The Orchard deducts 30 percent of the wholesale price as its distribution fee and charges a $90 fee to activate a new release.
- CD Baby (www.cdbaby.net) sells CDs by independent artists at its retail site, www.cdbaby.com. The company sets up a Web site for the artist, with sound clips and descriptions. It takes credit card orders for CDs online or through a toll-free phone number, and does the shipping. CD Baby sells the CD at the price you set and then keeps $4 for every CD sold.
- GigAmerica (www.gigamerica.com) provides complete services (including distribution, manufacturing, and promotion) for unsigned artists. You send in your master recording and GigAmerica helps promote and sell it. The company informs you of your break-even price; you can set the price you want GigAmerica to use over and above break-even to ensure you earn a profit.
- Grokster (www.grokster.com) connects and promotes unsigned artists to their free-file-sharing audience. To use their services, you provide them with a link to the files (songs) you wish to share and to your Web site, along with a bio. They include your information in an e-mail newsletter and provide a forum in which you can interact with other Grokster users. They also allow you to send messages about your upcoming concerts or new recordings to anyone who has downloaded your music.
- AudioGalaxy (www.audiogalaxy.com), a leading free-file-sharing site, provides services for independent musicians. In addition to providing a forum for showcasing independent music, it allows musicians to set up their own AudioGalaxy Web sites and sell music from those sites. AudioGalaxy doesn't directly distribute artists' music, however.
- Cornerband (www.cornerband.com) offers musicians the opportunity to sell their music through KaZaA (www.kazaa.com), a leading search, play, and share site. You post an MP3, which is categorized with the music of well-known artists, increasing the likelihood that users will click on it. Users then sample your file; if they like it, they can order your CD, which Cornerband ships to them.
- MusicCity.com allows users to download your music a limited number of times, after which users pay for the right to download your music. When a user pays, you keep 70 percent of the sale. But MusicCity also charges you a fee to post a song ($125 as of this writing) and a higher fee to post an album of up to twelve songs ($495).

How to Get Your Music on an Indie Artist Site. What's involved in affiliating with a multi-artist site? The process usually starts with your opening their home page and clicking on a link that provides instructions.

In the case of IUMA, you fill out a form online and sign a licensing agreement that outlines the terms of your affiliation. You're given a login and password that provide access to their Artist Uplink site, where you set up your own editable Web page (IUMA can build it for you for a fee.) You need to provide at least one MP3 file and one JPEG or GIF image. (IUMA also can convert your music to MP3 for a fee.)

The Orchard has you send them an e-mail containing the following information: contact name, artist name, title of release(s), contact information, and the name of your manufacturer.

Most indie-artist sites require setting up an account and uploading (or simply mailing) music files and artist information and supplying a link to your Web site (if any).

For CD distribution sites, such as CD Baby, you mail in a set number of CDs for them to sell, along with promotional information.

Some sites, including CD Baby and MusicCity.com, charge you a fee for their service. Here are some basic items you'll need in order to sign with a multi-artist Web site:

- Access to a personal computer and the software needed for uploading music and other information to the Internet
- Finished copies of your CD, or MP3 files of your music
- Bio information on your act
- Any tour news or other information that you wish to post

Check with individual sites to find out their affiliation procedures.

CONVENTIONAL WISDOM

If resources are limited, focus your marketing effort on a narrow target audience of most-likely customers.

BREAKING THE RULE

On the Internet, aim wide and narrow simultaneously. Mass-market sites will categorize you in the appropriate niche anyway, which will send their wide audiences in your direction. Separately, you can narrowcast your marketing to a specific audience segment.

Mainstream Subscription Sites

Following the first pioneering free-file-sharing ventures, the major labels began participating and collaborating in fee-based subscription sites to take advantage of online distribution while controlling the rights and commercial transfer of songs in their catalogs. In a 2002 *New York Times* article, analysts described such subscription sites as the wave of the future. The jury's still out, but finding a way to harness such sites' distribution power is a key challenge for marketers.

How Mainstream Subscription Sites Work. Essentially giant databases of songs, different sites provide users with different but similar options for accessing their music. As of this writing, leading subscription sites include MusicNet, Napster/press*play*, Rhapsody, MusicNow, and EMusic, each with its own approach to selling.

- MusicNet, AOL's music service, is a partnership between AOL Time Warner, Real Networks, BMG, EMI, and Zomba. For a monthly fee, the user gets a limited number of streamed songs and music downloads. A higher fee buys the user an unlimited number of both. For more money, the user can burn ten songs per month onto CD.

- Napster 2.0, not the original file-sharing site but a renamed iteration of the subscription service press*play* (www.pressplay.com), was conceived as a provider of a full menu of Internet purchasing options: songs for a fee per download (like Apple's iTunes), a subscription service, and Internet radio, with access to about 500,000 songs..

- Rhapsody, an offering of Listen.com, offers a basic service of customizable Internet radio stations—essentially an online jukebox. A higher monthly fee allows unlimited streaming of music from its catalog, plus permission to burn songs to CD for an additional per-song fee. Rhapsody offers music from all the big labels: Sony, BMG, EMI, Warner, and Universal. Rhapsody also offers its "content partners" services that include tracking playback, reporting usage, and paying royalties for each song streamed; providing links to retail and e-tail sites where consumers can purchase CDs; and using Rhapsody to promote other albums and artists on your label.

- MusicNow (www.musicnow.com) provides Internet radio for a basic fee. Paying higher fees get you unlimited streaming and temporary downloads. An extra per-song fee is charged for portable downloads.

- EMusic is a product of Universal Music, and it offers access to the music of hundreds of independent labels. Its monthly fee allows unlimited music downloading. EMusic claims it divides half its profits among its pool of artists.

How to Get Your Music on a Mainstream Subscription Site. Since these sites are generally run by the major labels, they are generally off-limits to artists not signed to one of the labels or their subsidiaries.

However, MusicNet claims to "welcome music from both major and independent record labels." They provide an online form to fill out and submit if you want to license your music to them for distribution.

Rhapsody offers "content partner" arrangements that involve their paying you a royalty for each song streamed. You'll need to contact their "content" contact for information on how to work with Rhapsody.

EMusic, which showcases a wide range of outside-the-mainstream artists, asks labels interested in partnering to submit information about their products, including

Some music streaming sites fall under the category of Internet radio, a format of streaming that offers less choice and less interactivity than more jukebox-like sites like Rhapsody. There are two kinds of Internet radio: traditional radio stations that also transmit over the Web, and Internet-only radio stations.

All companies that stream music must obtain a license from the recording owner (and pay separate fees to songwriters and publishers, as detailed in Chapter 16). The owner may grant or refuse that license, as desired. But Internet radio stations that meet certain criteria may be entitled to obtain a statutory (compulsory) license—a license that the recording owner is *required* to grant. Such sites pay blanket fees to an organization called SoundExchange, which in turn pays royalties to the record companies that own the recordings. The statutory license is billed as a more efficient way to pay for music if the site is streaming a lot of it: the site pays one blanket fee to one organization rather than separate fees to all the different recording owners.

The criteria for a Webcaster's eligibility to use the statutory license include:

- Providing noninteractive, nonpersonalized programming
- Abiding by time restrictions for play of multiple tracks from particular albums or by particular artists
- Not providing song playlists in advance

(Webcasters who don't meet these criteria, such as Rhapsody, which permits user choice of streamed music, must obtain a license directly from the individual owner. That's why you see corporate "partnerships" between music sites and large record companies: a single fee to the large record company pays for its entire catalog of music, or a portion of it, which beats the hassle of paying a thousand separate companies for a thousand different songs.)

Laws governing these statutory licenses are the Digital Performance Right in Sound Recordings Act of 1995 and the Digital Millennium Copyright Act of 1998. They are quite complicated. To learn more about them, contact the RIAA (Recording Industry Association of America) or visit their Web site at www.riaa.com.

To learn about receiving royalties: Visit the RIAA's Web site and read about SoundExchange. Then visit the SoundExchange site at www.soundexchange.com. It's free to become a member, and SoundExchange not only sends you royalties but handles direct payment to your recording artists, taking that burden off you.

It's worth noting here that while Internet radio stations are required to pay licensing fees to record companies, over-the-air "terrestrial" stations don't have to pay them. (See Chapter 12 for more about radio.) This inconsistency is described by the RIAA as "an historical accident.... The industry fought unsuccessfully to change this anomaly while broadcasters built very profitable businesses on the creative work of artists and record companies. The broadcasters were simply too strong on Capitol Hill."

the number of artists on the roster and the volume of releases per year. EMusic takes this information into consideration before agreeing to a deal.

Mass-Market Online Retailers

The Internet is a virtual shopping mall of retail outlets for music, ranging from sites that include music in a larger mix of products—sites such as Amazon.com and Barnes & Noble—to music specialists such as CDnow (part of Amazon.com) and Wherehousemusic.com. Some of these sites have brick-and-mortar counterparts; others exist only on the Internet.

How Mass-Market Online Retailers Work. These sites began as storefronts and ordering systems for physical CDs stored in warehouses. Increasingly, they are a combination of that and all-electronic channels for purchase and transmission of music.

They offer music in all available formats, purchasable by credit card online or via toll-free phone number. Many offer free downloads of songs as samples that expire after thirty days—just to provide a taste to induce purchase of a CD.

CDnow, for example, sells physical CDs, cassettes, and vinyl records. But it also offers digital downloads of products.

Tower Records also offers free downloads as promotion. You can order product by credit card online, by phone, or by fax.

Wherehousemusic.com sells downloads along with standard CDs and other music formats. The purchase procedure is the same for all formats. Wherehouse also provides links to the various kinds of music players currently available for playing back downloads.

How to Get Your Music to Mass-Market Online Retailers. Because many online retailers function as virtual storefronts for brick-and-mortar operations, you get on their sites the same way you get into stores: by going through a third-party distributor.

Such sites are served by the Big Four distributors: WEA, Sony, Universal, and BMG. Access to those companies is limited to their subsidiary record labels—not to independent musicians.

But there are other options, too.

Tower Records, for example, works with smaller distributors such as Alternative Distribution Alliance (ADA) and Bayside, its own distribution arm. (This is also true for their brick-and-mortar stores.)

Other sites accept music from such other non–Big Four distributors as Baker and Taylor, Alliance, City Hall, Ryko, and Koch International. (See the Appendix for a detailed list.)

Ask the retailer for a list of the distributors it works with. This can be as easy as phoning a site's toll-free customer service number and telling the agent that you're a businessperson with music you'd like to sell on the site and would appreciate guidance on how to go about it. The right staffperson will be more than happy to share information with you.

Methods of working with distributors are discussed in Chapter 7.

The Internet has tended to inspire innovative approaches to nearly every aspect of music transmission, and music retailers haven't been immune. Promising developments include:

- Retailer partnerships with such indie-accessible online distributors as CD Baby, in which members of the indie distribution site automatically get sold on the mainstream retail site.
- Programs such as Amazon.com's Advantage for Music, which allows independent musicians to have a Web page on Amazon and CDs for sale stocked at their distribution center. Amazon takes care of the ordering, the shipping, the inventory control, and the billing. They classify your title in the genre you suggest, and add personalized information to your title's details page. Amazon keeps 55 percent of the price you set for your CD.

These are further steps toward leveling the music playing field, providing more advantages for up-and-coming artists or labels.

Niche-Market Online Retailers

Just as you should try to sell in brick-and-mortar stores that may not specialize in music but that serve your target audience, do the same on the Internet. If your music is for kids, for example, approach sites that sell children's merchandise. If you specialize in roots rock from the 1950s, see if you can sell CDs on a site that peddles fifties memorabilia.

To find appropriate sites, go to your favorite Internet search engine and type in a keyword or phrase for your specialty—for example, "Brazilian culture," if your music is samba oriented. The first, most popular merchant sites on the list of results are the ones you might consider contacting.

Remember that although the Internet is an important outlet for your music, it's also a virtual version of the conventional marketplace, roiling amid the same commercial forces and teeming with the same number of competitors. It's a challenge to get noticed on the Internet; upcoming discussions focus on how to go about it.

Chapter 10

Promoting the Product: Publicity

omewhere, a recording of music that could ignite the next big media frenzy is sitting
n CD form on a record store shelf, awaiting purchase. But will customers buy it? Will
ales transactions occur, setting the star-making machinery in motion—and eventu-
lly putting money in the pockets of the people who created the work?

Not necessarily. Not unless the seller makes customers aware of the music's avail-
bility and of its value as a purchase. Without that, the CD will end up as little more
han a piece of random plastic lost in the industrial scrap heap.

That's where promotion—the last of the Four P's of marketing—comes into play.
romotion, in brief, is activity designed to stimulate demand for a product.

Promotion starts with the product selling points identified during product devel-
pment (see page 38) and translates them into memorable, brandable messages and a
narketable image (Eminem as vitriol-spewing rapper, for example). It then makes use
f the entire media system—print, audio, visual, and multimedia—to communicate
he message, project the artist's image, and broadcast the sound in as many ways, and
o as many potential customers, as possible.

In music, promotion has several components, including publicity, Internet
ommunication, radio play, television exposure, sales incentive programs, live per-
ormance, and advertising. Each of these types of promotion, in turn, has its own set
f components.

A complete promotion program makes use of all available tools, techniques, and
utlets. In the case of a new CD release, for example, a promotion campaign might
nvolve the following activities:

- Convincing magazine, newspaper, Web, radio, and TV journalists to
  cover the artist and CD
- Scheduling in-store appearances to sign autographs
- Offering free downloads over the Web for a limited time
- Securing "featured title" treatment on retail Web sites
- Placing ads in publications that reach the targeted audience
- Convincing radio music directors to add the music to their playlists
- Making sure the music is featured at store listening posts
- Getting the music played in non-music stores frequented by target customers

The goal, of course, is to boost not only one-time sales but also multiple sales over the long term. That means that promotion has to be an ongoing, long-term process, not just a one-shot effort.

Whether you're able to make use of all available promotion methods will depend on your resources, both human and financial. But whatever your capabilities, you'll be devising a campaign that draws from options detailed in this and the next three chapters. The first option on the list is publicity.

PUBLICITY: FREE ADVERTISING

The most available form of promotion is publicity, because it's free.

Publicity is the process of increasing public awareness of the product by getting editorial coverage in the media (as opposed to paying for ads). It's about gaining exposure through magazine articles, record reviews, photos in the news, and other means. In short, publicity is the art of attracting attention via the information outlets that consumers routinely use.

The value of publicity is no mystery: When people read or hear about a musician or recording, they develop both an awareness and an opinion of the subject matter. If that opinion is positive, there is increased likelihood of a sale.

The publicity seeker has a three-part job: (1) get the most possible coverage of the artist/product in a broad range of media; (2) get coverage in the most appropriate media; and (3) attempt to control the content of the coverage.

Getting *the most possible coverage* translates into reaching the largest number of people. Getting *coverage in the most appropriate media* means focusing on publications and programs that cater directly to the target audience. And *controlling the content of the coverage* means making sure that articles communicate the desired message. (Publicists can do this to a surprising degree, by funneling article ideas to "sympathetic" editors and by suggesting desirable "angles" for articles, to cite just two methods.)

Interdependence of the Media and the Publicity Seeker

The importance of the media to the marketer is substantial. The media provides the mass-communication channels through which marketers can publicize their products. The media also provides feedback—via reviews—about how the product is perceived in the marketplace. (The marketer can, if so inclined, use this feedback to suggest changes in future products, such as a different musical or lyrical direction in an artist's future recordings.)

But what about the other way around? What's the value of the CD marketer to the media? Is the marketer-publicist always in the weaker position of having to beg for media coverage?

Actually, no. And here's why: Media people have a job, and that job is to feed the public's giant appetite for information. In the music world, the public hungers for facts about new music and about artists and their lives, opinions, and personalities. That information—the subject matter—comes from the music makers and their reps.

esentatives. Without it, the media would have nothing to report or write about. The ublicist provides news about upcoming releases, which the media then reports. The ublicist also provides the media with access to the artists, for interviews and in-depth eatures. In other words, the media *needs* the publicists for its lifeblood.

The point is that the media and the record seller have a mutually beneficial relationship. And awareness of this interdependence can guide the publicity seeker's ttempt to get coverage. "What type of article can I suggest that would be of interest ⊃ this editor and his or her readers?" is the thought that should be foremost in the ublicist's mind when planning a pitch.

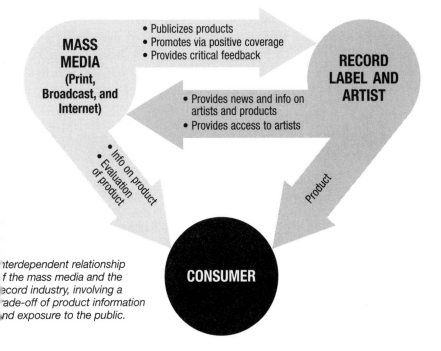

MASS MEDIA (Print, Broadcast, and Internet)

- Publicizes products
- Promotes via positive coverage
- Provides critical feedback

RECORD LABEL AND ARTIST

- Provides news and info on artists and products
- Provides access to artists

- Info on product
- Evaluation of product

Product

CONSUMER

iterdependent relationship f the mass media and the ecord industry, involving a ade-off of product information nd exposure to the public.

HE MEDIA AND ITS PARTICIPANTS

ledia is the collective term for the agencies of mass communication. Its individual ·articipants—editors, reporters, critics, columnists, and commentators—are often lescribed as the gatekeepers of public opinion. Their job is to monitor the constant vorldwide flood of new data and report only the information deemed most appro- ·riate for targeted readers, viewers, and listeners.

What kinds of media should you target when trying to get publicity? That will lepend on the kind of audience you are trying to reach. Each media entity has an ntended audience, whether it be a mass audience or a small group interested in a pecific topic, a print-oriented audience or a Web-savvy crowd.

The communication outlet you choose for your publicity campaign will be drawn rom three main categories: print, Internet, and broadcast.

Print Media

Newspapers and magazines publish information about music from a variety of perspectives, depending on the audience. Print publications of value to publicity seekers fall into the following categories:

Daily Newspapers. Audience: general readers from a national, regional, or local base; broad, rather than targeted, readership.

General Interest, Lifestyle, and Entertainment Magazines. (*People, Interview, Details, Entertainment Weekly, Cosmopolitan, Vogue, Vanity Fair, Newsweek, Esquire, GQ, Playboy, Ebony, New Yorker, Time, Maxim, Seventeen, Cosmo Girl,* and others).

Audience: broad national readership that conforms to the particular editorial focus; for example, *Time/Newsweek* to general readers, *People* mostly to female readers, *Entertainment Weekly* to pop-culture consumers, *Esquire/GQ/Playboy/Maxim/Details* to men, *Cosmo/Vogue* to women, and *Seventeen/Cosmo Girl* to teenage girls.

Newsweeklies (*Village Voice, Boston Phoenix, SF Weekly, Bay Guardian,* and others).

Audience: young, urban, sophisticated, culturally aware readers, primarily from local, but also from national and regional bases.

Music and Pop-Culture Magazines (*Rolling Stone, Spin, Vibe, New Musical Express* (U.K.) and others).

Audience: young adults with strong interest in pop culture and music.

Genre-Based Music Magazines (*Down Beat, Jazziz, Option, Country Music, The Source, Rap Pages*).

Audience: fans and aficionados of specific musical genres.

Promotional Magazines (*Request*).

Audience: customers of chain record stores.

Magazines for Music Hobbyists and Professionals (*Keyboard, Guitar Player, Guitar World, Modern Drummer, Computers and Music, Electronic Musician, Mix,* and *Musician*).

Audience: players of instruments, recording engineers, and other active music makers.

Magazines for Record Collectors (*Goldmine, Discoveries*).

Audience: collectors and aficionados of "oldies" and rare discs.

Trade Publications (*Billboard, Radio and Records, CMJ New Music Monthly, Music Trades, Hollywood Reporter, Variety*).

Audience: music-industry professionals, including record company personnel, radio program directors, music promoters, managers, and marketers.

Internet Sites

The World Wide Web has spawned a host of publications that are essentially hybrids of print and broadcast. Many combine text coverage of music (news, feature articles, and reviews) with audio and video clips. Publicity outlets on the Web include the following:

- Web-based music magazines and news sites (Launch.yahoo.com, MTV.com, VH1.com, virginmegamagazine.com, CountryStars.com)
- General-interest Web 'zines that include coverage of music-related subject matter (Salon.com, Slate.com)
- Web editions of many of the publications listed in the "Print" section above
- Blogs—personal Web logs that can attract large numbers of readers, becoming potential publicity bonanzas for artists who are mentioned and recommended

Broadcast Media

Deejays, veejays, commentators, and talk-show hosts on radio and television often have musical artists as guests or interview subjects. (In terms of radio, we're talking here not about airplay of the music itself—that's discussed in Chapter 12—but about coverage of the artist or music in the form of news, commentary, or interview.) Some outlets also have a music-news or trivia feature. Programming of value to publicity seekers is generally of the following types:

Radio

- Commercial talk radio, with occasional musical guests
- Commercial music radio, providing occasional interviews with and live performances by musical guests
- All-news radio, with occasional coverage of music and entertainment news
- Variety programs featuring musical guests (*A Prairie Home Companion,* for example)
- Public radio programs occasionally featuring musical guests (NPR's *Fresh Air,* for example)
- College radio programs, featuring interviews with and live performances by musical guests

Television

- Network late-night talk shows (*The Late Show with David Letterman, The Tonight Show, Late Night with Conan O'Brien,* and others)
- Network morning news programs, with occasional musical guests (*Good Morning America, Today*)
- Network prime-time news "magazines," occasionally covering music topics (*60 Minutes, Dateline, PrimeTime Live, 20/20*)

- Network prime-time "showbiz" news programs (*Entertainment Tonight, Access Hollywood*)
- Network daytime talk shows, with occasional musical guests (*The Oprah Winfrey Show*)
- Cable talk shows, with occasional musical guests.
- Cable music programming (MTV, VH1, The Box, Black Entertainment Television [BET], Country Music Television [CMT], Great American Country [GAC])

TYPES OF MEDIA COVERAGE

The kinds of articles or information that editors and producers choose to provide depends on their intimate knowledge of what audiences want. And what audiences want tends to fall into the following categories:

- News about current or upcoming products and ongoing career activities (for example, a change in musical group personnel, or a switch to a new record label)
- Performance schedules (as provided in entertainment calendars)
- Personality profiles, with in-depth information about an artist's life, opinions, beliefs, and tastes
- Reports on broad musical styles and trends (for example, the increase of interest in female pop artists in the late 1990s)
- Reviews of recordings and live performances

TOOLS OF THE PUBLICITY SEEKER

Before setting out to publicize a new release, you, the publicist, have to become familiar with the standard tools of the trade, and learn how to use them like a pro. The key items include reference tools, such as media lists; the press kit—your primary "calling card" for getting the attention of media representatives; and finally, press releases and public service announcements, the simplest devices for getting instant exposure.

Media List

First, identify the media people and businesses to contact when sending out information about your release or other product. Do this by assembling a media list—a database of names, addresses, phone numbers, and e-mail addresses of publications, radio programs, television programs, and Internet sites that would be open to covering a product such as yours. The list should also include the names of individual editors, reporters, critics, commentators, and producers who would be your personal contacts when pitching items and stories. (By the way, this is your third important list, the others being a mailing list of customers and a list of retail accounts. See page 10 for more information on mailing lists.)

If possible, store the media list both on paper and in a computer database for easy updating. And guard it with your life. It takes time and energy to assemble one of these lists, and when you do, it will be a one-of-a-kind, custom list for your product—not something you want to have to dig frantically for when preparing to send out a pitch.

Begin building a list by checking Web sites for the e-mail addresses of their editors and content producers, and by phoning newspapers and appropriate magazines based in your region and getting the names and addresses of their current music critics or art-and-entertainment editors. Then invest a few long-distance charges or use the Web to obtain editorial contacts for the more prominent national and international music media.

You can supplement this start-up list with information from such sources as the *Gale Directory of Publications*; the *Standard Rate and Data (SRDS)* directories *Consumer Magazine Advertising Source, Newspaper Advertising Source, Radio Advertising Source, TV & Cable Source,* and *Interactive Advertising Source*; and the Internet's MediaFinder (www.mediafinder.com). There are many other resources; look in the library and on the Internet.

Once you've assembled a basic list, keep it up to date. Job turnover in the media world is high, and the editor who loved your last concert may no longer be working at the same publication. Whenever you become aware of a new name, or an individual's move to a new organization, update your list. And most important, keep notes on your list about the individuals who have reacted positively to your product, as well as the people with whom you have established positive relationships. They will be key allies to contact in future publicity efforts.

Press Kit

The essential tool for presenting your product to the media is the press kit. It's the standard device employed by marketers and publicists when disseminating a substantial amount of information in a single mailing. It can be used to promote an individual CD release, a newly formed music group, an entire company, or any number of other newsworthy products or entities.

Whatever the musical product being promoted, the press kit is its "ambassador" to the press, and the kit's professionalism and quality have a direct impact on how the product itself is perceived. For that reason, the kit should be made as attractive and informative as possible.

Press kits can be in electronic form—on DVD, CD-ROM, Web site, or as an e-mail attachment—or in the traditional print format. Electronic press kits typically contain electronic versions of almost everything included in a printed press kit, as we'll now cover in detail.

The typical hard-copy press kit is composed of the following elements: a jacket, with pockets on the inside for inserting other elements; a cover letter (also called a pitch letter); a fact sheet; a bio or product description; publicity photographs; press clips; a CD (if that's what's being promoted); a DVD of visual performance and interview clips (optional but recommended); and additional attention-grabbing item (optional). Let's investigate these press kit components one by one.

Jacket. As described in Jim Pettigrew's book *The Billboard Guide to Music Publicity,* th jacket is, "in a media sense…the sexy costume in which your client goes onstage. I the part of the kit that gives the crucial first impression." The jacket is a combinatic of an attractive cover and a holder for all the other press kit items. The front is ofte decorated with a printed or stick-on logo, or it might have more elaborate artwork a full-color photograph. On the inside, it has pockets or fold-up flaps, in which yc insert the bio, press clips, and other items. The standard size of a jacket is 9 by 12 inche

(Bear in mind that you're free to devise alternatives to jackets if you're inclined save money and conserve paper.)

Cover Letter. Also called the "pitch letter," this is the first item that is read—it's th introduction to the press kit—and the greeting should include the name of the ind vidual recipient. (Your database software should allow you to merge a standard lett with names and addresses on your media list when printing, so that each letter w be personalized.)

The format of the cover letter is the same as that of a standard business letter. Wri it as clearly and concisely as possible, opening with a statement of what the letter about ("I'm writing to let you know about Artist A's new CD release") and why would be of interest to the recipient ("a step in a new musical direction that you readers will want to know about"). The remainder should expand on why the top would be of interest, and the letter should close with an invitation to actic ("Contact me if you'd like to work on scheduling a story for your publication [c program]. I look forward to speaking with you about it in the near future"). Und your signature, print "Enc." to indicate that there are "enclosures" (other press k items) included for review.

Publicists also use pitch letters alone—not as part of a press kit—to pitch stori to the media. And as veteran publicist Mark Pucci says, "By and large, a lot of it done by e-mail." This makes it especially important to be as succinct as possible.

"These days everybody's got short attention spans, even shorter than they we before, so you've got to get in and get out real quickly. You've got to have a 'pitcl ing' mind," Pucci says, "getting that pitch done and refined down, distilled down t its essence."

For more information about formatting and optimizing e-mail messages, see pag 163 in Chapter 11.

Fact Sheet. This is a simple one-page list of key facts about the product. It is perfe for use by a busy radio or TV commentator who has to interview a guest but hasn had time to do background research. The fact sheet provides the main discussio points at a glance. The sheet is also useful to members of the print media when the have to fact-check articles.

Some press-kit components: a bio, a publicity photograph, and press clips.

his electronic press kit,
ored on CD-ROM,
ntains video interviews
d concert clips.

© Blind Pig Records

At the top, print "Fact Sheet," followed by the name of the product or artist. In vertical column on the left side of the sheet, print item headings—Title of Ne[w] Album, Title of Single, Style of Music, Band Members, Record Label, Unusual Fact[s] or any other items that you think would be important to note—in bold type. Nex[t] to each heading, print the corresponding information, in short-and-sweet form. A[t] the bottom of the fact sheet, print the name and phone number of the person t[o] contact for more information, e.g., "Contact: Bob Roberts (212) 111-0000."

Bio. The bio or product summary is the central nervous system of the press kit. It [is] the fleshed-out description of the subject at hand, namely, the artist or product bei[ng] promoted. It will not only be read by numerous decision makers who may kno[w] nothing about the topic, but may also be printed word-for-word by small new[s] papers who want to run an article but are short on writers. For these reasons, the bi[o] needs to be publication quality—a concise, informative, and entertaining piece [of] copy. In form, the bio should consist of the following:

- *Introductory statement:* Communicates the essence of the product's unique-ness (or persona, in the case of an artist). The statement focuses on the key selling point that you identified during product development and have since translated into an image or easy-to-communicate concept.
- *Summary of current activity:* Quickly provides the reader with information about the new CD, upcoming tour, or whatever else you consider to be the immediate focus of your current promotion.

In this bio promoting a new CD, the key selling point is that the artist is "a living American music treasure."

HIGHTONE RECORDS

RAMBLIN' JACK ELLIOTT

Perhaps more stories have been told about Ramblin' Jack Elliott than any other contemporary American music artist; but one thing's for sure: he is a living American music treasure. A major figure in the folk movement of the 1950s, Ramblin' Jack has been called "a wandering, true American minstrel" by play-wright Sam Shepard. He learned his craft from the legendary Woody Guthrie, with whom he became a close friend. He has influenced several generations of singers, from Bob Dylan and Tom Waits to Beck and John Wesley Harding. His 1995 album, *South Coast,* won the Grammy Award as Best Traditional Folk Album. And now, with the debut of his HighTone Records CD, *Friends of Mine,* Jack has crafted his most ambitious work in a long line of creative visions.

Much has been said about Jack's early life: he got the cowboy bug at the tender age of nine; he ran away from home at 15; he learned cowboy songs and banjo from a rodeo clown; and, upon returning home, found an old guitar and started practicing.

Around 1951, Jack heard his first Woody Guthrie recording and—thoroughly inspired—sought out Guthrie himself. For the next few years, the two trav-eled the country together, as Jack absorbed the style and essence that made Woody Guthrie such an original

music icon. In 1954, after Woody was hospitalized for the disease that killed him in 1967, Jack continued to travel, playing the gospel according to Woody.

In 1955, Jack went to Europe, where he developed his own style and turned on a new audience to Guthrie's music. Upon returning to the States in 1961, Jack found the folk music boom in full swing and himself as one of its heroes. He lived in Greenwich Village in the early '60s, where he played the famous folk venues at the center of the folk revival. In 1965, he moved to California, and in the mid-'70s he joine[d] Bob Dylan's Rolling Thunder Revue. Jack received th[e] Bill Graham Life Achievement Award at San Francisco's Bay Area Music Awards in 1996.

As the title *Friends of Mine* suggests, Ramblin' Ja[ck] is joined on this CD by his friends: Guy Clark, Nan[ci] Griffith, Arlo Guthrie, Emmylou Harris, John Prine, Peter Rowan, Rosalie Sorrels, Tom Waits, Jerry Jeff Walker, and Bob Weir. The songs on *Friends of Min[e]* demonstrate the breadth of American music roots—folk, blues, country and western—that encompass [the] style of a true original: Ramblin' Jack Elliott.

- *Historical background:* Fleshes out the story. When did the musical group first get together? Why did it form? What were some of the key events in its development? Who helped them? When? These kinds of topics can be addressed here.
- *Additional information:* Fills out the picture of the artist or product with nonessential information. Special interests, unusual or influential experiences, favorite recording techniques, bits of philosophy—all are potential mentionables in this section, but bear in mind that not all readers will make it this far.
- *Closing passage:* Draws the bio to a satisfying conclusion. One way to do this is to restate the opening idea in a new way. Another is to end with a quote that provides a sense of summary or finality.

Speaking of quotes, use them liberally throughout the bio. Words taken directly om the mouth of the artist or another personality tend to add liveliness to these nds of written pieces. (A pertinent quote is often used *directly after* a point made in e text, to expand on or support the point. But avoid repetitively alternating text d quotes.) The quotes can be obtained through an interview with the artist or from st articles.

Putting together quotes is only one part of the bio preparation process. Whoever writing the bio—and it could be a hired freelance professional or you the mar-ter—will have to start by gaining thorough familiarity with the musician, the usic, and the image or main message that has been developed by the marketing am. This is done in several stages: (1) reading past literature about the artist and usic, including magazine articles and any promotional material already developed;) interviewing the artist to find out as much as possible about his or her personal-y, musical approach, and background; and (3) listening to the music. Overall, it's sential that the image presented in the bio be in sync with the image presented in other promotional materials.

blicity Photograph. Another essential part of the press kit. The standard format is 8-y-10-inch black-and-white glossy. (Sometimes it's worth providing a color slide for se on magazine covers or in color interiors. But since this is expensive, do it only r established acts or when you are reasonably certain of getting coverage.)

Digital photos in JPEG format are currently very much the rule in Web-based omotion and publicity. Plan on scanning your photos or having them shot with a gital camera.

The tone, style, and mood of the photo should support the image and personal-y of the artist or the character of the music. If the selling point of the music is that is charming and upbeat, the photo should be charming and upbeat. If the chief sales oint is the artist's guitar technique, show her with a guitar. If the song lyrics deal ith the problems of living in the city, show the artist against a stark urban back-ound. In sum, make the photo clearly convey the intended image at a glance.

Use a professional photographer with experience in the music business. You ca find one by skimming through music magazines and looking at the credits for tl photos that you like, and then calling the editorial office to find out how to conta the photographer(s). Another method is to consult such directories as the *Recordi Industry Sourcebook* and *Klik Showcase Photography*.

When discussing the shot with the photographer, make sure you clearly comm nicate the idea you'd like the shot to convey. If the final product conflicts with yo intended message, then you'll have wasted your money.

The photographer owns all rights to the photograph except for those that yo explicitly purchase. Your basic payment covers publicity uses—that is, use in prom tion packages and "editorial uses in regular issues of newspapers and other regular published periodicals and television news programming" (standard wording print on many promotional photos). For other uses, such as on album covers and in adve tising, the photographer normally requires a higher fee. It's important to state yo intended use when you first hire the photographer, and to put it in writing.

The publicity stills you distribute should show, at minimum, the name of the art or product, the name of the manufacturer (that is, the record label in the case recordings) and its contact information, and the copyright date and owner (the ph tographer, unless you have purchased the copyright as part of the agreement).

Press Clips. These are simply sample reviews or positive articles written about tl product, which you cut out, tape neatly to a sheet of 8 ½-by-11-inch paper (with tl publication name and dateline at the top), and photocopy.

Video Clips. Footage of performances or interviews is not essential but goes a lo way toward rounding out the picture of the act for the media recipient. But on include video clips if they're expertly produced—which doesn't necessarily me. Hollywood- quality production but does mean clean visuals, crisp editing, a smooth transitions. Provide it on DVD rather than VHS.

Additional Promotional Items. You may want to include other items that will help make the package memorable for the recipient. These might include buttons, stic ers, or trinkets of various kinds. Since editors receive (and often toss) so many of the items, it's best to avoid them unless the item is truly imaginative. At the very least, should be closely tied in with the concept of the band or product.

When preparing press kits, keep in mind that hard-and-fast rules about forma and presentation don't exist. Feel free to innovate, to mix up and combine componer as your imagination dictates. But whatever you do, design your kit for maximum ea of use by the recipient.

Press Release

When publicists set out to inform the media about a specific event, such as a ne product launch or an upcoming tour, they use a tool called a press release. This straigl orward, single-page (except for complex topics) device is designed to spark interest, opefully resulting in a magazine article or some other type of media coverage.

The format of a press release is as follows:

- The phrase "For Immediate Release" is often positioned in the upper left corner, followed by the date. (An alternative place for the date is at the beginning of the body copy, used with the location. Example: "New York, July 9, 2003").
- In the upper right corner, give the name of the contact person followed by his or her telephone number.
- Start the announcement with a succinct headline, typed in capital letters and centered above the body copy. If the message is complicated, add a subheading that supplies further explanation.
- The "lead" or opening text should summarize the topic, covering the "Five W's and an H" (Who, What, When, Where, Why, and How—not to be confused with the marketing Three W's and an H mentioned in Chapter 3). An explanation, with pertinent details, should follow.

A press release announcing the availability of a rare Roy Orbison recording is 10wn below.

Mailings for Entertainment Calendars

Listings of concert and club dates in "calendar" sections of newspapers and magazine and on radio are the most basic form of publicity. To get listed in print, send a simpl notice showing the name of the act, the venue, and the date, and include a publicit photo. For radio do the same, but add a copy of your fact sheet.

Public Service Announcement (PSA)

Public service announcements are simple notices of upcoming nonprofit or charit events, and they are sent out to noncommercial electronic media. A public servic announcement should be no longer than one paragraph, covering the Five W's an an H. It should include a short headline and should also provide the name and phon number of the person to contact for more information.

Mail, Fax, Phone, E-Mail, Web

Today's tools of transmission are numerous. Use the full range of communicatio options to your advantage when making pitches and follow-ups.

Publicist Marc Lipkin does just that: "We work to get as much coverage and air spac and newspaper space as there possibly is out there to get…. By *work* I mean sendin review copies to major press people, followed up with phone calls and e-mails, to g as many reviews of that brand-new record as soon after the release date as possible."

Many artists and record labels also use the Web as a site for press materials, supply ing downloadable photos, sound samples, video clips, bios, and recent press releases.

PUBLICITY TACTICS AND TECHNIQUES

The approaches used in generating publicity are as numerous as the kinds of produc pitched to the buying public. In music, the differences between approaches depen largely on whether the artist or product is new on the market or well established, an on whether the publicity campaign will be local, regional, or national. In *The Billboa Guide to Music Publicity*, Jim Pettigrew offers detailed information about how t conduct campaigns under these different circumstances. The following discussion limited to broadly applicable tactics and techniques.

Learn About the Product and the Audience. The first task in any publicity campaign is t gain a clear understanding of the product's (the artist's or the music's) selling poin and sales "hooks." Equally important is having a clear picture of the targeted audi ence. Obtain this information by interviewing the artist and others involved in th enterprise, and by reviewing paperwork prepared during the product developmen phase of the overall marketing campaign (see Chapter 4).

Target the Right Media Outlets. When planning gets under way, it's vital to aim for th appropriate media. Create a custom media list of the magazines, newspapers, We sites, and broadcast programs that your intended customers read and watch. Th doesn't only mean music-oriented media: *Target all possible media outlets.* If you know the nonmusical interests of your audience, you can plan to reach the audience through specialty publications and programs that cater to those nonmusical interests. For example, if you know that the audience of your speed-metal band includes a large number of hot-rod enthusiasts, it would be appropriate to pitch an article about the band to the editor of the top hot-rod magazine.

Time the Coverage for Maximum Impact. Aim for media coverage that coincides with live performance dates, or with the release of a new CD. In the case of live dates, send press kits to local media well before the date, and offer editors press passes to the performance.

"We press-release every tour date about a month or five weeks in advance," Marc Lipkin says. "We do hard mail releases, with photos and copies of the CD where necessary."

Think Like an Editor or Producer. Publicists have an important and constructive role to play in the media realm apart from simply promoting their products. They feed story ideas to editors, writers, and producers who are in constant need of new content. Publicists are sources of information. For that reason, you, the publicist, should be able to put yourself in editors' and producers' shoes. Learn to speak their language, since part of your task will be to work with them to make articles and programming happen. Know what makes an article or an Internet feature interesting to readers. Be able to extract interesting "angles" from the activities of the artist you're representing, so that when you pitch an idea you're offering something more specific than just another "great band with a new CD." For example, you (or someone acting on your behalf) might pitch an article about an unusual event in an artist's life, or a nonmusical interest or activity of the artist that matches a magazine's focus.

Start with Who You Know. When you are ready to contact the media, focus first on columnists, editors, writers, and commentators with whom you've had previous positive contact. Short of that, start with the "best bets"—the people whose work (which you know about from regular reading) indicates a preference for the kind of music you're promoting.

Before contacting these writers, come up with angles about the product that would make good subjects for articles in their individual publications. In other words, tailor your pitch to each individual as much as time allows.

Make your pitch to these people by telephone. If they're interested, tell them you'll supply any materials or information that they need.

Follow Up. After mailing press kits to the names on your media list, follow up by telephone with as many of the recipients as possible. Ask if they received the press kit. Offer to provide additional material, such as photos and extra CDs. Find out whether they're interested in covering your act. If they'd like more time to think about it, make a note of that, and follow up with another call after a mutually agreed upon interval.

"We don't just send these materials out and let them find their place on som editor's or writer's desk," Marc Lipkin says. "We follow them up with phone call: Some people may call it harassment, but I just think of it as doing my job."

Also follow up after a concert that a writer has attended as your guest. Make sur that all went smoothly. Ask if the writer needs any additional material or would lik to schedule an interview with your artist.

The key in following up is to be helpful. Approach it as an opportunity to assis the editor in doing his or her job.

Work with the Editor or Producer. The concept of working in partnership with editor: writers, and producers is an important one in the world of publicity. The most effec tive publicists have a reputation for being informative, responsive, and ready to mee needs for interviews, photos, copies of CDs, and whatever else is called for.

When you contact people in the media, offer to work with them on developin story ideas. Mention the availability of the artist for interviews. Ask if color slides c other items are needed. In short, make the process of preparing an article or story a easy for the editor as it is within your power to do.

Make the Media Person's Job Easy. To expand on the last point, one of the mor headache-inducing aspects of the editor's or content producer's job is having to hur for, order, and wait for artist photos, bios, fact sheets, and CDs. The Internet can serv as the answer to their prayers, if the publicity seeker uses it effectively.

Singer Jacqui Naylor makes editors' jobs easier by packing her Web site with an information an editor may need, downloadable at the press of a button.

Management companies and publicity firms also strive for press-friendliness o their sites. "We have a Web site, too," publicist Mark Pucci says. "If somebody wante to find out something about the [trio] Flatlanders, for instance, they can go to ou site and get a bio that's downloadable, an update on what's going on with the banc and pictures to download. If they want more detailed information, they can go to th [linked] New West Records Web site, where you've got a Flatlanders video, MP3 file: and tour itineraries. For journalists out there I think it's a godsend."

Establish Positive Relationships with People in the Media. This will occur naturally : you follow the previous guidelines in this section. Having good, mutually trustin relationships with professionals in the media sector will help immeasurably in an publicity effort. Being able to phone up and run an idea by a familiar editor is sever: shortcuts past the anonymous cold call and the faceless press kit added to the edito rial slush pile.

Building trust, says Marc Lipkin, can be as basic as "showing up for meetings o time...trying real hard to work with people...making things happen."

"There's not a phone call I don't return or an e-mail I don't answer," Lipkin say:

Bundle" Interviews When Possible. In the right circumstances, you can maximize exposure by doing several interviews at the same time.

Press conferences are one way to do this. Another is to attend a music conference covered by the press and set up multiple interviews—as publicist Pucci did for the Flatlanders at a South by Southwest conference: "We took advantage of all the journalists coming there by setting up a schedule for the guys to do in-person interviews with people. Then we set up a lot of conference calls with various press people from around the country. Often we'd do six or seven interviews at a time for up to thirty minutes each, then do the next call."

Stay Abreast of the Media. New information channels, from underground 'zines to midnight talk shows, come and go with startling speed. If you blink, you may miss an outlet that would be perfect for promoting your act. So keep your eyes open. Read trade magazines to stay on top of the changing mediascape. Surf the Internet for new music sites. Regularly peruse new and old publications to get a handle on their latest slants, and to learn about the interests of their writers. And when you find important new information, update your media list.

INDEPENDENT PUBLICISTS

At a certain point in the success curve of your enterprise, your publicity needs will become more than you or your staff can handle. It is at this point that you should consider hiring an independent publicist. Indie PR people are professionals who are intimately familiar with the tools and techniques of getting exposure for clients on a regional, national, or international basis, and who know how to coordinate their plans with those of other personnel involved in the promotional campaign (such as artist management, record company staff, and radio promoters). Publicists can be put on retainer for as long or short a period of time as they are needed in a campaign.

You can find the names of publicists by asking around and by looking in directories like the *Recording Industry Sourcebook*.

Chapter 11

Promoting the Product: Online Techniques

The good news for independent musicians, small record labels, and established companies: The Internet is an exciting sales vehicle. The bad news is that tens of thousands of others use it for the same purpose. Attracting attention from the middle of this crowd is as challenging as doing it in the brick-and-mortar marketplace.

The bottom line is that even if you have a presence on the Internet, no one will notice it unless you inform them and attract them to you—in other words, promote yourself.

Fortunately, the Internet can be an effective, low-cost starting point for your promotion because it offers so many communication options. Using these creatively and energetically will add a valuable extra dimension to your marketing campaign and boost your profile—on or off the Web. (Remember: The Web isn't a substitute for the promo and networking you'll still need to do in the real world of nightclub bookers, store owners, radio programmers, and media personnel.)

Interactivity is key to Internet promotion. Direct two-way communication and feedback help you and your audience get closer. And e-mail is still the "killer app" in the world of instant promotion.

Here's a summary of Internet promotion options:

- Setting up your own Web site and using it effectively
- Using e-mail and e-lists to inform target customers about your music—and to find out more about them
- Affiliating with *appropriate* multi-artist sites that provide promotional services
- Posting your music on a free peer-to-peer file-sharing site
- Promoting on mainstream and niche Internet retail sites

USING YOUR OWN WEB SITE AS A PROMOTIONAL TOOL

Creating a Web site dedicated to your music isn't always necessary. Without one you can still use e-mail or Web ads to promote your CDs and gigs, and you can affiliate with an already established multi-artist site. But having your own Web site provides you with maximum control over the "look and feel" of your message, as well as its

ontent. It also gives you and your audience a home base on the Web, and it serves as
 hub from which to extend your communications reach, like tentacles, out to other
Web sites. Given the time and know-how (or the means to access others' know-how),
reating a home Web site can be a valuable investment. (There are several economical
Web-building programs that offer templates of a Web site's key pages and features.)

Here are some guidelines for dynamic, actively promotional sites. If you think a
atic site that shows your name, image, bio, and contact information—a no-frills
Web presence"—is enough, skip to the section entitled "The Basics" (below).

The Basic Structure of a Web Site

Web-surfing veterans are familiar with the elements of a typical Web site:

- A home page—the first visual the fan sees upon visiting. It offers one
  or more hyperlinks in the form of words or graphics the visitor uses
  to reach other locations on the Web site.
- Additional pages accessed by clicking on home-page hyperlinks. These
  linked pages may include photographs; information on you, your music,
  and upcoming gigs; special promotions or coupons; and more.
- Product listings and a method of ordering; otherwise, a link to another
  location where products are available for sale.
- Links throughout to other related or affiliated sites on the Internet.

But it's what you *do* with these elements that makes the difference between a fan-
uilding, sales-generating site and one that's dead in the cyber-water—unnoticed,
ninteresting, and nonproductive.

When planning and designing the site, focus on the following goals:

- Holding visitors' attention
- Closing the sale
- Building one-to-one relationships with fans
- Building your brand

Holding Visitors' Attention

ust like an advertisement, your site has only a couple of seconds to grab a visitor's
ttention and hold his or her interest. If the visitor wasn't directed to your site, the
kelihood is that he hit on it by accident. That means his finger is on the mouse and
eady to click elsewhere at the first sign of boredom. Don't let him click! Provide him
vith an instant reason for sticking around.

he Basics: Visual Appeal, Clear Messages, Easy Navigation. Give newcomers a visually
r conceptually gripping first impression. If they already know who you are, a logo,
n image from the latest CD cover, or a familiar catchphrase (for example, a line from
ne of your songs) can do the trick. But if they're strangers, you'll need to spark
heir curiosity and make them want to explore further. Be creative. Be different. Be

eye-catching. Or even, as CD Baby's online marketing writer Derek Sivers has advised, *be weird*. ("Real people respond better to the weird fun stuff.")

Only use imagery you know will appeal to the existing or prospective target audience—the people who like your kind of music and your kind of style. As in product packaging and advertising, match the image to the music and your personality. You can use a funky roadhouse design for a blues band, a glamour shot for a cabaret performer, high-tech imagery for electronica, moody shadows for a plaintive poet singer, a colorful fifties diner setting for a pop group. But avoid sending the wrong message with your site's opening visual. Don't use image contrary to what you're really about.

Getting people to stay is sometimes as simple as providing a clear, unambiguous statement of where they've landed—"Home of the Howard McGillicuddy Band"—along with a quote from a positive review. (With a simple GIF animation program you can offer several different quotes, setting them up so that as one fades out, another fades in.) The right tagline or subheading can suggest a strong emotional benefit. "Mood adjustment the way you like it," for example.

Speaking of messages, writing for the Internet is not the same as writing for print. On the Internet, where long attention spans don't exist, your messages have to be succinct. Avoid long stretches of text like the one you've been reading.

New West Records' home page combines news, product highlights, a list of artists, and clear cues for ordering and for learning more.

Write statements that *pop* off the screen. Use bullets for emphasis. Write as if speaking. Speak as if to a guest in your home. Offer hospitality. Be helpful. Give visitors clear information at a glance. Tell them where they are. Tell them why they should stay. Tell them what else there is to see and how to find it. And tell them how to get back to where they were.

The last points have to do with navigation design. Don't frustrate visitors by allowing them to get lost on your site. Instead, offer clear subject headings, common-sense hot buttons, an easy way to get back to the home page, and logical links to other related sites.

Put important information near the top of the page so people with small computer screens won't miss it. (Jakob Nielsen's Web site, useit.com, is a good source of information on how to make sites user-friendly.)

Beyond the Basics: Keeping Them Coming Back. Don't be satisfied with offering a one-time thrill, never to be repeated. You should make visitors want to come back to the site again and again. Turn their initial curiosity into growing, long-lasting interest. Do this by providing content that (1) appeals to your target audience, (2) changes frequently, (3) offers added value they can't find anywhere else, and (4) is offered as enticing tidbits, rather than all at once.

First, **give visitors what they want,** whether it's information about band-member hobbies, anecdotes from the studio, or song lyrics and recording credits. Your knowledge of fan and customer preferences (see "Building One-to-One Relationships" on page 159) is the force that should guide many of your content choices.

The most effective Web sites typically include the following:

- Biographical information
- Current news about the artist
- Tour schedules, or a list of upcoming club performances
- An e-mail option for fans, allowing them to send messages to the artist
- A separate page and e-mail option for bookings and the press, enabling producers, reporters, and editors to get information and send business-related messages
- A chat room, where fans can exchange messages and build community
- Information about recordings available for purchase, along with ordering instructions
- Production notes on recordings, identifying singers and instrumentalists, producers and engineers, and dates and locations
- Song lyrics
- Audio clips of old songs and sneak previews of works in progress
- Video clips of the artist
- Audio interviews with the artist
- Links to other sites of interest, such as online stores, other artists' sites—anything the proprietor of the main site thinks will be of interest to a fan

Second, **keep the site fresh and up to date.** Because the Internet is a time-sensitive medium, nothing drives a visitor away faster than a site that's obviously out of date. Key information to update regularly includes:

- upcoming concert or nightclub dates
- new songs for 30- or 60-second sampling
- updated photos and videos for download
- chat rooms

Third, try to **offer valuable features and information unavailable anywhere else.** Then if people want the feature, they have to come to your site. Products for sale, of course, should be made available in as many outlets as possible, so don't put them into the category of "unavailable elsewhere." But ideas such as the following would be worth considering:

- News about the artist's activities
- Personal letters or messages from artist to visitors
- Special deals such as concert ticket discounts for site subscribers, prime seating at performances, or presale of concert tickets
- Contests, with prizes such as meeting the artist or tickets to a performance combined with a restaurant coupon
- Downloads or streams of works in progress or alternate mixes of songs
- Rare photographs

Jazz singer Jacqui Naylor provides a separate page for the press, where she posts recent press releases that can be used by editors at newspapers, magazines, and Web sites. (For more information about press releases, see Chapter 10.) Naylor also offers downloadable photos at low, medium, and high resolution, for editors and others to use in their articles (after getting permission). Naylor, a former marketing director, knows that this tactic provides an important service for the press, making it easy to get information and images for articles rather than having to order such materials by phone from the record label or a press agent and then wait for them to arrive by mail.

Fourth, **offer features and information sparingly, rather than all at once.** If the site is aimed at encouraging repeat visitors—especially if they're paying for subscription—you'll want to make them hungry for more. (And multiple "hits" make your site more attractive to potential affiliate partners.)

For example, you can:

- offer downloadable volumes of live recordings rotated on a monthly basis
- offer lyrics for only one song at a time, or one album at a time
- provide an artist's autobiography, one chapter at a time
- provide an artist's journal from a current tour, one episode at a time

Closing the Sale

Some marketers will tell you to provide an option to purchase on every page of your Web site. That may be overkill for an art-comes-first audience, but at the very least our site needs to provide multiple opportunities to purchase your music. The site's content and design should motivate the customer to buy with tasteful but persistent "calls to action."

Maybe you don't sell your music directly, but rather through another outlet such as an online retailer. Then use your site to promote the new (or old) album by offering free 30- to 60-second samples of selected songs, on a page with prominent links to the retailer's ordering page.

If you're selling directly from your site, provide clear methods of ordering products. Many acts use an 800 number for quick and easy purchases. You can also set up your site so fans can securely key in credit card numbers for instant ordering. (Chapter 9 has more about options for ordering.)

For incentives to buy, you can do the following:

- Provide quotes from reviews
- Offer descriptions of the music (less convincing than independent reviews)
- Offer discounts for purchasing from your site (without undercutting business partners—retailers—who may also be selling your music)
- Offer special sales with specific deadlines ("10% off if you order by December 1")

But whatever you do, *ask for the order.* Clearly tell people what you want them to do ("order now").

When asking for the order, you don't have to make it pushy or a hard sell. Some potential customers may reject that approach. You might want to follow the example of Jacqui Naylor, who fosters a sophisticated, low-key promotional tone that matches her music. Where she sells CDs, she suggests that they're "available for purchase now" with a link to the retailer.

Of course, you'll want to sell more than recordings. On a list of upcoming concerts or nightclub dates, include links to the concert hall or club—or ticket broker—so your visitor can buy a ticket right away.

Building One-to-One Relationships with Fans

One-to-one marketing relationships with customers are what make online promotion so valuable. The typical music fan likes to feel close to the act and its music. The more personal the relationship, the more loyal the fan. Your interactive Web presence will go a long way toward building close seller–customer relationships.

Interactivity has five components:

1. Allowing visitors to get in touch with you and join a community of like-minded music lovers
2. Helping you learn about what visitors want, so that you're better equipped to provide it to them
3. Getting visitors' opinions about your music, creating their buy-in and sense of active participation in your world

4. Getting visitors to "opt in"—that is, agree to future mailings and communications from you

5. Letting visitors learn more about you than they would elsewhere

The tools to foster interactivity include e-mail, chat rooms, and forms.

Fostering Interaction by E-Mail. Increase customer contact by permitting visitors to e-mail you directly from the site. You can reply to e-mails directly, or as their volume increases, program an automatic response mechanism that acknowledges receipt with a common message. (A third alternative is to list your answers to FAQs—frequently asked questions—based on actual fan e-mail. You'd set up an FAQ page and update it frequently.)

"Autoresponses" can be a mixed blessing. They make your life simpler, and some people prefer receiving any response—even an automated one—to getting no response at all. But a "form letter" can also cool off the hottest fan. To avoid this word the message carefully so it's general enough to apply to any message, yet as conversational and personal-sounding as possible: "Got your e-mail message. Thanks for taking the time to get in touch. We've been busy recording our new CD and playing a heavy concert schedule, which means we won't have the time to send you a detailed reply. But it's great to know you're there, and you can count on our working hard to bring you the best music we can come up with. Keep letting us know what you think."

Make sure your message reflects your personality—the same personality that comes through in your music and visual images. One way to keep it "real" is to read the message out loud to yourself until it sounds like something you'd say in conversation.

If possible, your response should also help you get valuable information about the visitor. For example, end the message by suggesting they sign up for your mailing list to receive special announcements or news about upcoming concerts and CD releases. To opt in to your mailing program (important to you so your messages aren't perceived as spam) they just need to give you their full name and e-mail address. Once this is done, you've established a win-win arrangement. The visitor benefits from getting valuable information, and you get the visitor's contact information and opt-in.

Setting Up an On-Site Chat Room. Fans like to feel as though they are part of a community. Posting a message on your site gives them a sense of bonding with you and other fans, which can change them from casual listeners to diehard fans and maybe more. You gain insights into your core audience by following their discussions. And of course you can drop in the occasional message-from-the-artist or make publicized "personal appearances" in the chat room to stir up some excitement.

Using Online Forms and Questionnaires. Another tool for building visitor interest and involvement—and finding out about their tastes and preferences—is an onsite form or questionnaire. Set them up for any number of purposes: to subscribe to your site, o order merchandise; to answer specific questions you develop to get feedback about your music; to vote on songs to play at your next big concert; or to enter a contest.

Whatever the questionnaire's purpose, *always* ask for the respondent's name and e-mail address, and provide the opportunity to opt in to your online communications (as well as the possibility of opting out).

Building Your Brand

Your *brand* is the specific, unique, consistent, memorable idea that sums up you and your music. It's no coincidence that America's most successful companies have all had very strong brand recognition, usually supported by a logo and visual imagery (see page 60 for more about brands). Your brand must be used consistently in packaging, posters, other merchandise, and ads to become firmly implanted in the buying public's consciousness. Branding is very important for Web sites, too. Use photos, a style, and color schemes on your Web site that are familiar from your other promotional materials.

Attracting Attention to Your Site

So now your Web site is set up and the key features are in place. But what if no one sees it? For the maximum promotional benefit, you've got to attract attention to your Web site and make people want to make that critical first visit.

What can you do to get potential customers to visit your Web site? There are a number of options.

- *Submit your Web address to leading search engines and directories.* By registering, you'll ensure that the search engines will display a link to your Web site when someone types in its title or name. You can go to each search engine's home page and select "submit or add URL" (URL being your Web page address, known in Netspeak as a Uniform Resource Locator). Some search engines require you to pay for registration—several hundred dollars, in some cases.

  It's important to optimize the chances that Web surfers will find your site near the top of any search engine's keyword-driven list of Web pages. You also want to optimize the chances of a user choosing your site among any other similar ones on the screen. The main tools for doing this are the title of your site, the title tags of your Web pages, and the words you use at the top or beginning of each page. These keywords are what search engines find and display when they list you. Make sure they identify you and your purpose as clearly as possible: "McGillicuddy Official Site," "McGillicuddy News," and "McGillicuddy Reviews" would be good identifiers for McGillicuddy fans, as an example.

  Marketers can pay certain search engines, on a per-keyword basis, to make sure a site appears at the top of the browser's list when a user types in a keyword. This arrangement is sometimes called a *sponsored keyword search*. You pay per click—50 cents to $10 and more, depending on the keyword. Obviously, this can be prohibitively expensive for a small business.

- *List your Web site address on all other publicity and sales materials.* Include it on your CD packaging. Mention it in your outgoing voicemail messages. Put it everywhere, including on your stationery.
- *E-mail everyone you know—and everyone on your mailing list—to tell them about the site.* Include the hyperlinked URL in the e-mail.
- *Get press coverage and reviews of your site.* Anyone helping with publicity should get the word out—via e-mail, snail mail, or faxed press release—that you're on the Internet. Magazines and news outlets—especially Internet and computer "infotainment" publications and programs—review sites for their audiences, and they are always in need of new ones to report on. (As always, remember to design publicity pieces with the publication's preferences and audiences in mind.)
- *Get the URL linked on as many other sites as possible.* If you choose the sites wisely, this greatly enhances your site's visibility and increases the number of ways people can find out about you. Make sure you're on sites that reach your target audience—which will include various "lifestyle" as well as music sites.

  To identify sites that might want to link to yours, type in a keyword or phrase that most matches your music, like "political folk music," and then look at the first sites that appear on the search engine's list. These top-listed sites are quite likely the most visited sites, and therefore the ones you should try to get your link on. E-mail the site's webmaster to pitch your site and offer something in return. Be cooperative, not competitive. For example, suggest a trade deal in which you'll set up a link to a partner's site and they'll link to yours (and maybe provide an enthusiastic endorsement).

  Having your page linked from as many other sites as possible does more than bring you valuable traffic from those sites. The number of such links is also used by at least one major search engine when it ranks sites—the more sites that have links to yours, the higher your site appears in their directory.
- *Advertise on larger and more established sites, as well as on niche sites.* There are numerous Internet ad formats, and several ways to pay for ads. With the right choices you can make the ad work for you and your budget. (See pages 119 and 193 for more information on Web advertising.)

  Use the same call to action that you would in a print ad. Include a hyperlink, and set up a page where the user will be taken by the click—a *landing page*—that references the ad. (Providing a counter on this page will enable you to track responses.)

Measuring Your Site's Success

After your site has been online for a while, you may want to get a sense of how well it's attracting visitors. Weighing its value against the time, effort, and cost of building and maintaining it means measuring ROI—return on investment.

How do you evaluate this?

- *Use an onsite counter to track the number of hits or visitors to your page or site.* (Keep in mind, however, that a *hit* represents only a stop-off at your site, regardless of that hit's outcome.) The counter won't provide an exact measure of "interested" visits, but it will give you a general idea of how many times your server was queried for your page. (Not all ISPs offer counters, so check to make sure.)
- *Provide a "guest book" for your visitors to sign.* A guest book is basically an e-mail form on your page to record the visitor's name, e-mail address, and other general information that you might use in later marketing. (Because this involves an action on the part of the visitor, it signals interest—and opting in to your mailing list. It's a key indicator of your site's effectiveness.)
- *Track sales generated from your site, and compare them with site costs.* But remember, the value of your site is also measured in promotion—how many people are exposed to your message—and in converting first-time visitors to long-term adherents. The site may also be your most valuable marketing research tool because it gathers information about who your audience is and what they want. Don't forget to include these factors in any evaluation of your site's success.

POPULAR PERCEPTION

E-mail marketing is an experimental, outside-the-mainstream technique.

ALTERNATE REALITY

E-mail has become a standard part of the marketing mix.
In 2002, veteran singer-songwriter James Taylor included a direct-marketing e-mail blast that reached a reported million recipients as part of the marketing campaign for his album *October Road*. It probably played a key role in the album's success, overcoming Taylor's lack of exposure in more youth-oriented radio and other media.

USING E-MAIL TO PROMOTE YOUR MUSIC

E-mail offers a powerful way to get your message out to a lot of people at a minimal cost. It's best used to complement your standard media promotion and print-based direct marketing, whether or not you have your own Web site.

But you have to contend with some challenges. First, billions of e-mail messages are sent each year, making it difficult to get yours noticed. And along with fear of viruses, some marketers' deceptive practices have fueled a backlash against commercial e-mail—popularly termed *spam*—that makes it less likely recipients will open messages from someone they don't know. These obstacles should be on your mind as yo plan the writing and the mailing of your e-mail messages.

Basic Principles of Successful E-Mailing

Having tested e-mail tactics with varying degrees of success and failure, savv marketers offer the following pointers:

- *Target your e-mailings carefully.* To avoid having your messages discarded as junk mail, send them only to recipients who you know are interested— or are likely to become interested—in your music.
- *Offer what data shows the customer wants or is interested in.* Whether it's an announcement of a new CD or a discount on concert tickets, reward recipients for their interest.
- *Give recipients a reason to open the e-mail with a good subject line.* (See page 165 for more about subject lines.)
- *Avoid obvious hype or ad-speak.* Blatant hard-sell copy may turn off readers. Instead, treat the e-mail as a person-to-person tip or timely message that shares useful information.
- *Make it easy to respond.* Provide your clickable URL and other contact information in your text.
- *Provide an opportunity to opt out of future mailings.*

The last item is key to ethical e-mailing. From ISP spam filters to myriad requests that the Federal Communications Commission place sharp restrictions on commercial e-mail, the battle is on to protect consumers from deceptive e-mail practices. Such practices include

- overall deception, causing economic or other harm to the recipient
- misrepresenting the sender (the true source of the e-mail is other than the one stated)
- misrepresenting the content (opening the e-mail sends the recipient to a site other than what is stated in the subject line)
- not providing reliable contact information
- not providing a reliable opt-out system (the recipient may opt out but continue to receive mailings)

Take pains to keep the content and the intentions of your e-mail marketing straightforward and above-board, with clear potential value to every recipient.

Purposes and Types of E-Mail Communications

The essential purpose of e-mail marketing is to widely disseminate a promotional message or series of messages. In addition, an e-mail is a way to create an opportunity for contact between your customer and you.

Announcements, Offers, Reminders, and Confirmations. Most e-mail marketing is devoted to letting customers know about a product offering, whether it's a new CD, an upcoming concert, a Web site, or a special promotional offer such as a time-sensitive discount or a contest. Reminders or autoresponses are good ways to follow up on those types of e-mails.

E-Mail Newsletters. Sending a regular e-mail newsletter is an effective way to foster long-term, ongoing relationships with customers, which translates into building a fan base. With your newsletter, you provide a benefit to recipients in the form of "inside" information on an artist's current and upcoming activities. Although often time-consuming, it keeps you in constant contact with fans so you stay on their mental "radar screens."

A interactive newletter can also make it easier to gather demographic information from recipients. For example, a reader poll—with results posted in the following issue—can pull in fans' opinions on any number of subjects. Posting feedback about the newsletter itself will give readers a sense of ownership and community, while helping you keep customer contact information current.

And by including links to the artist's Web site, and to sites that sell the artist's CDs or offer downloads, your newsletter can help increase traffic to the places where it will do you the most good.

E-Mail Press Releases. Just as you send printed press releases by fax, so can you send digital press releases by e-mail. (For details on using press releases, see page 149.)

Content of Customer-Targeted E-Mail Messages

Every component of an e-mail message deserves your attention: the subject line, the from field, the To and CC or BCC fields, the message itself, and other must-include items such as hyperlinks, your contact information, and an opt-out button.

Subject Line. Remember the last time you got an e-mail from someone who obviously didn't know you, with its subject line screaming hype in capital letters? Chances are you deleted it without hesitation.

That's why the subject heading of a promotional e-mail is so important. It has to briefly summarize the e-mail's message and immediately attract the attention of a recipient inclined to be interested: "Reserve great Beck seats cheap." "Sample new Springsteen song for free."

The subject line should tune the recipient in to station WIIFM—"What's in it for me?"

Good subject lines are short, preferably under fifty characters, so they can be read easily and fit in the subject windows of most e-mail programs.

Another tip: It's better not to capitalize the first letter of every word in the subject line, to make it look less like an advertisement. Rather, it should suggest a personal message with only the first letter of the first word and any proper nouns in upper case.

Sender Field. If recipients recognize and value the name, they're more likely to open the e-mail. Put the name of the band or artist in the sender field.

Recipient Fields. You'll be sending e-mails to many recipients but doing it with single command by listing a single group address you've set up containing multiple individual e-mail addresses. For any number of reasons, you may not want recipients to see who else you're mailing to.

Message. The body of the e-mail message should be brief—short enough to make its point within a small e-mail window on a small computer monitor. Some marketers say that the first three lines are the ones that count. The following elements are essential:

- *Tell the recipient why the e-mail has been sent.* "You're receiving this because you've been a core supporter."
- *State the offer or make the announcement.* "Advance copies of our new CD are available at a special price." Don't bury the main message in a lower paragraph. Put it up near the top of the e-mail message.
- *Include a call to action, with a hyperlink or e-mail address.* Tell the e-mail recipient where they can make the purchase or take advantage of the offer.
- *The reader has to be able to do it with a quick click*—without having to type a complicated URL into an Internet address window.

Insert line breaks around the call to action, to emphasize it and separate it from other parts of the message. Sometimes special characters like asterisks can help draw attention, but use them sparingly.

Also remember that the tone of the message should be personal and direct, not stiff or pushy. Word it as if you were tipping off a friend to some cool new information.

Option to Opt In or Opt Out. Put the recipient in control of communication with you and thereby avoid creating a base of recipients annoyed at being spammed by you. Do this by letting the recipient indicate a preference for either receiving your future e-mails or being deleted from the mailing list.

The wording can be as simple as "If you want to continue receiving news about our music, click here," or "If you'd rather not receive further e-mails, click here."

Giving not just the chance to opt *out* but also the opportunity to actively opt *in* gives you more certainty of the subscriber's interest. You can add even more certainty by providing a *double opt-in*—a confirmation e-mail that asks the recipient to confirm a second time that he or she wants to receive future e-mails.

Signature. E-mail programs allow you to create an automatic signature that prints in every e-mail you send out. Make sure to include one that has all your contact information, including a clickable e-mail address or URL, so it will be easy to contact you.

Who to Send E-Mail To

The opt-out option alone can't prevent some recipients from reacting negatively to promotional e-mails. The only sure way to get a positive response is to limit your list of recipients to people who are "friendly" or are likely to be.

Earlier sections of the book address the process of building mailing lists (see pages 42 and 107). E-mail addresses should be included in the contact information you collect. You may also have e-mail addresses from personal contacts or your Web site, if you have one. (One ingenious marketer gathered e-mail addresses by offering a free CD to the first ten people who submitted their e-mail address, generating many submissions.)

Providing an opportunity to "receive news messages and special offers by providing us with your e-mail address" encourages the customer's opt-in.

As with off-line marketing, you will have at least two e-mail lists—one with customer addresses, another with media addresses—for starters. Mailing lists can also be rented from an existing music publication, a successful music site, or a commercial broker—such as TargitMail, Netcreations, and YesMail—that specializes in e-mail address lists.

Another option is participating in online newsgroups that match your target audience. If a key member of your support group happens to be a member of a related newsgroup, you might ask that person to include a plug for you on the next message they post to the group. If you're already a member of a newsgroup, you might post a notice about your music and send an MP3 to interested members.

But the best e-mail campaigns usually start with a "house list"—hard-core fans and enthusiasts whose names and addresses you've collected since becoming serious about marketing.

There are companies that specialize in managing your e-mail marketing, from providing lists to handling the mailing to tabulating results. But this outsourcing option is recommended only if you are well along in your career, with the financial resources to make it worthwhile.

Follow-Up E-Mail

You can reinforce your original message by sending a follow-up e-mail. This can be the kind of autoresponse mentioned earlier in this chapter.

An autoresponse can serve a number of purposes. It can confirm an opt-in to future mailings. It can acknowledge an opt-out, asking for feedback on the reason for opting out, and inviting the recipient to opt in in the future. The autoresponse can also mention other products, tell more about your upcoming plans, and restate all your contact information.

You can program autoresponses yourself, or you can hire a commercial vendor to handle them for you. Whether you do the latter depends on the size of your marketing budget.

A good way to find an e-mail marketing company is through an Internet search engine. One great overall source of information about e-mail marketing, including the names of specific service providers, is ClickZ (www.clickz.com).

Measuring E-Mail Success

How many recipients opened your e-mail? How many clicked on your link and then bought a CD? There are ways to find out.

Click-Through Rate. Create a new page on your Web site—a *landing page*—that corresponds to your e-mail message. It could have text such as "Thanks for checking this out. Here's the next step." The link you provide on your e-mail message jumps the reader to the landing page. A "hit counter" on the page will tell you how many click-throughs you got from your e-mail.

Conversion Rate. The number of click-through visitors that go on to buy your CD, order your MP3, or subscribe to your site—in other words, do what you asked them to do—is the basis for the *conversion rate*. Tracking sales from the landing page tells you the conversion rate of your e-mail campaign. (Five sales in 100 click-throughs would be a 5 percent conversion rate.) A good conversion rate is one that brings you revenues that exceed your costs.

Any of these measures will help you make sure you're using e-mail skillfully and more importantly, whether it's worth further time, money, and effort.

PROMOTION USING ESTABLISHED MULTI-ARTIST WEB SITES

In Chapter 9 you read about selling music through established multi-artist sites. You can also affiliate with one of these sites to promote your products, in addition to or instead of having your own Web page.

Aligning with such popular sites can get you exposure to a vast array of potential new listeners who can preview or buy your product easily and safely. But a multi-artist site might amount to a cyber-maze of hundreds of bands, with potentially negative side effects ranging from getting entirely overlooked to being perceived as just another "wannabe." To prevent this from happening you'll need to go into overdrive to position yourself as being different from all the rest.

Multi-artist sites offer a range of services, from categorizing you by genre to providing statistics on your popularity.

Hosting a Web Page. Many such sites help you set up a Web page and let you submit music files, photos, and bio information, which they feature so visitors can learn about you.

Adding You to a Search Engine. Sites may also help visitors find you by name or by song. There may be a link to your Web page within the music category descriptions.

Providing Market Research Tools. Some sites offer a database of national media and venues as well as other promotion support.

Offering Special Promotional Boosts. One site allows you to post MP3s, then links them stylistically to the music of well-known artists whose fans may then be drawn to your page.

Measuring the Success of Your Affiliation. Many sites offer a "statistics" option to allow you to view how many downloads and page views you're getting.

Here are examples of promotional services offered by a couple of sites current as of this writing:

- Grokster specializes in distributing and promoting unsigned artists. You provide Grokster with a link to the files (songs) you wish to share, along with a bio and a link to your Web site. Grokster includes your information in an e-mail newsletter and provides a forum in which you can interact with other Grokster users. The site also allows you to send messages about your upcoming concerts or new recordings to anyone who downloads your music.
- AudioGalaxy allows you to share your music for free with its thousands of users.
- MusicCity.com, a pay-to-be-featured site, places a picture and a promo line in their "more artists" section. You get a page with two pictures, a bio, Web links, and a place for your music to be downloaded.
- The independent-artist distributor CD Baby (which also charges users) sets up a Web page with photos, descriptions, and reviews to sell your music and link it to its galleries and search engines.

PROMOTION USING MAINSTREAM RETAIL MUSIC SITES

Today's Internet retail sites—Amazon.com, Tower Records online, and others—are essentially vast databases of music for sale. In ever-changing programs like those in brick-and-mortar stores, they provide extra promotion of a small selection of releases. With elaborate home pages, call-out boxes, lists of what's new, and extra-large hyperlinks—the e-tailers' versions of window displays, front-of-store racks, and end caps—these sites draw attention to featured artists and albums.

Internet retailers' promotional packages can be broad in scope. As an example, Amazon.com offers

- visibility on your music genre's home page
- e-mail announcements about your new releases, targeting customers interested in your music genre
- "Buy X, get Y" promotions, offering discounts when purchasing two items at once

The road to getting special promotion on a mass-market Internet retail site is similar to that for an on-the-street store: you pay promotion dollars, sometimes called "co-op funding" or "paid placements," to the site. But more and more mainstream retail sites are offering cheaper promotional services for small labels and independent musicians who have neither the money nor the clout to get the V.I.P. promotion treatment cited above.

Amazon.com, for example, has a member program in which it's possible to sell and promote music through their site other than via "paid placements." Amazon enables you to set up a product "detail page" showing your CD cover and offering information about the tracks and how to order. As part of its marketing support, Amazon also offers promotion through its Digital Music Network, which lets you upload MP3 tracks of your music and make them available for free download to help drive sales of your CDs.

Tower Records provides an affiliate program—as do many Web name-brands—that links your Web site to theirs and pays you a percentage of click-through sales. (And being associated with a well-known brand may increase your site's credibility.) On your Web site you display a choice of links: a Tower Records banner, a search box, or a specific recommended title.

Affiliate programs are long shots in terms of concrete results, and they can hurt you if association with them damages your "street cred." But they can also be modestly profile-boosting components of a larger promotion program. (The affiliate program guru Declan Dunn, found on the Web at www.activemarketplace.com, is a good source of information about online partnerships.)

A few large retailers have begun to cut deals to sell and promote music already affiliated with the indie Internet distributors. This points to broader avenues of promotion in the future for up-and-coming artists.

Keep on top of currently unfolding programs, both by reading trade magazines and by talking to live human beings in the promotion departments of retailers. Many of these people are more than willing to share what they know.

Wherever your music is posted, whether on your own site or elsewhere, undertake an Internet-based communications campaign to build exposure and possibly profits. The Internet is no longer merely an "extra" or an optional tool. Internet promotion is now fully integral to any artist's broad-based marketing strategy.

Chapter 12

Promoting the Product: Radio, Video, and Television

Airplay—the broadcasting of music on radio for free listening—has played a crucial role in the popularization of musicians since the 1920s. Similarly, television performances have, since the 1950s, converted many previously unknown artists into household names.

This aspect of music promotion isn't about getting news coverage, and it's not about building an interactive presence on the Internet. It's about *getting your music heard in the mass media.*

It's never been easy. "The hardest part of promotion is getting a record played," according to Richard Palmese, head of promotion at J Records.

For new music in particular, breaking into traditional radio (as opposed to Internet radio) has become more difficult over the years, for three reasons:

1. More musicians, which means increased competition.
2. Industry deregulation, reducing restrictions on how many stations a network can own, leading to control of the industry by a few corporate owners and leaving fewer entryways for untested music.
3. Increasing power of independent promoters who get placement of songs on the radio for fees that are beyond the reach of most indie artists.

Television appearances have been just as difficult for new artists to secure. But the rise of cable television has at least increased the number of outlets available to performers, even if many of those outlets are outside the radar of mass audiences.

With that as the background, let's look more closely at the role of airplay and TV in music marketing and promotion.

RADIO PROMOTION

In popular music, radio airplay is an invaluable promotion tool. It ranks among the Big Three of commercial activity in music, the other two being record sales and live performance. Having a number one hit single in *Billboard* magazine's Hot 100™ popularity chart—a measure, in part, of radio airplay—has long been considered one of the highest achievements in commercial music.

In classical music, jazz, and other commercially marginal genres, radio play is not as much of a factor in promoting sales of recordings, simply because those types of music get less radio play. Still, whatever airplay they eke out gives a vital boost to retail sales.

The promotional value of radio play is easy to understand: Listeners are exposed to the music, and if they like it, the chances that they'll buy the recording improve.

There are cases of performing artists making money without benefit of mainstream radio hits. One of the best examples is the Grateful Dead, which became one of the top concert draws in the world despite having only one top-40 radio hit in nearly thirty years of recording. But the general rule is that radio is a key part of the marketing program, even if it's airplay outside the commercial top 40.

If a recording is well served by exposure over the radio, what can the marketer do to make sure it happens? The answer is: promote the record to radio stations. (Although radio play is itself a form of promotion, the term *radio promotion* refers to the task of convincing radio decision makers to play the record.)

First off, marketers have to be aware of the architecture of the radio industry, including the types of broadcasters in operation and the kinds of programming they offer. With this information, marketers can better target stations that reach the artist's target audience.

Types of Radio Broadcasters

The radio industry is subdivided into two main sectors: commercial and noncommercial.

The commercial sector consists of national radio networks (such as ABC), regional radio networks, local independent stations, and syndicators. (Syndicators are production companies that package programming, which is then sold or licensed to radio stations. Shows may include announcers, music, interviews, and other elements. They allow time for insertion of commercial messages by the local stations.)

The noncommercial sector includes college and university stations, PRI (Public Radio International) affiliates, National Public Radio (NPR) members, regional networks (such as Minnesota Public Radio), and other small networks (such as Pacifica Radio).

The marketer will be looking at the full range of station types for airplay opportunities. For the start-up record label or the independent artist, the best opportunities for breaking into radio, generally speaking, will be found in the noncommercial sector.

Radio Markets and Programming Formats

Within the commercial and noncommercial radio sectors, there are thousands of stations in operation in the United States, programming in dozens of different formats.

What is a *format*? Essentially, it's the category of programming—classic rock, country, easy listening, or something else—chosen by a radio station's owner to attract its targeted audience.

What governs the choice of format? To get the answer to this, you have to look closely at what makes the radio industry tick. And that insight, in turn, will reveal much about why it can be so difficult for an unknown artist to get airplay on national commercial radio.

In the commercial sector, the governing force essentially boils down to this: Radio stations are in business to make a profit, not necessarily to showcase the best records. Their money comes from advertisers, who pay the stations to run ads. Radio stations need to attract advertisers. To attract advertisers, they need to get *market share*—that is, a significant portion of the targeted audience. The larger the market share, the more money the station can charge for advertising.

Basically, then, commercial radio is in the business of providing advertisers with the largest possible number of ears to listen to their ads.

Advertisers, in turn, choose the stations that offer the best opportunities to reach the correct demographic for their products.

What's a *demographic*? It's the set of statistical characteristics—such as age, gender, education, and economic status—defining a population segment. This should sound familiar; as discussed in Chapter 4, you, the marketer, are often in the business of aiming your product at audiences with particular demographic characteristics.

Just like product marketers, radio has its target audiences. Through research, the radio industry has subdivided the human race into demographic markets—specific population segments that programs will attempt to attract.

The two primary markets that radio stations target are the youth market and the adult market. Stations further subdivide these according to a variety of demographic characteristics.

The radio person selling time to potential advertisers has to convince them that at a certain time of day the station can deliver X number of listeners within a targeted demographic—listeners, say, between ages 18 and 24, who make between $25,000 and $50,000 a year, and who are inclined to buy the potential advertiser's kind of products.

(Market or audience share of a particular station—that is, a station's portion of listeners who have their radios turned on at a given time—can be determined by outside firms, like Arbitron, that collect data using controlled samples of listeners. Stations check their success in reaching targeted audiences by periodically checking their Arbitron rating—the radio equivalent of television's Nielsen ratings.)

To attract listeners within the chosen demographic, the station chooses the type of programming—the format—that appeals to the largest segment of that demographic. For the youth market (late teens through mid-twenties), for example, roughly 90 percent of programming is derived from commercially released records dominated by pop music and its derivatives. Programs feature deejay "personalities." The tastes of the adult market, on the other hand, have been tougher to pinpoint. The general view has been that post-teens prefer "softer" music.

Within those broad guidelines, the following music formats have proven the most commercially viable:

- *Commercial Hit Radio (CHR)* (also known as Contemporary Hit Radio and Top 40): Current mainstream pop hits.
- *Rock:* New music by such straight-ahead rock artists as Bruce Springsteen, Red Hot Chili Peppers, Korn, and Tool.
- *Classic Rock:* Old music by such "classic" favorites as the Who, the Beatles, and the Rolling Stones.
- *Alternative Rock* (also called Modern Rock and New Rock): New rock artists and performers whose music is considered non-mainstream. Aimed at young audiences.
- *Adult Contemporary (AC):* Smooth, mellow rock and oldies—artists such as Celine Dion, Michael Bolton, Sting, Phil Collins, Don Henley, Linda Ronstadt, Enrique Iglesias, and Rod Stewart. For ages 25 to 54.
- *Adult Top 40* (otherwise known as Hot AC, Adult Standard, and Adult Hits): Hits by artists who appeal to more "mature" listeners than artists in the Alternative or Modern Rock category; examples are Sheryl Crow, the Dave Matthews Band, and Tori Amos.
- *Adult Album Alternative (AAA)* (also known as Adult Alternative): Music aimed at maturing audiences who retain their interest in rock (an audience termed the "gray-haired ponytail set" by one radio station); examples of artists in this left-of-center category are Van Morrison, Bonnie Raitt, U2, Elvis Costello, and Mark Knopfler.
- *Soft AC and Easy Listening* (sometimes considered two different categories): Even mellower music for the adult market (the Carpenters, Helen Reddy, John Denver). Includes pop instrumental music, sometimes called "beautiful music." For those aged 55 and older.
- *Smooth Jazz:* Includes such "light" jazz artists as Kenny G, Pat Metheny, Fourplay, and Tom Scott.
- *Country:* A range of styles subdivided into such categories as Country Rock and Pop Country. There are about 2,000 country-oriented stations in the U.S., mostly in the South Atlantic and West South Central states. It's the "second most likely to succeed format," according to one survey.
- *Urban* (also known as Rhythm and Blues, R&B, and Black Music): Includes new rap, hip-hop, R&B, and dance tracks. Examples of artists popular in 2002 include Mos Def, Wu-Tang Clan, Busta Rhymes, and Alicia Keys.
- *Urban Adult Contemporary (Urban AC)* (also known as R&B Adult, Rhythmic, and Urban Oldies): Includes soul music and other sounds aimed at the maturing "urban music" audience. Chaka Khan, Prince, and Luther Vandross are some artists who have been placed in this category.

There are numerous other radio formats. Here are some of them:

Classical	Jazz	International
Oldies	Nostalgia	Latin
Pre-Teen	Religious	Variety

Radio stations change format frequently—sometimes as often as once a year—depending on changing market trends, the amount of competition from other stations, and the preferences of new owners.

Bear in mind, too, that the names of formats change over time. What is now called Easy Listening was once called Middle of the Road (MOR). What is now called Urban was at one time called Rhythm and Blues. It's a good idea to keep an eye on *Billboard, Radio and Records,* Radio Business Report (www.rbr.com), Radio-locator (www.radio-locator.com), ArtistDirect.com (http://ubl.artistdirect.com/music/ubl/radio), the *CMJ Directory,* Broadcast Data Systems' list of formats (www.bdsonline.com/stations/index.html), and other trade information sources so that you stay up-to-date on the latest terminology.

One indicator of the importance of listener preferences in station programming is the practice of employing what is called reverse programming. Research has shown that many people will tend to listen to a radio station—let it drone on—until they hear something they *don't* like. Consequently, some stations attempt to determine not so much what their listeners will like, but what they won't like, and then avoid it. Such reverse programming is used when a station wants to maintain current audience share, rather than build a new audience.

So that's the backdrop to the music decision-making process that occurs in the commercial radio sector. The station formats and demographics will be your guide in choosing target stations for your promotion effort.

How Do Stations Choose Records?

Now let's look at the day-to-day, week-to-week factors influencing the choice of whether to give airplay to a particular record, assuming that it conforms to a station's format.

Programmers are often under pressure from station owners to play it safe—which is why they're unlikely to experiment with an untested record. They like to play records that have already begun to build some momentum, or that have a good chance of making it. Evidence of success comes in the following forms:

- The record is already successful on other stations.
- The record is by an established artist with a track record of hits.
- The record is already on sales and airplay charts in trade magazines and tip sheets.
- The record is currently generating sales in record stores.
- Listeners are calling the station to request the song.
- Market tests indicate that listeners like—or do not dislike—the recording.
- The record is being recommended by a promoter—a record company representative who shows up weekly at the radio station to push new records.

"Very few radio programmers rotate records by gut," J Records' Richard Palmese told *New York Times* writer Lynn Hirschberg in 2002. In the same article, Hirschberg describes Clear Channel Communications—owner of 1,200 stations—testing a song by playing it on the radio a few hundred times during off-hours and then conductin "call out" research—phoning listeners at random and playing ten seconds of the son If enough respondents recognize it and like it, Clear Channel adds it to the playlist.

Once stations have determined that a song is worth adding, they create their ow weekly playlists, with indications of how often a record should be played. Those ne the top are considered to be in *heavy rotation*. Those in the middle are in *medium rot tion*. Only a handful of new songs are added to a playlist each week.

Needless to say, it is extremely difficult to break into that list. The way to start to learn who makes the decisions.

Who Chooses the Music to Play?

The person responsible for making up the weekly playlist of a station or cluster stations is the program director (PD). The PD oversees a music director (MD). It is th MD's responsibility to deal with programming details—that is, keep abreast of curre releases, read the trades, and meet with record promoters. (Music directors generall set aside specific hours each week to talk to promoters and label reps.) The MD the makes recommendations of records for the PD to add to the playlist. At smalle stations, a single person may serve as both program director and music director.

Decisions about playlists are increasingly being made by regional program directo or by corporate owners of networks of stations—owners who choose the music to b played on all their stations. Obviously, this represents a contraction of the broadca distribution channel, making it more difficult for makers of unusual or innovativ music to get their records played on the radio.

Independent Promoters

At the beginning, you may be handling radio promotion yourself by contactin college stations. But at some point in your campaign you'll find it necessary to hir an independent promotion firm to take over the tasks of meeting with programmin staff, making follow-up calls, and handling other promotional details. The nee usually arises when your campaign has already generated some momentum an begun to move from regional to national, or noncommercial to commercial.

At this time, the placement of songs on commercial top-40 and rock radio handled virtually exclusively through the independent promotion system. Inde pendent promoters establish close relationships with stations and networks—ofte with owners or general managers rather than the lower-level program directors—tha may involve making promotional payments for adding songs to playlists. An inde pendent promoter may gain a "lock" on a station or cluster of stations and become kind of exclusive gateway between the stations and the record labels who want the songs played on those stations. With fewer "clusters" around, as mentioned early i the chapter, the indie promoter with a lock on one wields a huge amount of clout– and can command huge payments from record companies.

Costs for independent promotion vary depending on the radio market sector. Yo might hire a firm to target college radio for a month for a fee of $1,500. On the hig

nd, indie promoters may charge major labels well over $250,000 for each single that
they successfully place on top-40 radio nationally, including up-front fees and $1,000
to $8,000 per station "add." That's not a misprint. The largest indie promotion firms
currently include Tri-State Promotions and Jeff McClusky & Associates.

To find a promotion firm, ask around. Get recommendations from managers of
successful artists involved in music similar to yours. Look on the Internet using the
keywords *independent record promoters*. And hunt through directories such as the *Recording
Industry Sourcebook* and online listings on sites like MusicIsland (www.musicisland.com)
and Artist Direct (www.artistdirect.com).

Promotion companies that help independent artists reach college and community
radio include Advanced Alternative Media (AAM), Fanatic Promotion, McGathy
Promotions, Planetary Group, The Syndicate, Team Clermont, Triage, and Vision Trust.
Look for them on the Web.

But again, you might want to hold off on hiring an independent promoter until
you've laid the initial promotional groundwork yourself.

How to Promote to Radio

"Getting on the radio is like mounting a military campaign," according to marketer
Tom Colson of J Records.

If you don't yet command an army, how should you approach the job of promoting a record to radio? Apart from adhering to standard industry protocol, there
are some guidelines to follow that will increase your chances of success. Among them:
start small, target the right stations, present a convincing promotion package, establish
positive relationships with people in radio, and coordinate radio promotion with the
other parts of the marketing campaign.

The Basic Process. Before approaching a station with product, it's important to find
out the name of the person to contact at the station and the best time to make
that contact.

Ideally, you'll telephone this person first. (In the case of mass radio promotion, the
first step may be to mail a promotion package—a basic one-sheet and a CD.) In the
telephone call, briefly describe who you are and the record you're representing, and
then ask if you can make an appointment to meet with the music director. If the
answer is negative (possibly because the MD's time is all booked up), ask if they would
like you to mail them a promotion package and a copy of the record.

If you're ultimately able to set up an appointment, bring promotion materials
along with copies of the recording. At the meeting you'll discuss the recording with
the music director, the goal being to make the MD want to add the song to the
station's playlist. Listen to the music with the MD, and go through the promotion
material, emphasizing information that will convince the MD of the disc's potential
for popularity. Points to mention include radio play on other stations, touring dates
or live performances in the region of the station, press and media coverage and advertising, and sales activity in local stores.

That's the general order of events. Now here are some tips for improving you chances.

Start Small. Your best bet, if you're not an established label, is to start locally. Aim fir at college and community stations in the artist's home region—the area where th artist performs regularly. That way you'll have a built-in promotional angle to prese to music directors. ("The artist has been performing here for years—has regular dat lined up for the next month, in fact—and has a large local following.") Starting sm: has the additional benefit of ensuring that local radio play and live performances ha a reciprocal promotional benefit.

While you're at it, it wouldn't hurt to encourage audiences at live performanc to call local radio stations to request airplay of the single.

As touring expands to new regions, expand radio promotion to stations in tho regions. (Keep in mind that with expansion will eventually come the need to empl indie promoters—unless you, the marketer, can clone yourself to handle sever regions simultaneously.)

Target the Right Stations. As with publicity, it's important to aim for outlets that rea your targeted audience. (After all, it wouldn't make much sense to promote an ele tronic noise band to a mainstream country music station.)

The way to ensure an appropriate match is to do some preliminary researc Check radio station directories that list stations by region, by format, by audience, ar by market share. There are books that serve this purpose, including the *Radio Pou Book,* the *Broadcasting and Cable Yearbook,* and Gebbie Press's *All-in-One Media Directo* Also, the World Wide Web has several media lists that sort stations by various criteri They include the BRS Radio Directory (www.radio-directory.com), the Gebbie si (www.gebbieinc.com/radintro.htm), Radio-Locator (www.radio-locator.com), ar the Ultimate Band List (ubl.artistdirect.com).

Make a list of radio stations with the format most likely to accept your produc

Within each radio format are key stations that report their weekly playlists current or new songs (and how often they're playing the songs) to music trade ma: azines and other organizations, which then use that information, along with oth data, to compile their charts of currently popular records. Because the charts ha such a potent effect on the success of a record, getting your song added by those k reporting stations should be a priority.

According to Tim Kolleth, head of radio promotion at Alligator Records, "Th important thing is, basically, decide who you want to target, what format you pe ceive the music succeeding at most, make sure all the reporters that affect the char receive a copy, then make sure they listen to it come hell or high water."

For more on the intricacies of this process, see Kolleth's interview on page 277

The *Billboard* magazine weekly Hot 100™ Singles chart collects the radio portic of its data from the electronic sampling service Nielsen Broadcast Data Systems (BDS BDS samples some 1,100 stations in 128 markets, in about ten overall formats, broke ıt into subformats. (*Billboard* also collects playlists from selected stations BDS doesn't ɔver.) The specific stations BDS logs are listed on its Web site, www.bdsonline.com. ɹadio promotion on the mass-market level should obviously target these BDS-ɔonitored stations.

'esent a Convincing Promo Package. The promotion kit presented to radio stations— ther in person or by mail—consists of essentially the same material used to attract distributor. Rather than a full press kit, use a one-sheet and a copy of your CD. (See ɪge 95 for more about one-sheets.)

It's extremely important that the one-sheet present a convincing summary of the t's previous successes and potential for continuing growth in popularity. It should early highlight the points that will be of key interest to station music directors, such previous radio play, distribution strategy, current tour plans, and track record of ɪedia coverage.

Marketers sometimes try to make promo packages more memorable by including inkets or novelty items of some kind. They can lean toward the ridiculous, earning ɪe derision of radio staff, or they can cleverly tie in with the artist's image, achiev-g the desired effect of getting positive attention. Singer Jacqui Naylor, for example, cluded red roses in her mailings of a CD that emphasized red in its packaging.

ːtablish Positive Relationships with People in Radio. Music directors at radio stations e besieged with people promoting records. Chances are they'll give preference to

---

NIELSEN BROADCAST DATA SYSTEMS (BDS)

Nielsen Broadcast Data Systems, owned by VNU, Inc. (the parent company of *Billboard* magazine and also the owner of Nielsen SoundScan), is a computer-based system of tracking radio play of individual songs. It is used by *Billboard* in the compilation of its music charts, and by ASCAP in its survey of radio airplay for purposes of calculating performance royalties payable to its members.

The information is also used by radio programmers to help them decide what to play on the air (essentially, what others are already playing), by record executives who want information on the radio play of their tracks, and by many others.

BDS works by monitoring radio station airplay and matching music it "hears" with music that is stored in its database. It can output the music title, date of performance, and time of performance, thus yielding highly accurate information for use by those whose business decisions rely on radio airplay data.

BDS can only track airplay if it has a "fingerprint" of the music in its system. To get your track into their records, send submissions promptly to BDS, 8100 NW 101 Terrace, Kansas City, MO, 64153, Attn: Encoding Department. For more information, visit www.bdsonline.com.

those whom they trust, or with whom they have established good relationships. Yo should aim to be among that group.

Building trust means consistently demonstrating professionalism in your interactio with station personnel: following up on mailings, being proactive without being push knowing the station's format and demographics, knowing your product inside and o so that you can answer questions, being knowledgeable about the music business ar current musical trends, and generally showing that you know what you're doing.

Building a relationship has more to do with the "people" side of the equation. Th introverts among us may bemoan the fact that "it ain't what you can do, it's who yo know," but the fact remains that in the music business—as in many other businesses— "who you know" goes a long way toward getting the job done. In radio promotio you need to be outgoing, sociable—the kind of person to whom someone would be happy to extend an invitation to meet again a week later, or the week after that. those calls.

Networking, socializing, providing favors—all are unofficial ways people grea the rusty wheels of business and commerce the world over—whatever the industry Like it or not, you the promoter-marketer-salesperson will have to put on your par clothes (figuratively speaking, of course) and become a glad-hander. A people perso

So go ahead. Take that music director to the occasional lunch. But don't forg to enjoy yourself in the process. This is the music business, after all. It's supposed be fun!

Coordinate with Other Parts of the Marketing Campaign. The most effective radio pl occurs in synchronization with live performances and other types of promotion. A components of the campaign then work together to create a kind of media blit Audiences see ads for concerts, hear the music on the radio, read reviews of th record, watch an interview on local cable TV, become hyperaware of the presence this music entity, and ultimately buy the record.

- When you undertake a promotion to radio, time it so that any radio play will occur simultaneously with a live performance in the station's region. And make sure the music director is aware of the upcoming performances—it'll make the MD more likely to want to play the record.
- Make sure that if a station plays the record, the listener will be able to buy the record. Have it stocked and available at retail stores or on the Web
- Keep marketing team members—including distributors and retail accounts—abreast of any station adds and news about airplay activity.
- Compile a *radio report* to circulate among marketing participants. (This is a fourth important marketing list for you to maintain—others being lists of customers, media, and retailers.) In the radio report, list
  - each station contacted
  - date of contact

- action resulting from contact ("will review," "no answer," "will add," "in light rotation," "in heavy rotation," and so on)
- comments of radio staffperson ("great record, I'm a big fan," "not the kind of thing we play")

Marc Lipkin of Alligator Records describes how that label handles synchronizing promotion:

> "We have a separate radio department, a retail department, and an advertising department. We all work together. We have weekly staff meetings at 4:00 on Friday afternoons. We all go around and tell each other what's coming up, [such as] a big feature in the Chicago Tribune that's running a week from Friday.
>
> "If there is, our radio department will get on the phone with a station like WXRT and say, 'Hey we've got this feature coming. Are you guys playing the record? Let's work out something together. There's a big show coming up in two weeks. Let's see if we can work out some kind of promotion together.'
>
> "The retail department will then go to the local retail stores and talk to whoever the buyers are for the big chain stores and say, 'We've got this major feature running on December 14. Can we make sure we've got stock in the stores?' Because once people see this feature and hear the song on the radio, they're going to want to buy the record. And if we can finally get the consumer to buy the record and there's no record in the store, well, we lose bad.
>
> "It works both ways, too. If our radio guy says that WXRT here in Chicago just added the new Shemekia Copeland record, that helps me to go to the Tribune and say, 'Hey, have you heard the new album yet? XRT just added it and she's coming to town in a week.'
>
> "Every piece of the puzzle has to work together, or you're just spinning your wheels."

Handling Rejection. What if you can't generate any radio interest? Keep in mind that even if radio stations reject a record initially, it's not necessarily the end of the road. They might add the record to their playlists sometime later, if they see that live dates and press are generating growing audience demand.

For example, the Gin Blossoms single "Hey Jealousy" couldn't get airplay on alternative radio. The band continued to tour and generate word-of-mouth interest. Months later the song was picked up by a Los Angeles rock station. The airplay translated into growing record sales, which caused the song to be added by several more stations. More touring success combined with more radio attention and more record sales, all adding up to a successful—if slow-to-pick-up-steam—marketing effort.

So don't treat an initial lack of radio enthusiasm as a rejection. View it as an impetus to work on building an audience, gathering press coverage, and marketing locally

until you generate so much grassroots excitement that radio stations will be compelle
to take a second look.

College Radio as Career-Launching Pad

For both the start-up record peddler and the more established marketer, college radi
is often where all radio promotion begins. National commercial radio is largely inac
cessible to those not affiliated with major labels. College radio, on the other hand,
within reach.

Where commercial radio is singles oriented, college radio is more freewheeling i
its programming, offering a wider selection of music than commercial radio and the
providing better opportunities for smaller acts to get airplay. Often, success at the
college-radio level snowballs into acceptance by commercial radio.

Where commercial radio programmers deal primarily with indie promoter
college radio deals also with artists, label reps, and managers.

College radio is also used by major labels to test-market their acts before promo
ing them at the national commercial level. The songs that college radio chooses
play, and the geographical locations of listener interest, help guide subsequent ma
keting and promotion decisions by the record company marketing team.

Stephanie LeBeau, head of a San Francisco–based independent promotion compan
called Vision Trust, specializes in college radio, and she emphasizes its importance t
the careers of developing artists:

> "[In the case of more-established labels] college radio is the first market
> all artists/bands are sent to. Some call it a test market. The reason this
> is the first market is that it is a free format and [the deejays] can play
> whatever tracks they wish. The stations are supplied with records, and
> it is up to the volunteering music director to pick and choose what music
> will best suit his or her market.
>
> "The end result [of college radio promotion] is to create a buzz, build
> awareness, and build a solid foundation from which the artists/bands
> can grow. For some majors it's not only to create a buzz but also to help
> sort out [identify] the commercial hit track. The label will usually have
> the single chosen, but then the information coming back from the college
> market could change the track or confirm it.
>
> "The better the artist does at college radio, the more ammo, if you
> will, the label will have at getting national commercial [radio] interest.
> [In the case of small-label and indie promotion efforts, college radio]
> informs the artists/bands of where their markets are, what the popular
> tracks are, and indeed if they have a market. They can use the infor-
> mation collected and schedule a tour, get consignment with retail stores
> (because now they know where a buying market is), or even get a
> distribution deal. The [college radio play] information also shows a

buyer/investor that the artist/band is worthy of further investing with the potential of making their money back.

"Our job [as college radio promoters] is to make sure the music director— who is a volunteer in most cases—doesn't let the release we are representing slip through the cracks, the black hole, which could mean [being used as] a coffee coaster in the lobby or sold to the nearest used-record-store bin."

"The average college radio station receives anywhere from 50 to 100 CDs per week. That is one reason the life of records in this market is so short. The other reason is that the deejays can play whatever tracks they fancy. Which means the record will burn out at a faster rate. Every week is crucial. The life ["impact time"] of a record in this market is 10 weeks. At the end of the promotion the label or artist will still continue to get played, but the impact time is gone.

"If the band can afford to hire a college independent radio promotion company, it may prove money well spent, especially when you consider the long-distance calls and the impact/life of your record at the stations. The music director will also take your CD more seriously coming from a person they trust. Most music directors don't like talking to band members, because they are not objective and usually do not know what the radio station is currently playing or when the MD holds their office hours. They would have to do weeks of research just to obtain that information. But of course, if there is a dedicated band member who will take the time to do all the grassroots work, like readers of this book, they may be able to accomplish a lot on their own."

VIDEO AND TELEVISION AS PROMOTIONAL TOOLS

How do videos and television fit into the music marketing and promotion picture? What impact do they have on the distribution and consumption of popular music?

Like radio, they provide outlets for getting music to the ears of consumers. Unlike radio, they provide the added promotional power of visual information, filling out the consumer's mental picture of the artist.

Performers for whom visual exposure has been vital—or extremely valuable— including the following:

- The Beatles, whose appearance on *The Ed Sullivan Show* in 1964 made them household names in the United States
- Jennifer Lopez, whose films and videos meshed with her albums to create a multidimensional persona
- Tina Turner, who staged a comeback in the mid-1980s with the help of video

Handled intelligently, videos and television can make the difference between relegation to the commercial fringe and acceptance by mass audiences.

Video Promotion

Since the launch of Music Television (MTV) in the early 1980s, the music video ha
become a staple of the music business. While they won't necessarily "break" an arti
or directly affect record sales, videos are generally thought to have an important ind
rect impact on solidifying and increasing sales. They are indispensable for increasin
name recognition and shaping an artist's public image and personality.

But music videos have thrown more weight on the shoulders of musical per
formers. In the mass-market pop realm, at least, it's no longer enough to be musicall
proficient; the artist now also requires a visual image that permits exposure in
variety of visual as well as audio media. The dawn of the music video was also th
dawn of the cross-media marketing vision that now dominates the entertainmer
industry. For example, Madonna—one artist—generates revenue streams throug
recordings, videos, movies, television guest appearances, the Internet, magazine arti
cles, and books.

For the beginning act, a commercial video isn't essential. The Gin Blossoms, fc
example, initially "had no need whatsoever for a video other than it's occasionall
useful, whether it's a sales presentation or in some remote local show. We didn't thin
MTV for a second," label executive Jim Guerinot told writer Bud Scoppa for a
article for ASCAP.

Only after the marketing-promotion machine has been in motion for a while—
generating radio airplay, press coverage, and the rest—will it be time to approach th
video programming giants for a shot at adding a clip to their rotation schedules.

In the meantime, shooting some digital video for streaming on the artist's Web sit
is a good way to get started.

When it comes time to prepare a video, follow all the guidelines you applied t
other promotional materials. Make sure the style and mood of the clip match th
image and personality you are trying to convey. Make the look of the video reflec
the nature of the artist and music—just like CD packaging and print ads.

CONVENTIONAL WISDOM

Videotape your performances as a tool for honing your visual presentation.
Study videos of your live shows as a reality check for how you look and present
yourself. Eventually you may even come up with broadcast-quality footage. If so,
promote it to local cable stations for possible programming.

Television Promotion

Now for television itself. How important is it? Let's put it this way: if an artist per
forms on *The Late Show with David Letterman*, *The Tonight Show*, or *Saturday Nigh
Live*, it means one of two things: (1) it's a new artist who, through the appearanc
will instantly become known to millions, or (2) it's an already famous artist who

rough the appearance, will promote a new record to millions. TV is one power-
ul promotion tool.

To promote to television, follow the general approach used for both publicity and
adio promotion.

Contacting programs involves sending press kits and video clips—on DVD or
CD-ROM—to individual TV producers. As with publicity and radio promotion, the
press kits should provide convincing information about sales success, media coverage,
opularity, and so on. (The producers want to know that an audience exists for the
lip they are being asked to broadcast.) After mailing, use follow-up telephone calls
ɔ verify receipt and determine the degree of interest.

As with radio, start small, mainly because you'll have to; the national programs will
arely consider you unless you've established a track record. At initial stages, think in
erms of local cable programs—any type that broadcasts video clips or includes
ausical guests.

Target appropriate programs. Channel-surf until you're familiar with all the rele-
ant programs on the dial. (For categories of shows, refer to the list in "Broadcast
Media" on page 141.) Find out the name of the producer of each show, so that when
ou establish contact you're able to do it person-to-person rather than send your
naterial to "whom it may concern."

Create a database of television production companies, allowing fields for names
f individuals, contact information, representative shows, date of most recent action
ıken ("mailed promo kit," "spoke to producer by phone," for example), and result
f action.

Your responsibilities don't end at the point of "making the sale." As a marketer,
ou've got to work this new injection of promotional fuel to the advantage of the
ntire marketing machine. When producers indicate interest, work with them to
nsure that the video programming or the on-air performance occurs on a date (or
ates) around the same time that a recording is available in stores and tracks are
etting played on the radio. When this works well, as mentioned earlier in the chapter,
ou'll achieve a full-blown media blitz.

While you're proactively seeking television coverage, there's always the chance that
'V may come after you, if you've been doing your homework in other sectors of
our marketing. This happened to publicist Marc Lipkin:

> "I went to Shemekia Copeland's debut in Atlanta, and one of the local
> papers, maybe Creative Loafing, gave her a small blurb that I had set
> up with a writer. I had supplied him with the material and given him
> info on the gig.
>
> "The blurb was read by a producer for CNN, who said, 'Oh that
> sounds interesting.'…We produced this seven-minute feature on Shemekia
> that ran not just on the CNN Entertainment Weekly show in prime
> time, but they had it run on the morning show. They cut it up and put

*it on Headline News in a two-minute version, and even a 30-second
version that ran on airlines' in-flight entertainment.*

*"I mean, we're still getting mileage out of this, and I had just sent
out a press release with a phone call, and the local writer said, 'Hey, I
never heard of her, but the record sounds good. I'll do a blurb for it.'*

*"I also had her on the WGN morning news show, and the booker for
that show is coming to the gig tonight and bringing a bunch of her friends.
And one of her friends is the senior talent producer for* The Oprah
Winfrey Show. *I've been trying to break through to Oprah for ten
years now. I couldn't even get a call back from these people. But now
I have a stroke of luck tonight, a senior producer coming to her gig."*

Chapter 13

Promoting the Product: Sales Incentives, Live Shows, and Other Methods

There are always more ways to promote. A marketing-promotion campaign uses a wide range of tactics, all carefully coordinated to reinforce each other and add punch to the overall effort.

Along with ongoing press coverage, Internet promotion, direct mail, radio play, and television exposure, you'll frequently want to hot-wire the marketing program with special promotions to achieve short-term ends—such as promoting a new CD a month from now in a town where the act is booked to perform. In-store sales promotions and spot ads in local media are two of the options you have available.

Other strategies worth adding to your repertoire include reaching more people by cross-promoting—that is, partnering with another business that reaches the same kind of audience as you but a different segment of it. Another is to engage in what might be termed "extreme networking"—attending industry conventions and trade shows to meet a lot of businesspeople in a short time, both to stay abreast of industry trends and to meet potential business partners.

It's also important to be aware of the promotional power of performing live. Artists are doing more than playing songs when they're up on stage—even though giving the best possible performance has to be the main goal at that particular moment. In effect, they're selling themselves as performers.

Let's look at these promotion techniques in greater detail.

SALES PROMOTION

Certain types of promotion are designed to encourage immediate sales or draw attention to the product via methods other than publicity and advertising. Such programs fall in to the category of sales promotion.

Sales promotions are generally of two types: (1) programs aimed at members of the distribution channel, such as wholesale distributors and retail outlets, and (2) programs aimed directly at consumers.

Distribution Channel Promotions

As mentioned in Chapter 7, when stores stock your CD, you want to have their display it prominently. That also goes for Internet retailers, as discussed in Chapter 11. In other words, you want the stores and e-tailers to give your music special treatment.

But stores have no vested interest in doing this; all they care about is that products—*whatever* they are—are selling. Add to this the heavy label competition for limited display space and you might quickly conclude that you'll have to give retailers some kind of incentive to specially promote your product. You'd be right.

What kinds of benefits can you provide to retailers so that they will agree to give you prominent display space? There are several that are standard.

One is a reduction in price for an order of recordings in return for prominent display in the store. This can run you anywhere from several hundred dollars for a CD promotion in a single store to many thousands of dollars for a promotion in multiple outlets of a national chain. It would buy you space in window displays, listening booths, wall displays, end caps, and tables for a period of several days to a week. You pass this price reduction on to the retailer via your distributor.

In addition, you can promote your album through the record store using what is called co-op advertising. Here's how it works: The retailer places a newspaper ad that plugs both the store and several CDs being sold there. (You've seen these ads: Sam Goody touting a handful of new albums, for example.) You pay for the portion of the ad that features your product. The retailer pays for the entire ad and then deducts your share of the cost from its account with your distributor. The distributor, in turn, deducts this amount from what it owes you. The retailer often coordinates the ad with a prominent in-store display and a product discount.

Several of the larger record-store chains publish magazines to promote new music that they sell. For example, Musicland puts out *Request. Pulse!* was published by Tower Records for 19 years. Part of retail promotion is getting the stores to cover your product in their magazines. Your incentive package can include a request that the store provide such coverage.

Consumer Sales Promotions

Sales promotion programs can be aimed directly at consumers. Giving prospective buyers an extra "push" is often what's needed to get them to make a purchase. There are any number of ways to do this, and marketers are constantly coming up with new ones. Here are some incentives that are fairly common:

- Tear-out coupons, printed in newspapers or other media, that offer money off the selling price of products purchased within a specified time period
- Direct discounts off the retail price, indicated with stickers on the products themselves
- More product (such as a bonus track on a CD—a new studio recording added to a live album, for example) without an increase in price
- A premium (such as a poster) included with the product at no extra charge

- Two products (such as a full-length CD plus a CD single) for the price of one
- Merchandise (such as T-shirts, coffee mugs, and cigarette lighters) either given away or sold
- CD samplers (containing several tracks from a new album) given away at retail stores, timed to coincide with radio play and a concert
- CD sampler giveaways at concerts
- Contests, coordinated with local radio stations and retail stores
- Creating artist or label "V.I.P. groups" on a Web site, and providing members with special deals, such as free merchandise

LIVE PERFORMANCE AS PROMOTION

When you perform in front of an audience, you are engaged in a form of promotion. You're communicating with an audience in a way that, hopefully, sells them on you and your music. They may, as a result, want to seek out your new CD. At the same time, you may gain increased media coverage in the form of reviews and personality profiles in the press.

Typically, tours are scheduled to coincide with the release of a new recording to set in motion a two-pronged marketing blitz, each component reinforcing the visibility of the other.

Because of the promotional value of touring, record labels often provide financial tour support (repayable by the artist out of record royalties). The investment pays off in the form of a steadily growing audience base, which eventually translates into record sales.

This process worked for the Gin Blossoms, as explained by Jerry Weintraub, A&M Records Vice President of Artist Development, in an article written by Bud Scoppa for ASCAP:

> "I was into that band hundreds of thousands of dollars in tour support—
> they were our road dogs. The Gin Blossoms could play anywhere, at any
> time. Some of those shows they had to do I wouldn't wish on anybody.
> But it paid off.
>
> "The band was really super—they did it in a van; they worked. It was
> a healthy commitment of cash because it took so long; relatively, on a per-
> week basis, it was modest. But when you have a band that's willing to go
> through that kind of ordeal for as long as they were willing to go through it,
> the cash added up.
>
> "The thing that kept happening, though, that made it worthwhile, where
> it became clear to us that we needed to keep doing this, is there was growth.
> We were getting growth in terms of, oh, 200 people at a show is now 320
> the next time they show up. Then they'd go support someone, go back in
> that market again and it'd be 500 people, support someone, come back
> and it would be a sell-out. It was truly artist development at that point—

the band growing and developing an audience. Develop an audience base and the record sales will follow.

"We hung out long enough to get the lucky break that you eventually need to break a band. It was all about the touring. It was keeping the band on the road until the radio climate started to change. The marketplace shifted a little bit in our direction, and we were still around. We hadn't abandoned hope."

The media value of touring is that it functions as a news event, which can serv as the basis for a publicity campaign. An upcoming live appearance in a region c locale is an ideal "story" for a publicist to pitch to editors and producers of loc: newspapers and electronic media.

To more directly promote a new recording via live performance, you can use th appearance as an opportunity to distribute copies of the CD—if you work with record company, clear it with them first—as well as posters, bumper stickers, and an other collateral material. It's standard to announce songs "from the new CD" onstag Having the venue play tracks from the recording before and after the stage act would n't hurt, either.

CROSS-PROMOTION

In the business realm, the last few years have been a time of corporate partnerships– separate companies sharing certain resources for mutual benefit, each helping t extend the other's marketing reach.

Here's how this applies to you: One of the more imaginative, and increasingl prevalent, promotional techniques is *cross-promotion*. It involves partnering with anothe business entity to promote each other's products simultaneously. Costs are shared b both partners, and each benefits from access to the other's customer base.

An example you've probably noticed is the cross-promotion of a new movie an a fast-food chain, such as McDonald's. You'll see television ads touting free movie related merchandise when you buy certain meals at the fast-foodery, for a limite time. The restaurants themselves feature in-store point-of-purchase promotion; items, posters, and other attention-getting devices. The benefit to the restaurant is a: increase in customer traffic because people are attracted by the gifts. The benefit t the movie is that more people become aware of it. Both partners win.

One music-related cross-promotion involved three partners: Windham Hi Records, Macy's department store, and Tower Records. The three set up a deal i which any customer buying a CD player from Macy's (from one of 23 stores i California) would get a free Windham Hill sampler CD plus coupons from Towe Records for discounts off Windham Hill products. To attract attention, Macy's spon sored an in-store concert by a Windham Hill artist, included the label in its print ad and used in-store display advertising. Tower also set up special in-store Windham Hi promotional displays.

All three businesses stood to gain from this deal: For Macy's, there was the potential for selling more CD players thanks to the giveaway CD and coupons. For Windham Hill, there was exposure to Macy's' huge customer base and increased sales due to the coupons given away by Macy's. For Tower Records there was the chance to sell more of its Windham Hill product.

A successful cross-promotion is one where the partners cater to the same general audience but reach different segments. That way, each gains access to the other's segment and thus increases the size of its customer base. As Windham Hill marketer Roy Gattinella told *Billboard:* "[Macy's] wanted to tie in a label, and Windham Hill is fairly obvious because you figure the Windham Hill buyer and Macy's customers are demographically similar."

When considering cross-promotion, think of an audience segment you'd like to reach that lies outside your usual distribution channel—or decide to reach your current audience more effectively. Then think of a business that caters to those people. Imagine ways in which both your business and the other would benefit from cross-promotion. Use that concept as the basis for a proposal to the other business.

Another Windham Hill cross-promotion was with a Napa Valley winery, Sterling Vineyards. Sterling, recognizing the demographic similarity of Windham's customers and its own, sponsored a tour by Windham Hill musicians to benefit tree-planting groups across the United States. It then co-sponsored a Windham Hill CD featuring music from the tour. (For more information about CD "partnerships," see "Custom Albums" on page 223.) Each partner's visibility extended to the other's core customers, and both benefited from association with an environmental cause.

ADVERTISING

In music promotion, paid advertising is used to supplement publicity, radio promotion, and all other programs aimed at drawing attention to the product.

There's a distinction between direct-response ads (discussed in Chapter 8), which are designed to get direct orders, and informational, image-promoting, or product-announcing ads. The latter are for pure promotion, rather than promotion-plus-distribution.

There are two major downsides to advertising. One is that it can be expensive. Another is that customers may dismiss it as "hype." (Ads are less convincing than, say, a review in a newspaper—a problem that can be mitigated by using endorsement quotes in the ad.)

The basic purpose of advertising is to assist in the sale of the product by increasing awareness of it and by making it attractive to a targeted audience.

Types and Costs of Advertisements

There's a long list of possible ways to advertise your music, all of which boil down to these categories: (1) display ads in newspapers and other print media; (2) direct mail pieces such as brochures (see Chapter 8 for more information); (3) flyers for placement in cafés and other public places; (4) outdoor billboards and signage; (5) transit ads (in buses, taxis, trains, and subways); (6) Internet ads of various kinds; and (7) commercial on radio and television.

A budget-challenged independent artist or label faces limited options: national television ads, obviously, are out of reach, as are full-page ads in large daily newspaper and national consumer magazines. But local radio and cable TV offer more affordable options that also permit precise targeting of listeners and viewers. Similarly, specialty magazines that target a narrow band of readers can offer ad rates within the realm of indie-label possibility.

In the media, ad costs vary tremendously and are affected by a number of factors.

Print Media. Factors affecting cost include

- the size of the publication's audience (circulation)
- the size of the ad
- whether the ad is black and white or color
- the number of times the ad is run (frequency discounts apply)
- the position in the publication (back and inside covers are more expensive, for example; and when there's competition for prime space, publications usually give preference to repeat customers)

Broadcast Media. Factors include

- length of commercial
- size of audience reached (represented by rating points, with one rating point representing 1 percent of households in the targeted broadcast area)
- demographics of audience
- geographic area reached, called the DMA (designated market area) in spot TV and ADI (area of dominant influence) in radio
- frequency (the number of times the commercial is broadcast)
- time of day, or *daypart,* of the broadcast (for example, in radio, "morning drive" time is more expensive, and in TV, "prime time" is more expensive); in TV, prices also vary seasonally, with the fourth quarter being the most expensive
- CPP (cost per point): the dollar price of one rating point, based on the value of the program, station, or market
- GRP (gross rating points): the total number of rating points purchased by the advertiser multiplied by the number of times the ad is broadcast; a calculation of an ad's intended exposure and thus a measure of an ad buy's strength
- specificity of timing; radio offers options of less flexible but cheaper programming packages in which the station chooses times: ROS (run of show), BTA (best time available), or TAP (total audience plan)
- economic conditions, affecting negotiability of pricing

nternet. Factors include:

- type of ad, whether a
  - banner, positioned somewhere on a Web page either horizontally or vertically
  - pop-up window, which opens in front of a Web page
  - pop-under window, a less intrusive version of the pop-up, since it opens *behind* the Web page
  - display ad, whether horizontal or vertical
  - interstitial—an ad page that appears for a few seconds when a user jumps from one page to another
  - superstitial—a TV-like commercial that runs between page loads
  - floating ad—a moving image that appears on the screen
- type of site, whether a high-traffic one or a niche site with low traffic
- position on the site, whether on the home page or a secondary page
- CPM, or cost per thousand impressions—that is, the number of times the ad is delivered
- CPA, or cost per action—*action* referring to either a customer click or a customer order
- a combination of CPM and CPA—say, a fee per CPM plus an extra amount when a customer takes an action
- size of the ad
- economic conditions, affecting negotiability of pricing

The following tables provide sample ad rates in various media.

TYPICAL PRINT MEDIA AD RATES (2002)*

Media Type	Smallest Ad	Largest Ad
Newspaper		
College	$12[†]	$1,512[††]
Community	$35[†]	$4,410[††]
Small Daily	$100[†]	$9,400[††]
Major Daily	$300[†]	$37,800[††]
Magazine		
Specialty (50,000 circulation)	$1,500	$5,700
Regional Consumer (150,000 circulation)	$2,500	$10,000
National Consumer (700,000 circulation)	$10,000	$48,000

* Black-and-white ad, one time only.
† Per standard advertising unit (SAU), a.k.a. standard column inch, which measures 2 $\frac{1}{16}$ inches wide (one column) by 1 inch deep.
†† Full page (broadsheet size), or 126 SAUs.

TYPICAL BROADCAST MEDIA AD RATES (2002)

Media Type	Less Expensive	More Expensive
Television (30-second ad)		
Network	$3,000* (daytime, off season)	$14,000* (prime time, high-demand season)
Spot (per market)	$40* (daytime, small market)	$1,300* (prime time, major market)
Cable	$1,000 (daytime, network)	$20,000 (prime time, premium network)
Radio (60-second ad)	$2,000 (light buy†, small market)	$90,000 (heavy buy†, major market)

* Per rating point, or 1% of households in the area of broadcast. Advertisers typically buy multiple points to achieve higher exposure; 100 GRPs (gross rating points) would theoretically cover all households in an area. 500 GRPs would theoretically expose those households to an ad five times.

† Effectiveness requires multiple airings of an ad, generally a minimum of 20 per week on two to three stations. In this example, a light buy is 24 airings in a week on one station (about $85 per spot in a low-rated market); a heavy buy is 144 airings in a week spread over three stations (about $625 per spot in a high-rated market). Price variances also depend on the time of day of the broadcast.

TYPICAL ONLINE MEDIA AD RATES (2002)

Type of Ad	Low-Traffic or Less Targeted Site*	High-Traffic or More Targeted Site*
Banner Ad	$5	$75
Text Ad, Keyword-Linked	$20	$80
Pop-Up Window	$10	$75
Pop-Under Window	$2	$5
Interstitial	$30	$45
Superstitial	$30	$45
Floating Ad	$25	$35

* In CPM, or cost per thousand impressions.

For ad rates of specific print publications, visit their Web sites or look in the Standard Rate and Data Service (SRDS) directories *Consumer Magazine Advertising Source* or *Newspaper Advertising Source*. For radio, television, and Web rates, contact the station, network, or site directly.

Placement

It's essential for the effectiveness of advertising that the ad be placed in media that reach your target audience or potential new audience members.

Choose your target carefully, based on research discussed in Chapter 4 (see page 41). Find the media outlets that directly reach the target audience, whether the outlet is a specific program on a local cable TV station, a popular local radio station, a niche magazine, or an alternative weekly newspaper. Contact the outlets, order their rate cards, and compare prices. Choose the outlet—or, better, combination of outlets—that offers the most cost-effective means of reaching your audience.

An alternative to target advertising is high-dispersion advertising, where you seek to build audiences by aiming for the maximum number of different consumers. The best media for this are network television and large-circulation consumer magazines. Not surprisingly, the costs of placing ads in these media are high—prohibitively so for independent musicians.

Message

In fashioning the message to be delivered in the ad, keep in mind that the overall purpose is to spark interest and create positive feeling about the product, and to provide the impetus to buy it.

The central message of an ad is often referred to in ad-speak as the Unique Selling Proposition—the notion that the product has something appealing that makes it different from other products. In the product development phase of your marketing effort (discussed in Chapter 4), you identified your music's selling points and the characteristics that made it different from other products. In an ad, you'll have to boil those characteristics down to one simple, powerful, and convincing message.

Ideally, the message will speak—directly or indirectly—to the self-image and preferences of the target consumer group. (Remember Apple Computer's ad line "Here's to the crazy ones"?)

For more discussion of ad copy and content, see page 118.

Other Advertising Approaches

There are various ways to advertise without breaking the bank.

One is to use *co-op advertising,* where a marketing partner places an ad that includes your product and either charges you for that portion of the ad or works out some other compensation arrangement (see the discussion on page 188).

Another is *per-inquiry* and *per-sale advertising*—arrangements in which you place an ad in a magazine without paying an up-front fee. Instead, the magazine takes payment only when the ad generates a lead (per-inquiry) or a sale (per-sale). Payment per inquiry is a set amount. Payment per sale is in the form of a percentage of the retail price of the product.

TRADE SHOWS AND CONFERENCES

There's a networking aspect to promotion—getting out into the marketplace and meeting potential business partners one-on-one to talk about your act. It happens as a part of doing business—you chat with people on the phone, see them at clubs, and meet them for lunch or dinner. This is part of establishing a presence in the industry. Unfortunately, it's not always easy to focus specifically on networking, given the sheer time and effort your daily tasks require.

But there's a way to do it—and do it on a macro level. Trade shows like South by Southwest, CMJ, NAMM (the National Association of Music Merchants), and NARM (the National Association of Recording Merchandisers), offer opportunities to meet many professionals in targeted sectors of the industry over several days in a single loca tion. You get two benefits: (1) you learn what's going on in the business marketplace what others are doing, and what they're looking for; and (2) you talk and promote t these people, increasing your (or your product's) visibility in the industry.

South by Southwest, for example, provides new musical acts with the opportunit to be heard by, and network with, record companies, producers, and managers wh might be able to provide career assistance.

But because of the size and frenetic energy of these shows, it's easy to get over whelmed and lost in the crowd. It's important to plan ahead so that this doesn't happen

Rather than randomly participate in trade shows, first research the ones mos likely to meet your needs—the ones attended by the people you want to meet whether foreign distributors, CD manufacturers, reps of chain retailers, or whoevei If you can, set up appointments with individuals ahead of time. Have a specific agend of what you want to accomplish at the show—for example, line up four or fiv potential distributors, or talk to journalists, or find partners for possible cross-promo tion initiatives. And come armed with plenty of business cards, one-sheets, and CDs Don't plan on having any left when you leave.

Artists and labels aiming to book showcases at trade shows should visit trade show Web sites for guidelines on submitting music samples and applications for consideration

CONVENTIONAL WISDOM

Succeed by attracting as large a share of the existing market as possible.
Many marketers aim primarily at typical music buyers, competing with other marketers for their attention in standard music outlets.

UNCONVENTIONAL WISDOM

Go where others haven't gone, and find new audiences. Create new markets.
Windham Hill, for example, found new markets for their records by promoting in book-stores, health-food stores, and other non-music outlets. As marketing expert Regis McKenna put it in *On Achieving Excellence:* "Marketing should focus on market cre-ation, not market sharing. Rather than taking a bigger slice of the pie, [marketers] must try to create a bigger pie."

SAMPLE PROMOTION STRATEGIES

Creative, imaginative promotion professionals draw from all of the methods discussed thus far to develop campaigns carefully tailored for the specific product with which they are working. And, as pointed out previously (several times, because it's important for you to grasp), successful architects of promotion campaigns often look beyond the standard approaches to find innovative ways to gain exposure to new audiences and places where commercial transactions occur.

The following strategies are from actual campaigns.

or a New Blues Record Release

- Sent CD mailings to national blues societies, with mail-back surveys that supplied information on blues retail outlets, newsletters, and radio. Used the information to create a marketing database.
- Sent CDs to nationally syndicated blues radio shows.
- Sent a two-song CD sampler to blues radio stations and blues clubs in 13 focus markets.
- Set up a CD sampler giveaway to visitors at Riverwalk Blues Festival in Fort Lauderdale.

or the Release of an Album by Canadian Band I Mother Earth

- Worked Florida radio stations on the song "One More Astronaut," sending out promotional items and following up with faxes and phone calls.
- Coordinated July 4 radio performance with an autograph session following at a Blockbuster Music tent that included a portable listening station featuring the new release.
- Set up a fundraising event (cross-promoting the album *Scenery and Fish*) with the organization Save Our Everglades, involving retail, radio, the press, and the local I Mother Earth fan club. (See the flyer below.)
- Set up an opportunity for the public to e-mail an astronaut on the Mir space station via I Mother Earth's Web site. Listed the opportunity with all available Internet search engines.

Flyer cross-promoting an album and a fundraising event.

For Another Album Release

- Set up CD sampler giveaways at retail stores in the radio airplay markets to promote the current focus track.
- Set up cross-promotions with coffeehouses and restaurants in several markets, using specially produced samplers and coasters.
- Booked listening booths at most of the stores affiliated with the Coalition of Independent Music Stores (CIMS) to ensure visibility during the holiday buying season.

For the Japanese Band Skoop on Somebody

- Targeted working women (in Japan) by aiming for media exposure in women's magazines.
- Set up live performance in Tokyo's Marunouchi central business district.

So use your imagination. Start with the ideas explored above and use them as springboards to your own promotional planning. Think beyond the traditional channels through which music flows. Think of all the ways music gets to people's ears: on airplanes, in supermarkets, in boutiques and other clothing stores, on obscure cable TV shows, on Web sites, in hip hotels, in coffee bars, in movie theaters—wherever people congregate in public or receive information. Then find ways to get your music into those environments. (Think of yourself as a new-millennium version of the early-1900s song pluggers described in Chapter 1.)

The idea is to create new markets. You still need to get across to the existing music-consumer base, but with innovation, hard work, and luck, you'll also be able to uncover a whole new cache of listeners.

Chapter 14

Working the Live Performance Market

Playing live is the most basic way to get music to the marketplace.

The nightclub or concert stage is where the initial "sales pitch" is made, for most musical artists (the exceptions being certain media personalities who are sold first on disc and video). The stage is an ideal site for test marketing: The music is played and the audience either likes it or doesn't. The audience also accepts or rejects the *way* the music is presented—that is, the artist's stage presence, visual image, and personality.

Traditionally, it all starts here. If the music proves saleable at a given venue, other live performances follow. If the artist builds an audience, sales of recordings follow. If the recording is successful, more recordings and higher-level concerts follow. And on it goes, until the continually successful artist becomes an established headliner, marketable in all sectors of the music marketplace, from large performance venues to new media to broadcasting.

As a tool in the total marketing program, live performance serves two purposes: it earns money directly and it promotes other products the artist has on the market. (See page 189 for more on the promotional value of live performances.)

CONVENTIONAL WISDOM

Before issuing a CD, a performer has to build a following by performing live. In the past, musicians began by working steadily in clubs, building popularity at the local and regional levels in the hope that a record company would eventually take notice and sign them to a recording contract.

ALTERNATE REALITY

A musical act may release a CD prior to embarking on a steady live performance schedule. Some clubs, in fact, won't book an act that doesn't have a CD on the market. (The practice of releasing a record first has roots in the distant past: The 1967 Summer of Love song "A Whiter Shade of Pale" was recorded before the artist, Procol Harum, had assembled a touring band.)

As a direct source of income, live performing—even if only on the local level-can keep a music career afloat for years. It's a major part of the musician's finar cial pie.

As promotion, it's especially valuable for up-and-coming artists who don't yet ha extensive radio play, where it can provide the spark needed to ignite record sales. Suc was the case with singer-songwriter Jewel: "When she was on the road she was sellir records," said A&R rep Jenny Price to ASCAP's Bud Scoppa. "She was getting ve little radio airplay—she was selling at least 1,000 records a month from basically ju live shows."

There are several levels of live activity. The first is that of the start-up or local ac The next step up the success ladder involves performing regionally in concerts an large showcase clubs. The third level is that of the headlining recording artist, involv ing large-scale touring.

While there isn't always a clear separation between these levels (for example, regional act may also open for a major artist on a national tour), each move up th ladder requires some adjustment in marketing strategy.

For purposes of the following discussion, let's assume that the "product" has alread been developed—that is, the musician has already achieved a performance-ready lev of competence, complete with a repertoire, a set list, the needed personnel, a sense c how to "put on a show," and all the necessary instruments and sound equipment.

NEW OR LOCAL ARTISTS AND LIVE PERFORMING

Many successful music careers start out at the level of playing at nightclubs, hote lounges, restaurants, weddings, office parties, and private get-togethers in area immediately surrounding home locales. Other careers both start and end at th level. Either way, nearly every musician deals with it at some point along th career trajectory.

Booking Performances at the Start-Up or Local Level

Getting the job for the local or beginning artist is most often a do-it-yourself proces

Friends and acquaintances are the first source of work. Musicians can put out th word that they're available and thereby line up bookings at private parties, schoc dances, and other types of local functions.

Booking work in commercial venues like nightclubs requires a more professiona approach. It includes the following steps:

- Burn a demo CD, using three or four representative songs or compositions and putting the best first. (Be prepared to program different CDs for different prospective employers, depending on their music preferences.) The demo can also be in the form of MP3 files, which you can e-mail to a club owner upon request, or have posted on a Web site to which you send the interested club owner.

- Create a basic promotion kit, which should include the demo CD plus an 8-by-10-inch photograph, a fact sheet describing the artist and listing past engagements, several press clips if available, and a folder to put it all in. (See page 143 for detailed information on professional press kits.)
- Identify the target audience and the clubs, cafés, and other venues that cater to it.
- Telephone or visit each venue to get the name of the person who does the booking. Or check the venue's Web site, if it has one.
- Mail press kits to those individuals or deliver the kits in person. Your press kit may also be online, in which case, send a simpler promo piece that sends readers to your Web site.
- Follow up by telephone several days later. Offer to provide additional information, if needed, including professional references. If no bookings are offered, ask if a future callback would be advisable. Make note of the answer, and follow up at the appropriate time.
- Start and maintain a running list of venue contacts, with fields for club name, contact person, address, phone number, last date of contact, and comments.

VENUE MASTER LIST

Venue	First Name	Last Name	Address	Phone	Date	Comments
Johnny's	John	Doe	1234 1st St.	222-1111	11/12/02	Left press kit
Red Barn	Rhett	Barnes	1 Broadway	123-5432	11/13/02	Will call back
Rhodehouse	Fred	Rhodes	44 Waller	333-1234	11/15/02	Set audition for 11/22

Pricing and Payment at the Start-Up or Local Level

The amount of money that can be earned at the start-up or local level varies considerably. On the low end, a member of a performing group might leave a local club gig at 3:00 a.m. with a total of $15 in the pocket. On the high end, a corporate party might pay several thousand dollars for a small group. Here are some ballpark examples:

- Subway platform or business-district street during rush hour: pocket change, up to quite a bit more if you're in New York's Grand Central Terminal and people really like you
- Small restaurant, Sunday brunch: low hundreds for a duo, several sets

- Folk music or jazz club/café, evening performance: low hundreds for a single or small group, one to three sets
- Rock club: low hundreds for a small group, one to three sets
- Wedding: several thousand dollars for a quartet or quintet, two to three sets
- Corporate event: low thousands for a quartet or quintet, two to three sets

Parties, weddings, and restaurants generally pay a flat fee. When you get into the realm of nightclubs, however, there are numerous possible approaches to handling payment, as follows:

- Flat fee.
- Percentage of the door. The performer gets paid only from ticket sales or the cover charge, at a rate typically somewhere between 15 and 50 percent (this figure is negotiable). (For example, if 25 people show up, the cover charge is $10, and you're getting paid 50 percent of the door, you'll be paid $125.) If the club expects to make most of its money from alcohol and food sales, you may be able to negotiate a higher percentage.
- Flat fee or a percentage of the door, whichever is greater.
- Flat fee *plus* a percentage of the door.
- One hundred percent of the door, after deducting a "house fee." The club would require a specified dollar guarantee, to be recouped from ticket or cover charge receipts. After recoupment, all "door" money would go to the performer. (This arrangement requires prior agreement on whether the house gets paid its guarantee if the door receipts don't cover it.)

There are many, many variations on these methods of payment. Generally, avoid paying the house to let you use their facilities (unless you're staging a promotional showcase event, as described on page 266). And if payment is a percentage of the door, go all out to get as many people as possible to show up.

When you book an appearance, make sure to have a contract written up. It should specify—at the very least—the location and date of the engagement, the schedule and hours of the performance, the amount of compensation, the method and timing of compensation, and the names, addresses, and signatures of both purchaser and performer.

Promoting Performances at the Start-Up or Local Level

In club work, attracting customers is vital not only when the performer is paid a percentage of the door (where earnings depend on attendance) but also because a booker's willingness to rehire the performer may depend on it.

To promote a performance, prepare informational postcards or flyers with the gig's location, date, time, and door charge and mail them to friends, family, acquaintances, names on your mailing list, and anyone else who might be remotely interested.

Post flyers in windows and on the bulletin boards of record stores, cafés, and any other appropriate commercial and public spaces that will allow them. Posting on college campuses is a great way to reach large numbers of concert-goers.

Get the performance listed in entertainment calendar sections of local media. Do this by sending newspapers and local magazines a simple notice showing the name of the act, the venue, and the date and time. Include a publicity photo if there are enough extras. For radio do the same, but add a copy of the artist fact sheet.

If you have a Web site, list the date in the Upcoming Gigs (or whatever you happen to call it) section.

Encourage coverage in the local media by sending simple promotion kits to local music writers. Follow up by telephone and offer them press passes to the performance. After the gig, seek them out to thank them for showing up (if they did) and offer additional information if they'd like it. If you don't hook up with them at the venue, phone them thank-yous as soon as possible. Demonstrating professionalism and concern just might nudge a writer toward deciding to write a review.

CONVENTIONAL WISDOM

Job One for the club musician is to keep the crowd happy. The club musician is in partnership with the club owner. If the band holds the crowd and the crowd buys drinks, the club owner makes money, is happy, and rehires the band. Bands should strive, above all, to win the audience over.

BREAKING THE RULE

The seventies proto-punk band Suicide routinely shocked its audiences with its confrontational stage show, often driving people away from the club. Silver lining: though rarely hired, Suicide eventually became regarded as art-rock innovators and performance pioneers.

Onstage Marketing

The task of marketing doesn't stop when the performer steps out onto the stage. Any attempt to win over the crowd is, in fact, a form of marketing. Performers should use all the skills at their command to "close the sale" onstage in a manner appropriate to the setting and in keeping with their artistic vision and musical style.

Choice of music, choice of attire, style of stage presentation, tone of between-song comments, attitude toward audience—all add up to a "message" that sums up the artist. And it is this message that you'll reinforce in every aspect of your marketing program.

MIDDLE-LEVEL ARTISTS AND LIVE PERFORMING

Let's define a middle-level artist as one who has prior experience at the start-up level, has developed an original approach to music, and has a recording in distribution, but hasn't yet reached the national headliner level.

Such artists are usually attempting to expand their market to include new geo graphic areas. Instead of staying close to home, they travel in cars and vans to club dates and concerts booked in a multi-state region. Their goal may be to "break out" and get known on a national level.

Venues include large nightclubs, midsize concert halls, and college gyms and auditoriums.

With luck and the right connections, the middle-level performer can end up as an opening act on a major tour or as one of numerous artists on a national package tour, gaining impetus for a step to the next level of success.

Booking Performances for the Middle-Level Artist

While artists often handle bookings themselves at this level, it's also common to get work through a personal manager or a booking agent.

A booking agent lines up engagements, handles the contracts, collects the money and pays the musicians after subtracting a commission that is usually 10 to 20 percent of gross earnings. (If your personal manager handles bookings, the percentage will be whatever he usually charges. Dedicated booking agents, however, are regulated by the American Federation of Musicians [AFM] and allowed maximum percentages that depend on the type of gig: a higher percentage for a one-nighter, a lower percentage for a steady engagement.)

When booking shows, the agent or manager will make sure that the venues (or headlining acts on a major tour) are appropriate for the performer. For example, no hard-core country music roadhouses for a hip-hop act.

The agent will also strive to set up an itinerary that won't saddle the performer with unreasonable travel demands.

To find a booking agent, consult such directories as the *Billboard International Talent and Touring Directory* and search the Web using the keywords "booking agents." Look at directories published by the concert-tour trade publication and Web site *Pollstar,* including its *Agency Rosters* and *Talent Buyer Directory* (details at www.pollstar.com). You can also check the American Federation of Musicians Web site at www.afm.org/booking.htm to find regional listings of AFM-approved agents.

As you did with record distributors, make sure to target booking agents who handle music similar to yours. Don't get hooked up with an agent who doesn't under stand your music—or who might accidentally book the Touchy-Feelie Soft Band into a headlining gig at Mel's Heavy-Metal Head Bashery.

Be prepared to provide a prospective booking agent with your promotion kit including plenty of evidence—such as a list of places you've played—demonstrating that the booker will stand to make money from working with you.

For college bookings, which are a good source of income for mid-level perform ers and which you can book yourself, find databases of colleges and look for the names of the people who schedule their entertainment. Send one-sheets—with your Web site URL where your songs can be checked out—to each college contact. Follow up with phone calls.

Pricing and Payment for the Middle-Level Artist

With extensive road work comes extensive spending—for hotels, food, gasoline, and a full-time road manager at the very least. On a bare-bones budget, one week's worth of expenses for five people could total $3,200 ($700 for food, $1,400 for hotel rooms, $300 for gas, and $800 for the road manager's salary). An artist's record company will sometimes provide tour support—in other words, foot the aforementioned bills—and recoup the costs from the artist's record royalties.

For the musicians to earn even minimal pay over and above costs—even when traveling on the above shoestring budget—performances would have to bring in at least $800 to $1,000 a night, six nights a week.

The formulas for payment typical at this level are the same as listed in the start-up act section: a flat fee, a share of the gate, a guarantee against a share of the gate, or a guarantee plus a share of the gate.

Unless a CD is getting noticed and beginning to sell, the amount of money earned may not be significantly more than for a start-up or local act. It's not unusual for a traveling performer, lacking CD sales, to play in a remote club to an audience of five.

The moral is: don't expect to make much money on the road unless your CD is selling. If it isn't, treat the road work as necessary promotion to make sure the CD eventually does sell. (Many are the bands who have paid dues on the road and reaped the benefits years later.)

A college may pay a band $1,000 and a solo performer $500 (being a solo performer eliminates a lot of overhead and can be a lucrative—if lonely—choice of career). A band newly signed to a major label may earn $1,000 to $2,000 per club date. For an act whose recording is selling well, the financial picture is quite a bit different. The act will be able to play large clubs and amphitheaters and gross several thousand dollars per night.

THE AMERICAN FEDERATION OF MUSICIANS

The American Federation of Musicians (AFM), also known as the musicians' union, sets standard minimum hourly pay rates (called *union scale*) for its members for live performances, recording, and work in various media. The union also provides standard employment contracts, and it franchises booking agents "who meet the highest levels of professional service."

Membership in the union becomes important at the large-nightclub and concert-hall level of performing. But even non-union members working in situations outside the union's jurisdiction (private parties, small coffeehouses, and so forth) can get a sense of what to charge and how to do business by referring to the union's pay and contract guidelines.

For more information, call (212) 869-1330, or check www.afm.org.

Pricing of tickets for concerts depends on going rates, what the customer willing to pay, and the performer's preferences. Some performers like to keep tick prices low in order to make access affordable to as many customers as possible. (Th band Fugazi, for example, played only at clubs that charged no more than $5 ticket—at a time when the band's records were selling well into six figures.)

Partial payment—usually 50 percent—is generally made in advance, with th balance paid at the time of the performance.

BETTER GIGGING THROUGH CIRCUITRY

Once upon a time—in particular, from the 1940s through the '70s—there thrived the "chitlin circuit," an informal network of nightclubs and theaters that snaked through the American South and parts of the urban North and provided steady bookings primarily for black performers.

These days there are other "circuits" that performers can plug into for regular roadwork.

- **Nightclub chains.** This book's author once performed regularly in a regional chain of upscale steakhouse/nightclubs. Middle-level performers can tap into such a chain, do well in one of its venues, and gain the trust and regular patronage of the chain's owners or managers.
- **Lounge circuit.** Show bands and top-40 acts find steady sources of work in hotel lounges, casinos, and resorts from the West Coast to the East.Identify employers by visiting Web sites of major chains such as Six Continents Hotels and Marriott, then contact the relevant individual—usually the manager of a local franchise. Do well in one, then build word of mouth that gets you into others.
- **Cruise ships.** As with the lounge circuit, nightclub bookings on cruises require a deep repertoire of current top-40 hits and standards from all eras, to please the multigenerational clientele. This is journeyman work, not for those who crave coverage in the alternative press and recognition for artistic innovation.
- **Theme parks.** Disney World, Universal Studios Hollywood, and other theme parks provide paycheck possibilities for performers willing to give customers the music they want. The "Mickey Mouse Club Theme," anyone?
- **Festivals.** Jazz musicians survive on the festival circuit, which can offer a steady schedule of bookings all around the world. Other music styles, from bluegrass to hard rock, have festivals of their own. Name recognition is normally required of performers, but breaking acts with good press and solid music can land slots as warm-up acts, which can lead to better things later. Surf the Web for music festivals and see where you might fit in.

Promoting Performances for the Middle-Level Artist

Promoting on the road involves a lot of advance planning. Press kits should be sent, entertainment calendar notices mailed, and ads placed well in advance of each and every personal appearance. If possible, an advance person should be working ahead of the tour to put up posters and flyers and contact the local media in towns soon to be reached. Radio interviews and record-store appearances should be set up, if the act's CD success warrants it.

Those invited to appearances should include—in addition to members of the press—local record-store owners, key personnel from the distributor, and radio deejays.

NATIONAL HEADLINERS AND LIVE PERFORMING

With national recognition, substantial radio play, and unit CD sales in the tens of thousands, the performer has graduated to the level of national headliner. Tours at this level generally cover midsize venues (anywhere from 1,500 to 5,000 seats) and larger.

With CD sales at the platinum (one million copies) or multiplatinum levels, the headliner is operating at the "superstar" level, able to fill arenas and stadiums that can seat many thousands of fans.

At this level, a tour is a complex and expensive operation. In addition to the performers, numerous personnel are involved, including tour management, road manager, road crew, sound and lighting technicians, advance person, and possibly a full-time tour publicist. For top-level acts, there may be additional participants, such as a tour photographer, a writer assigned to cover the tour for a national magazine, a video or film crew shooting a documentary, and so on. The logistics of running such an operation involve coordination of air or land travel, hotel bookings, local press coverage and advertising, rehearsals and sound checks, and payments.

CONVENTIONAL WISDOM

Tours are set up mainly to promote a recently released album.
Bruce Springsteen toured to promote his album *The Rising* in 2002. His previous tour had been coordinated with the release of the 1998 set *Tracks*. Between album releases, he tended to stay off the road.

BREAKING THE RULE

The Grateful Dead toured constantly, whether or not they had a new record out. Their success, in fact, rested more on live shows than on recorded music. With only a single mainstream radio hit in their 30-year career, they routinely ranked among the world's highest-paid entertainers.

Booking Performances at the National Headliner Level

A certain amount of strategizing goes into choosing venues to book and markets to cover in a tour. There are several key issues involved:

- The cachet of the venue. A beautifully remodeled state-of-the-art concert hall will reflect better on the artist than a seedy, dilapidated amphitheater
- The venue's proximity to the site of another concert on the tour. Multiple appearances in the same geographic area could split the audience, resulting in empty seats
- The amount of time since the artist last performed in the geographic area. If the last appearance was too recent, there may not yet be enough demand for another concert (a problem called *market saturation,* as is the problem cited above).

Performances at the headlining artist level are booked through local, regional, or national concert promoters. Promoters are essentially concert *producers:* they book the venue, handle associated costs, and take the financial risk. Their profit comes from a percentage of ticket sales after expenses have been recouped.

The long-established operation Bill Graham Presents (BGP) is an example of a concert promoter that operates regionally—primarily in Northern California. Clear Channel Communications promotes concerts internationally (and also operates dozens of venues and owns some 1,200 radio stations, making it the kind of vertically integrated company described on page 84.)

Costs for the concert promoter include renting the hall; paying personnel (stage crew, security, box office); renting equipment (lights, sound, instruments); and additional payments for advertising, ticket printing, ticket agency fees, catering, insurance, and ASCAP/BMI licenses for public performance of the music. (See page 235 for more about performance licenses.)

Concert promoters deal with the artist's representatives—the booking agency or personal management—when putting a concert together.

Pricing and Payment at the National Headliner Level

The standard payment arrangement for a performer at this level is a guarantee against a percentage of net profits (net profits being ticket receipts after the promoter's expenses have been deducted). (Acts with clout can sometimes get payment on gross income.) Such guarantees can run in the range of $20,000 to $100,000 per concert, depending on ticket prices, which can range from $20 to $300. A typical split of profits is 85 percent to the artist and 15 percent to the promoter. If final sales are less than the guarantee, the artist gets to keep the entire guarantee. (That's why it's called a guarantee.) If final sales are *greater* than the guarantee, the artist gets additional money to make up the difference between the guarantee and the total percentage of profits due the artist.

The promoter pays the booking agent a deposit of 50 percent of the guarantee, usually one month before the concert date. The balance is payable—in cash or by cashier's check—after the performance.

Personal appearance contracts at music's upper levels can get complex. In addition to covering the basics, a contract will often include a lengthy rider or addendum addressing such issues as rehearsal times and locations, accommodations and dressing rooms, compensation for travel and cartage, additional music equipment, other technical requirements, and provisions for cancellation due to weather or *force majeure.* Generally, no point should be overlooked in detailing the artist's and promoter's requirements in the contract.

PACKAGE OR MULTIARTIST TOURS

Traveling shows of multiple, like-minded musicians have been a staple of the live performance scene at least since the minstrel shows of the mid-1800s. More recently, we've seen Ozzfest (heavy metal), Lollapalooza (varieties of indie rock), and the Lilith Tour (women).

Such tours are a great way to spread costs among many, to maximize exposure to large audiences (the collective fans of all name acts on the lineup), and to jump-start careers for up-and-coming performers.

Promoting Performances at the National Headliner Level

Because concert tours can have such a profoundly beneficial effect on record sales, promoting each appearance effectively is of key importance.

The steps to take are much the same as for the middle-level artist (see page 207). In the case of national headliners, however, promotion at different legs of the tour is often handled by different offices or individuals, coordinating their efforts to do the following:

- Book television appearances and radio interviews on both national programs and those in local markets (the latter timed to coordinate with local concerts, of course).
- Set up special promotions with record stores, radio stations, and other related businesses (not limited to those focused on music—see pages 196–198 for some ideas).
- Set up feature stories with entertainment editors in the local press. The goal is to have artist profiles appear in newspapers a week or so before the live appearance. The goal is also to have reviews appear after the performance.

Take care of all of the above well in advance. Press kits to local radio and TV should be mailed four to six weeks in advance of the local appearance. Kits to newspapers should go out three to four weeks in advance. National television an magazines should be contacted months before the tour begins, because of th booking and production lead time they need.

CORPORATE SPONSORSHIPS

The high cost of touring has already been mentioned. One way some artists have c these costs is by gaining the sponsorship of a corporation. The sponsor underwrit some of the costs of the tour in return for plugging the corporation's product v onstage banners or displays, inclusion of the company logo on tour posters and in ac and other artist-corporation tie-in strategies.

The downside is that, just as in advertising, the performer may suffer from assoc ation with the product.

But sensible matches of artists and corporate entities have long served as viab methods of subsidizing the arts while burnishing the reputations of the business The JVC Jazz Festival is just one example of this.

Chapter 15

Expanding the
Marketing Program

After you've dealt with the basics of the music marketing program—product development, packaging, pricing, distribution, and promotion—you have the option of expanding the program. This means finding additional ways for your basic product—in this case, the recorded music and the artist who made it—to bring in money.

Keep in mind a point made earlier: recorded music is a piece of raw "content" that can be packaged, repackaged, and delivered to customers in any number of ways. We've already taken a look at the different configurations in which a recording can be presented, from CDs to DVDs (see Chapter 4 for details). Now the focus will be on the different *sources of income* for the use or sale of a piece of musical content beyond the primary sources discussed in preceding chapters.

The current world of entertainment is exploding with multiple media and varied means of delivering content to consumers. Movies and movie soundtracks, television (including commercials), video outlets, compilation albums, custom records, transmittable digital files, and more—all make use of music. That means each is a potential source of money for the sellers of music.

And beyond the music itself is the potential for making money from the likeness of the performer, on T-shirts, mugs, posters, buttons, calendars, and other retail merchandise.

Expanding marketing beyond selling CDs in stores is becoming more important than ever. "There are all sorts of licensing opportunities out there," licensing executive Bob DePugh says, "and as the retail climate changes so drastically, with the consolidation of retail into fewer and fewer hands, and as it becomes harder and harder to get especially back-catalog titles into a store where somebody can find them, alternate streams of revenue become ever more important."

Since a complete marketing program means wringing every conceivable dollar from your basic product, let's take a closer look at the different sources of those dollars and what can be done to tap them.

These discussions are intended as introductory overviews. Some of the sources—especially television and movies—involve business complexities that can't be fully covered in a single chapter. We suggest that you consult more detailed information sources before starting to do business in these areas. The books *This Business of*

Music and *This Business of Television,* both published by Billboard Books, are goo places to start.

Another note: The licensing arrangements discussed in this chapter are just exam ples of typical deals. In the marketplace itself, "there's every variation you ca imagine," as Bob DePugh says. You get what you can negotiate.

And a final note: As you read through this chapter, keep in mind that the re enues discussed represent only one kind of earnings—those for recordings ar recording artists. The other kinds are writer and publisher earnings, which are di cussed in Chapter 16. I'll remind you of this every few pages or so, just so you dor get confused.

DVD AND VIDEO

As discussed in Chapter 12, videos can provide substantial promotional benefit However, they can also serve as sources of income through sales of digital video dis (DVDs—also called digital versatile discs) and VHS videocassettes. Be advise though, that it's the rare artist who earns back the cost of video production throug DVD and video sales. (And video production costs are charged back to the artist the mainstream music biz, recouped from royalties—sometimes from both video a album royalties.)

Up-and-coming artists are rarely in the business of selling videocassettes ar DVDs. Most of those available in retail stores are "long form," consisting of collecte single-song videos or full-length concert performances. New artists simply don't ha enough single-song videos (if they have any at all) to compile into a long progran (Years pass before enough songs accrue to justify a video compilation.) Nor do ne artists have the broad popularity necessary to create demand for a concert video.

But for established performers, DVD/video is yet another way to repackage mus in order to generate sales.

DVD/Video Revenue Potential

There are three main ways to make money with video:

1. You are the producer and seller of the DVD/video (in other words, it's issued under your label) and your money comes directly from product sales.
2. You sell someone else the right to manufacture and distribute your video, and your money comes from a licensing fee or royalty.
3. Your audio recording is used in someone else's video and your money comes from licensing fees or royalties.

Sales of Your Own Video. If you're the owner (that is, the maker and seller) of the vide you'll deal either with short-form video (one song) or long-form video (usually a ful length concert video, a documentary about the artist, or a compilation of short video

Long-form video revenues come mostly from retail sales to record/entertainment chains (like Tower Records and Virgin Megastores), video stores, supermarkets, and specialty stores. Through these outlets, DVDs and videocassettes are sold or rented to customers for home play on DVD players or videocassette recorders (VCRs).

As of this writing, a typical long-form music video retails for $19.98. DVDs sell at retail prices ranging from $19.98 to $24.98. Subtracting dollars for retail outlet and distributor may yield around $8 to the video maker, on a suggested retail list price of $19.98. Subtracting a recording artist royalty of, say, $2 leaves $6. Say the video is a compilation of 10 songs. The publishers of those songs must be paid royalties (if not a one-time buyout fee, described on page 233)—let's say 10¢ per song (for each video distributed). That's $1 total, leaving you $5. Out of that, you'll need to subtract the cost of production, and here's where the fun begins: It's not unusual to accrue $100,000 in production costs for a single-song video. A compilation of 10 songs, then, might involve $1 million in combined production costs. To break even, you would have to sell a very large number of copies (even if you recoup production costs from the recording artist's royalties).

Other sources of income for both long- and short-form videos include broadcast on network, local, public, and cable television and exhibition in nightclubs. Note that, in general, the airing of short-form videos on local TV generates no payment to the record company; such uses are considered promotional.

Short-form videos are the lifeblood of such cable music channels as MTV and GAC. MTV has been known to pay millions of dollars to a major record label for the exclusive right to broadcast a specified number of videos for a specified period of time. For the most part, however, labels provide short-form videos to these channels—and to other broadcasters—for free.

Licensing Fees from a Separate Manufacturer-Distributor. If you're granting a license for someone else to manufacture and distribute the video, your income will be a royalty, from which you will pay the recording artist 50 percent of your *net receipts* (the money you receive minus your expenses).

You may be granting a license to a producer to use your short-form video in a compilation of numerous short-form videos. In this case, your royalty would be prorated—that is, reduced proportionate to the total number of short videos included in the compilation. For example, if there are 10 short videos including yours, you'll receive one-tenth of the total royalty. (Another, less common, method of prorating is to provide a reduced royalty proportionate to the duration of your video relative to the total time taken up by all videos.)

Use of Your Recording on Someone Else's Video. If you're simply licensing a master recording of a piece of music for someone else's use in a video (usually a video version of a television show or movie), the money could come in a couple of different ways, based on your issuing what's called a *master use license*. If the original licensing agreement was for a motion picture, which is now being issued as a video, the video licensing fee would most often have been included in the single "buyout" (all inclusive) license granted to the movie production company. (For more about license for movie use, see "Movie Revenue Potential" on page 217.) If the original agreement was for a television program, the home video rights might bring you a licensing fee of between $3,000 and $7,000.

How to Generate Video Revenues

For retail sales of DVDs and videocassettes, the marketing methods used are much the same as those discussed in Chapters 7, 8, and 9. To find distributors that specialize video, ask at local video outlets and look on the Internet using the keywords "video distributors" or "video distribution." You can also look in Yahoo's directory und Business and Economy > Business to Business > Entertainment and Media Production > Film and Video > Distribution. Take a look, too, at UC Berkeley's database of distributors: www.lib.berkeley.edu/MRC/Distributors.html.

Another option is to try to license your video to one of the major-studio video labels (an arrangement not unlike the pressing-and-distribution deals mentioned on page 104). Find these studios by investigating the sources cited above.

To get a video on MTV and other music television channels usually requires prior success in record sales—as do most other types of video success. You can take a long shot and mail press kits and video clips to producers of programs on these channels but before establishing a sales track record your best shot for video play is on local cable stations. Contact them as you would one of the major channels—supplying press kits and video clips as directed on station Web sites or to personnel listed in major cable TV directory (see Appendix, page 289). Again, short-video airplay on such stations is considered promotional and will probably net you no money.

In the case of licensing an existing audio recording to other video producers, that usually only happens when someone comes to you with a request to use your recording. For details, see the "Television" and "Movie" sections that follow.

TELEVISION

Like DVDs and videos, television can be a tool not only for promotion but also for generating money.

Television Revenue Potential

Television uses of your basic musical product generally fall into the following categories

- Use of an existing audio recording in a television program either as a theme (for example, Tears for Fears' "Everybody Wants to Rule the World" used in *The Dennis Miller Show*) or as background during a scene
- Use of a recording in a soundtrack album for a TV show
- An appearance by a performer as a guest on a television program
- Use of a short-form (one song) video on a television program, or a full-length video as the main content of a program

Television Use of an Existing Recording. If your recording is chosen for use in a television program, you will issue a master-use license and charge a licensing fee. This may range from $500 to $10,000, depending upon the term of use (typically five years); type of use (main theme or background); the popularity of your recording; the frequency of use (every episode of a series, or once only); the duration of the use (that is, how many minutes or seconds of the music will be played); and the success of the television show itself (if the show has already proven it has "legs," you may be able to charge more).

The most basic licensing fee typically covers use in free television only. The buyer may be granted options for additional uses, requiring payment to you of additional fees. Such "extras" may include use in a soundtrack album, a home-video release of the show, a foreign theatrical release (such as of a made-for-TV movie), a pay-TV broadcast, or a cable TV showing. This add-on approach differs from movie licenses, which are generally "buyout" deals encompassing all possible uses in one blanket agreement.

From your licensing dollars you would subtract expenses and then pay usually 50 percent of the remainder to the recording artist—who may be you.

(Here's the reminder I promised: Note that we're talking here only about fees for a *master recording*. Songwriter and publisher fees are separate. See Chapter 16 for information about these types of payments. There are also separate payments required for all union participants in the recording.)

Television Soundtrack Albums. Occasionally a successful TV series will issue a soundtrack album (*Ally McBeal* and *Dawson's Creek* have done this, for example). If your recording was used on the show, the TV production company may want to use it on the album. In this case, you, the recording owner, would demand a licensing royalty prorated according to either the total number of songs on the album or the percentage of total album playing time taken up by your song.

Artist Appearances on Television. What if the recording artist gets hired to appear on a television program—say, to perform a song on a late-night talk show, a series, a variety special, or a made-for-TV movie? Unless the recording artist is a celebrity, payment will be the standard "scale" hourly rate of one of the following three unions: the American Federation of Musicians (AFM), the American Federation of Television and Radio Artists (AFTRA), or the Screen Actors Guild (SAG). (Celebrities are paid more than union scale.)

The question of which union governs a TV performance is somewhat complicated, but here's how it works in general: If the performer is an instrumentalist only, the payment is through the AFM. If the featured performer is a singer, he or she is paid through AFTRA or SAG, depending on the kind of television production (AFTRA for videotaped or live programming; SAG for programming shot on film). For detailed information about the pay rates and rules of these unions, phone them at their main offices or visit their Web sites, which are listed in this book's Appendix.

Note: A consolidation of AFTRA and SAG has been under discussion for some tim and may be in place by the time you're reading this.

Television Use of Music Videos. As mentioned previously, prerecorded short-form videos played on one of the cable music channels such as MTV or on other T' broadcasts will generally yield no income, unless it is part of a blanket fee paid by music channel for the use of many videos for a specified time period (an arrange ment not normally available to small record labels). Some channels or programs tha depend on videos for their programming may be willing to pay for videos tha they've concluded will attract viewers.

How to Generate Television Revenues

Generally, television uses of recordings and performers are generated by televisio producers based on their familiarity with a particular recording or artist and the desire to license a particular song or book an appearance. That is, television uses ger erally don't occur unless the musical product is already on the market and ha attracted some attention, so that producers know it's out there. Bear in mind, thougl that many TV production companies balk at paying the fees commanded for h music and are more than willing to go with a lesser-known song for less money. Th key for you is bringing that music to the attention of producers.

To encourage the use of a recording in a television show, start by studying currer programming to learn what kinds of music they use. When you find a show that use songs like yours, send a promotion kit to the show's executive producer. Include link to your MP3s on the Internet. Follow up with a sales call.

Keep a list of the people and companies you contact, just as you have done fc media contacts, radio contacts, and retail contacts.

Also, stay up to date on the kinds of programming that production companies an studios have in preproduction. You can do this by consulting such sources as *Varie* (www.variety.com) and the *Hollywood Reporter* (www.hollywoodreporter.com). you have a recording that would be ideal for a show, contact the production office t let them know. (*Don't* contact them just to promote a scattershot of random track only do it for a track or tracks that you strongly feel are appropriate.)

To promote the use of a video on programs that regularly feature them (such ; those on cable music channels like MTV), mail press kits and video clips to the prc ducers of targeted programs.

You can also take steps to generate interest in a performer as a potential TV shov guest. Do this by sending press kits and video clips to producers of appropriately tar geted programs, concentrating on local cable programs if the act is new. (See page 18 for more information on getting media exposure.)

Representation of the artist by a well-known, full-service talent agency such as th William Morris Agency, International Creative Management (ICM), or Creative Artis Agency (CAA) can be very helpful in getting television work. These agencies have tie to all entertainment media, and offer their clients the inside track to activity in these area

MOVIES

Film companies often use new or existing songs, in addition to background scores, to serve as a main theme or to add flavor to particular scenes. And more and more, movie companies are boosting their revenues by releasing soundtrack albums of featured songs and music. For the owner of a recording, use of it in a movie and subsequently on the movie soundtrack album can be a very substantial source of income. Movie soundtrack albums often reach the top of the sales charts. (*Pulp Fiction, Purple Rain, Titanic,* and *O Brother, Where Art Thou?* are some examples.) Even minor songs in a film are potential moneymakers if included on a hit soundtrack album.

Movie Revenue Potential

Typical money-generating movie sources include the following:

- Use of a new recording as a theme or in the background (for example, Madonna singing "Die Another Day" for the 2002 James Bond film of the same name or Celine Dion's "My Heart Will Go On" for 1997's *Titanic*)
- Use of an existing recording as a theme or in the background (for example, "You Sexy Thing" in 2001's *Rat Race,* "Can't Take My Eyes Off You" in 1997's *Conspiracy Theory,* and "I Say a Little Prayer" in 1997's *My Best Friend's Wedding*)
- Use of a recording on a movie soundtrack album
- Use of a performer in a movie

Movie Use of a New Recording. If a production company wants you to record a track for use as a title or background theme in a movie, you'll negotiate a fixed fee, which can range from a miniscule amount for an indie film to half a million for a superstar signing on to a big-budget feature. If you're the artist, you'll need to clear soundtrack album rights, and probably share royalties with your record company if it's different from the one releasing the album.

Movie Use of an Existing Recording. If a movie production company wants to use one of your preexisting recordings in a movie, you issue a master-use license and collect a fee, which may be anywhere between several thousand dollars (or much less for a low-budget movie) and several hundred thousand dollars depending on whether the song is well known, whether it is used as a theme or in the background, how long it is played, and how many times it is heard—and depending, of course, on the overall budget of the film project. Additionally, you may opt to negotiate a lower per-song amount if a movie studio agrees to use several of your songs in a single film.

Unlike most television licenses, the movie license has no time restriction (it's "in perpetuity"), and movie license fees tend to be buy-out fees—that is, they cover all other uses the movie studio might want to exploit, including home video and television broadcast. From the licensing fee, the recording owner pays a royalty—generally 50 percent—to the recording artist (which, of course, is not an issue if the owner is also the artist).

Keep in mind that, as in television, the movie production company will also have to get permission from the writers and publishers to use the music, and will have to work out separate licensing deals with those entities (who could also be you). You'll find more about this topic in Chapter 16.

Movie Soundtrack Albums. If the movie studio wishes to use your recording on soundtrack album, you may negotiate a royalty per unit sold. The amount generally will be prorated according to either how many tracks are on the album or the percentage of total album playing time taken up by the individual track. For example using the first method, if the total royalty is 12 percent of the retail price and your track is one of 10 on the album, your royalty would be 1.2 percent of the retail price. Now let's fantasize that the album is as successful as 1987's *Dirty Dancing* soundtrack which sold 10 million copies. At a $17.99 retail price (for the CD), you'd earn $2,158,800 for that single song.

Artist Performances in Movies and on Soundtrack Albums. What if the movie studio wants the artist to perform onscreen in the movie? This, essentially, is a deal that does not include the record company, since it's for the performer rather than a recording. The artist's fee for such an onscreen appearance can range from union scale (the appropriate union being the Screen Actors Guild) to upwards of $100,000 for superstar performer.

The movie company may want to include the audio of this new performance on a soundtrack album. The artist royalty for this use would generally range from 10 to 18 percent of the retail price, depending on the artist's level of popularity (translation: clout), and the royalty would be prorated. (In addition, the artist will have to consult with his or her label for permission to be included on this soundtrack if it is being released by a different label. And the royalties may be sent to the artist's own record label, who may take a cut.)

How to Generate Movie Revenues

It's usually the movie production company, rather than the owner of the recording, that initiates a deal to use a recording or a performer in a movie. For that reason having the product out in the market where people will hear it is a near prerequisite for getting movie play.

To take an active role in promoting the product to movie makers, try to keep abreast of current films in preproduction by referring to the *Hollywood Reporter Variety,* and other trade information sources. Contact a film production office only if you feel strongly that your recording would be appropriate for their film.

An additional tactic is to keep a list of music supervisors—the invaluable professionals whose job is to plan the program of songs to be used in a movie and to acquire the rights to use those songs. Music supervisors tend to move from movie to movie, and keeping tabs on them—and promoting your music to them—is one way to increase the chances of getting your music chosen. (Music supervisor re listed in the *Film and Television Music Guide,* available in print or on disk at www.musicregistry.com.)

Bob DePugh takes this active approach. "We have quite an extensive list of film companies and television production companies and music supervisors that we mail out all our new releases to," he says. "[We] call on almost a monthly basis to see what they're working on, what new projects are coming up, what we can do some things for. You develop a lot of personal contacts."

It's not uncommon these days for a music supervisor to subcontract a single record label to provide all the songs to be used in a movie and on a soundtrack album. This makes the music supervisor's life easier: there's only one deal with one label rather than a lot of complicated little deals with separate labels for different songs. It's good for the label, too: the label has the potential opportunity to include songs by some of its lesser-known artists, thus giving them a promotional boost. The label can offer an "all-in" deal of reduced per-song licensing fees if the music supervisor agrees to use several of its songs in a single movie.

Because movie music deals are so complex—requiring, at the very least, the approval of record label, artist, music publisher, and songwriter—movie producers are more likely to work with music suppliers who know how to smooth out the process and who are easy to deal with. You should aim to be that kind of person.

There is no hard and fast rule about how songs get chosen for movies. In the case of writer-director Quentin Tarantino, who places a lot of importance on the choice of music, "a good half of the songs are usually ones in my collection," as he told Neil Strauss of the *New York Times.* Director Gus Van Sant, on the other hand, tends to choose music as an afterthought; in one case he reportedly picked a song by taking the top tape from a pile of music being considered for a movie.

The moral is: Serendipity sometimes does play a role. And all you can do is make sure your music is in the right place when the serendipity starts kicking in.

(A point to bear in mind here: In these days of corporate vertical and horizontal integration, it's not uncommon for a movie studio and a record label to be owned by the same umbrella corporation. In such a case, music may be chosen in part because it is owned by a music subsidiary of the corporation.)

To arrange for performer appearances in movies, either send press kits directly to production companies or go through a talent agency or entertainment attorney with strong ties to the film industry. Ideally, for this purpose, the performer's talent agency is one of the full-service firms such as those mentioned in the preceding section on television. These agencies serve both the music and film industries and can easily make links between one and the other.

COMMERCIALS

You've undoubtedly heard hit songs revived as product themes on television commercials: Bob Seger's "Like a Rock" for Chevy Trucks, Van Morrison's "Moondance" for Infiniti, the Rascals' "A Beautiful Morning" for the Gap—the list goes on. For the owners of those songs, such commercial uses can mean a jackpot of high earnings. A well-known recording used in a national TV and radio ad campaign can earn as much as $500,000 per year (in combined record company and music publishing fees).

Because of this expense, pre-existing songs are most often used by advertisers with large budgets. Which means they'll be on the lookout primarily for proven hits. (That's not to say that a music-savvy ad creative director won't occasionally want to indulge his or her taste for a particular little-known recording and use it in a commercial. It happened with music by cult singer-songwriter Nick Drake.)

Ad Music Revenue Potential

When an agency requests the use of a preexisting recording in a commercial, the owner of the recording issues a master use license (the fee for which can be anything from very little for a small-town radio ad to an astronomical figure for a national media campaign).

The license to use the song in a commercial should provide specification of the following points:

- *Term of use:* usually one year or less, with options to license for additional periods of time
- *Number and type of commercials produced:* for example, one 30-second TV ad, one 60-second radio spot, and so on
- *Kinds of media used:* free TV, basic cable, pay cable, radio, print
- *Territory:* a specific city, a state, a region, the entire United States, Canada, other countries, throughout the world
- *Exclusivity:* prohibiting the use of the song in other ads, whether *all* other ads or just ads for competing products

If you're fortunate enough to have an advertiser requesting the use of your recording, carefully consider the ramifications of having your song associated with the product. The target audience you have so carefully cultivated in your marketing program may be put off by the commercial, resulting in damage to the artist's public image. On the other hand, the amount of money offered for the ad use may outweigh all other considerations in deciding whether to go ahead.

How to Generate Ad Music Revenues

Don't expect to hear from an ad agency unless your recording has already earned its rightful place in the mass public's collective memory—which is often where ad copy writers look first when hunting for musical ideas.

On the other hand, if you have a CD or digital files of recordings that sound catchy or gripping enough for the ad airwaves, there's little reason not to submit copies or downloads to creative directors at advertising agencies. This works best if the recordings sound appropriate for specific types of products—a propulsive techno groove for a car ad, an expansive orchestral sound for an airline—and you know which agencies handle those types of products. You can inform yourself about what going on in the ad world by referring to such trade information sources as *Advertising Age* and the Internet's MediaFinder (www.mediafinder.com).

It doesn't hurt if you know someone who works in an ad agency—perhaps a producer, copywriter, or creative director—who knows your work and will give your music a listen. On rare occasions, a prerecorded song that's unsolicited—even a song that's not a hit—will strike the powers-that-be as having just the right message for an upcoming ad campaign.

COMPILATION ALBUMS

Increasingly popular are albums and boxed sets that feature collections of recordings—sometimes by different artists—that share a common theme. These compilations have proven to be an effective means of making new money with old, or previously packaged, recordings. They cost less to create than new recordings, because they don't require spending money on new music production.

For the artist included on a compilation album, it's a chance to make money and gain exposure to markets he or she might not ordinarily get into.

Compilation recordings are generally of the following types:

- *Record label retrospectives.* Motown, Atlantic, Stax, and Chess are just a few of the labels that have repackaged their hits into historical collections.
- *Artist retrospectives.* Individual artists with extensive track records are often the subjects of multi-disc collections. Bob Dylan, Miles Davis, Eric Clapton, and John Coltrane are examples of leading artists whose performances have been collected in new album packages. Record labels have occasionally sought profits by releasing retrospectives of songs by newer or less widely popular artists.
- *"Greatest Hits" collections.* The most common type of compilation is a repackaging of a single artist's past hit songs.
- *Style retrospectives.* Historical music styles have proven to be popular themes for compilation albums. Examples include garage rock of the 1960s, rhythm and blues hits of the 1950s, and big-band jazz of the 1930s.
- *Theme collections.* Compilations are sometimes created around musical themes, such as cult rockers, popular television themes, and psychedelic surf music.
- *Nightclub or package tour collections.* Popular nightclubs may issue compilation CDs of tracks by artists who have performed on their stages. (San Francisco's Up and Down Club is one example.) Similarly, traveling roadshows may issue CDs compiling tracks by their performers. The Lilith Fair tour, for example, did this successfully.
- *Tribute albums.* Increasingly common are albums that feature songs of an influential artist, as recorded in new versions by other performers. Jimi Hendrix, Jimmie Rodgers, the Grateful Dead, Hank Williams, and

Richard Thompson are just a few of the artists who have been the subjects of tribute albums.

- *Corporate promotional compilations.* A company may want to assemble a CD bearing its logo to market to core customers and attract new ones, using artists that have the appropriate appeal. The company might give it away as a promotional item or premium, or, if it's in the retail business, it might sell the CD along with its other products.

Compilation Album Revenue Potential

There are two main ways to make money from compilation albums: (1) you're the producer and seller of the entire compilation album, or (2) you're licensing one of your recordings for use on someone else's compilation album.

If you're creating a compilation album and you own the master recordings, your income per album will be the same as for a new recording plus the money you save by not having to pay for new music production. (You will, of course, have to pay royalties to the recording artists as well as mechanical royalties to the publishers of all the songs. See page 232 for more about mechanical royalties.)

If you're creating a compilation album and you are obtaining licenses for track from other sources (Rhino Records is a company that specializes in this approach) you won't be paying for new music production but you will be paying a per-unit royalty to the owners of the masters, usually with an advance. (The rate depend on how many songs are on the album and whether the album will be sold at full price, mid-price, or budget price.) You will also have to pay mechanical royalties to the publishers.

If you are licensing your recording (one song, say) for use on someone else's compilation album, you will be the recipient of the per-unit royalty described above, half of which is payable to your recording artist.

How to Generate Compilation Album Revenues

Because of the savings on production, the business of putting out compilation album may be attractive to label owners or to people with expertise in packaging CDs, from concept to song selection to licensing to manufacturing and finally to distribution and promotion. If so, your approach to distributing and promoting will be essentially the same as for standard, new albums, as described in Chapters 7 through 13.

On the other hand, you may have a single recording you'd like to get on someone else's compilation album. How do you go about it? The process may be out of your hands. Producers who handle such projects come up with the concept and then find music that fits. You may happen to exemplify a historic musical style that a producer now wants to revisit on disc. Or you might have been in one of the bands that launched the punk club CBGB in the 1970s, and a producer wants one of your songs for his *Best of CBGB* project. It takes a combination of popularity, affiliation and fate to create the conditions in which you'll get tapped for a compilation disc If it happens, great. (Just make sure the project casts you in a positive light.) If it doesn't happen, don't lose any sleep as you get on with marketing strategies over which you can exert more control.

CUSTOM ALBUMS

A relatively rare—but lucrative—marketing avenue is the sale and creation of custom albums. This kind of marketing activity is often categorized as a "special sale," since it occurs outside standard music sales channels. It's best suited for producer types with expertise in packaging compilation albums, or for record labels interested in exploiting B2B opportunities, or for musicians with a flair for salesmanship combined with a knowledge of CD manufacturing and a desire to branch out into the business world.

A custom album is one that a record or production company (or individual) specially produces for, and delivers to, another company or business entity, whose name goes on the product and who distributes it through the company's own channels. Such companies often have these albums created as a special supplement to their own product line, or as a premium to give to employees or customers.

Here's an example: The Bank of America had a custom CD created to give to senior customers who opened new CD (certificate of deposit) accounts. Artists were chosen to appeal to the targeted demographic.

Another example: The national home furnishings retailer Pottery Barn sold a CD, under its own label, titled *Martini Lounge*. The CD compiled cocktail lounge–type songs by the likes of Dean Martin, Peggy Lee, Rosemary Clooney, and Esquivel. Pottery Barn displayed the CD in baskets on a table alongside various martini-oriented products like glasses and trays. The idea was to sell the customer on the idea of purchasing an entire martini "environment"—music included. *Martini Lounge* was prepared for the Pottery Barn by EMI-Capitol Music Special Markets.

Custom-Album Revenue Potential

Custom albums offer the record company or producer (let's call it the *seller*) the opportunity to make a clean profit. The seller charges the corporate customer a fee that covers all manufacturing costs (including licenses, royalties, packaging, pressing, and whatever else) and includes a markup.

How to Generate Custom-Album Revenues

Start by making a list of high-profile companies and envisioning the kinds of music that would match their products or services. If you find a promising prospective customer, present them with a proposal for an album custom-programmed according to their specifications. Offer a list of potential tracks, and work with the customer to narrow the selection down to a list of primary and secondary choices (in case masters are unobtainable for all the primary choices). Determine how many copies of the album the customer would like to order. Prepare a manufacturing budget that covers everything—including shipping to the customer's warehouse. Add your desired markup to the total manufacturing cost, and use this as the total fee for your service.

NON-MUSIC MERCHANDISE

Merchandise other than CDs that incorporates the artist's name or likeness ca
provide significant supplementary income.

Retail and promotional merchandise can include logo-bearing T-shirts, sweat
shirts, jackets, tote bags, coffee mugs, mouse pads, notepads, pens, refrigerator magnet
buttons, stress balls, calendars, posters, souvenir publications, bumper stickers, an
more. The imagination's the limit.

Merchandise serves as both an important promotion tool and a source o
money—even if the performing artist is not a national headliner. It's promotiona
because the purchaser wears the logo-bearing T-shirt and the button, decorates his o
her car with the bumper sticker, posts the poster—all of which advertises you to th
public. And not only is this advertising free, you've been paid for it (assuming they'r
not giveaway promotional items).

For merchandising on an epic scale, we need only cite the case of Kiss, the ban
famous for its comic-character makeup and stage shows so elaborate the musi
seemed almost beside the point. Over the years they've amassed a department store'
worth of paraphernalia, all still available on their Web site.

A mere sample listing of Kiss products should be enough to keep the averag
band's heads swimming with ideas for possible items to market:

- *Apparel.* Sun visors, camisoles, underwear, lingerie, jackets, shorts
- *Accessories.* Wallets, beanies, magnets, key chains, personal checks
- *Home decor.* Wall clocks, doormats, telephones, "Kissmas" ornaments,
  figurines, pillowcases, toothbrush holders
- *Toys.* Kiss creatures, band member busts, bobbleheads
- *Collectibles.* Trading cards, lunchboxes, model cars, skateboards,
  commemorative plates, autographed figurines

For the artist still focusing mostly on music, a few T-shirts and mugs may be sufficient, at least for the time being. As for sales outlets, there are several choices. Som
merchandise sales occur through normal retail channels, including stores and mai
order. Other sales occur in connection with live performances and tours.

Merchandise at the Do-It-Yourself Level

If you plan to handle merchandise on a small, start-up scale—say, setting up a tabl
at nightclub shows and selling paraphernalia along with CDs—there are som
simple options.

You can find manufacturers to produce your T-shirts, posters, keychains, and
refrigerator magnets per your design, at prices that leave room for you to add a markup that won't send buyers running to the exits.

Look for merchandise manufacturers on the Web by keying in your desired item
along with the word "manufacturers." Also, the music-career-advice site StarPolish
(www.starpolish.com) has a database that provides a good starting point.

It's important realistically to assess what kinds of items you need to produce and how many you need to manufacture. Don't produce more than you think you can sell, or than you're willing to give away.

Initially, choose a single item—such as a T-shirt—with the best potential for sales. Since it's going to carry your name and image, make sure to coordinate its visuals with other promotional material, from CD covers to posters to Web site graphics.

Remember: Selling a piece of merchandise bearing your logo boils down to getting paid to advertise yourself. Don't let the opportunity slip through your fingers.

Higher-Level Merchandise Sales Through Retail and Mail

On a higher commercial level—that of established artists—the process can get more complicated. The seller of the artist's likeness and name—which could be the record label or the artist, depending on who holds the rights—issues a license to and receives a royalty from a retail merchandiser (a company that manufactures and distributes the merchandise). This royalty is generally in the realm of 10 to 20 percent of the wholesale price for retail store sales, and 25 percent for mail-order sales.

If the seller (the rights holder) is the record company, it pays the recording artist a royalty that is normally 50 percent of net receipts.

If the artist has retained the right to peddle his or her own name and likeness, the royalty will go directly from the merchandiser to the artist.

The seller (label or artist) usually receives an advance against royalties, the amount of which can range from very little for an unestablished act to hundreds of thousands of dollars for an established artist.

Higher-Level Merchandise Sales at Performances

At the established-artist level, impressive amounts of money can be earned through the sale of tour-related merchandise bearing the name and/or likeness of the performer. This includes material like posters, sweatshirts, program booklets, and just about anything else deemed saleable to a fan hyped up on concert excitement.

The artist licenses the right to use his or her name and likeness to a merchandiser. The merchandiser handles manufacturing and arranges for sale of the items at concert halls, paying the artist an advance against a royalty in the area of 25 to 40 percent of gross sales. (The sales onsite are usually handled by the concert hall, which charges its own "hall fee" of between 20 and 40 percent of gross sales.)

Such agreements tend to run for a term of one year or until the advance is recouped, whichever is longer.

One of the dangers of a merchandising agreement is that the final product may conflict, in design or quality, with the kind of image the artist is trying to project. For this reason it's wise to retain some degree of creative control over the product and to stipulate as much in the merchandising contract.

Another pitfall is that some merchandisers require exclusivity, meaning you're prohibited from selling similar products in the vicinity of their merchandise stands for a given period of time (which could, of course, cut into their sales). But what if you already have merchandise on the market, which you're selling through stores in nearby town? If so, it's important that this merchandise be excluded from any exclusivity agreement with the tour merchandiser.

How much money can be made? If 10,000 T-shirts sell for $25 each over the course of an entire tour, and the royalty is a middling 30 percent of gross sales, you'd receive $75,000. ($250,000 X 30% = $75,000.)

And that's just for T-shirts. Don't forget the sweatshirts, caps, mugs, brandy snifters, cigarette lighters, wall posters, refrigerator magnets, buttons, mittens—whatever.

It's something to aim for, isn't it?

Chapter 16

Generating Revenue from Writing and Publishing

n addition to making money from recordings, you can generate earnings from music writing and publishing. Smart performers who have the skill to write their own material do so energetically, knowing that it can open up new and lucrative revenue streams.

Before examining specific revenue sources, let's look at how music writing and publishing fit into the overall marketing scheme.

In the music business, the product sold directly to the consumer is most often the musical performance, in whatever format chosen, from live presentation to audio CD to audiovisual software. Most marketing focuses on such sales to consumers.

But a great deal of money-making goes on beneath the surface consumer world. It happens in the world of business-to-business commerce, where a product is sold by one business to another for further processing and resale. (Like lumber sold to a cabinetmaker, who will use it in building a cabinet and then sell the cabinet to the public.)

One of the primary music business-to-business products is the raw, unrecorded music composition, known in legal parlance as *intellectual property*. The owner of this property is said to hold the *copyright* to the property—that is, the right to reproduce, publish, and sell the work. The copyright holder is the original author or another entity to whom the author has assigned the copyright.

As owner, the copyright holder is entitled to make money from the property. This is done by selling the right to use the property in some way. The permission to use is called a *license*. The copyright holder grants a license to another business (say, a record company) to process the product further (e.g., to record a song) and then to sell it to the public or to another business.

The song "Yesterday," by Lennon and McCartney, is an intellectual property. It's been recorded hundreds of times by a variety of artists. Each one of those recorded renditions represents a separate licensing of the song by one business (the owner) to another business (the record label), each license bringing new money into the coffers of the "Yesterday" owners.

In the marketing program discussed up to this point in the book, the assumption has been that you are marketing a musical product in the form of a recording or a musical performing artist. But what if you own a music composition, because you wrote it, co-wrote it, or at some point obtained the rights to it? In this case you'll be able to draw earnings that are separate from those for recording or performing.

If you're a combination songwriter, recording artist, and performer, those writer earnings will be *in addition* to the recording and live-performance earnings. That's why smart performers who *can* write *do* write.

If you're both the record-label owner and the music composer-publisher, you get to keep the money that would otherwise be paid to an outside writer and publisher.

The main sources of income for music writing and publishing are summarized in the upcoming discussion and diagrammed below. (Because the details are too complex to cover fully in a single chapter, you're advised to consult additional information sources that focus specifically on the individual topics.) But first let's briefly revisit a subject introduced back in Chapter 2—that is, music publishing.

Examples of income-generating uses for a song.

WHAT IS MUSIC PUBLISHING?

In essence, music publishing is the set of business activities aimed at exploiting a music composition for profit. (In the music business, the term *exploit* doesn't have its usual negative connotation; here it simply means "to put to productive use.") These activities usually include, but aren't necessarily limited to, marketing, promotion, publication of printed music, collecting fees and handling the money, and overall business administration.

The corporate music publisher relies on various individuals and departments to handle these functions.

- *Chief executive.* He or she guides the entire company and shares in all the major decisions, including signing new songwriters and composers, pairing songs with artists, and solving strategic problems.
- *Professional manager.* The person in this vital position is constantly on the lookout for music compositions that may have potential for commercial use in all manner of markets and styles of arrangement, from elevator music to heavy metal, country, and jazz. The professional manager signs songwriters, matches songs with recording artists, and may help the songwriter-artist-producer team in carefully shaping lyrics and arrangements to bring out a song's hit power. Professional managers are often aided by personnel who review new songs and make recommendations for acquisitions.
- *Business and legal affairs.* This department handles the publisher's contractual matters and advises on business decisions large and small, from specific wording in a writer contract to buyouts of entire song catalogs.
- *Copyright department.* Personnel in this area handle registration of the company's songs with the U.S. Copyright Office, file for copyright renewals, and register songs with performing rights organizations such as ASCAP and BMI.
- *Royalties and accounting.* This is an exacting area that involves keeping track of advances to songwriters, company expenses, and taxes; reviewing royalty statements from music licensees; and calculating and making payments to songwriters.

Signing with a Music Publisher or Doing It Yourself

Many musicians decide to do their own music publishing rather than pay a portion of royalties to a separate publisher. This works best when the musician-songwriter isn't especially interested in trying to convince others to record new versions of the songs.

It's best to work with an established music publisher when you want active promotion of your songs in the music market but don't have the time, energy, industry contacts, knowledge of money sources, and business expertise offered by a professional publisher (see figure on page 230).

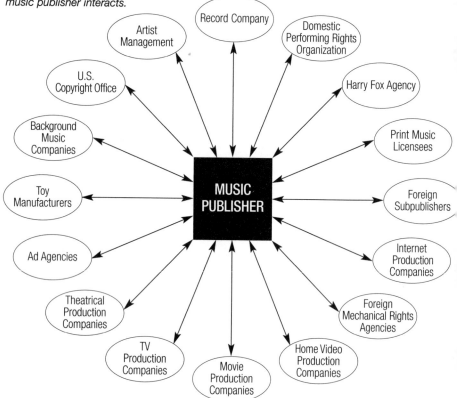

Types of businesses and organizations with which a music publisher interacts.

Standard Writer-Publisher Royalty Shares

The usual writer-publisher split of royalties is 50-50. That is, the publisher gets half and the writer gets half. If there are two writers, they would split the writer share, in whatever percentages they agree are reasonable.

Often, two writers of a song have their own separate publishers. In this case, the standard royalty shares would be

Publisher 1:	25%
Writer 1:	25%
Publisher 2:	25%
Writer 2:	25%

That is, the publisher percentages match the corresponding writer percentages. (Note that BMI expresses these shares as totaling 100 percent on the publisher side and 100 percent on the writer side for an overall total of 200 percent. So the above xample would be expressed on a BMI song clearance form as Publisher 1, 50%; Vriter 1, 50%; Publisher 2, 50%; Writer 2, 50%.)

Royalty division can get more complicated. If authorship of the song is divided etween three writers, two of whom split half of the writer share and one of whom wns the other half—and each writer has her own publisher—the royalty division rould be as follows:

Publisher 1:	12.5%
Writer 1:	12.5%
Publisher 2:	12.5%
Writer 2:	12.5%
Publisher 3:	25%
Writer 3:	25%

THE HARRY FOX AGENCY

To facilitate the licensing of their compositions for certain uses, music publishers may engage the services of the Harry Fox Agency, a subsidiary of the National Music Publishers' Association (NMPA). The Harry Fox Agency serves as a clearinghouse representing thousands of music publishers, and its service is useful to both music customers and music copyright holders. For customers, it provides a single place to go to obtain licenses and offers a standardized procedure for requesting licenses and paying fees. For copyright holders, the agency does all the paperwork related to licensing, collects and distributes the royalties, and audits the books and records of licensees. The agency subtracts commissions from its royalty payments to publishers.

The Harry Fox Agency handles the following kinds of music uses:

- On CDs, tapes, and records distributed to the public for private consumption
- In movies, television, home video, and commercial advertising (Harry Fox provides information only)
- In background music and syndicated radio
- In recordings made outside the U.S. and imported to the U.S. for sale

Note that these uses all involve *fixing* the composition in some playable form. The Harry Fox Agency does not handle licensing for the *performance* of music on radio or television or in concert (although it does license U.S. theatrical motion picture performing rights). Performance licensing is handled by performing rights societies such as ASCAP and BMI (discussed on page 234).

For more information about the Harry Fox Agency, call (212) 370-5330 or visit www.nmpa.org/hfa.html

There are any number of variations of this royalty division, depending on th number of writers and publishers and the percentages of the song that they own.

Now let's go on to the various sources of revenue available to music publishe and writers. Keep in mind that in nearly all cases the fees collected are shared by put lishers and writers per the above guidelines.

MECHANICAL LICENSING FEES

Whenever an audio recording is created and distributed, the writer of the music (; opposed to the performer on the record, although they are sometimes the sam person) is due some money. So is the publisher that represents the writer.

The license for this kind of use is called a *mechanical license.* More specifically, mechanical license covers the incorporation of a copyrighted music composition int commercial records, tapes, and CDs to be distributed to the public for private use.

As an example, if Bonnie Raitt records a song by John Hiatt for her new albun her record company must obtain a license from, and pay fees to, Hiatt's publishin representatives.

When a record company wants to use your song on a record, it informs you, you publisher, or an organization called the Harry Fox Agency (see the description o page 231) of the intended use. (If you have previously recorded and distributed th song, you are *required* to grant a mechanical license to anyone else who wants t record it, as long as they pay the required fees. Underscoring this requirement, th license is called a *compulsory mechanical license.*)

The standard fee payable by a licensee to the copyright holder is, as of Januar 2004, 8.5¢ per composition or 1.65¢ a minute of playing time, whichever is greate for every CD, tape, or record that is manufactured and distributed. This royalt rate is the statutory, or compulsory, rate established under the United States Copy right Act. It is adjusted every couple of years to reflect changes in the Consume Price Index.

The licensee may negotiate with the copyright holder for a royalty rate lower tha the statutory rate. Mechanical royalty rates are generally set lower (usually 75 percen of the standard rate) for reduced-price records.

If you are a recording artist who writes your own songs (in music-business parl ance, such a song is called a *controlled composition*), you should be aware of on common record-company practice related to mechanical royalties. When artist written songs are included on an album, you'd think that a record company woul pay the artist separate royalties covering recording (artist royalties) and songwritin (mechanical royalties). And they do. But record companies often include a "con trolled composition clause" in the recording agreement, setting the mechanica royalty at a reduced rate—usually 75 percent of the minimum statutory rate, with total album limit of 10 times the per-song royalty (even if the artist includes mor than 10 original songs on the album). Artists with clout can sometimes negotiate higher percentage.

SYNCHRONIZATION LICENSING FEES

In the music business, the term *synchronization* means combining recorded music with visual images. Copyright owners have the right to grant synchronization licenses for uses of their compositions in movies, television, and home video.

Movies

A synchronization fee for the use of a song in a movie is negotiable and can total between $10,000 and over $50,000. The amount depends on such variables as the movie's production budget, how well known the song is, whether the song is sung onscreen or used as background, the duration of the use (in minutes and seconds), the term of use, the territory of use, and whether the movie company guarantees inclusion of the song on a soundtrack album. (If the song will be used on a soundtrack album there will be separate mechanical royalties for the song owner, which is why owners sometimes agree to reduce the sync licensing fee if a soundtrack album will be issued.)

Television

Synchronization fees for the use of compositions in television series, special programs, or made-for-TV movies can range from several hundred dollars to many thousands of dollars per composition. The amount depends on many of the same variables cited in the preceding section about movies. Some other variables include whether the program will be released on home video, broadcast in additional media, or released in foreign movie theaters. Typically, the licensee will initially pay for a specified set of conditions and request an option to buy more as needed.

No sync license is required if the show is broadcast live or "live on videotape."

Home Video

A synchronization fee for the use of a composition in a home video is paid in one of the following ways: a per-unit royalty (usually from 8¢ to 15¢ per song); a single buyout fee covering all quantities sold; or a rollover advance covering a set number of copies, with additional amounts payable for additional specified quantities sold.

COMMERCIAL ADVERTISING LICENSING FEES

Licensing fees payable for the use of a composition in commercial advertising can range from a few thousand dollars to upward of half a million dollars. The amount will depend on such variables as how well known the song is; the advertising budget; the type of media (free television, basic cable, pay cable, radio); the geographic territory of use (local, regional, national, international); the term of use (usually one year, with an option to extend the license); the number of commercials produced in various formats (such one 30-second TV ad and one 60-second radio ad); and whether the advertiser wants exclusivity.

By the way, although television commercial licenses are synchronization licenses, radio commercial licenses are *not* synchronization licenses, because radio doesn't

ASCAP AND BMI

A vast number of music performances occur in an equally vast number of electronic media outlets and public establishments every day. If every radio station, television station, Web site, mobile entertainment provider, and concert promoter had to obtain licenses directly from the individual owners of all the songs they wanted to broadcast or perform—a process known as *source licensing*—the task would be enormous. That's where ASCAP and BMI come in.

The American Society of Composers, Authors and Publishers (ASCAP) and Broadcast Music, Inc. (BMI) call themselves performing rights societies. They represent many thousands of music creators and publishers, and serve as one-stop clearing-houses for the collection of performance licensing fees from music users and the distribution of royalties to members whose works are performed.

Instead of granting separate licenses for individual compositions, ASCAP and BMI issue blanket licenses to music users. A *blanket license* allows the licensee to use all the songs in a society's repertoire for a single fee, paid yearly in most cases. The fee paid by radio is based on a station's annual revenue. The fee calculation for TV is more complicated, involving a single industrywide fee that's allocated among individual stations based first on the size of the station's geographical market and second on the individual station's viewer share within that market. (Stations may opt for a *per-program license,* a cheaper option than the blanket license because it covers more limited or incidental uses of music, as in a single program.) Other types of licensees—nightclubs, concert halls, and retail stores, for example—pay based on such factors as the size of the establishment or audience and the manner in which the music is performed, whether live or recorded, audio only or audiovisual.

For the Internet, license fees are determined by BMI on the basis of the Web site's gross revenues or a "music area calculation" that involves figuring music area revenues as a fraction of gross revenues. ASCAP calculates rates using a variety of criteria, including revenues and number of music transmissions.

Out of the pool of collected license fees, ASCAP and BMI pay royalties to writers and publishers. Dollar amounts of royalty checks depend on several factors. A factor for traditional media is the total number of times individual compositions are performed in a specific time period, which ASCAP and BMI calculate using surveys and airplay-logging systems. Other factors include the type of use, the medium in which the composition was performed, the size and importance of the logged station or outlet, and (in the case of TV) the time of day of the performances.

If writers and publishers want to make sure they are paid for performances, they essentially have to join either ASCAP or BMI (or a third, much smaller performing rights society called SESAC). Once affiliated, the writers and publishers register each of their published songs with the performing rights society.

To find out more about the societies and their services, contact ASCAP's membership office at (212) 621-6000 or BMI's Writer/Publisher Relations department at (212) 586-2000, or visit them online at www.ascap.com and www.bmi.com.

ontain visual material. Radio involves *transcription licenses,* as does background music,
iscussed next.

ACKGROUND-MUSIC REVENUE SOURCES

ackground music—as supplied by such companies as Muzak—is music played in
ores, malls, restaurants, hotels, offices, airlines, elevators, and other public places, as
vell as over the telephone when callers are put on hold. It is meant to accompany
ctivity, to relax people, to override ambient noise, to create a pleasant atmosphere,
nd to enhance the image of the business using the background music. For that
eason it is sometimes called *functional music.*

The creators of background music normally record their own versions of music
or which they have obtained what are called transcription licenses.

The method of remunerating the copyright holder for a transcription use varies
epending on the background-music company seeking the license. One method is a
xed payment for the use of a song over a set period of time. Another method is a
enny-rate royalty on each copy of a transcription recording sold or leased by the
ackground music company to its commercial clients.

In general, suppliers of background music seek material that listeners already
now. But if you are interested in tapping into the background- or functional-music
narket, research suppliers on the Internet and make contact to find out how you can
e of service.

ERFORMANCE LICENSING FEES

n addition to owning the rights to grant mechanical and synchronization licenses for
he use of his or her music, the copyright holder owns what are called performing
ights. The term *performing right* refers to the right of the copyright holder to grant
censes for public performances of the music, whether the performance is over the
irwaves, on the Internet, in concerts, or in various types of public venues, from
estaurants to shopping centers.

That means that if a singer's recording of your song is played on the radio, you get
noney. If it's streamed on the Internet, you get money. If the singer sings it in concert,
ou get money. If the song is played on TV, you get money. If it's played in a disco,
ou get money. And so on.

Let's make sure we're clear on the difference between *mechanical/synchronization*
ses of music and *performances* of music. The former refers to the incorporation of the
nusic into a product such as a compact disc, movie, or TV show, for which the music
wner gets paid. The latter refers to the actual playing of music on radio, television,
r elsewhere, for which the music owner also gets paid—separately. For example, a
V producer will pay a music publisher for a sync license to use a song in a program.
eparately, the TV station that broadcasts the program will pay a different fee—for
erformance rights.

Performance licensing fees are collected from music users and distributed to copyright holders by performing rights organizations, of which ASCAP and Broadcast Music, Inc. (BMI) are the largest. (See the sidebar on page 234.)

Music Uses That Generate Performance Royalties

Because there are so many contexts in which music is performed, and because there are so many different royalty rates depending on the context, I'll simply summarize here the array of possible performance royalty sources.

- Radio—network and local
- Television—network and local
- Cable services—premium (like HBO) and basic (like MTV)
- Web sites, including Internet radio
- Musical events and concert halls (for more about performance licenses as an expense incurred by concert promoters, see page 208)
- Restaurants, nightclubs, discos, bars, health clubs, hotels, amusement parks, retail stores, shopping malls, stadiums
- Jukeboxes
- Circuses, theme shows (beauty pageants, ice shows), Las Vegas-type revues
- Conventions, expositions, trade shows
- Music services such as background music, airline music, music-on-hold, wireless phone ringtone providers

In all of these cases, the proprietors pay license fees to one of the performing rights organizations (or to the jointly run Jukebox License Office, in the case of jukebox performances), which in turn pay royalties to affiliated writers and publishers.

Performance Subcategories Used in Determining Royalty Rates

Royalty amounts payable to writers and publishers vary depending not only on the context or medium (as listed above) but also on the type of use in the given medium. Here are types of uses listed in BMI's payment schedule:

- Radio feature performance—a performance lasting "90 seconds or more and which is the sole sound broadcast at the time of the performance"
- Radio theme—"a work used as the opening and closing of a regularly scheduled program"
- Television feature performance—"a performance of a work which is the focus of audience attention at the time of the broadcast"
- Television theme—a work "which is regularly associated with a television program and identifies that program to the viewer when used as the opening and/or closing music"
- Television background music—"music [that] is not the focus of attention yet nonetheless is used to set the mood of the scene"
- Web site use where the music is the primary feature
- Web site use where the music is a secondary feature

(ASCAP, in its definitions of Web site uses, differentiates between "noninteractive" music transmissions—that is, nondownloadable and nonselectable streaming audio—and music transmissions that are "interactive," meaning downloadable and selectable.)

MARKETING AND PROMOTING IN THE MUSIC PUBLISHING ENVIRONMENT

It's been said before in this book, and now I'll say it again: marketing and promoting music for use within the industry—that is, for use by record companies, movie and TV producers, performing artists, and others—depends a lot on who you know. That's why established music publishers are well positioned to do this sort of work. They have connections throughout the industry—managers, producers, A&R people, and others, whom they contact periodically to check on their current music needs and to make them aware of songs that might be appropriate for their use.

So the primary guideline for anyone embarking on an attempt to license songs is to build a network and a list of music-industry contacts: Remain in touch with these contacts in whatever ways possible—via telephone, through the mail, and by attending trade shows, conventions, and other industry events. Read trade publications in the fields of music, movies, and television regularly to stay abreast of upcoming projects that might require music such as yours. Be proactive in ascertaining and offering to meet the music needs of potential clients. And build a reputation for reliable and knowledgeable service.

Perhaps the most direct way to promote a song is to contact a friend or associate who also happens to be a recording artist and offer your song for his or her use. But don't be offended if they decline. Business is business, after all.

THEATER MUSIC

Occupying a somewhat out-of-the-way sector of the music marketplace is theatrical music. It's out of the way in the sense that there are fewer money-making opportunities in the theater world than in the standard music market of recording artists, albums, and touring. The most significant amounts of theater music money are earned in the Broadway show sector, where in recent years we've seen the likes of *Rent, The Producers, Phantom of the Opera,* and the Abba musical *Mamma Mia.* Unfortunately, there are relatively few Broadway shows produced and fewer that are successful. Still, theater music is a potential source of money for songwriters, and for that reason it deserves a mention.

If You Are the Writer or Co-Writer of a Show

Money can come to writers of musical shows in a number of ways and from a variety of sources. They include option payments from a producer for the right to produce the show; an advance based on capitalization of the show; royalties during the main run of the show (usually 3 to 4.5 percent of gross weekly box office receipts until costs have been recouped, and 4 to 6 percent thereafter); royalties from the touring version of the show; monies from revivals and amateur productions of the show; mechanical royalties from an original cast album; performance royalties for songs from the album; mechanical and performance royalties for cover versions of songs from the show; synchronization fees from movie versions of the show and from uses of songs in other movies; mechanical royalties from a movie soundtrack album; performance royalties for songs from the movie soundtrack album; and monies for home video, television uses, commercials, and a host of other sources.

For more information about payments to writers of theatrical music, contact the Dramatists Guild of America at (212) 398-9366 or check their Web site (www.dramaguild.com).

If Your Song Is Used in Someone Else's Show

If a producer decides to use your pre-existing song in a show, the payment to you is often a fixed dollar amount, paid weekly. Another way is to pay you a percentage of the weekly gross box office receipts, prorated according to the total number of songs used in the show or according to the duration of the song in relation to the total running time of all music in the show.

PRINTED MUSIC

As previously mentioned, another source of income in the music publishing business is the selling of music in printed form. The chances are slim of an independent or up-and-coming musician—particularly in the pop-music field—selling printed versions of original songs. It's lucrative only when the public already knows the songs. But in the interest of completeness, here are a few different ways in which printed music can be presented:

- Sheet music of a single song
- Folios (collections, including record album songbooks)
- Music collections for educational purposes
- Music collections for various vocal and instrumental combinations: choral group, band, keyboard, guitar, brass, strings, and so on

Printed music can be aimed at different markets. Sheet music and collections of popular songs appeal to amateur singers and instrumentalists, who number in the tens of millions in the United States. Certain types of song collections are aimed at the high school and college band market. Miniature scores are widely used for study in college music classes. Instrumental sheet music may be used by serious amateurs or practicing professionals.

If you perceive a market for a certain kind of printed music and you wish to enter that market as a publisher, there are two main ways to go about it: (1) you, the publisher, handle the entire publishing process; or (2) you enter into an agreement with a separate company to handle certain aspects of the publishing process.

Handling the Complete Print Publishing Process

In this case, you oversee the complete preparation of the printed music. Here are some of the steps that are involved:

1. Obtain the rights to use the music, if you are not the original publisher or writer. (A copyright notice for each piece of music must be printed in a prominent place on the publication.)
2. Have the music arranged for the intended use (whether solo guitar, piano, vocal plus guitar, string quartet, or some other configuration).
3. Have the music professionally typeset, using either traditional engraving or computer-based (desktop publishing) methods.
4. Arrange for the preparation of an attractive cover design.
5. Estimate the number of copies to be printed, based on your knowledge of the size of the audience.
6. Negotiate an agreement with a distributor, establishing a retail price that ensures you make a profit after the distributor takes a cut.
7. Arrange for printing, binding, and delivery to the distributor.
8. Arrange to pay royalties to the composer of the music (if you're not the composer). This amount depends on the type of publication, but generally runs between 10 and 15 percent of the wholesale selling price (minimum rates set by the Songwriters Guild of America, www.songwriters.org). For collections of songs, the total writer share will be divided among all the participating writers.

Bear in mind the following general rule about sales of printed music: Publishing sheet music of current hits can be highly risky; the song's popularity may have dwindled by the time you reach the market. On the other hand, long-established hits—"standards" in music parlance—can continue to sell for many years. And additional money can be made by repackaging such songs for different types of users: school bands, community choirs, guitar students, and so forth.

Having Other Companies Handle Aspects of the Publishing Process

You may have neither the expertise nor the inclination to handle such tasks as music preparation, production, and printing. If this is the case, you may opt to have an independent folio publisher-distributor handle these responsibilities. The organization may serve as either a licensee or a selling agent.

License Arrangement with an Independent Publisher-Distributor. In this situation, you license an independent publisher-distributor to handle and pay for production and printing and to handle distribution. It pays you, the publisher, a royalty (a portion of which—generally 50 percent—goes to the writer). The royalty amount depends on the type of publication, as follows:

- For regular (piano-vocal) sheet music of a pop song, around 20 percent of the retail price

- For band arrangements, choral arrangements, and other separately printed copies, 10 to 15 percent of the retail price
- For folios, 10 to 12 ½ percent of the retail price, prorated. (If the folio is a "personality folio"—with a single artist's songs from a single album or several albums—an additional royalty of 5 percent is payable to the artist)

Joint Venture with an Independent Publisher-Distributor. It's also possible to set up a joint venture with an independent publisher-distributor licensee. In this case, you and the partner split the profits after the costs of production and printing have been recouped and after the deduction of an administration fee for the partner publisher-distributor.

For listings of companies that specialize in producing and distributing sheet music, look in *Billboard's International Buyer's Guide* (published annually).

If Your Song Is Used in Someone Else's Publication

You may not be interested in publishing music via any of the above approaches. Still another publisher or producer may want to include one or several of your songs in some type of published product. Here are a few of the possibilities:

Printed Music Collections. In such a case, you would receive a royalty prorated to reflect the percentage of the total collection represented by your music. That is, if your song is one of 10 compositions used, you get one-tenth of the total available royalty.

Music and Lyrics Printed in Magazines. For the use of your lyrics in a magazine, the payment to you is a lump sum, usually in the range of $100 to $500 (per issue). This amount may be higher if your song is a major hit, or if the magazine has high circulation.

For the use of both music and lyrics in a magazine, the payment to you is sometimes a pro rata share of a royalty.

Lyric Reprints in Books. Book publishers sometimes request permission to print song lyrics—in total or in part—in a novel or nonfiction book. The fee is a lump sum, the amount of which depends on a number of factors including the number of lyric lines used, the context in the book, the size of the budget, whether the book is hardcover or paperback, the number of copies printed, and the territory of publication. A minimum fee would be around $100.

There are innumerable other possible uses for printed lyrics, from greeting cards to calendars to product packages. Don't worry too much about promoting your material to producers of such products. If your composition is famous enough to boost the value of a product, the producers won't hesitate to contact you. Your job is to make your music well known, so that commercial demand for it will be as high as possible.

Chapter 17

Marketing and Promoting Music in Foreign Countries

The burgeoning global market offers music makers tremendous potential for increasing revenues. In addition to worldwide retail sales, touring income, and licensing fees, the international market can provide certain types of revenue streams that are not available domestically—such as radio and TV performance royalties for record companies.

Entertainment companies of all kinds have increasingly come to rely on international sales as a major source of income. Performers are groomed for multinational appeal. Artists who don't catch on—or have gone out of fashion—in one territory may still be able to generate revenues in another. Movies are created with international audiences in mind (action films do particularly well, since they use minimal dialogue).

To increase their ability to market such products across international boundaries, large conglomerates establish foreign offices or gain ownership of foreign media companies, and smaller companies build global networks of business partners.

The reward for developing a worldwide marketing program can be very significant, even for an independent label: in the case of the blues label Alligator Records, for example, 10 to 20 percent of its business comes from international sales.

Music—the so-called international language—is especially well suited for selling all over the world. It provides enjoyment that can transcend cultural differences. Western pop music, in particular, is in ever-growing demand among worldwide populations.

So thinking globally is a natural way to extend a music marketing program. To begin, however, you need to understand both the means of building a worldwide presence and the kinds of business conventions that govern international music commerce. The following discussion summarizes key aspects of global marketing.

ESTABLISHING AN INTERNATIONAL PRESENCE, ONLINE AND OFF-LINE

The Internet, of course, is the key to making your music available worldwide with a minimum of effort.

Amazon.com, for example, has sections of its site devoted specifically to such countries as Japan, Germany, France, and Austria, with instructions in the languages of those countries. And recall the case of the small New Albion label getting orde from Australia and Uruguay as soon as it launched its San Francisco–based site.

The Internet is particularly useful as an international marketing tool for non mainstream product. As former Liquid Audio marketing VP Scott Burnett put "The ones that have the most promotional money get marketed and get retail spa [in chain stores]. So the Internet becomes the enabling vehicle to allow for prom tion and marketing of content that you wouldn't traditionally find front and cent on the shelf at Tower, [such as] talent from another country."

That conclusion is echoed by Taku Harada, an entertainment product manager Amazon Japan: "In the off-line shops, they mainly supply the best-selling and items. But in the online shops we need to supply a wide variety of products. The be CD sale this year in Amazon Japan was Yo Yo Ma's *Best of Yo Yo Ma*. This couldr happen in off-line stores."

So if you're working outside the major-label circle, following the Internet distr bution and promotion approaches described in Chapters 9 and 11 are ways to beg increasing your international presence.

But in global commerce, the traditional brick-and-mortar retail store and ma media network is still a marketing force to be reckoned with, and faced head-on.

To establish a commercial presence in a foreign territory so that you can tap t sources of income available there, you'll need to affiliate with, or gain representatic by, distributors and publishers that handle the territory.

There are different types of organizations that do this. Giant media companies li Sony and BMG have international reach, so that if you're signed with or distributed one of those companies you generally have access to its worldwide marketing mech nism. Smaller companies may operate on a regional basis, with capabilities extending several countries. Finally, there are companies that do business in only one country.

Building an International Distribution Network

If you're not affiliated with one of the media giants, you'll most likely end up workir with several different companies. For example, you may want to partner with a mult national company to do business in only those countries in which it has proven effe tive. In other countries, you'd deal with separate companies that have been successf in your targeted region.

Many small record labels, such as Alligator Records, choose to build networks foreign representatives on a country-by-country basis. Alligator's director of licensin Bob DePugh, explains his label's approach:

> *"At this point we're licensed in France by Night and Day, in Australia by Shock Records, and in Japan, Blues Interaction has licensed a couple of dozen titles. Off the top of my head, those are the only licensed arrange-ments that we have overseas at this point.*
>
> *"We were licensed in Canada by Warner Music—they had some changes in internal policy and that came to an end last year, so we're*

exporting now through Distribution Fusion III in Canada, which is working quite well.

"In Europe we're imported and distributed by different companies in different countries. For instance, in the U.K. we go through Proper Music Distribution; in Scandinavia we go through the Amigo Network; Munich through Benelux Records; Spain we go through Disc Medi; Germany we go through Edel Contraire; and in Italy we're through IRD.

"We also do some exporting to Japan through a company called SuperStop. And a few of the Eastern European countries: A&N in Greece, Karsay in Hungary, Classic Music in the Czech Republic, and I'm sure I'm forgetting someone.

"And we do a lot of licensing at this point in South America in Chile through a company called Distribuidora Belgrano Norte."

Finding the right partner companies is of key importance. You'll want to find organizations that have proven track records of success marketing music like yours.

One way to start is to look into some of the organizations mentioned by DePugh, above, listed in this book's Appendix (page 292). Another is to pick up a recording of music similar to yours, call the publicity office of the record company that released the disc, and ask for the names of the companies that handle foreign distribution. You can then place exploratory phone calls to those companies and follow up by mailing them promotional materials (the same type that you would use to present your music to a domestic distributor, as described on page 94).

The Internet is another effective source of international distribution information. Look in the music and entertainment sections of leading search engines, or type in such keywords as "music distributors" and "international music distributors."

You can check directories for the names of foreign companies and then research their track records and music specialties. *Billboard's International Buyer's Guide,* for example, lists international record labels, music publishers, distributors, professional associations, PR and record promotion firms, and other types of companies.

Attending music-industry conferences and conventions is a way to speak directly with attending distribution and label personnel and ask them for referrals to reputable foreign business entities. One such conference is MIDEM (International Music Market), which is held each January in Cannes, France. The U.S. trade shows and conventions cited on page 195 are also good potential networking opportunities for those seeking to find international partners.

If you can't attend such shows, look at their Web sites. For example, MIDEM's Web site, www.midem.com, provides a list of exhibitors at its most recent show. Company names are listed by country, helping you target potential partners more precisely.

Again, it's essential, before establishing a business relationship with a foreign organization, to thoroughly research its track record and reputation. You'll be entrusting the company with your music, and for that you need nothing less than the best.

Keeping in Contact with Network Partners

As circumstances change, business partners may alter their agreements—or even pull out of agreements. But there's always the possibility of renewing deals, so remain in touch and on good footing with network members. Contact them regularly important sources of information about business opportunities and trends in the regions—and reciprocate by being informative about your domestic business environment and conditions.

According to veteran licensor DePugh:

> *"We do stay in contact with people. If a company decides they just aren't in a position to do the importing at some point, we never entirely turn our back on them. Friendships remain, contacts remain, and we stay in touch with people.*
>
> *"It helps that we also have a publishing company here in Alligator called Eyeball Music, and we publish about 25 percent of the repertoire that appears on Alligator Records. As a publishing company you have subpublishers around the world that are a great source of information on what's going on in the local marketplace. You get an objective viewpoint from your subpublisher contacts"*

Accommodating Regional Customs, Laws, and Business Practices

People new to international marketing may find themselves confused by the negotiating styles of businesspeople in other countries. Some cultures, for example, may favor communication that is more reserved, less forthright, than others—a difference that can lead to misunderstandings in trying to reach business agreements. It takes time and experience to develop sensitivity to these differences, but being ready for them is essential when embarking on a global business initiative.

Regional regulations and business practices are also crucial factors in working across geopolitical boundaries. MTV Japan programming vice president Tomoyo Ueno confronts them when attempting to deliver Japanese MTV content overseas. "Like the language, business customs are different.... [For example] program producing fees differ,...pricing for leisure [activities] differs, thus causing a local gap. These are the walls we face. It's the eternal theme for marketing overseas."

But some practices can be remarkably similar across borders. HMV Japan product manager Yutaka Oikawa describes his store as doing essentially what Western retailers do:

> *"Cooperate with the label. Place [tracks] in CD players for sampling songs or DVDs. Schedule an in-store event [timed with the record release]. Also an in-store digital satellite program, HMV-TV, is broadcast live in all the stores all over the country, with which we [promote products] to the customers in stores. We also give away monthly free papers that include information on in-store events, artists, and products we recommend."*

Learn about the cultures and trade practices of target countries by checking international business sites on the Internet. One, the International Business Resource Connection (www.ibrc.business.ku.edu), offers cultural overviews of countries worldwide, focusing on business customs and practices. Another, the World Chambers Network (www.worldchambers.com) provides access to chambers of commerce worldwide.

Monitoring International Economic Trends and Emerging Markets

Study political and economic events in countries where you do business, or are planning to. Volatility in these areas can affect your business investment there and require a change in marketing plans.

Keep an eye, too, on emerging markets in developing countries. You may find exciting fresh sources of revenue as new markets open to your domestic product.

Bob DePugh of Alligator Records keeps tabs on the climate for trading around the world:

"The international business is down from what it was say four or five years ago, the main difference is being in the Far East and in South America.

"We had a huge boom in Argentina six or seven years ago through Distribuidora Belgrano Norte, and we sold just a ton of records. Their market just kind of opened up to us and we really had some boom years there before the Argentine economy kind of collapsed.

"And in the Far East it was much the same thing. At one point we were distributed through Silk Road in Hong Kong and through Rock Records in Taiwan, and that branched out into Singapore, Malaysia, and Indonesia. But when the general music recession fell upon us four or five years ago, East Asia and South America were among the places hit the hardest. So those are, I guess you could say, only shadows of their former selves.

"But these things do tend to come in cycles, and eventually there are new consumers in the marketplace; if a market goes down economically they do always tend to rebound, and you find new partners eventually, and you start from scratch and build up again.

"As far as markets in developing countries, you're kind of always looking everywhere. I'd be hard-pressed to mention one market that is seriously viable at this point, where we're not involved. We've lost some markets like South Africa over the last few years, simply because the general business has gotten so bad. And when the general market suffers, anyone who's got kind of a niche market like us tends to suffer, because it's just not economically viable for people to bring our product in.

"But you're always watching those areas and waiting for the economy to get a bit better so you can get a toehold in that market."

FOREIGN DISTRIBUTION AND SALE OF MUSIC PRODUCTS

To get your records into foreign stores, you'll need to work with distributors that can service those stores. As mentioned previously, if you're not affiliated with an international media conglomerate with its own foreign branch affiliates, you may find it necessary to work with a number of independent foreign distributors on a country-by-country basis.

Once you have identified reputable foreign distributors, you can enter into any of several different types of arrangements, including the following:

- Licensing the foreign distributor to manufacture and distribute your product
- Exporting your product through a foreign distributor
- Setting up a joint venture with a foreign record label

It's entirely possible that a record company may not only work with several different foreign companies but also have different types of business arrangements with different companies, depending on what makes the most financial sense. For example, in one territory it might be more profitable to license a record company to manufacture and distribute, while in another territory the best arrangement is a simple export deal. Alligator Records takes this approach, as its founder and president, Bruce Iglauer, explains:

> *"We do a number of different things. We have some license deals. We used to license everywhere, and sometimes we would actually have the companies in foreign countries physically producing the albums. Sometimes we would act as their supplier, but they would buy from us at a pressing cost and then pay us a royalty after they made the sale.*
>
> *"More and more now, we've moved to exclusive exportation deals. And we export at sometimes some attractive prices. But we're still making our money rather quickly, rather than waiting for licensing deals and royalty statements.*
>
> *"The disadvantage [to exporting] is that we don't get any advance, which you normally get on a licensing deal. We also have to provide them with a budget for advertising. You know, if you have a licensee you expect them to do advertising, radio, and press promotion at their expense. You've got an importer, you're going to expect that you can do it at your expense, which would be just like a U.S. distributor."*

Licensing Foreign Companies to Manufacture and Distribute Products

In this very common arrangement, the record owner (you) grants a foreign record label a license to issue your recording in its local territory. The *licensor* (again, you) provides the *licensee* (the foreign label) with a master recording, from which the licensee manufactures copies and handles local distribution and promotion.

Such licensing often involves distribution using the foreign company's—not our—label. Alternatively, the record may be distributed under a split label—that is, using both the licensor's and the licensee's labels.

The licensee may prepare a new album cover, in some cases using photos and artwork from the original cover, or it may order printed covers from the licensor. The licensing agreement may also permit the licensee to change the track order, add tracks, or remove tracks.

Compensation paid by the licensee to the licensor is generally an advance against *the equivalent* of 8 to 26 percent of the local retail list price, less taxes and packaging costs, for 90 to 100 percent of records sold. (Sometimes payment is based on 100 percent of records sold minus promotional copies and returns.)

The words *the equivalent* are used above because, frequently, the royalty is computed not on the retail price but on what is called the *published price to dealer* (PPD), which is roughly equivalent to what in the United States is called the wholesale price. When this is the case, the royalty percentage is set higher so that the amount earned is equivalent to 8 to 26 percent of retail.

In another type of licensing deal, the licensor provides manufactured albums to the licensee, who buys them at the manufacturing cost and then pays a royalty on sales. This arrangement makes sense when estimated sales are not high enough to justify the foreign label bearing the cost of local manufacturing.

Depending on the previous sales track record of the album, you may be able to negotiate a sizable advance against projected royalties. In any event, a record of previous sales is usually necessary to attract the interest of a foreign distributor, just as it is with a domestic distributor.

Exporting Products to International Distributors

In some cases, it makes the most financial sense for the record owner to export its finished recordings to a foreign distribution company, who simply distributes.

In the export scenario, the exporter (you) sets a price that permits a reasonable profit above manufacturing cost. (That price will be roughly the same as the distributor wholesale price you charge domestically.) One independent record label set its export price at roughly 50 percent of the domestic suggested retail list price. That same label offered some foreign distributors an additional discount of 15 to 20 percent. In other cases the label provided foreign distributors with an advertising allowance in the form of a discount off the export price. Arrangements vary from company to company. Typically, though, the foreign distributor pays for freight and duties. Also typically, the exporting label is responsible for paying mechanical royalties (since it is the manufacturer of the product).

Joint Ventures with International Companies

The owner of a recording may want to exert more control over how a product is manufactured, marketed, and distributed in a foreign territory. An effective way to do this is to set up a joint venture with an internationally active major or independent label. In such cases, the two business entities share resources, control, costs, and profits (For more information about joint ventures, see page 105.)

Performance Royalties for Record Companies

In many countries outside the United States, record companies are paid royalties when their recordings are publicly performed—say, broadcast on radio and TV. (In the U.S., only writers and publishers get radio and TV performance royalties—although Internet radio now pays record companies.) Such performance fees are generally shared by licensees and licensors, typically on a 50-50 basis.

Recording Artist Royalties for Foreign Sales of Music Products

Royalties payable to a recording artist on foreign sales of various types of music products are generally lower than domestic royalties. And as with domestic royalties, they vary depending on the type of product.

Artist Royalties for Foreign Record Sales. Artist royalties on foreign sales of records vary depending on the territory. They also vary depending on whether the record company markets through a foreign affiliate or licenses through an independent label in the territory.

In general, the royalty rate on records sold in Canada is 85 percent of the U.S. rate.

For records sold in what are termed major territories (the United Kingdom, France, Germany, Italy, the Netherlands, Australia, and Japan), the rate is generally 60 to 75 percent of the U.S. rate.

For records sold in the rest of the world, the rate is generally 50 to 60 percent of the U.S. rate.

Foreign royalties are negotiable, of course, depending on the recording artist's track record of product sales and his or her popularity in particular territories. (The more popular the artist, the greater the artist's negotiating strength.)

Artist Royalties for Foreign Merchandise Sales. Artist royalties on foreign sales of tour-related merchandise (see page 225) are around 80 percent of the domestic rate (which, in turn, is generally 25 to 40 percent of gross sales).

Artist royalties on foreign sales of retail merchandise (see page 225) are also around 80 percent of the domestic rate. (The domestic rate, in this case, is 10 to 20 percent of the wholesale price for retail store sales.)

FOREIGN EARNINGS FOR WRITERS AND PUBLISHERS

Earnings for music writers and publishers (as differentiated from record companies and recording artists) come from the same types of uses in foreign territories as they do domestically:

- Manufacture and distribution of recordings (mechanical uses)
- Incorporation of music in visual works (synchronization)
- Public performances

(For basic information about writer and publisher revenue sources, see Chapter 16.)

There are several different ways for domestic publishers to secure representation f their catalogs—and ensure collection of their earnings—in foreign territories:

- Through a multinational publisher
- Through a network of local subpublishers
- Through a joint publishing venture
- Through a combination of the above

Multinational Publishers

f the foreign representative is a multinational organization, songs are exploited, and oreign earnings are collected, through its affiliated offices in various countries. For ne writer or publisher dealing with such an organization, this may be the most con-enient way to ensure blanket coverage of numerous territories. The risks are twofold: 1) certain local offices of the multinational company may not be particularly effective, nd (2) the song or catalog may not get the attention it would in a smaller company, esulting in missed marketing opportunities.

Foreign Subpublishers

'or the smaller domestic publisher, earnings are usually collected on a territory-by-erritory basis by foreign *subpublishers*—that is, local foreign publishers with whom ne domestic publisher has set up what are called subpublishing agreements.

Subpublishers perform the same tasks in their territories that domestic publishers o at home, from promoting songs for potential new uses to collecting and paying ut royalties. Foreign subpublishers generally retain between 10 and 25 percent of noney earned (including the writer share), remitting the remainder to the domestic ublisher. (Thus, foreign royalties received by domestic writers are generally less than neir domestic royalties, because the total amount of foreign royalties—of which vriters get 50 percent—is reduced by the amount kept by the subpublisher.)

The subpublisher share may be higher under certain circumstances. This is some-mes true in the case of performance royalties, because the writer share of these roy-lties is paid directly to writers (through performing rights societies) rather than to ne subpublisher, thus justifying an increase in the subpublisher's percentage to com-ensate for the overall 50 percent reduction (the writer portion) in the total amount n which they calculate their share.

Subpublishers also tend to take a higher share of earnings for local cover versions ne subpublisher procures. The share is generally 40 to 50 percent. The justification is nat in such cases they are taking a more active role than when simply collecting oreign earnings for a domestically recorded song.

Subpublishers often pay advances to original publishers, against expected earnings. The amount of an advance usually depends on the perceived value of the catalog.

Subpublishing agreements may cover an entire catalog, a few songs, or even one song.

At-Source Royalty Calculation. In some cases a foreign subpublisher will have a foreign licensee in another country collect earnings for that country and submit them to the subpublisher. The foreign licensee may retain a percentage before submitting monies to the subpublisher, who then deducts its percentage before forwarding monies to the domestic publisher. This, obviously, would reduce the overall amount of money received by the domestic publisher and, ultimately, the writer. For this reason, some subpublishing agreements include an "at-source" provision, stipulating that the domestic publisher's percentage will be based on the total amount earned at source, before the sublicensee deducts its percentage.

Joint Publishing Ventures

As with foreign record distribution, a foreign publishing operation can be set up as a joint venture, with responsibilities, costs, and profits split between the domestic and local foreign partners.

Territory-by-Territory Publishing Arrangements

Another option for exploiting songs in foreign territories is using a combination of the previously described options—that is, using a multinational publisher in some territories, and using separate subpublishers in territories where the multinational offices are not particularly effective (or don't exist).

Mechanical Royalties for Music Distributed Internationally

Mechanical royalties, again, are monies paid by a record company to a publisher for the use of a song on a record.

In most foreign countries, mechanical licensing fees for songs used on records are collected from record companies by the local mechanical rights collection agency, which then distributes the money to publishers who make claims for those songs. (U.S. publishers can deal directly with these agencies rather than having a foreign subpublisher deal with them; the Harry Fox Agency [see page 231] can also act as a representative for a U.S. publisher, since it maintains reciprocal representation agreements with affiliated collecting societies in the world's major music markets. For information on foreign affiliates of the Harry Fox Agency, check the Web at www.harryfox.com:80/foreignsoc.html.)

Foreign mechanical earnings sometimes go unclaimed by original publishers. Accrued money for unclaimed songs is eventually distributed to local publishers in amounts proportionate to individual publishers' percentages of total mechanical earnings.

Mechanical license rates differ in different countries. Typically, the rate per track is a prorated percentage of the published price to dealer (PPD), which is roughly the ame as what the U.S. terms the wholesale price. (Canada, like the U.S., computes mechanical fees on a penny basis.)

Synchronization Fees for Audiovisual Works Distributed Internationally

Licenses of music for use in TV shows, movies, and home videos originating in specific countries are issued by the subpublishers in those countries (if subpublishers are used). Since this is work performed by the subpublisher, the amount it retains before submission of money to the domestic publisher may be higher than the usual 10 to 15 percent—sometimes 50 percent.

License agreements for home videos of movies and TV programs produced in the U.S. tend to be for the entire world. That is, generally the producer will pay the U.S. publisher the established rate regardless of the country of sale. This way, producers avoid having to deal with many individual foreign subpublishers.

Payment for Foreign Performances

Foreign territories have their own performing rights societies like ASCAP, BMI, and SESAC. (For foreign societies affiliated with ASCAP, for example, see www.ascap.com/about/affiliated.html.)

For performances of U.S. works, local performing rights societies collect money from local users and pay publisher shares to local subpublishers (or, for music with no local subpublisher, directly to the original publisher's domestic society—ASCAP, BMI, or SESAC) and writer shares to ASCAP, BMI, or SESAC. The rights societies then distribute collected foreign royalties to their members.

Unlike in the United States, royalty-generating performances in foreign countries include movie theaters. Fees are based on one of several possible formulas, including a percentage of net box office receipts or a dollar amount per seat times the total number of seats in the theater.

"Black box" collections—money collected for songs not identified as having ownership—go into general funds that are eventually distributed to local publishers.

Printed Music Sold in Foreign Territories

A domestic publisher may arrange to have a foreign subpublisher manufacture and sell sheet music of its song. In this arrangement, the subpublisher typically pays the domestic publisher 10 to 12 ½ percent of the suggested retail price. In the case of a folio consisting of multiple works owned by different publishers, this royalty is paid out on a pro rata basis.

Lyric Translations

Obviously, a song may be easier to exploit in a foreign territory if it is translated into the local language. For this reason, subpublishers retain the right to hire local translators.

Local writers who translate lyrics get a percentage of the subpublisher's share of earnings—or the domestic publisher's, depending on the arrangement—for local mechanical and synchronization uses and for sales of printed music. For performances, local performing rights societies deduct the translator's percentage from payable write royalties, submitting the remainder to the domestic performing rights society. Per centages vary depending on local practice and the negotiating strength of the translato

INTERNATIONAL TOURING AND LIVE PERFORMANCE

As in domestic touring, foreign tours are generally set up to coincide with the releas of an album.

While international headliners routinely book world tours, mid-level performer may limit foreign performances to those territories in which they have had succe with distribution and sales, and in which they have received some press attention.

An interesting case of selective popularity is that of jazz musicians from the Unite States, many of whom find more enthusiastic audiences in foreign territories—sa Europe and Asia—than they do in their homeland. There have also been many case of rock performers who have gone out of fashion in one part of the world and ye are able to mount hugely successful tours in other regions.

Bookings for foreign performances may be handled by foreign agents, foreign sub agents of domestic booking agencies, or large domestic agencies—like Williar Morris, ICM, and CAA—that have foreign offices. Tours can also be booked by artis or their managers dealing directly with foreign concert promoters. For small banc who haven't yet achieved national success in their homeland but still wish to boo live dates in foreign countries, it's important to line up that first series of dates—a tas made easier with the assistance of an enthusiastic contact in the foreign country wh can put in a good word or traffic promo materials to clubs—and then do well at th gigs and get positive press coverage. The resulting buzz can power an increasingl potent booking campaign, and open doors to some of the booking agencies men tioned above. Many bands have done it—the 1990s "sadcore" band American Musi Club, not known much outside of San Francisco, managed to build a sub-followin in England, and singer Huey Lewis's early band Clover—another unknown outsid of its regular Northern California haunts, made inroads into the U.K. thanks to connection with producer Nick Lowe. By targeting receptive foreign markets an building up personal and company contacts connected to those areas, artists in th middle of the commercial market can lay the groundwork for a fruitful internationa marketing campaign.

Chapter 18

Monitoring and Managing the Marketing Program

Marketing a music product is a complex operation. It encompasses numerous activities, from product development to distribution to promotion—all of which work together to support a sales-generating whole, functioning like a well-oiled machine.

But the machine, once assembled and turned on, can't be left untended. It requires constant upgrading and modification. Promotional strategies may have to change. New distribution methods may have to be adopted. The musical approach may require adjustment.

In other words, the music marketing program has to be monitored and managed to ensure its ongoing effectiveness.

Before looking at what's involved in fine-tuning the marketing machine after it has been set into motion, let's assemble an overview—a marketing management master list—of the essential marketing tasks discussed in preceding chapters.

THE MARKETING MANAGEMENT MASTER LIST

A "big picture" view of the entire marketing enterprise is essential in working the individual parts so that they fit and support the whole. Use the following checklist as a tool for keeping tabs on where you are in the marketing program and what you still need to do to manage it effectively.

Some of the steps in this checklist apply to those aiming to build a record company. If your goal is simply to market your own music, or to market music to a degree that falls short of creating a record label, extract from the checklist only those items that apply to your unique situation.

Market Research

- Target your market: identify the audience to which you plan to sell music.
- Estimate the size of the audience.
- Research the interests of the target audience.
- Identify the ways the audience satisfies those interests; identify the stores audience members frequent, the magazines they read, the Web sites they visit, and so on.

- Plan to sell the music through those stores and media.
- Identify appropriate distributors that service those stores.
- Initiate contact with distributors and find out what they need from you in order to establish a business relationship.
- Assemble a customer list, initially culled from personal contacts and later to be supplemented with rented mailing lists, if necessary, for specific marketing actions. Update it frequently.
- Assemble a list of performance venues and their personal contacts, for use in getting bookings. Update it frequently.
- Assemble a media list that includes the information sources—newspapers, magazines, Web sites, radio, and television—used by the target audience. Update it frequently.
- Assemble a list of retail outlets—independents stores, local chain outlets, and more—whom you will make contact with over the course of your marketing effort. Update the list as needed.
- Assemble a list of radio stations, focusing on station formats that will air your kind of music, and identifying key stations in your target markets ("key" meaning stations that report playlists to trade magazines that publish influential weekly airplay charts). Update the list as needed.
- Assemble lists of movie and television production companies and music supervisors, for use when sending out your music for consideration. Update it frequently.
- Identify the qualities of your product that will be most attractive to your targeted audience. Plan on emphasizing those qualities in product packaging, promotional material, and ads.

Business Preliminaries

- Obtain a Fictitious Name Certificate from your local county clerk's office to establish your business's name as a DBA (doing business as).
- Obtain a Universal Product Code (UPC), which you'll use on all your products, from the Uniform Code Council.
- Obtain a seller's permit (resale license) from your state board of equalization if you're operating in a state that has sales tax.
- Consider registering your business name (trademark) with the U.S. Patent and Trademark Office.

Product Development

- Decide on your basic physical product format—usually CDs and digital files for Internet transmission.
- Assemble a final list of the music compositions to be included in the product.
- If you are the writer and/or publisher of any of the music, register it for copyright protection through the U.S. Copyright Office.

- If you are the writer and/or publisher of any of the music, join one of the performing rights societies—ASCAP, BMI, or SESAC—and provide them with clearance forms for each music composition to be included on the album.
- If you are the publisher of any of the music, consider engaging the services of the Harry Fox Agency for help with administering mechanical licenses for uses of your music by others.
- For compositions on your CD that are not written or published by you, obtain mechanical licenses from the copyright holders. This involves contacting the Harry Fox Agency or going directly to each copyright holder not affiliated with Harry Fox.
- Become a member of SoundExchange to make sure you get paid royalties for Internet radio play of your recordings (see page 134 for more about SoundExchange).
- Set a release date for the recording. This will govern the scheduling of your promotion plans.
- Assign the album a unique catalog number.
- Obtain a bar code (digitally or in the form of film) from a local supplier.
- Plan and execute the preparation of packaging and promotion materials, emphasizing in their design the qualities of your product that will be most attractive to your targeted audience.
- Anticipate, to the extent possible, all of your near-future print needs (including, for example, direct-mail flyers and brochures) and have them designed and produced at the same time as product packaging, to save money.
- Estimate the number of CDs you will manufacture, based on your estimate of the size of the audience. Allow for many extras to use as giveaways and promotional copies.
- Get bids from several different disc manufacturers, and choose the one that offers the combination of price and service that best meets your needs.
- Determine the suggested retail list price (SRLP), based on your cost, customer expectations, and competitors' pricings.
- Register the track with Nielsen SoundScan and Broadcast Data Systems to make sure your retail sales and radio airplay are accurately tracked.

Distribution

- Decide on a distribution approach: reaching retail stores through standard distribution channels, using direct marketing, employing the Internet, or a combination.
- For direct marketing, and for sales of CDs over the Internet, create an ordering and fulfillment system: deal with product storage space, postal regulations, toll-free phone numbers (if desired), and credit card ordering systems (if sales volume warrants).

- For Internet distribution, set up your own Web site and work with other online outfits that draw music customers.
- For direct marketing, plan and execute the preparation of mailers, a brochure, direct-response advertising, or other sales tools.
- Look into record clubs and gift catalog companies that might have an interest in selling your product via mail. Provide them with information on your product.
- Prepare a product information sheet (a "one-sheet") to use when trying to interest a distributor in taking on your product.
- Line up a distributor. If necessary, handle distribution yourself on a local basis, and over the Internet, until you have a track record that will attract distributors' interest.
- Start with local and regional distribution; build up to national (and international) later.
- Use restraint when deciding how many copies to press in the first run. If you press too many, there may be lots of copies returned unsold. Pressing fewer will help ensure sell-though, a distributor reorder, and the distributor's timely payment for the first order as an incentive to get you to press more copies.

Promotion

- Plan and execute Web-based promotion.
- Aim to obtain prominent display of your album and promotional materials in retail stores.
- Consider buying co-op advertising through retail stores.
- Prepare press kits.
- Schedule concerts, nightclub dates, and other personal appearances to coincide with the release of the album.
- Mail press kits to the local press and other media several weeks in advance of personal appearances. Follow up to ensure receipt and to (tactfully) urge coverage.
- Place ads for performances and the recording in local and national media, as affordable.
- Arrange special promotional events—such as record store autograph sessions—to coincide with local performance dates.
- Sell the recording at live shows, if it doesn't conflict with label strategy.
- At live performances, provide a mailing list for audience members to sign.
- Direct publicity efforts at regional and national publications as touring expands.
- Set up cross-promotions with other business entities that cater to the customer group that you're targeting.

- Work hard to come up with imaginative, innovative ways to promote your product.
- Choose songs to promote to radio. Promote them to radio by starting with local and regional college and noncommercial stations. Focus on key stations that report to publishers of popularity charts. Get songs into the hands of radio program directors one month before release date.
- As popularity increases, prepare a promotional video.
- Promote the act to television by starting with local and regional cable programs. Work up to national programs.
- As the marketing program broadens, engage the services of independent publicity and promotion firms.

Expanding the Marketing Program

- Develop additional formats for the delivery of your music, possibly including DVDs.
- Promote your music to all possible business customers, including producers of television, movies, commercial advertising, and compilation albums.
- Create non-music merchandise and sell it at your shows. At a higher commercial level, license the artist's name and likeness to manufacturers of merchandise to sell at retail and on tour.

Managing the Money Flow

Set up a system for handling the following types of payments in a timely manner:

Incoming Payments (Accounts Receivable):

- Retail sales revenues for all product formats. Payable to product owners (such as record companies) by distributors (for store sales) and by individuals and credit card companies (for direct mail and Internet sales)
- Live performance fees. Payable to the artist by nightclub owners, booking agencies, and other customers.
- Television appearance fees. Payable to the artist by producers, booking agencies, and advertising agencies.
- License fees for uses of the recording on television, in movies, on the Internet, and in other contexts. Payable to the owner of the recording by television and film production companies, Web sites, and advertising agencies.
- Royalties for uses of the recording on Internet radio. Payable to the owner of the recording by Web sites or SoundExchange.
- License fees for use of the artist's name and likeness in non-music merchandise. Payable to the record company or to the artist by merchandising companies.

- Royalties for public performances of music compositions (whether on radio and television, on the Internet, in concert, or in other public settings). Payable to writers and publishers by ASCAP, BMI, or SESAC.
- Royalties for mechanical uses of music compositions (in records, tapes, and CDs). Payable to publishers by record companies (often through the Harry Fox Agency).
- Royalties for synchronization uses of music compositions (in movies, television, and home video). Payable to publishers by production companies and advertising agencies.
- Royalties for transcription uses of music compositions (in background music and syndicated radio programming). Payable to publishers by production companies and syndicators (often through the Harry Fox Agency).
- Royalties for printed versions of music compositions. Payable to publishers by independent print-music publishing companies.

Outgoing Payments (Accounts Payable):

- Payments for production and manufacturing (of all product formats), including recording, packaging, and duplication costs.
- Artist royalties.
- Mechanical royalties for uses (on records, tapes, and CDs) of compositions owned by others. Payable to publishers (often through the Harry Fox Agency).
- Synchronization royalties for uses (in audiovisual products) of compositions owned by others. Payable to publishers.
- Licensing fees for uses (say, on compilation albums, or as sound samples) of pre-existing master recordings. Payable to owner(s) of the recording (usually a record company).
- Promotional costs, including materials, postage, advertising, and services of independent publicists and promoters.
- Fees for legal and financial advisors.
- Payments of salaries, rent, telephone, utilities, equipment, and other overhead.
- Taxes.

NAVIGATING THE SHIFTING CURRENTS OF THE MUSIC MARKETPLACE

Managing an in-motion marketing program requires knowledge and decisiveness. To illustrate, let's expand the "marketing machine" metaphor a bit: Picture the machine as powering a forward-moving enterprise.

The marketer is essentially the navigator. Like the captain of a new ship crossing uncharted waters amid changing weather conditions, the marketer constantly monitors the "seaworthiness" of the enterprise amid a changing business climate and then adjusts course as necessary.

Monitoring the progress of the marketing enterprise provides information on (1) the success or failure of marketing efforts to date, and (2) changes in the marketplace. These factors will, in turn, guide decisions about future courses of action.

Monitoring Progress

Obtaining information about the progress of the marketing plan is a relatively straight-forward process. It involves paying close attention to the impact of the marketing effort on several fronts, including live appearances, the press, retail sales, and electronic media.

Determine a reasonable amount of time for the marketing and promotion effort to take hold ("reasonable" can mean anything from months to years, depending on your level of patience), and then focus on the following questions (not all of which will apply to all types of performers):

- Do audiences respond positively to the performer in concerts and other live appearances?
- Is the act able to obtain regular and frequent bookings?
- Has attendance increased at live appearances over time?
- Has the act graduated from small venues to larger ones?
- Has the act made progress in expanding from local appearances to regional and national bookings?
- Has the act received press coverage?
- Has press coverage been positive? Negative? Mixed?
- Is the act getting attention on the Internet, measured in downloads, visits to the act's Web site, and statistical reports on multi-artist sites?
- Have distributors shown interest in handling your product?
- If stores have stocked your CDs, are they selling, and at what rate?
- Do SoundScan reports indicate weaknesses and strengths in different markets?
- Has radio shown interest in playing your music?
- If there has been radio play, has there been a corresponding increase in retail sales and concert attendance?
- Has there been progress in expanding from college, local, and non-commercial radio to national programs and networks?
- Has the act been listed in sales and radio-play charts in trade magazines?
- Has there been interest in the music on the part of movie producers, television producers, printed-music publishers, other artists, other record companies, and other types of business customers?

and, most importantly,

- Are checks coming in?

The answers to these questions should give an accurate indication of your progress to date.

Now what do you do about it?

Responding to Successes and Failures

Different outcomes of marketing efforts require different approaches to moving forward.

But whatever your particular outcome may be, it is better to have prepared for a range of outcomes ahead of time—with a corresponding range of courses of action—rather than be caught by surprise and have to improvise less-than-ideal changes in strategy on the spur of the moment.

You should have plans in place for dealing with best-case, worst-case, and most-likely scenarios.

The Best-Case Scenario. In the best-case scenario, marketing efforts have yielded positive results at each stage of the operation. In such a case, management decisions should focus on either maintaining the present level of activity or expanding the marketing program—whichever is preferred.

Expansion might mean finding new ways to promote the artist or exploit his or her success—through books, for example, or some other side product line (example: the neckties based on designs by the Grateful Dead's Jerry Garcia). Expansion might also mean spinning off new musical projects, such as collaborations with other artists or explorations of new musical approaches. (Think of Paul McCartney's and Billy Joel's forays into "classical" music.) Expansion could also involve moving into new geographical territories.

Whatever the expansion plan, care should be taken not to alienate the core audience. Elvis Costello's collaboration with a classical string quartet on the album *The Juliet Letters* worked because it was in keeping with his style-surfer reputation. Middle-of-the-road crooner Pat Boone's 1997 foray into heavy metal did not work; it offended his conservative Christian loyalists.

Maintaining the present level of activity is also an option. But doing so may not be as simple as it sounds. External factors may enter into the picture and require action.

The Worst-Case Scenario. What if the marketing effort has reached the stage of distributing products to stores, but the sales are minimal, and intensive live performing over an extended period of time seems to be having no beneficial effect on sales?

At some point, the decision may have to be made to end the program and do what is necessary to cut further losses. This may involve a cessation of promotion spending and the establishment of steep price discounts to help sell off the remaining product.

Most people are familiar with "cutout bins" in record stores, where albums sell for a dollar or so. This is where records go that have been deleted from record company catalogs and tagged as "excess inventory"—in other words, left for dead. This is the final option for squeezing any last pennies out of a failed album.

But it's not over till it's over. There is always the possibility of restarting from scratch with the same artist: reworking the music, rebuilding the image, aiming for a new market, and hoping that customer memories are short.

The Most Likely Scenario. Typically, marketing efforts yield mixed results. An artist may do well in live performances while having difficulty in getting radio play. A record may be successful in one region and have no impact whatsoever in another. Critics may praise the product, yet record sales are not up to par.

Every record release and artist promotion has its own unique set of problems. For that reason it would be pointless to try to address every possible scenario here. The main point to keep in mind is that if an artist is doing well in one sector of the marketplace, it's an encouraging sign: it means that with patience, hard work, and creative thinking, there's a decent chance that in time you'll win over the holdouts. For example, many a performing artist has worked on the road for years before getting the attention of radio programmers and national record buyers.

In such cases, keep adding to the promotion kit: update bios and fact sheets to include the latest successes, add new press clippings, and include samples of new recordings. Use the kit to keep in contact with sectors of the market that you're trying to enter. As the artist's track record lengthens, chances increase that formerly reticent observers will finally see the light and show some enthusiasm.

Responding to Changes in the Marketplace

The success or failure of a marketing effort is affected not only by the pros and cons of the product itself (and the marketing plan) but by factors related to the external environment. Such factors include shifts in public tastes, changes in consumer buying patterns (such as seasonal fluctuations), economic booms and downswings, technological developments, and evolving trends in delivery systems. Any new factor that can potentially influence the short- or long-term success of the marketing program should be analyzed and, if necessary, met with a shift in marketing strategy.

Chapter 19

Twenty Profile-Building Ideas to Use Right Now

1. Give away samples of your music. If you're starting your music venture from scratch (at least from a business standpoint), consider distributing samples of your music for free to as many listeners as you can reach. This is what Netscape and other companies did with their new products to get them initially accepted and used by a wide audience. The money came later.

It makes some sense. After all, if you're willing to give radio stations a song to play for free, counting on it as promotion, why not treat, say, file-sharing the same way?

For starters, you might send two of your best MP3s via e-mail to people who know you—personal contacts, alumni from your high school and college, and members of your Internet newsgroups, for example. Ask those people to pass the songs on to others who they think might like them.

Most important, let recipients know how to get—at a price—the rest of what you have to offer, whether by visiting your Web site, logging on to another Internet sales site, or simply phoning you.

It's the beginning of a grass-roots awareness campaign.

Opposing point of view: There's a school of thought that says never, ever give your music away. A famous jazz saxophonist, for example, used to say he never picked up his instrument unless someone paid him to. Others advise to avoid giving away even to family and friends, to have them, too, pay for your music.

Whether you choose this route or not boils down to personal inclination. But keep in mind that if you have no audience and no one knows you, you won't be able to sell anything. Giving away samples early in your venture at least gets your name out there and lays the groundwork for future sales.

2. Set up a Web site devoted to your music. It doesn't have to be elaborate—although the more attractive and professional looking the better. Provide free downloads. In addition, offer options for purchasing your music—say, an album's worth of your songs. The option can be as straightforward as your phone number or as automated as filling out an online form.

- Include descriptive information about the musician and the music.
- Link to as many other sites as possible.
- Send the URL to as many recipients as possible, and include the URL in

every communication that you transmit, from e-mail to outgoing voicemail message to business card to mailers to CD packaging.

. Turn your Web site into an online press kit. After you've set up a basic, functional Web te for delivering your music, fine-tune it into a press kit to which you can always efer potential business contacts, including the media, booking agents, club owners, istributors, and radio programmers.

- Have the Web site press kit function as a complete overview—informational, visual, and musical—of the artist.
- Provide a bio—both a brief summary and a more detailed version.
- Provide photos that media editors and producers can download for publishing in their publications.
- Provide an e-mail option to enable business entities to contact you about permission to use photos, notification of planned stories and features, queries about nightclub bookings, and any other business matters.
- Provide a news section. It should feature the most current news, written in the form of a press release, so that it can be downloaded and used verbatim by newspapers, magazines, and other media. Also include an archive of recent news, containing the "press releases" previously posted.
- Include positive quotes from independent sources (reviews). Use them throughout the site.

. Display CDs on mass-market Internet retail sites. Some large sites, including Amazon.com, accept products directly from independent sellers. Amazon's Advantage Program, for example, allows you to sell through them on a consignment basis, without having to go through third-party distribution. They let you set up a title etail page for which you provide your own marketing copy. When copies sell, they pay you 45 percent of the price you set for your CD. You'll be able to tell your audiences to "look for the CD on Amazon."

. Affiliate with alternative distribution sites online. Take advantage of independent-artist services that allow you to link your site to theirs, set up your own page on their site, or simply post your MP3s on their site and then sell through them on financial terms that vary from site to site. Current site options include CD Baby, GigAmerica, AudioGalaxy, and Cornerband. They reach millions of music fans.

. Use an e-blast to announce your presence to the world. Is it worth a hundred of your dollars to e-mail a thousand targeted people with information about your CD along with a sample track? How about $200 to reach 2,000 people? If you think it may be, rent a list of e-mail addresses from a relevant magazine, organization, or Web site, or from a commercial list broker that can offer addresses of people likely to appreciate your style of music.

- Make the message memorable (which may mean funny, off-the-wall, and colorful).
- Make sure the e-mail includes a hyperlink and a direct way to order the CD.

7. For your next big gig, execute carefully timed promotion. Make sure that anyone like to be interested in the gig is well-informed about it through several sources. Hit the with an ad (even if it's small) in a local newspaper several weeks in advance of th date. Send a press release to newspapers in the area with specific who–what–when where data for the papers to include in their entertainment calendars. Two weeks advance, send flyers to everyone on your mailing list—and media list—who is base in the gig's geographical area. Post flyers in restaurants, cafés, stores, and colleges, and c outdoor walls in the vicinity. One week before the show, send e-mail announcemen to names on your e-mail list(s). If you can, set up an interview on community c college radio—you'll need to lay the groundwork for this far in advance—as close t the show date as possible. Have the interviewer play some tracks, and during th interview tell listeners to come to the show.

Repeat this process for all your live engagements, to the extent possible.

And when the rooms fill up, don't forget to play as if your life depended on it!

8. Sell merchandise at shows. Set up an easy-to-see merchandise station at your show and sell CDs, T-shirts, bumper stickers, and whatever other items you can creative and attractively concoct. It brings in money and serves as promotion, broadcastin your name out into the world traversed by those who own and display the items.

9. Meet your audience. Make your relationship with fans (and fans-to-be) face-to-fac and personal. At your merchandise table at shows, sit there after your set, talk t people who stop by, and offer to sign the CDs and items they buy. Provide a sign-i book for people who want to receive notice of news or upcoming dates, and allo space for addresses, phone numbers, and e-mail addresses. And give something awa such as a poster, or a postcard with an eye-grabbing image and, on the back, fac about your new CD and how to order it.

10. Find individual investors. If you have people who believe in your music, you may b able to tap into them for capital with which to fund your next album project or som other step in your professional development. In setting up such a deal, clarify two thing (1) the return on investment, whether a percentage of revenues generated by the funde activity (such as a specific CD project) or a fixed dollar amount; and (2) the possibilit of the investor not getting paid back at all due to the high risk of the business.

Finding an investor may sound far-fetched, but it can be done, even by an unsigne band. I once worked in a band that was bankrolled by an individual investor. All ban members drew a weekly salary, whether or not the act performed in a given week Expenses, stage clothing, and professional recordings were covered by investment funds

11. Find a corporate sponsor. You may be able to set up reciprocal arrangements with businesses that match your image and sensibility. An example would be a compan that provides you with services, equipment, or financial support in return for you featuring their name on your Web site and promotional materials, allowing them t reach a new customer base that fits their target demographic. To find such a company start with known fans of your act: it may be that one of them runs or works for company and may be happy to work with you on a sponsorship deal. Otherwise, research companies that match your audience, and present them (or one) with a proposal that clearly indicates how they'll benefit from exposure to your audience. *Important:* Make sure the company profile matches the personal image you're trying to project.

2. Self-recording? Don't think demo. Think finished product. In the past, recording yourself tended to mean doing it as a demo, with the hope that a finished version would come after a real record company decided your demo merited a contract. But today, the tools of high-end record production are at your fingertips, and major record companies are at arms' length. So there's every reason to treat your recording project as the "real thing" rather than a rough sample to get you a deal. This *is* the real thing. From here on in, approach every home-studio recording as a market-targeted professional project. Think of it as *the album,* or *the single*—not *the demo.* Similarly, think of it as your task to get it to the marketplace. And if you're determined to sign with a major, a finished master recording may help seal the deal.

3. Meet or touch base with one or two music-industry professionals each week, starting now. If you're not known by people in a position to help, you'll never get help. Conversely, the more people who are aware of you (and like you), the better the chances of your name coming up when an opportunity arises. So make it a routine to meet or reconnect with one or two music professionals at least every few weeks, and add them to a cumulative list from which you can choose people to periodically touch base with. Seek out such people at professional music-business or songwriting workshops, at industry conferences, and through friends—and friends of friends. When meeting someone, introduce yourself in a way that connects. ("I'm a huge admirer of that box set you put out." "I'm a friend of Frank, your engineer over at ProSonic Sound." Be friendly; express interest in what *they're* doing. And without being pushy, let them know what you're up to, and impress them with your personality. Have business cards—or more imaginative contact cards—available to give to anyone you meet face to face. If they express interest in hearing your CD, *follow up quickly.* Don't let the connection slip away.

The word for this, of course, is *networking.* Treat it as an essential and ongoing part of getting known as a musician.

4. Recruit a "street team" of marketing interns. You need help, and young people need work experience. Put those two needs together and you come up with the "intern," the student or entry-level worker whom you can hire to carry out some of your marketing tasks for free (at least initially) in return for the career experience, a letter of recommendation from you, and perhaps some of your CDs or merchandise. You benefit by (1) delegating nonstrategic tasks and (2) adding to the growing legion of people emotionally invested in your success, as interns will likely become.

Recruit interns by posting "Marketing interns [or 'marketing assistants'] wanted" notices on college and high school bulletin boards, in record and music stores, and on your Web site, and by putting the word out among current fans. Review résumés an interview applicants before hiring.

The kinds of work you might assign to interns includes mailing CDs and me chandise, distributing posters and flyers throughout areas where you have booking and calling stores and radio stations to request your music.

You can count on an intern who enjoyed working for you to proudly build u the experience to friends. Word of mouth spreads. The intern's friends come to shov and buy your music. You've started a new ripple of interest on the grass-roots level

15. Line up some music students. A musician who has the time can develop hard-con followers by taking on private students. Motivated music students often bond wit their instructors, especially if the instructor has a distinctive and effective teaching styl The students will attend the teacher's shows and buy the CDs, becoming, in effec champions. (One musician I know attracted a cultish following of students. The spread the word about him. The musician became something of a local legend, able t book high-profile gigs in part because his students could be counted on to fill seats.

16. Address an important public issue as part of your music promotion. If there's a publi issue you care strongly about—whether in politics, economics, education, health, c the arts—consider using your platform as a performer to publicize your views on th matter. You might earmark a portion of receipts from ticket or CD sales as a dona tion to an organization aligned with your position. Address this in your marketin communications. You'll not only act on an issue you care about but also connect wit others who share your views. Your involvement in the issue can also serve as a topi to pitch to editors and writers in your publicity campaign.

17. Book your own showcase performance. If you're having trouble getting booked int targeted venues, consider renting out a hall and producing your own show. Cut cost if you want, by doing it on a co-op basis, with one or two other acts.

Choose a hall that is conveniently located, large enough to handle the crowd yo plan to attract, and attractive enough to show you in a positive light.

You're in control, so you present yourself as you dream of being presented, wit lighting and a stage setup tailored to your musical persona.

The key to making it work is to promote it well ahead of time (see item 7) an do everything in your power to have the event covered by the press, even if it's jus a local college paper.

A showcase is also a good way to present yourself to potential distributors or othe business backers or partners. Make sure you invite anyone you know in this category

Set a reasonable ticket price, and assign a trusted party with the task of sellin tickets at the door.

Don't forget to set up a merchandise table and to man it after the show, chattin up the audience and signing CDs.

Note: "Showcasing" also refers to the act of performing live for a record executiv to "close the deal" after the label has expressed interest in you because of your dem CD or your indie success.

8. Appeal to fans of musicians you sound like. Say your music sounds like a mix of Artist X and Artist Y. It makes sense that X's and Y's fans might like your music, too, if they only knew about it. So consider posting messages in chat rooms on the most popular Web sites devoted to Artist X and Artist Y. (This probably requires subscribing to the site or joining a newsgroup.) Make the subject heading of the message appeal to the specifics of the sound your music shares with the artist—something like: "If you like [song title], check this out." The body of the message should be friendly, simple, nonhyperbolic, and informative: "People say our band's music reminds them of Artist X but also has a bit of Artist Y plus something they've heard nowhere else. You might like it. Listen to samples at our Web site: [supply URL]."

Some official sites prohibit posting commercial solicitations, so make sure the message isn't a "buy this" pitch. The idea is, you're tipping off like-minded people to something they might appreciate.

9. Piggyback on the distribution plan of an established indie label. Having difficulty lining up a distributor—maybe because you have limited product (like, only one CD)? Get around it by finding an indie label that already has distribution and is willing to add your CD to its catalog.

10. Invent a new way to present your music. This is where you throw out the rule book. Sit back and let your imagination run wild. Allow yourself to explore the most outlandish, off-the-wall "what if?" scenarios your mind can conjure. Something entirely new may come out of it—or at least something old done differently and better. If it does, and if you make it happen, it could provide an impetus for potential buyers to look your way.

What about mixes made to order (the customer wants louder guitar; he gets a version that has it)? Or providing separate tracks that the customer can personally mix—with extra instruments costing extra? Or offering personalized versions with a lyric altered to include the customer's (or someone else's) name? These aren't exactly new ideas, but they and others like them can point the way to new avenues of thinking.

The business of music marketing and promotion is volatile, all right, but the flip side of volatility is positive change in the form of innovation. Maybe you'll be among the visionaries and determined marketers who find ways to broaden the field, who manage to open up whole new panoramas of profit possibilities by using their imagination and wits.

On your way to that point, watch what others are doing, learn from them, stay up to date on new technologies, and keep your marketing gears in motion.

Chapter 20

Talking Shop: Interviews

MARKETING YOURSELF AS AN INDEPENDENT MUSICIAN
Jacqui Naylor, Singer and Recording Artist

You're a jazz singer from the San Francisco Bay Area with two CDs, an expanding performance schedule, and many enthusiastic reviews to your credit. Anything you'd like to add to that description?

JN: My third CD was just released. It's a jazz-pop crossover recording comprised mostly of original music. I guess that now makes me a jazz-singer/songwriter, for lack of a better term.

Provide a little background on your pre-performer work life and how you made the transition to a music career. You've worked as a marketing director, haven't you?

JN: Yes. I was the director of marketing for a clothing company for many years and had worked at an advertising agency before that. My degree is actually in marketing and it wasn't until my last year of college that I became interested in acting and singing through classes there.

I went on to study at ACT [American Conservatory Theater] and took a jazz vocal class at the San Francisco Conservatory, where I met my vocal mentor and teacher, Faith Winthrop. I studied with her privately for the next five years. During that time, I continued to work full-time in marketing.

I never intended to make a career of music until the day Faith called me with a gig she couldn't make. I was terrified but took the gig, had a great time, and came home with a check. I was hooked.

Has your experience as a marketer had an impact on how you handle your music career?

JN: Absolutely. As an artist, I just want to make music and tell a story with my voice that strikes an emotional connection with people. But as a marketer, I know I need to ask myself, 'Is my music as good as it can be? Is there anyone who really wants to hear it? What price would they pay for it? How many ways can I let them know about my music? And where do they want to purchase it?'

As I answer these questions, I can set goals and make artistic and business choices that make them attainable.

Looking at things from a marketing perspective reminds me that choosing the right distributor is just as important as practicing scales if I want to make music that connects with people.

Describe your process of "graduating" from small clubs to better-known jazz venues. Did it just happen, or did you take specific marketing-related steps to help it happen?

N: A little of both, actually. I'd been wanting to make the jump but wasn't really sure how it would come about. I kept knocking on the bigger doors, but with little success.

Meanwhile, I just kept refining my craft at the clubs around town, creating tighter sets—mini-shows with more defined solo sections, patter, and a stronger stage presence.

I also decided I wouldn't wait for concert venues in San Francisco to notice me and began securing shows in Los Angeles at the more prestigious venues on a monthly basis.

This was difficult, working two markets at the same time. But I had a good car, good charts, and a cheap hotel. I was also able to find great musicians there to work with.

Of course, I still lost money, but I was making a name for myself in L.A. I made sure to send any reviews I received not only to the press in San Francisco but to those clubs I had been trying so hard to get into.

Around this same time, I was asked to perform at the Jazz and Cabaret Convention at Town Hall in New York City. It wasn't a paying gig, but I felt it was an opportunity to begin establishing myself as a rising national artist and not just a San Francisco or West Coast singer. I saved my money and brought my trio from the CD with me, wanting to make the strongest impression I could on the two songs I was to sing.

I came home to a phone call from the Plush Room, San Francisco's most famed vocal concert venue, offering me two weeks at their club. He had heard me in New York, even though I had been down the street for four years.

The club requested that I not perform at a public venue for two months in San Francisco on either side of the dates to ensure the maximum audience during my run. I started turning down my regular San Francisco gigs and put all of my energy and resources into PR and marketing for the Plush Room dates. I knew this was my chance to make the leap.

Some questions about making and releasing records: Do you release your albums independently? If so, what distribution channels do you use? What challenges and obstacles have you confronted? And what advice do you have for musicians who want to release their own albums?

N: I was very fortunate to have financial help from my family to make my first record, and I was determined to make a CD that could be picked up by a major jazz label with minimal effort on the label's part.

I secured the best San Francisco players, recorded at Different Fur [Recording Studio], and had it mixed by Phil Edwards from Concord Records and mastered by George Horn at Fantasy.

Like most artists, I was sure I'd get a deal. After many press kits, phone calls, plan rides, meetings, and negotiations, I came very close to a deal with Atlantic—and ha met with the president of jazz A&R from every major jazz label.

When it became clear that the Atlantic deal was not all I had hoped, I went aft independent labels. But I felt that most of them didn't have much to offer me that wasn't already doing myself.

So I started my own label and began looking for distribution. Easier said tha done. I learned quickly that any good distributor, one that'll do what they say an pay you even remotely close to on time, wants a catalog from more than one arti and a guarantee of a marketing budget and a steady stream of releases.

This, of course, makes sense. But I just had *me,* with my one record that I had sum every dime into.

I had to sell this record and sell a lot of them. I sold them at shows. I sold ther on Amazon. I sold them to hotels, florists, and specialty stores. I sold them on con signment to every major record store I could get into. And to get into stores an assure I'd sell records, I traded in-store appearances for listening stations.

For my second release, I recorded a live album at the Plush Room. Again, I wer after major and independent labels and distributors, came close to deals with Warne Max Jazz, and other independents, but in the end chose to sell my record directly.

I released the third title on my label in June of this year, and have secured financi backing for the marketing of the record and some corporate sponsorship for touring

With three CDs, a marketing budget and plan, and a commitment to release title regularly from myself and other artists, I'm negotiating with good independent dis tributors.

My advice on making and releasing independent records: Keep recording cost down to ensure recoupment on investment, and explore every possible channel fo sales and distribution. Determine to have success in one market and grow from there

What specific actions do you take to (a) promote live appearances, (b) promote albums, and (c) cultivate an audience?

Regarding the latter, I've noticed that you sell and sign CDs at some of your club appearances, which would seem to be a good way to make a personal connection with listeners.

JN: I feel that everything eventually boils down to helping my listener or potenti listener feel that they are in some way connected to me.

And you're right: going out into the lobby and making myself available to sig CDs and say hello certainly does this and helps build my audience. I also really enjoy i

The same is true of the way I go about promoting a live performance or CD Ultimately, from the huge quantity of music available, I'm asking someone to liste to *me*—to come out and hear *me.* I believe that the only way to do that is to estab lish a relationship with my market, and that has to start before they even hear me.

I think it's also worth saying that my market is not just the buying public but a the people who help me relate to them—like the staff at my label, but also the press e staff at the venue, the deejays, the clerks at the record stores, and the owner of the afé down the street that let us put up a poster.

And how well do the materials I give these people tell the story about me and my music? How attractive is that poster, business card, letterhead, CD artwork, postcard, ress release, CD giveaway, co-op ad?

And how good is the story? I try to find an angle when promoting a show or CD hat also supports my image and beliefs as an artist and those of my market.

What about strengthening your image through cross-marketing?

N: I've found cross-marketing to be a great way to do this—and to target specific market segments.

For example, with my second CD, *Live at the Plush Room,* I helped raise money or Music in Schools Today, a nonprofit that I care about, while also aligning myself with a corporate sponsor that supported my image.

Lexus pre-purchased CDs for their customers in exchange for their name and logo n the CD and press materials for the release and concert. Of course, they were also ffiliated with a good cause and the nonprofit. I got my CD inside of a Lexus and am ble to give 30 percent of sales from that CD to Music in Schools Today.

My new CD includes an original tune recorded for World AIDS Day in conjunction with Artists Against AIDS. This is something I feel very strongly about and am ersonally committed to. It also helps me reach a market I may not have reached before nd certainly helps to tell the story about who I am and build a relationship with my audience. When the new record is released, this is something that my PR person, radio promoter, and distributor will be able to use to set me apart from other artists.

Does radio fit into your professional plan at all? What opportunities does radio offer these days?

N: I think radio, both over the airwaves and on the Internet, still presents an important opportunity to reach a wider audience and help sell records. I'll definitely be outsourcing radio promotion with my new release.

Does the Internet play a significant role in your marketing mix?

N: Amazon continues to be my best-selling account, so I'm a large proponent of nternet promotion and sales. I also feel that having a Web site is incredibly important, nd especially for the press. Downloadable press kits and photos make their job easier.

Now that you've become established as a performer, are you conscious of projecting a pecific image or sensibility or point of view, and reflecting it consistently in your music, hoice of venues, album art, and promotional material?

N: I think developing a well-defined image is one of the most important keys to building a successful artist. Whether one does this independently or with a manager, t must be done.

I'm very conscious of how my image reflects my sensibilities, my aesthetic, and my beliefs as a human being. I say this because I think many artists may view paying attention to one's image as selling out in some way. I think it's quite the opposite, and that defining one's image can help an artist to focus all of their efforts to support who they are.

Choosing music, venues, corporate ID, album art, and other materials that support one clearly defined image can greatly increase the chances that you'll be remembered and understood as an artist and businessperson.

For example, *Live at the Plush Room,* while essentially a jazz album, also has some sexy, sophisticated modern jazz versions of some '70s pop tunes.

The cover features a modern-styled photo of me against a red curtain that's plush and soft looking. The red of the curtain also works well with the red in my logo and letterhead.

For a promotional kit, I packaged a scaled-down version of my one-sheet and press release with the CD in a clear plastic box filled with fresh rose petals.

I overnighted them, of course.

Related to that last question, when choosing songs to perform or record, do you base the choice entirely on your personal taste, or do you think about the marketability of the material, or both?

JN: As an artist and businessperson I definitely think about both.

Finally, any general advice you can offer talented musicians who are preparing to enter the field as professionals? Any important lessons you've learned?

JN: Read this book from cover to cover, even if you intend to be with a label or hire outside specialists.

Be educated, but put some of your energy and resources into getting to your market in ways no one else is. You'll stand out.

Never give up!

MARKETER'S ADVICE FOR EMERGING ARTISTS
oy Gattinella, CEO, Overdrive Entertainment

ou directed marketing for Windham Hill Records, then went on to EMI-Capitol. Tell us
bout your new, post-EMI venture.

G: It's a production and marketing company that creates original programming for
V and film and provides full-service marketing consulting for artists and corpora-
ons seeking to build their brands by reaching out to wider audiences.

While we work with many corporations in lots of categories, when we work with
tists it's primarily developing young artists. And we treat them as if they're a young,
udding brand, a small company that needs to grow. We help them sign with a label,
that's something they need to do or should do.

hat artist characteristics make your job easier?

G: There's a certain personality we look for in an emerging act. When speaking to
a artist for the first time I like to fast-forward and envision them in a few years. Can
ney communicate well? Do they do so cogently? Effortlessly, with a smile? Are they
ole to speak to the press? Are they able to communicate well with different people
different levels of the record company? Are they able to connect to an audience?
ou know, do they get it? Those are the personality traits that I look for.

hat else do you look for? What helps a new artist succeed?

G: Some point of differentiation. There's so much music out there, and so many
tists building their careers and playing great music, that unless you have a point of
ifferentiation for your audience to grab onto—to remember who you are and set
ou apart from everyone else—success is going to be hard to find.

The second big key is to build a local following. Any managers, record labels, or
nsultants like us are all looking for an artist who has a proven local following,
hether it's done through playing live incessantly in your market, getting local radio
rplay that can then spread to regional and national, or having a really interesting
ews story that generates local press and then hopefully national.

I'm working with one band that sold 15,000 units in a small college town here in
alifornia. No label, all self-produced, all self-sold off the stage. That's a lot in a small
own, and there are stories like that all over the country. That's the way an artist can
reak out, by creating a very large local following and then building it out from there.

Play anywhere you can—college campuses, radio stations, sponsored events; I
now people who would play at the opening of an envelope. Get ready to play wher-
ver somebody wants you to be. That's where you need to be.

nything beyond those fairly standard guidelines?

G: I'd recommend that artists try just about anything—whether it's enlisting friends
shoot really cheap on-the-fly video, or hooking up with the local manufacturer of
me kind of product.

I teach a college class on marketing, and I ask students what their favorite C[] are. One raised his hand and said it's a certain sampler CD put out by a brand of ba[] ketball shoes, clothing, and gear. It's a collection of various indie bands that the co[] poration handpicked, and it's become an underground classic.

How do you get on something like that? Well, there are lots of companies that d[] CDs like that. Those are great ways to hit your audience. You're following in the wa[] of a strong brand that's out there marketing themselves, and if you're being markete[] with them, it'll do great things to help market your band.

You mentioned video. Is that really something an emerging act should focus on?

RG: Think of it this way: If an artist has a friend who's in film school, owns a camer[] and can do creative stuff, you have nothing to lose to shoot something. Edit together in a way that looks completely different, that no one's ever seen before.

Will it air on MTV? Probably not. But this is such a visual medium, and we're [] so used to seeing things visually. A video can be put in front of people very quick[] and give an idea of what the act's like and what it sounds like. It's also helpful for[] band to see itself on the screen playing live.

And when labels get a packet, if it includes a video, trust me, everybody at the lab[] will watch the video. They probably won't play the music all the way through, b[] they'll spend three or four minutes to sit there and watch something.

And now that you can burn it on DVDs it makes it even easier.

So, to summarize your message?

RG: My message to young artists would be stay at it, stay on it, differentiate yourselve[] build a local following, be patient, and just don't give up.

Know the odds going into it, just like a high school basketball player looking t[] go to the pros should know the odds; they're seriously not in your favor. The sam[] thing goes for being a musician.

But the ones who have made it are the ones who have stuck with it and persevere[]

There are a couple of great examples today: the Norah Jones record, which [] blowing up all over. Here's a woman who a year and a half ago just got herself a gi[] at a restaurant in New York and played there every week. No one ever heard of he[] her chances were a million to one. But she built a huge following in Manhattan, an[] she's got herself a top-five record right now.

There's also a band here in San Francisco called the Donnas—four ladies all i[] their early twenties. They've been at it four or five years now and playing everywher[] And now they have a breaking video on MTV and are selling lots of records, and it[] happening for them.

So it does happen. I wouldn't be deluded to believe that it happens for everyon[] of course, but when everything's aligned, good things happen.

TACTICS USED IN MARKETING
Roy Gattinella, CEO, Overdrive Entertainment
Bruce Iglauer, President, Alligator Records

In the broadest sense, what is the task of the music marketer?

RG: The ultimate task is to take great music and get it out there so that people can hear it, enjoy it, and hopefully enrich their lives from it.

The first thing we do as music marketers—depending on the level you might be working with in the organization—is interpret the artist's music. Then we have to somehow convey and communicate the essence of their art to consumers—faithfully, and as compellingly as possible.

How do you go about doing that, specifically?

RG: The first thing that you do is sit with the artist, get to know them, get to know their music and where it comes from, and work with them to develop their careers in a way that you can best present them to their potential audience. That's the real key. And that [involves] lots of components.

There's visual marketing—how to present them visually. Everything from the graphic design and packaging of the product to the advertising and marketing message. If there are music videos, it extends to the production of the visuals of the music video itself.

Then singles need to be chosen for appropriate formats of radio.

Also, retail stores will be targeted to service the record to. If you've got an adult-oriented artist, you want to make sure Borders Books and Music, Barnes & Noble, and those kinds of accounts are covered. If you've got a rap artist, you want to make sure that your indies and your mom-and-pop record stores in urban centers are covered. These are only a few of the distribution challenges.

BI: There are a number of things that we do [at Alligator Records]. First of all—we spend anywhere from ten to twenty thousand dollars on a new release for price positioning, listening posts, end caps, and anything else related to retail placement.

Beyond that, one of the key things that we do is we have artists, at least for the most part with our current catalog, who tour just constantly. So a great deal of the advertising and the promotion is around live performance dates.

Typically, when an album is in its first four to six months, we'll support a number of the live performances with advertising, especially in weekly-type print media, or if we can find the right day of the week and the right show, sometimes we'll do radio advertising. Radio is very expensive.

For the most part, our radio play is now on AAA-format stations—Adult Album Alternative. And from time to time we'll support those stations by advertising, if we can afford it.

And we also do some sponsorships around gigs of Public Radio shows. You can't buy a real ad on a public station; you buy an announcement, or, you know, "Brought to you by a gift from Alligator Records, who wants you to know that Tinsley Ellis performing at the Variety Playhouse."

Beyond that, we feel that in order to play the majors' game we have to do a lot things that a lot of other labels think their distributors are doing.

For example, I have two people who do nothing all day but call retail stores. An the irony of that is that we don't sell to retail stores. We sell through distributors. We' a real independent company. We don't sell around our distributors at all. But we ca up stores and just talk to them about our new releases, about artists coming int town, about numbers on SoundScan reports. We talk about radio play in their mark or other media in their market. We invite them to gigs, basically greasing then Shmoozing them. Getting them to remember our product; talking to them abou bringing titles in. I don't think that there's anybody else at our level of the inde pendent industry who works so closely with retail.

We also think that we're in the business of career building, and we stick with ou artists for a very long time. And because our artists are genre specific, what we lear from one artist helps us with another artist.

GETTING MUSIC ON RADIO
Tim Kolleth, Head of Radio Promotion, Alligator Records

What's the role of a record company's radio promotion department?

TK: The radio promotion department plays a major role in exposing and introducing the artist/band to the largest possible audience it can. The ultimate goal is to heighten the awareness of a band and to help create a hit at radio. By and large, the public still makes decisions about purchasing discs and learning about bands based on radio airplay. Radio is still one of the best ways to directly connect with the music fans that purchase records and attend live shows.

If the band/artist is signed to a label, we'll assume that the distribution of their record is firmly in place and that copies of their new release are available or will be available at finer record stores across the country.

Most songs are worked to radio prior to their availability in stores. Some labels work the first single of a record several weeks in advance of the street date (the day a record is available for sale). This helps build awareness of a record, and it also allows for retail to consider ordering more product if radio is responding and an overall buzz is being created.

Radio helps create the buzz and drive the momentum.

As you might imagine, a lot of thought goes into picking the right song and the appropriate radio format to promote the record to.

The selection of the right song can be a laborious process, involving several departments at a label, including radio promotion, marketing, retail, A&R, and so on. The artists and artists' management also have input and certainly have opinions regarding this matter. Ultimately, everyone wants to make the right decision and select The Hit. It can be a very tough decision to make, with the success of the entire project hanging in the balance.

By the time a record is delivered to the label and a song is selected as a single, the label has a pretty good grasp of what radio format it will be sending promo discs to.

It's the radio promotion department's job to get the discs in the hands of the right stations at the right time. One of the most important aspects of being a signed act is that you have a label staff working your record that has strong personal relationships with key decision makers at radio. The power of a label's radio promotion department is the power of its relationships with radio and with the many stations it works with across the country. Labels have vast databases of contacts and addresses to ensure the appropriate people get the appropriate discs.

All stations are not created equal, as you might imagine. Radio promotion departments mainly work "reporting stations." These are stations that are allowed to report their playlists or spins/rotations of current music to major radio trade magazines. Stations are allowed to become reporters mainly because of their impact and importance in their market or region. Stations that report to trade magazines affect the radio airplay charts. The charting of a record is basically the scorecard by which success is measured at radio. You can talk to a bunch of stations that don't report, but the airplay isn't registered on the national charts. It's almost like the tree-falling-in-the forest scenario: It'll be heard, but are there enough people around for the sound make an impact in the big picture?

The radio airplay charts are tabulated every week and published in the trade magazine or through an online tracking service provided by the trade magazine.

So the promotion department first focuses on the reporting stations in the various formats because they affect the charts.

Once the programming department of each station has a copy of your record, it the job of the promotion department to get with the music or program director each station either on the phone or in person to make sure they have heard the record and to get input from the programmer regarding airplay. Your goal is to get an add An add means that the radio station has made the commitment to officially play an report the airplay of your record to the charts of the various trade magazines.

Radio has a process they follow when adding records. Each Monday or Tuesday (depending on when the trade magazines want their reports), stations officially add new songs to their playlists and begin spinning them and assigning them to certain rotations. Mondays and Tuesdays are known as add days. An add date is the label's way of targeting a specific day for airplay to begin on a new project. When all of the stations have reported their new adds for the week, the totals are tabulated, and ultimately one release a week is deemed the "most added" across the format.

Being the most added record is the first step toward ascending the radio chart and it's a surefire way to get noticed by the entire format—especially by the station that didn't add you that week. Of course, getting an add at each station is just the beginning stage in the lifespan of your song on each station.

Again, the reporting stations are important to contact and work because they directly affect the national charts, and the use of your record's chart position is a major tool for gaining more attention and getting additional stations to add your songs. lot of these stations tend to watch what others do, and the charts and the trade magazines allow them to keep track of what their peers are doing.

Perception is a huge factor in promoting a record. Program and music directors are really aware when there's a push happening by the label. They deal with label promotion people all the time, and when a label person comes with a priority to them they're hopefully going to listen to it with strong consideration. The involvement independent promotion companies also tips programmers off to the importance certain projects (more on that later).

Getting radio airplay involves a similar approach with each record. Basically, you get the record into the hands of the decision makers, you select an add date (the date you want every station at the format to add your record), the label may hire the best independent promotion firms to augment the promotion staff, and collectively they tediously and thoroughly call, fax, e-mail, and visit each station in person to get the important points across about why they should add your record into rotation instead of a pile of other songs/CDs.

Do record labels have to work with, and pay for, independent promoters?

K: Yes. In fact, most of your promotion budget can get used up paying for their services and providing "support" (hint, hint: dollars) to the stations they work exclusively. The relationship between an independent promotion company, the labels, and the stations is important to know.

Essentially, independent promoters, or "indies," are hired guns. Labels hire them because of their influence, expertise, and knowledge of the format and because they have spent years maintaining and building relationships with the key decision makers at the various stations.

Many indies strike exclusive deals with certain stations that contribute to the charts. When an indie has an exclusive deal with a certain station or stations, it usually means that they are the only independent firm who can talk with the station about new music.

For this exclusivity, the indie pays an advance to the station of a certain amount of money each year, or they pay a certain monthly stipend. The money collected by the indies from the labels in the form of "support" is funneled back to the stations for its own promotional efforts. Exclusivity allows the indies to infiltrate the programming arms of the stations they have deals with. When an indie has an exclusive deal with a station they definitely have the ability to affect some of the programming decisions. Exclusivity also allows the indies to pitch to the station just the songs they are getting paid/hired to work, as well as be the first to know what songs are getting added at each station.

If you hire an indie that has exclusive deals with the stations you need airplay on, there is a high likelihood you'll pay for each and every add. Many are calling this legal payola, and the practice is widely debated across the industry. The long and short of all of this is that if you want radio airplay it will cost you and your label handsomely. It's not just about how good a song is, unfortunately.

If your company isn't paying some of those independent promotion firms to contact the stations for you, then your likelihood of making a substantial impact at any format is limited. It's very simple: If an indie has an exclusive deal with multiple stations and you are not hiring that indie, there is a good chance you will be shut out at those stations. There are still stations that add records because they like them, even if their exclusive indie isn't working them, but the indie will still try to find a way to bill the label for the add. Either way, if you don't pay, you still may get the add, but the indie will spread the word around to the other stations they work with, and you'll ultimately get shut out down the line.

Working a record to radio these days is all about opening up the artist's and label's wallet in the hopes that the record takes off. Call it a gamble or an investment, but you'll need the funds to get a song off the ground at radio. That's reality.

A lot of great songs make the radio, but they don't make it for free. A lot of great songs don't make the radio because the labels just can't afford the promotional rollout.

Of course, the music has to be there to begin with or it will get shot down imme diately, even if you do hire the best indies money can buy.

Every artist who is inspired to make a record thinks that what they do has valu and worth, and they measure it against the songs they hear on the radio. It's some times easy to forget that for every song you're trying to push there are maybe hundred other bands/songs and twenty or thirty other labels trying to work the sam people for the same small number of slots at each station.

So the promotion talent you surround yourself with is vital to your development growth, and success at radio.

LICENSING MUSIC TO TELEVISION AND FILM
Bob DePugh, Director of Licensing, Alligator Records

How important is licensing to film and TV in the grand scheme of a music marketing program?

BD: Over the past couple of years this has become kind of a phenomenon. With the success of some big soundtracks and the higher visibility of music and bands in film and TV projects, people are a lot more aware of this avenue of the business than they were a couple of years ago. Bands starting out now, even before they have a record deal, are aware of the possibilities of licensing in film and TV. They know what it can do for their careers and the money and publicity it can generate. So there are a lot more people eyeing and competing for those placements now than there were five years ago.

When you talk to a music supervisor or someone in a film or TV production office, it's just amazing the amount of material that arrives on their desk each week. It's like they're a record label. They're getting 50 to 100 unsolicited CDs a month or a week. Every unsigned band is sending their demo into Fox TV, hoping that somebody will hear it and put it on the air.

If these people get hit with so much material, how do you get their attention?

BD: The only way to get them to listen to you—especially if you're not a name artist or if you're a niche label like us—is to build up a personal relationship with them.

People never want to admit that what they're involved in is sales, but that's such a strong element in almost anything you do, even under the banner of publicity. Are you on somebody's mind, on their current list? And have you proven through the course of years that you're easy to work with and you're dependable, that you can provide what you say you're going to deliver?

What about some other revenue streams?

BD: We have a Web site where people can get back catalog titles. You can get into that mail-order system through our Web site, and that's a good selling tool for us.

In terms of other revenue streams, there are jukeboxes. In the old days you would sell one record and it would be played on the jukebox forever. Now there are jukeboxes that exist solely on a hard drive, and you receive a royalty every time the song is played.

You can license your masters out for downloads and streaming on the Internet, which provides sometimes a big, sometimes a tiny revenue. There are Muzak companies, and you know Muzak is a lot hipper than it used to be.

It's part of the tragedy of growing older, that all the music you loved as a teenager is suddenly piped to you out of the ceiling.

I don't think rock is dead, I think it's on a kind of strange marketing life-support.

GETTING COVERAGE IN THE MEDIA
Mark Pucci, Publicist, Mark Pucci Media
Marc Lipkin, Publicist, Alligator Records

Mark Pucci, tell us a little about your journey from working at a major label to running an independent publicity firm.

MP: I've been in this business in two different incarnations, so to speak. The first tim started in 1979, as Mark Pucci Associates. Then, late in 1991, I went back to work fc Capricorn Records in Nashville as vice president of publicity and eventually becam vice president and general manager of the label. I left that at the end of 1995 an restarted my company under the name Mark Pucci Media. We've been concen trating exclusively on music this go-around, for the most part doing entire labels at all possible.

My tastes tend to run more towards the "rootsy" side of things, so we're primaril doing things in the area of Americana, alt country, roots rock, blues, some jazz, an some rock things.

I've represented probably over 100 artists over the years.

How has the publicity side of the business changed since you started out?

MP: So many of the magazines and a lot of the newer things that have come alon over the last five to ten years are so pointed toward the gold- and platinum-sellin acts with the videos—the Christina Aguileras of the world—and we're probably th furthest away from that kind of thing that you can imagine. It's that much more dif ficult to make some kind of impact with these publications, some of which we don even attempt anymore, because we know they're just not interested in what we'r talking about.

It's difficult for the client to hear that sometimes, especially if they don't have whole lot of knowledge or experience in things. They'll say "We want to be in *Rollin Stone* and *Spin,* on Jay Leno and MTV." But there are certain things that just exclud you automatically from that, unfortunately.

Also, the media is changing on a daily basis. Things come, things go, people mov in and out, and it's difficult sometimes just to keep up with things.

How has technology affected the way you do business?

MP: There are still things that have remained the same, physical things that are sti around, but there's so much more done electronically these days. Some of the peopl we work with don't even have hard copies of photos; everything's done with JPE(files and downloaded. In the old days you had to rely on FedExing stuff and spend ing money that way, when now it doesn't cost you anything to send a JPEG to some body. And it's instantaneous.

The ways of reaching people are so much quicker and more cost-efficient, an you can do so much more. People seem to forget that before we had all these grea things to make our jobs so much easier, we spent a lot of time just trying to get things to people.

Everybody has a Web site, and we have one, too. We link our Web site to the sites of clients, so if somebody wants to find out something they can go to our Web site and get everything we have there, and then maybe get something from the client's site that we don't have, such as downloadable music.

Marc Lipkin, as a label-based publicist, how do you make promotion material get attention?

ML: A writer's a very busy person; an editor's a very busy person. We want to make their decision making easy. To that end, every press kit we send comes in a bright green folder. That green folder is usually identifiable on a very busy writer's or editor's desk full of mail and press kits. If I call and say, "Did you get the material on Koko Taylor?" and they say, "I don't know if I saw that or not," I say, "Well, look for that bright green folder with the Alligator logo on it." They'll go, "Oh yeah, there it is," and they'll pull that folder out.

It's got a bio for them, it's got every bit of information on the gig, including show timing and ticket prices, and there's a photo for them. And now in the age of e-mail, if they need color art we send an e-mail attachment with a high-resolution JPEG they can print.

What else do you do to "grease the wheels"?

ML: Our track record and reputation are good, and we work very hard to not mess up that reputation. Publicity is very much about integrity and trying real hard to work with people, because essentially they're doing you a favor. We get a feature in the *Chicago Tribune,* we're not paying ad space for that. They're giving us a feature, and we're going to do everything possible to make sure that writer's needs are met and that he's having a pleasant time doing it.

As a publicity person you really have to think about not just those editors' needs, but their job definition, the structure they're in that they have to answer to.

For example, I've been here about ten years and I think we've had maybe five records in that time reviewed in *Rolling Stone.* But I understand how magazines work and shows like Letterman work. They have advertisers to answer to, and they've got people spending a lot of money for thirty seconds of TV space wanting to know why Garth Brooks isn't on every night.

It all comes down to honesty, too. I don't see doing something unethical or wrong just to get a story. The Jay Leno show was coming to Chicago maybe five years ago, and I called his booker and said, "Listen, if you come to Chicago you've got to have blues. This is the home of the blues. Here are our artists: We've got Koko Taylor and Lonnie Brooks and these living Chicago blues legends."

She says to me, "That's great, how do I get in touch with Buddy Guy?"

So, even though Buddy Guy isn't an Alligator artist, I said, "Here's the manager's number. Buddy's great to work with, and you won't go wrong booking him. Thanks anyway. If something falls through and you need an Alligator artist, I'm here."

She can't always book my artists or even always take my calls, but she knows I'm someone who's not going to steer her the wrong way just to get one of my artists on the show. You may lose a feature on Thursday and then a week from Friday you may get the cover.

Publicity is a very important cog in the marketing machine. While a review in *Rolling Stone* doesn't get people out to buy a record immediately, everything's building block. When the producer of the Conan O'Brien show sees a review in *Rolling Stone,* you're one step closer. Every little piece is a building block to the next little piece.

Things can fall in your lap, but sometimes you've got to make them fall into you lap. You don't win the drawing unless you've got an entry in the drawing.

Appendix: Marketing and Promotion Resources

Advertising

Advertising Age
www.adage.com
Weekly trade magazine covering ad agencies, their clients, and their ad campaigns.

Advertising on the Internet, 2nd Ed.
Robbin Zeff and Brad Aronson
New York: Wiley, 1999.
Addresses online ads and direct marketing, audience targeting, and Web measurement.

Adweek
www.adweek.com
Trade magazine of the advertising industry.

American Association of
Advertising Agencies (AAAA)
405 Lexington Ave., 18th Fl.
New York, NY 10174
(212) 682-2500
www.aaaa.org
National trade association representing the advertising business.

Co-op Advertising Sourcebook
New Providence, NJ: National Register Publishing
Lists 4,500 available co-op programs in 52 product classifications.

Standard Rate and Data (SRDS) advertising sourcebooks:
Consumer Magazine Advertising Source,
Newspaper Advertising Source,
Radio Advertising Source, TV & Cable Source,
and *Interactive Advertising Source*
Des Plaines, IL: SRDS
www.srds.com
Provides circulation/audience data and ad rates.

Audience and Market Characteristics and Research

Arbitron Inc.
140 W. 57 St.
New York, NY 10019
(212) 887-1300
www.arbitron.com
Provides business subscribers with reports on radio and television audience sizes, demographics, and viewing patterns.

DM2
(DecisionMaker Media Management—
formerly Cahners Business Lists)
2000 Clearwater Dr.
Oak Brook, IL 60523
(800) 323-4958
www.dm2lists.com
Commercial mailing list provider for direct marketing.

Encyclopedia of Associations 40
Farmington Hills, MI: Gale Group, 2003
Detailed information on nonprofit organizations, their purposes, their activities, and their contact information.

Hugo Dunhill Mailing Lists
30 E. 33rd St.
New York, NY 10016
(888) 274-5737
www.hdml.com
Commercial provider of mailing lists for direct marketers. Includes many music-related lists.

InfoUSA
(formerly American Business Information)
5711 S. 86th Circle, P.O. Box 27347
Omaha, NE 68127
(800) 321-0869
www.infoUSA.com
Commercial mailing list broker.

Market Data
www.riaa.com/MD-Tracking.cfm
The Recording Industry Association of America's electronic music market research newsletter.

MediaFinder
See Print Media.

Nielsen Media Research
770 Broadway
New York, NY 10003
(646) 654-8300
www.nielsenmedia.com
Provides business subscribers with reports on television audience sizes, demographics, and viewing patterns.

Nua.com
www.nua.com
Online source of information on Internet demographics and trends. Good for statistics on numbers of Web site visitors and online music users.

Standard Periodical Directory
See Print Media.

United States Census 2000
U.S. Department of Commerce
Bureau of the Census
www.census.gov
Statistics on makeup of U.S. population by sex, race, age, education, occupation, income, and other factors.

Government Agencies

Federal Trade Commission (FTC)
600 Pennsylvania Ave., N.W.
Washington, D.C. 20580
(202) 326-2000
www.ftc.gov
Trade regulation agency. Publishes a variety of documents on FTC rules.

United States Copyright Office
Library of Congress
101 Independence Ave., S.E.
Washington, D.C. 20559
(202) 707-5959
www.loc.gov/copyright
The place to go to register music copyrights.

United States Patent and Trademark Office (USPTO)
Crystal Plaza 3, Room 2C02
Washington, D.C. 2023,
(703) 308-HELP
www.uspto.gov
The place to go to register a trademark.

United States Postal Service
www.usps.com
Publishes the booklet *Designing Letter and Reply Mail* (Publication 25), which provides guidelines for businesses engaging in mail-order commerce.

Internet and Web Development

Electronic Musician
www.electronicmusician.com
Magazine focusing on electronic music techniques and equipment, including Web music production.

Music and Computers
www.computersandmusic.com
Web site for music software and hardware enthusiasts.

Network Solutions
487 E. Middlefield Rd.
Mountainview, CA 94043
(888) 642-9675
www.networksolutions.com
The place to go to register your Internet domain name.

Sams Teach Yourself Web Publishing with HTML and XHTML in 21 Days, 3rd Ed.
Laura Lemay
Indianapolis: Sams Publishing, 2001
Well-regarded book on creating Web sites.

Useit.com
Information on Web site design.

Internet Consumer Music Sites

Amazon.com
Leading online retailer of music, books, DVDs, and other merchandise.

Barnes & Noble
www.bn.com
Online retailer of music, books, DVDs, and other merchandise. Also long-established brick-and-mortar retailer.

CDnow
www.cdnow.com
(Now part of Amazon.com)
Sells CDs and DVDs online.

Emusic.com
Music downloads for a monthly fee. Plays the music of numerous smaller, independent labels.

Internet Underground Music Archive (IUMA)
www.iuma.com
Online music listening site organized by genre; also a promotion site for independent bands and musicians and a sales outlet through its owner, Vitaminic.

MTV.com
Cable television channel's Web site. Useful for music news and information about artists.

MusicNet
www.musicnet.com
Subscription-based digital music service.

Rhapsody
www.listen.com
A self-described "celestial jukebox," offering music streaming for a monthly fee.

Rolling Stone
www.rollingstone.com
Online version of print music magazine, plus downloads.

pressplay
www.pressplay.com
Mainstream music site, set to be called Napster 2.0 as of 2004.

TechTV.com
www.techtv.com/audiofile
Information source for MP3 and Internet music enthusiasts.

Tower Records
www.towerrecords.com
Online outlet of leading brick-and-mortar retailer of CDs and DVDs.

VH1.com
Cable television channel's Web site. Useful for music news and information about artists.

Manufacturing (Disc and Cassette)

Billboard's International Buyer's Guide
See Music Distribution.

Billboard International Disc-Tape Director
New York: VNU
More than 4,000 listings of audio and video manufacturers, duplicators, packaging suppliers, and production companies.

Discmakers
(800) 468-9353
www.discmakers.com
Complete CD, DVD, and cassette packaging for independent artists and record labels.

Oasis CD Manufacturing
12625 Lee Hwy., Box 214
Sperryville, VA 22740
(888) 296-2747
www.oasisCD.com
Full-service CD and cassette manufacturing and duplication company, with additional promotion and distribution services offered through partnering companies.

Marketing (General)

American Marketing Association
311 S. Wacker Dr., Suite 5800
Chicago, IL 60606
(800) AMA-1150
www.ama.org
Membership organization that provides information on marketing trends, research, tools, and best practices.

Catalog Age
www.catalogagemag.com
Trade magazine for catalog marketers.

Direct
www.industryclick.com
Magazine covering every aspect of direct
marketing, including direct mail, e-mail,
the Web, and regulatory issues.

Direct Marketing Association
1120 Avenue of the Americas
New York, NY 10036
(212) 768-7277
www.the-dma.org
Trade association for users and suppliers
in the direct, database, and interactive
marketing fields.

Direct Marketing Marketplace
New Providence, NJ: National Register Publishing
Annual directory of service firms and suppliers.

Do-It-Yourself Direct Marketing:
Secrets for Small Business, 2nd Ed.
Mark S. Bacon
New York: Wiley, 1997
Covers mail order, newsletters, print
advertising, and more.

The Fast-Forward MBA in Marketing
Dallas Murphy
New York: Wiley, 1997
Concise overview of essential marketing topics.

Inside Direct Mail
www.insidedirectmail.com
Monthly newsletter and Web site on all aspects
of direct mail. Includes "Who's Mailing What"
archive of real-world direct-mail pieces.

Marketing
Robert D. Hisrich
Hauppauge, NY: Barron's, 2000
Covers product planning, packaging, pricing,
advertising, promotion, and distribution.

MediaFinder
www.mediafinder.com
Web site with links to a range
of marketing resources.

The Portable MBA in Marketing, 2nd Ed.
Charles D. Schewe and Alexander Hiam
New York: Wiley, 1998
Overview of marketing strategy and practice.

SRDS Direct Marketing List Source
Des Plaines, IL: SRDS
www.srds.com
Annual directory of mailing list and
e-mail list rental sources and costs.

Words That Sell
Richard Bayan
New York: McGraw-Hill, 1987
Lists more than 2,500 words and phrases
that grab attention.

Marketing (Internet)

Actinic
www.actinic.com
Provider of software products for e-commerce,
covering such functions as catalog and
shopping cart setup and order processing.

AWeber Communications
www.aweber.com
Service that automatically sends your e-mail
messages to prospects at times you designate.

ClickZ
www.clickz.com
Online articles about all aspects of marketing
on the Internet, including the use of e-mail,
search engines, advertising, links, and more.

Cyberatlas
www.cyberatlas.com
Online provider of Web marketing
information and statistics.

Dan Janal's Guide to
Marketing on the Internet
Dan Janal
New York: Wiley, 2000
Guide to using the Internet as a selling tool in
order to build customer loyalty, conduct market
research, and achieve other marketing ends.

Forrester Research, Inc.
www.forrester.com
Conducts research on impact of technology
on businesses and consumers.

Jupiter Research
www.jupiterresearch.com
Provides businesses with research data and
tactical advice on marketing online.

Larry Chase's Web Digest for Marketers
www.wdfm.com
Weekly e-mail newsletter delivering short
reviews of sites dealing with direct marketing,
search-engine marketing, e-mail marketing
and related topics.

MarketingSherpa
www.marketingsherpa.com
Web site and newsletter providing case
studies and best practices data about Internet
and integrated marketing.

Microsoft bCentral List Builder
www.bcentral.com
Service for creating, sending, and tracking
professional-looking e-mail announcements
and newsletters and for managing mailing
lists and campaigns.

Nua.com
See Audience and Market Characteristics
and Research.

PostMasterDirect
www.netcreations.com
Provides e-mail list management, brokerage,
and deployment services.

Search Engine Watch
www.searchenginewatch.com
Information on using search engines to your
marketing advantage.

SparkLIST
www.sparklist.com
Outsourcing service for managing mass
e-mail messaging.

TargitMail
www.targitmail.com
Delivers e-mail marketing services to
optimize your customer lists and manage
your e-mail campaigns.

WebTrends
www.netiq.com/webtrends
Service that provides business customers
with reports on site visitor behavior to
evaluate effectiveness of e-business strategies
and campaigns.

Yesmail
www.yesmail.com
Specialists in "online relationship marketing,"
specifically using e-mail for marketing purposes.

Media (General)

All-in-One Media Directory
New Paltz, NY: Gebbie Press
www.gebbieinc.com
Print and online directory of radio
and TV stations, newspapers, magazines,
and news syndicates.

*Gale Directory of Publications
and Broadcast Media*
P.O. Box 9187
Farmington Hills, MI 48333
(800) 877-GALE
www.gale.com
Lists contacts for radio and television
stations, cable companies, and print media.

Movies, Television, and Video

All-in-One Media Directory
See Media (General).

Broadcasting and Cable Yearbook
New Providence, NJ: R.R. Bowker
Directory covering the radio, TV, and
cable industries.

Electronic Media
6500 Wilshire Blvd., Suite 2300
Los Angeles, CA 90048
(323) 370-2432
www.emonline.com
Weekly publication covering trends in television.

The Film and Television Music Guide
Los Angeles: Music Business Registry
www.musicregistry.com
Directory listing movie studios, the music
departments of TV networks and independent-
production companies, music supervisors,
and more.

*Gale Directory of Publications
and Broadcast Media*
See Media (General).

Hollywood Reporter
5055 Wilshire Blvd.
Los Angeles, CA 90036
(323) 525-2000
www.hollywoodreporter.com
Daily publication focusing on the film
and television industries.

Hollywood Reporter Blu-Book
Los Angeles: Hollywood Reporter
Annual print and online directory to
Hollywood entertainment industry,
including company personnel listings.

Nielsen Media Research
See Audience and Market Characteristics
and Research.

SRDS TV & Cable Source
Des Plaines, IL: SRDS
www.srds.com
Directory listing TV stations and networks,
providing names of personnel, coverage data,
market demographics, and other information.

This Business of Television, 2nd Ed.
Howard Blumenthal and Oliver Goodenough
New York: Billboard Books, 1998
Overview of distribution, programming,
production, and legal aspects of the
television industry.

Variety
5700 Wilshire Blvd., Suite 120
Los Angeles, CA 90036
(323) 857-6600
www.variety.com
Daily and weekly print and online publication
offering news and analysis of film, television,
video, and theater industries.

Video Business
5700 Wilshire Blvd.
Los Angeles, CA 90036
(323) 857-6600
www.videobusiness.com
Weekly publication and online source of
information on the marketing, distribution,
and sales of DVD and VHS, Internet video,
and digital video.

VideoLog
New York: Muze, Inc.
www.muze.com
Lists all videos available to consumers,
by category.

Music Distribution

AFIM Directory
Tempe, AZ: AFIM
www.afim.org
The Association for Independent Music's
directory of members, including distributors.

Alternative Distribution Alliance (ADA)
72 Spring St., 12th Fl.
New York, NY 10012
(212) 343-2485
www.ada-music.com
Independent music distribution.

Amazon.com
Online superstore that provides
a distribution program tailored
to independent sellers of music.

Baker and Taylor
2709 Water Ridge Pkwy.
Charlotte, NC 28217
(800) 775-1800
www.btol.com
Full-line distributor of books, music, and
videos to traditional and Internet retailers.

Billboard International Buyer's Guide
New York: VNU
Annual directory that lists distributors, wholesalers, manufacturers, duplicators, and assorted
other categories of music businesses.

Billboard Record Retailing Directory
See Music Retailing.

BMG Distribution
(212) 930-4000
www.bmg.com
Distribution arm of Bertelsmann
Music Group.

Caroline Distribution
6161 Santa Monica Blvd. #208
Los Angeles, CA 90038
(213) 468-8626
www.carolinedist.com
Distributor of independent labels.

CD Baby
925 N.E. 80th Ave.
Portland, OR 97218
(503) 595-3000
www.cdbaby.net
Sells CDs by independent artists through
retail site, www.cdbaby.com.

CDstreet.com
350 Manufacturing, Suite 111
Dallas, TX 75207
(877) 692-7999
www.cdstreet.com
Online music superstore and e-commerce site
designed to serve indie and emerging artists.

Cityhall Records
101 Glacier Point, Suite C
San Rafael, CA 94901
(415) 457-9080
www.cityhallrecords.com
Distributes independent record labels.

Cornerband
www.cornerband.com
Online outlet for posting and selling MP3s.

EMI Music Distribution
www.emigroup.com
The EMI Group's distribution network,
with centers around the world that service
retail outlets.

GigAmerica
1123 Broadway, Suite 317
New York, NY 10010
(212) 367-0826
www.gigamerica.com
Provides complete online services (including
distribution, manufacturing, and promotion)
for unsigned artists.

Grokster
www.grokster.com
Free file-sharing service that connects and
promotes unsigned artists to its audience.

Koch Entertainment Distribution
2 Tri-Harbor Court
Port Washington, NY 11050
(516) 484-1000
www.kochint.com
Independent alternative to traditional,
national major label distribution.

MusicCity.com
www.musiccity.com
Allows artists to share files online with listeners
who then have the option of purchasing.

NARM Distributor Database
www.narm.com
Member-accessible online database of
distributors and their music catalogs.

Navarre Distribution Services
7400 49th Ave. N.
New Hope, MN 55428
(763) 535-8333
www.navarre.com
Distributor to both traditional and
e-commerce retailers.

The Orchard
133 Fifth Ave., 4th Fl.
New York, NY 10003
(212) 529-9109
www.theorchard.com
Sells music by independent artists and
record labels to online stores as well
as to brick-and-mortar retail accounts.

Redeye Distribution
1130 Cherry Lane
Graham, NC 27253
(877) REDEYE 1
www.redeyeusa.com
Services indie retail chains, national
chains, one-stops, the Coalition of
Independent Music Stores, and others
sellers on- and off-line.

Ryko Distribution Partners
555 W. 25th St.
New York, NY 10001
(800) 808-RYKO
www.rykodistribution.net
Medium-sized independent distributor.
Uses WEA Distribution's pack, ship, invoice,
and collection infrastructure.

Select-O-Hits
1981 Fletcher Creek Dr.
Memphis, TN 38133
(901) 388-1190
www.selectohits.com
Well-established national independent
record distributor.

Sony Music Entertainment
www.sony.com
Distributes product of Sony Music's
record labels.

Triage International
See Radio.

Universal Music and Video Distribution
www.umusic.com
A division of the Universal Music Group
conglomerate, handling UMG's owned
and affiliated labels.

Warner-Elektra-Atlantic (WEA)
www.wea.com
The distribution operation of AOL
Time Warner's Warner Music Group.

Music Distribution, International

AMG Records
Rue de l'Artisanat 2
B-1400 Nivelles, Belgium
(32) 67 21 02 48

Amigo Musik
Box 4113
Renstiernas gata 12
S-10262 Stockholm, Sweden
(46) 8 55 69 69 80
www.amigo.se

Ankh Productions
38 Dafnis St.
15772 Zografou, Athens, Greece
(30) 1 65 45 747

Blues Interactions
Tomigaya 2-41-10
Shibuya-ku, Tokyo 151-0063 Japan
(81) 3 34 60 86 11
www.bls-act.co.jp

Caravelas Records (Brazil)
(55) 11 3272 8585
www.gravadoracaravelas.com

Classic Music Distribution (Czech Republic)
Biskupcova 26
130 00 Praha 3, Czech Republic
(420) 271 77 34 05
www.classic.cz

Discmedi
Ronda Guinardó
59 bis, Baixos
08024 Barcelona, Spain
(34) 93 284 95 54
www.discmedi.com

Discovery Records
The Old Church Mission Room
Kings Corner, Pewsey
Wiltshire SN9 5BS England
(44) 1672 563 931

Distribuidora Belgrano Norte
Zabala 3941
C1427DYI Buenos Aires, Argentina
www.dbn-discos.com.ar

Distribution Fusion III
5455 Rue Pare, Suite 101
Montreal, Quebec, Canada H4P 1P7
(514) 738-4600
www.fusion3.com

edel contraire
Neumühlen 17
22763 Hamburg, Germany
(49) 40 890 85 352
www.edelcontraire.de

Extraplatte
P.O. Box 2
A-1094 Vienna, Austria
(43) 1 31 01 084
www.extraplatte.at

I.R.D.
Via G. B. de la Salle 4
20132 Milano, Italy
(39) 02 2591 700
www.ird.it

Jupiter Distribuzione
Corso Roma, 66
128883 Gravellona Toce (VB), Italy
(39) 03 23 84 06 69
www.jupiterclassics.com

aronte
Alfonso XIII 141
8016 Madrid, Spain
34) 91 345 86 26

Munich Records
www.munichrecords.com

Night and Day
30 bis, rue du Bailly
93213 Saint-Denis la Plaine, France
33) 1 49 17 88 50
www.nightday.fr

Proper Music Distribution
The Powerhouse
Cricket Lane, Beckenham
Kent BR3 1LW, England
44) 0 208 676 5156
www.proper.uk.com

Shock Records
200 Beavers Rd., Northcote
Victoria, Australia 3070
(61) 3 9482 3666
www.shock.com.au

SunnyMoon Distribution
Keppentaler Weg 3b
55286 Worrstadt, Germany
(49) 06732 9361 0
www.sunny-moon.com

Music Industry (General)

All You Need to Know
About the Music Business, Rev. Ed.
Donald S. Passman
New York: Simon & Schuster, 2000
Engaging look at how the business works,
aimed primarily at artists.

ASCAP Web Site
www.ascap.com
Provides a range of information for music
professionals, especially in the "Music Meets
Business" section.

Billboard
VNU, 770 Broadway
New York, NY 10003
(646) 654-5000
www.billboard.com
Weekly trade magazine of music and home
entertainment; includes pop music charts.

Billboard Musician's Guide
to Touring and Promotion
New York: VNU
Lists more than 4,000 music–industry
contacts, for use in booking gigs, contacting
record labels, finding a manager, and other
business essentials.

CMJ New Music Report
151 W. 25th St., 12th Fl.
New York, NY 10001
(917) 606-1908
www.cmj.com
Weekly trade magazine for the new–music
industry, with radio and retail charts of
noncommercial and college music, profiles
of emerging artists, and other features.

How to Make and Sell Your Own Recording,
5th Ed.
Diane Rapaport
Englewood Cliffs, NJ: Prentice Hall, 1999
One of the first books on making records
independently; now in its fifth edition.

Internet Music Pages
www.musicpages.com
Internet links to businesses in every
sector of the music industry.

Musician's Handbook
Bobby Borg
New York: Billboard Books, 2003
A guide to the music business.

MusicIsland
www.musicisland.com
Online information source for
independent musicians.

Music, Money, and Success, 3rd Ed.
Jeffrey Brabec and Todd Brabec
New York: Schirmer Trade Books, 2002
Detailed information on the many ways
music can generate money.

Radio and Records
10100 Santa Monica Blvd., 3rd Fl.
Los Angeles, CA 90067
(310) 553-4330
www.radioandrecords.com
Weekly news magazine and Web site
serving the radio and record industries with
radio airplay data and other information.

Recording Industry Sourcebook
Vallejo, CA: Artistpro.com
Annual directory of record companies, publishers, managers, attorneys, and other music-related businesses.

StarPolish
www.starpolish.com
Online business information source, with the aim of "helping artists help themselves."

Taxi
www.taxi.com
Independent A&R company for unsigned artists and songwriters, offering a monthly newsletter and online business information.

This Business of Artist Management, 3rd Ed.
Xavier M. Frascogna, Jr., and
H. Lee Hetherington
New York: Billboard Books, 1997
An overview of the music business from the perspective of artist management.

This Business of Music, 9th Ed.
M. William Krasilovsky, Sidney Shemel, and John Gross
New York: Billboard Books, 2003
Overview of the music business with an emphasis on legal issues.

The Ultimate Band List
ubl.artistdirectcom
Internet links to music sites of all kinds, including record companies, radio stations, magazines, promoters, and venues.

What They'll Never Tell You About the Music Business
Peter M. Thall
New York: Billboard Books, 2002
A lawyer explains industry practices.

Worldwide Internet Music Resources
www.music.indiana.edu/music_resources
Vast database of information on all aspects of music industry.

Music Industry Conferences and Seminars

CMJ Music Marathon
151 W. 25th St., 12th Fl.
New York, NY 10001
(917) 606-1908
www.cmj.com
Annual convention for music professionals, artists, and fans, showcasing new music.

MIDEM
www.midem.com
Annual international music convention held in Cannes, France, offering attendees the chance to network with labels, agents, distributors, promoters, and production companies.

NAMM
(760) 438-8001
www.namm.com
Annual trade shows for music instrument and gear manufacturers and sellers. Includes performances by well-known musicians.

NARM/AFIM Convention
(609) 596-2221
www.narm.com
www.afim.org
Annual trade show for music retailers, wholesalers, distributors, and record labels.

South by Southwest Music Conference
P.O. Box 4999
Austin, TX 78765
(512) 467-7979
www.sxsw.com
Annual convention connecting artists with industry types, with performances, panel discussions, and "crash courses."

Music Retailing

Billboard Record Retailing Directory
New York: VNU
Seven thousand listings of independent
and chain stores, chain headquarters,
and e-tailers.

Coalition of Independent
Music Stores (CIMS)
www.cimsmusic.com
National network of independent music
stores offering store-based promotion
strategies for labels with developing and
established bands.

Independent Record Store Directory
www.the-ird.com
Online database of U.S. indie record stores,
searchable by location.

National Association of Recording
Merchandisers (NARM)
See Organizations and Trade Associations.

Organizations and Trade Associations (Music and Entertainment)

American Federation of Musicians (AFM)
www.afm.org
The musicians' union. Sets pay rates and
work standards. Represents more than
250 local unions in the U.S. and Canada.

American Federation of Television
and Radio Artists (AFTRA)
www.aftra.org
Union representing actors, singers,
broadcasters, and other types of
entertainment talent.

American Society of Composers,
Authors and Publishers (ASCAP)
One Lincoln Plaza
New York, NY 10023
(212) 621-6000
www.ascap.com
Music rights clearinghouse. Licenses
members' music for public performances.

Association for Independent Music (AFIM)
925 W. Baseline Rd., #105-G
Tempe, AZ 85283
(480) 831-2954
www.afim.org
Organization promoting the independent
recording industry.

Broadcast Music, Inc. (BMI)
320 W. 57th St.
New York, NY 10019
(212) 586-2000
www.bmi.com
Music rights clearinghouse. Licenses
members' music for public performances.

Coalition of Independent Music Stores (CIMS)
See Music Retailing.

The Dramatists Guild of America
1501 Broadway, Suite 701
New York, NY 10036
www.dramaguild.com
Professional association for playwrights,
composers, and lyricists.

Harry Fox Agency
711 Third Ave.
New York, NY 10017
(212) 370-5330
www.nmpa.org/hfa.html
Music licensing agency handling
mechanical rights and a range of
music uses for publisher members.

NAMM, the International Music
Products Association
5790 Armada Dr.
Carlsbad, CA 92008
(760) 438-8001
www.namm.com
Organization promoting the musical-
instrument industry.

National Association of Recording
Merchandisers (NARM)
11 Eves Dr., Suite 140
Marlton, NJ 08053
(609) 596-2221
www.narm.com
Trade association representing music
retailers, wholesalers, and distributors.

National Music Publishers'
Association (NMPA)
475 Park Ave. S.
New York, NY 10016
(646) 742-1651
Promotes the interest of publishers.
Parent organization of the Harry Fox Agency.

Recording Industry Association
of America (RIAA)
1330 Connecticut Ave., N.W., Suite 300
Washington, D.C. 20036
(202) 775-0101
www.riaa.com
Trade organization promoting the interests
of record companies. Certifies gold and
platinum record awards.

Screen Actors Guild (SAG)
5757 Wilshire Blvd.
Los Angeles, CA 90036
(323) 954-1600
www.sag.org
Film and television performers' union.

SESAC
55 Music Sq. E.
Nashville, TN 37203
(615) 329-9627
www.sesac.com
Music rights clearinghouse. Licenses
members' music for public performances.

Songwriters Guild of America
1500 Harbor Blvd.
Weehawken, NJ 07086
(201) 867-7603
www.songwriters.org
Provides contract guidelines and other
professional services for members.

SoundExchange
(212) 828-0120
www.soundexchange.com
Provides Internet licensing services
for member record companies and
artist representatives.

Print Media

All-in-One Media Directory
See Media (General).

*Gale Directory of Publications
and Broadcast Media*
See Media (General).

MediaFinder
www.mediafinder.com
Lists magazines, directories, mailing list
sources, and more.

National Directory of Magazines
Oxbridge Communications
www.mediafinder.com
Print and electronic publication providing
staff, circulation, advertising, and list rental
data for more than 17,000 publications.

*SRDS Consumer Magazine
Advertising Source*
Des Plaines, IL: SRDS
www.srds.com
Lists magazines by category (e.g., music) and
includes information on circulation and ad rate

SRDS Newspaper Advertising Source
Des Plaines, IL: SRDS
www.srds.com
Includes information on circulation
and ad rates.

Standard Periodical Directory
Oxbridge Communications
www.mediafinder.com
Provides circulation, advertising, and list rental
data for more than 75,000 periodicals.

The Ultimate Band List
See Music Industry (General).

Worldwide Internet Music Resources
See Music Industry (General).

Publicity

The Billboard Guide to Music Publicity, Rev. Ed.
Jim Pettigrew, Jr.
New York: Billboard Books, 1997
Describes the process of getting
media coverage.

Radio

Advanced Alternative Media (AAM)
W. 22nd St.
New York, NY 10010
(212) 924-3005
www.aampromo.com
Independent marketing and college
radio promotion.

All-in-One Media Directory
See Media (General).

Arbitron Inc.
See Audience and Market Characteristics
and Research.

ArtistDirect.com
http://ubl.artistdirect.com/music/ubl/radio
Internet listing of radio stations and Internet
stations by alphabet, genre, and network
or syndicate.

Billboard
See Music Industry (General).

*Billboard Musician's Guide to
Touring and Promotion*
See Music Industry (General).

Broadcasting and Cable Yearbook
See Movies, Television, and Video.

BRS Web-Radio
www.radio-directory.com
Web site listing radio stations by call letter,
state, format, and Internet presence.

CMJ New Music Report
See Music Industry (General).

Fanatic Promotion
630 Ninth Ave., Suite 1012
New York, NY 10036
(212) 974-8021
www.fanaticpromotion.com
Assists independent artists in national radio,
publicity, and retail campaigns.

*Gale Directory of Publications
and Broadcast Media*
See Media (General).

McGathy Promotions
www.mcgathypromotions.com
Handles radio promotion and other services.

Nielsen Broadcast Data Systems (BDS)
8100 NW 101 Terrace
Kansas City, MO 64153
Attn: Encoding Department
www.bdsonline.com
Automated tracking of music airplay, used
in tabulating pop charts and for research by
music professionals.

Planetary Group
P.O. Box 52116
Boston, MA 02205
(617) 451-0444
www.planetarygroup.com
Provides radio promotion and publicity for
independent and non-mainstream artists.

Radio and Records
See Music Industry (General).

Radio Business Report
6208-B Old Franconia Rd.
Alexandria, VA 22310
(703) 719-9500
www.rbr.com
Monthly trade publication and online news
and research source.

Radio-locator.com
(formerly the MIT List of Radio Stations
on the Internet)
www.radio-locator.com
Radio station search engine.

*Radio Power Book: The Directory of
Music Radio and Record Promotion*
Lists radio stations in 15 formats, with
Arbitron Inc. ratings for top 100 markets.

Radio Stations on the Internet
www.gebbieinc.com/radintro.htm
Links to U.S. radio station Web sites,
searchable by location.

SRDS Radio Advertising Source
Des Plaines, IL: SRDS
www.srds.com
Directory listing AM/FM commercial
radio stations, networks, and syndicators.
Includes information on stations'
programming formats and audiences.

The Syndicate
www.thesyn.com
Promoter to college and rock radio.

Team Clermont
www.teamclermont.com
Serves "new and adventurous artists"
with radio promotion and publicity.

Triage International
www.triagemusic.com
Provides radio promotion and distribution
services to independent record labels and
some major labels.

Tri-State Promotions
www.tspromo.com
Leading promoter of records
to the radio industry.

The Ultimate Band List
See Music Industry (General).

Touring and Live Performance

American Federation of Musicians Web site
www.afm.org/booking.htm
Provides regional listings of AFM-approved
booking agents.

Billboard AudArena Stadium
International Guide
New York: VNU
Lists more than 5,800 venues worldwide.

Billboard International Talent and Touring Guide
New York: VNU
Lists more than 17,000 performance venues,
agents and managers, merchandisers,
sound and lighting services, and other tour-
related personnel.

Billboard Musician's Guide
to Touring and Promotion
See Music Industry (General).

Pollstar
4697 W. Jacqueline Ave.
Fresno, CA 93722
(559) 271-7900
www.pollstar.com
Weekly trade publication and Web site devoted
to the concert industry, providing tour schedules, ticket sales results, and trade news.

Pollstar Agency Rosters

Fresno, CA: Pollstar
www.pollstar.com
Biannual listing of touring artists
and their booking agencies.

Pollstar Concert Venue Directory
Fresno, CA: Pollstar
www.pollstar.com
Biannual listing of amphitheaters, stadiums,
arenas, and theaters used by touring artists.

Pollstar Talent Buyer Directory
Fresno, CA: Pollstar
www.pollstar.com
Biannual listing of concert promoters,
nightclubs, colleges, theme parks, and
other buyers of talent.

The Touring Musician
Hal Galper and Bret Primack
New York: Billboard Books, 2000
Veteran jazz musician provides lowdown
on music roadwork.

Trade Organizations (General)

Uniform Code Council (UCC)
7887 Washington Village Drive, Suite 300
Dayton, Ohio 45459
(937) 435-3870
www.uc-council.org
Issues Universal Product Codes
(UCCs) for companies to use in
identifying their commercial products.

Visual Art and Graphic Design

American Institute of Graphic Arts (AIGA)
164 Fifth Ave.
New York, NY 10010
(212) 807-1990
www.aiga.org
National membership organization of
professional graphic designers. Provides
an online directoy of designers, searchable
by specialty.

t Directors Annual
ew York: Art Directors Club
ww.adcny.org
ollection of the year's most innovative
nagery in the fields of advertising, design,
ustration, video, and new media.

ack Book Illustration
ww.blackbook.com
ourcebook displaying the work of
ustrators available for advertising and
her commercial projects.

ack Book Photography
ww.blackbook.com
ourcebook displaying the work of
notographers available for advertising
nd other commercial projects.

raphic Artists Guild
12) 463-7730
ww.gag.org
romotes and protects the
conomic interest of its members.

raphic Artists Guild Handbook:
ricing and Ethical Guidelines, 10th Ed.
incinnati, OH: North Light Books, 2001
n essential source of information on
raphic design prices and trade practices.

lik Showcase Photography
ew York: American Showcase
ww.americanshowcase.com
nnual directory that showcases
umerous photographers and wide
ariety of photo styles.

howcase Illustration
ew York: American Showcase
ww.americanshowcase.com
nnual sourcebook of artists for packaging,
ollateral, advertising, and more, showing a
ide variety of illustration and design styles.

he Ultimate Album Cover Album
oger Dean and David Howells
ew York: Prentice Hall, 1987
ollection of album cover designs
panning 45 years.

Index